# ENFORCED DISAPPEARANCES

*Enforced Disappearances: On Universal Responses to a Worldwide Phenomenon* discusses the UN human rights (both treaty bodies and special procedures) response to the key challenges of missing persons and enforced disappearances, including reparations, family rights, involvement of non-state actors and the migration context. The book also includes several illustrative case studies from Latin America, Africa, Mexico, Western Balkans and the Asia-Pacific region, which demonstrate the current challenges and problems relating to enforced disappearances in domestic or regional settings. The book includes contributions from experts working across a global range of jurisdictions. This title is also available as open access on Cambridge Core.

GRAŻYNA BARANOWSKA is a professor at the Friedrich-Alexander-Universität Erlangen-Nürnberg and vice-chair of the UN Working Group on Enforced and Involuntary Disappearances. Previously, she was a senior researcher at the Hertie School and assistant professor at the Institute of Law Studies of the Polish Academy of Sciences. Her first book, *Rights of Families of Disappeared Persons* (2021), examined how international bodies in Europe address the needs of the families of forcibly disappeared persons.

MILICA KOLAKOVIĆ-BOJOVIĆ is a senior research fellow at the Institute of Criminological and Sociological Research, Belgrade, and the vice-president of the UN Committee on Enforced Disappearances. Her research interests and fields of expertise are focused on criminal justice, justice system reform, human rights and harmonization with international standards. Since 2021, she is also a member of the ICC Advisory Committee on nomination of judges of the International Criminal Court.

# ENFORCED DISAPPEARANCES

## On Universal Responses to a Worldwide Phenomenon

GRAŻYNA BARANOWSKA
*Friedrich-Alexander-Universität Erlangen-Nürnberg*

MILICA KOLAKOVIĆ-BOJOVIĆ
*Institute of Criminological and Sociological Research, Belgrade*

CAMBRIDGE
UNIVERSITY PRESS

CAMBRIDGE
UNIVERSITY PRESS

Shaftesbury Road, Cambridge CB2 8EA, United Kingdom

One Liberty Plaza, 20th Floor, New York, NY 10006, USA

477 Williamstown Road, Port Melbourne, VIC 3207, Australia

314–321, 3rd Floor, Plot 3, Splendor Forum, Jasola District Centre, New Delhi – 110025, India

103 Penang Road, #05-06/07, Visioncrest Commercial, Singapore 238467

Cambridge University Press is part of Cambridge University Press & Assessment, a department of the University of Cambridge.

We share the University's mission to contribute to society through the pursuit of education, learning and research at the highest international levels of excellence.

www.cambridge.org
Information on this title: www.cambridge.org/9781009461726

DOI: 10.1017/9781009461719



First published 2025

*A catalogue record for this publication is available from the British Library*

*A Cataloging-in-Publication data record for this book is available from the Library of Congress*

ISBN 978-1-009-46172-6 Hardback

CONTENTS

*List of Contributors* vii
*Acknowledgements* ix
*List of Abbreviations* x

1 Dealing with Uncertainty: On Addressing Enforced Disappearances Universally 1
GRAŻYNA BARANOWSKA AND MILICA KOLAKOVIĆ-BOJOVIĆ

2 Enforced Disappearances in Armed Conflict through the Lenses of the International Convention for the Protection of All Persons from Enforced Disappearance 19
IVAN JOVANOVIĆ

3 The Guiding Principles on the Search for Disappeared Persons: Origins and Impact 47
MARIA CLARA GALVIS PATIÑO AND RAINER HUHLE

4 New Technologies and Enforced Disappearances: The Working Group on Enforced or Involuntary Disappearances – Exploring a New World between Opportunities and Challenges 78
GABRIELLA CITRONI

5 The Fate and Whereabouts of Social Rights in the Practice of the Committee on Enforced Disappearances 103
ARIEL DULITZKY

6 NGO Contributions to Eradicate Enforced Disappearances in Latin America 130
HORACIO RAVENNA

7 Contemporary Disappearances in Mexico: A Conceptual Challenge for the International Framework on Enforced Disappearances 154

LENE GUERCKE

8 Disappearances of Migrants in Africa 181

EVA NUDD AND BARBARA LOCHBIHLER

9 Enforced Disappearances and the Right to Reparation in Western Balkans 203

MILICA KOLAKOVIĆ-BOJOVIĆ AND JASMINKA DŽUMHUR

10 The Strategies to Increase the ICPPED Ratification with Special Attention to the Asia-Pacific Region: Being a Party as an Incessant Act of Treaty-Making 242

KOJI TERAYA

*Bibliography* 269

*Index* 293

# CONTRIBUTORS

GABRIELLA CITRONI, PhD, is Adjunct Professor of International Human Rights Law at the University of Milano–Bicocca, Italy, Chair of the United Nations Working Group on Enforced or Involuntary Disappearances, an international legal advisor for the Latin American Federation of Associations for Relatives of the Detained-Disappeared (FEDEFAM) and senior legal advisor for TRIAL International.

ARIEL DULITZKY, PhD, is Clinical Professor of Law and the director of the Human Rights Clinic at the University of Texas, the director of the Latin America Initiative and a former member of the United Nations Working Group on Enforced or Involuntary Disappearances.

JASMINKA DŽUMHUR, PhD, is Human Rights Ombudsperson of Bosnia and Herzegovina, a vice-president of the UN Committee on the Protection of the Rights of All Migrant Workers and Members of their Families, a member of the UN Commission of Inquiry on Ukraine and former member and the vice chair of the UN Working Group on Enforced or Involuntary Disappearances.

LENE GUERCKE, PhD, is Senior Researcher at the UC Berkeley Human Rights Center.

RAINER HUHLE, PhD, is a human rights expert, co-founder of the Nuremberg Human Rights Center and former member and the vice-president of the UN Committee on Enforced Disappearances.

IVAN JOVANOVIĆ is a transitional justice and rule of law consultant.

BARBARA LOCHBIHLER is member and the former vice-president of the United Nations Committee on Enforced Disappearances.

EVA NUDD is legal advisor at the Danish Institute Against Torture and former legal advisor in REDRESS.

MARIA CLARA GALVIS PATIÑO, PhD, is Professor at the Externado University of Colombia and American University–Washington College of Law and former member and the vice-president of the United Nations Committee on Enforced Disappearances.

HORACIO RAVENNA, PhD, is Human Rights Professor, School of Social Sciences University of Buenos Aires and member of the United Nations Committee on Enforced Disappearances.

KOJI TERAYA, PhD, is Law Professor at Tokyo University, member of the United Nations Human Rights Committee and former member of the United Nations Committee on Enforced Disappearances.

# ACKNOWLEDGEMENTS

The research work of Grażyna Baranowska for this book was supported under the project 'State Obligations with regard to Missing and Disappeared Persons under International Law', grant agreement 2019/35/D/HS5/03700, by the Polish National Science Centre.

The research work of Milica Kolaković-Bojović for this book was supported by the Ministry of Science, Technological Development and Innovations of Serbia through Agreement on the Realization and Financing of Scientific Research Work SRO in 2024, no. 451-03-66/2024-03/200039.

The cover image is by Ana Batrićević.

# ABBREVIATIONS

| | |
|---|---|
| CAT | Committee Against Torture |
| CED | Committee on Enforced Disappearances |
| EC | European Commission |
| ECHR | European Convention on Human Rights |
| EU | European Union |
| FEMED | Fédération euro-méditerranéennecontre les disparitionsforces |
| GIZ | German Agency for Economic Cooperation (Deutsche Gesellschaft für Internationale Zusammenarbeit) |
| HRCt | Human Rights Committee |
| IACHR | Inter-American Commission on Human Rights |
| ICC | International Criminal Court |
| ICMP | International Commission on Missing Persons |
| ICPPED | International Convention for the Protection of All Persons from Enforced Disappearance |
| ICRC | International Committee of Red Cross |
| ICTR | International Criminal Tribunal for Rwanda |
| ICTY | International Criminal Tribunal for the former Yugoslavia |
| IHL | international humanitarian law |
| IOM | International Organization of Migration |
| NGO | non-governmental organization |
| NHRI | National Human Rights Institution |
| OHCHR | Office of the High Commissioner for Human Rights |
| UN | United Nations |
| UN TBs | United Nations Treaty Bodies |
| WBs | Western Balkans |
| WGEID | Working Group on Enforced or Involuntary Disappearances |

# 1

# Dealing with Uncertainty

## On Addressing Enforced Disappearances Universally

GRAŻYNA BARANOWSKA AND MILICA KOLAKOVIĆ-BOJOVIĆ*

Killer, you will be forgiven for everything.
Just tell me where you buried my son.
Did you put a Lab River stone on his chest?
Or did you pour sand from Sitnica River on it?
Maybe you laid him in my field?
How you condemned him, what guilt did you find for him?
What did you tell him at the end? Did you blindfold him?
Or did you boldly look a child in the face?
. . . Killer, you'll be forgiven for everything, just tell me where you buried him.
Under which tree did you end his life?
With what grass did you green him?[1]

—From the poem by Dragana Majstorović,
mother of a sixteen-year-old disappeared person in Kosovo Polje

### 1.1 Effects of Disappearances

Uncertainty. This simple word does not sound strong enough to describe all the seriousness and gravity of the consequences of an enforced disappearance. This human rights violation consists of an arrest, detention, abduction or other forms of deprivation of liberty by State agents or persons and groups acting with State authorization, support or acquiescence, followed by a refusal to acknowledge the deprivation of liberty or

* The opinions expressed in this chapter are strictly personal and do not in any way reflect the position of the CED and WGEID.

1 Dragana Majstorović is mother of sixteen-year-old Ivan Majstorović from Kosovo Polje (Serbia) who went missing in 1999 on his way to school. See www.recom.link/wp-content/uploads/2014/11/Transkript.pdf (trans. Milica Kolaković-Bojović).

by concealment of the fate or whereabouts of the disappeared person, which place such a person outside the protection of the law.[2] In this context, the meaning of uncertainty goes beyond the lack of information about circumstances of a disappearance and the unknown fate of a missing person. Uncertainty encompasses all the stress, pain, suffering and emotional imbalance caused not only to direct victims but also family members, relatives and others close to the disappeared person.

All disappearances of persons cause uncertainty to families, but *enforced* disappearances lead to an additional layer of uncertainty, as it is State authorities that should search for missing persons. However, the circumstances of disappearances are rarely clear, thus during the search process it usually cannot be conclusively established whether the person was *forcibly* disappeared. Because of that, according to the UN Committee on Enforced Disappearances (CED, the Committee) States should conduct search activities according to the enforced disappearances framework, even when the enforced disappearance has not been conclusively established yet.[3] Additionally, acquiescence is the attribution threshold for enforced disappearances under international human rights, thus – as also widely discussed by various authors in this edited volume[4] – disappearances committed by persons not formally affiliated with the State can be enforced disappearances. As such, we use 'disappeared persons' to apply to persons that went missing and may have been forcibly disappeared and 'forcibly disappeared' to those with regard to whom it has been established that they were victims of enforced disappearances.

Being an individual case or a part of a widespread or systematic practice, an enforced disappearance prevents all directly or indirectly affected persons from continuing with their lives normally. A mother whose son went missing after he had left home in El Salvador looking for a better life in Mexico explained to the Committee how this changed her life:

> I am searching for my son . . .. He was 18 when he went missing. So, by now, he is 27 years old. I said goodbye to him when he was still at home, and he never called. It has been very hard for me to have this empty space at home. A space that no one will ever fill. I am always looking and

[2] Article 2, International Convention for the Protection of All Persons from Enforced Disappearance (ICPPED), 1726 UNTS 3, 20 December 2006. For more on the definition of enforced disappearances, see, for example, H. Relva, 'Three challenges for the codification of Enforced Disappearances' *Droits fondamentaux*, no. 19 (2021) 5.

[3] UN Committee on Enforced Disappearances, Guiding Principles for the Search for Disappeared Persons (8 May 2019), UN Doc CED/C/7.

[4] See discussions in Chapters 2, 6, 7 and 10.

> waiting for him. For me, he is alive. Because I don't believe otherwise. I talk about him in the present tense. He is in my heart, thoughts, and prayers.[5]

A wife of a man disappeared in Pakistan shared her pain with the CED: 'It took me many months before I realized what had happened and that I needed to get up from bed and start searching for my loved one . . .. As I got up with extraordinary pain and determination, I started an endless, nerve-wracking battle in which I never rested.'[6]

The uncertainty also describes a legal vacuum because the unknown fate of a disappeared person has legal consequences and comprehensively affects the financial capacities of the whole family, especially when the main breadwinner went missing. Families often do not know whether the disappeared persons are dead or alive, which leads them to feel a sense of loss called 'ambiguous loss'.[7] Their access to property rights, childcare and various forms of social support and protection is frequently challenged by the uncertain fate of their loved one(s).[8] It tangles and breaks sensitive and priceless links between family members who desperately seek the truth.

A mother of a disappeared person from Mexico highlighted the impact this has on her grandchildren: 'My grandchildren can't understand that their parents were disappeared. They are convinced that they were abandoned. This makes them desperate, and they have lost touch with reality . . .. My eleven-year-old grandson is now involved in organized crime. He thinks they will give him news of his parents. I am desperate. The children of the disappeared are the forgotten ones of the system.'[9]

[5] Maria Elena Larios is a mother of Heriberto Antonio Gonzalez, eighteen-year-old boy who went missing after he left home in El Salvador looking for a better life in Mexico, testimony, 17th session of the CED, 30 September 2019, https://www.ohchr.org/en/stories/2020/05/un-virtual-meeting-gives-victims-chance-be-heard, DOA: 7 February 2022.

[6] Amina Masood, testimony, 21st session of the CED, 13 September 2021, https://www.ohchr.org/en/stories/2021/09/we-need-your-support-and-hope-see-our-dreams-coming-true, DOA: 7 February 2022.

[7] P. Boss, *Ambiguous Loss: Learning to Live with Unresolved Grief* (Harvard University Press, 2000).

[8] M. Kolaković-Bojović, 'Disappeared persons and the right to be considered alive – the current state of play in the Western Balkans' (2021) 4 *Yearbook. Human Rights Protection: Right to Life* 271, 272; G. Baranowska, 'The rights of the families of missing persons: Going beyond international humanitarian law' (2021) 55, 1 *Israel Law Review* 25.

[9] Comité contra la Desaparición Forzada, *Informe del Comité contra la Desaparición Forzada sobre su visita a México en virtud del artículo 33, par. 5 de la Convención*, CED/C/MEX/VR/1 (Recommendations), para. 87, 14.

Another Mexican victim, a minor, said: 'I never imagined I would be here with you now, talking about my mother's disappearance. I didn't think this was possible. It's not the kind of thing they teach you at school. When your mother suddenly disappears, you have no idea what to do. It's a nightmare that starts over every day.'[10]

The families clearly want to receive support and information about their disappeared loved ones.[11] The support may assume different forms, but we should remember that it may not mean financial compensation only.[12] Without proper institutional support, the families feel abandoned in their attempts to search for their loved ones. They need truth, justice, reparation.[13] On the international level, there are different perspectives on reparation from regional courts, which have a huge influence on the outcomes of cases for victims of enforced disappearances.[14] Not all families have the same needs, which both international and domestic courts must also consider.[15]

Today, the statistics regarding disappeared persons and victims' heartbreaking stories amount to millions around the world. In Mexico alone,[16] the number of disappeared persons has recently reached 100,000.[17]

[10] Comité contra la Desaparición Forzada, *Informe del Comité contra la Desaparición Forzada sobre su visita a México en virtud del artículo 33 de la Convención*, CED/C/MEX/VR/1 (Findings), para. 51, 9.

[11] S. Robins, *Families of the Missing: A Test for Contemporary Approaches to Transitional Justice* (Routledge, 2013); S. Robins, 'Toward victim-centred transitional justice: Understanding the needs of families of the disappeared in postconflict Nepal' (2011) 5 *International Journal of Transitional Justice* 75.

[12] S. Fulton, 'Redress for enforced disappearances: Why financial compensation is not enough' (2014) 12, 4 *Journal of International Criminal Justice* 769.

[13] See Chapters 5 and 9.

[14] G. Citroni, 'Measures of reparation for victims of gross human rights violations: Developments and challenges in the jurisprudence of two regional human rights courts' (2012) 5 *Inter-American and European Human Rights Journal* 49; R. Rubio-Marin, C. Sandoval and C Diaz, 'Repairing family members: Gross human rights violations and communities of harm' in R. Rubio-Marin (ed.), *The Gender of Reparations: Unsettling Sexual Hierarchies while Redressing Human Rights Violations* (Cambridge University Press, 2009).

[15] F. Mégret, 'The strange case of the victim who did not want justice' (2018) 12, 3 *International Journal of Transitional Justice* 444.

[16] See Chapter 7.

[17] For more about trends and statistical data on enforced disappearances in Mexico, see Comité contra la Desaparición Forzada, *Informe del Comité contra la Desaparición Forzada sobre su visita a México en virtud del artículo 33 de la Convención*, CED/C/MEX/VR/1 (Findings) 3; CED & WGEID Joint Statement, Mexico: Dark landmark of 100,000 disappearances reflects pattern of impunity, UN experts warn, www.ohchr.org/en/statements/2022/05/mexico-dark-landmark-100000-disappearances-reflects-pattern-impunity-un-experts, DOA: 4 July 2022; D. Wilkinson, 'Mexico: Forced disappearance, an ongoing crime' in *Lessons from a Human*

However, we must understand that despite the previous and unfolding crises of disappearances in several regions, enforced disappearances may occur anywhere and at any time. These are not isolated phenomena linked to a particular region, time and cultural, social or political background. Yet, each of these circumstances – individually or in synergy – may influence the occurrence and frequency of enforced disappearances.[18]

The diverse patterns of enforced disappearances, the growing community of those who suffered from them and the emerging situation in terms of global capacities to address all the challenges foreground the burning need to create a diversified response. This book contributes to those joint efforts to better understand – but also to improve – the universal legal responses to enforced disappearances. It demonstrates the practical functioning of UN standards and mechanisms and their relevance in specific regions and countries.

## 1.2 Current Developments and Legal Frameworks against Enforced Disappearances

International law avenues have been used for a long time to address enforced disappearances, with the first person being convicted by an international court for enforced disappearances in 1946. The German field marshal Wilhelm Keitel was sentenced in the Nuremburg trials, among other things, for implementing a policy for secretly transporting persons engaged in resistance activities in Western European territories, for whom the issuance of the death penalty by a court was uncertain.[19] However, subsequently, it was rather the human rights law than the

*Rights Catastrophe*, www.hrw.org/news/2018/11/26/mexico-forced-disappearance-ongoing-crime, DOA: 4 July 2022; L. Guercke, 'State responsibility for a failure to prevent violations of the right to life by organized criminal groups: Disappearances in Mexico' (2021) 21, 2 *Human Rights Law Review* 329; R. D. Saenz, 'Confronting Mexico's enforced disappearance monsters: How the ICC can contribute to the process of realizing criminal justice reform in Mexico' (2021) 50 *Vanderbilt Law Review* 45; I. Beltran-Gil, 'Double disappearance: A problem that increases the forensic crisis in Mexico' (2022) 5 *Forensic Science International: Reports Volume* 100256.

18 M. Kolaković-Bojović, 'The United Nations response to enforced disappearance: No victim left behind' (2021) *UN Chronicle*, www.un.org/en/un-chronicle/united-nations-response-enforced-disappearance%E2%80%94no-victim-left-behind, DOA: 4 July 2022.

19 B. Finucane, 'Enforced disappearance as a crime under international law' (2010) 35 *Yale Journey of International Law* 171; J. Nyamuya Maogoto, 'Now you see, now you don't: The State's duty to punish disappearances and extra-judicial executions' (2002) *Australian International Law Journal* 176, 179–81.

criminal law framework that developed rules regarding enforced disappearances, first on the regional and then on the international level.

### *1.2.1 Regional Developments*

While the book clearly demonstrates that enforced disappearances are a universal phenomenon that must be addressed with universal means,[20] the legal fight against enforced disappearances is undoubtedly connected with one region: Latin America. State authorities from the continent have in the 1960s and 1970s systemically employed enforced disappearances, which become a symbol of their rules. The very term 'enforced disappearances' (Spanish original 'desapariciones forzadas') was adopted to describe those events.[21] In response to those human rights violations, there arose powerful civil society initiatives, including the world-famous Mothers of the Plaza de Mayo: an association of women that demonstrated in Argentina in front of the presidential palace to petition for the live reappearance of their children.[22]

The families of the disappeared also brought the cases to the Inter-American Court of Human Rights, leading to the development of international case law on enforced disappearances.[23] The Court was at the forefront to recognize the right to truth of disappeared persons' families and developed impressive case law on reparations.[24] Furthermore, the

[20] In an earlier work, one of the editors compared enforced disappearances case law of organs with broad jurisdiction (Human Rights Committee, European Court of Human Rights) with organs with case law limited to a specific conflict (Human Rights Chamber for Bosnia and Hercegovina, Human Rights Advisory Panel in Kosovo, International Criminal Tribunal for the former Yugoslavia). The research demonstrates that specific conditions of the conflicts have not significantly influenced the elaboration and interpretation of the standards applied by each organ. Thus, we argue that a universal approach is possible. G. Baranowska, *Rights of Families of Disappeared Persons: How International Bodies Address the Needs of Families of Disappeared Persons in Europe* (Intersentia, 2021) 213–14.

[21] Report submitted by Mr Manfred Nowak, independent expert charged with examining the existing international criminal and human rights framework for the protection of persons from enforced or involuntary disappearances, pursuant to paragraph 11 of Commission resolution 2001/46 of 23 April 2001, E/CN.4/2002/71, January 8, 2002.

[22] Broader on the role of NGO's in the fight, see Chapter 6. See also V. Vázquez Guevara 'Prologue to truth: Argentina's National Commission on the Disappeared and the authority of international law' (2021) *35 Leiden Journal of International Law* 105–27.

[23] A. E. Dulitzky, 'The Latin-American flavour of enforced disappearances' (2019) 19, 423 *Chicago Journal of International Law* 423, 446–51.

[24] G. Citroni, 'Measures of reparation for victims of gross human rights violations: Developments and challenges in the jurisprudence of two regional human rights courts' (2012) 5 *Inter-American and European Human Rights Journal* 49.

Inter-American Court contributed to the adoption of the first international convention on enforced disappearances: the Inter-American Convention on the Forced Disappearance of Persons (1994).

The European equivalent of the Inter-American Court of Human Rights, the European Court of Human Rights, has also decided in enforced disappearances cases for many decades.[25] The vast majority of cases decided by the European court were disappearances that occurred during internal armed conflicts, in particular in Chechnya[26] and south-eastern Turkey.[27] Compared to the approach of the Inter-American Court, the European Court has been less favourable to applicants in such cases, in particular to recognize violations of disappeared persons' families.[28] The universal framework heads more in the direction of the Inter-American system, as the International Convention for the Protection of All Persons from Enforced Disappearance clearly recognizes disappeared persons' families as victims of enforced disappearances and provides them with the right to truth.

The legal framework regarding enforced disappearances has been strongly developed in the regional European and Inter-American system,

[25] With the first judgment in 1998, see *Kurt* v. *Turkey* App no 24276/94 (ECtHR, 25 May 1998). For more on the judgments, see S. Jötten, *Enforced Disappearances and EMRK* (Duncker & Humblot, 2012); Baranowska, *Rights of Families of Disappeared Persons*, 37–110.

[26] M. Imaeva, 'Deferring criminal accountability: Humanitarian resolution of conflict-related disappearances in the Caucasus' (PhD Thesis, Dublin City University, 2022). I. Lapitskaya, 'ECHR, Russia, and Chechnya: Two is not company and three is definitely a crowd' (2010–2011) 43, 2 *New York University Journal of International Law and Politics* 479.

[27] A. Reidy, F. Hampson and K. Boyle, 'Gross violations of human rights: Invoking the ECHR in case of Turkey' (1997) 15, 2 *Netherlands Quarterly of Human Rights*; D. Kurban, *Limits of Supranational Justice: The European Court of Human Rights and Turkey's Kurdish Conflict* (Cambridge University Press, 2020); B. Çalı, 'The logic of supranational human rights litigation, official acknowledgment, and human rights reform: The Southeast Turkey cases before the European Court of Human Rights' (2010) 35, 2 *Law & Social Inquiry* 311.

[28] O. Claude, 'A comparative approach to enforced disappearances in the Inter-American Court of Human Rights and the European Court of Human Rights Jurisprudence' (2010) *Intercultural Human Rights Law Review* 407; T. Feldman, 'Indirect victims, direct injury: Recognizing relatives as victims under the European human rights system' (2009) 1 *European Human Rights Law Review* 50; A. Murray, 'Enforced disappearance and relatives' rights before the Inter-American and European human rights courts' (2013) 2, 1 *International Human Rights Law Review* 57; I. Taqi, 'Adjudicating disappearance case in Turkey: An argument for adopting the Inter-American Court of Human Rights' approach' (2001) 24, 3 *Fordham International Law Journal* 940.

as vividly presented in the chapters of this edited volume. However, the phenomenon is worldwide, and as such, the universal response is particularly relevant to regions with a weak regional response. The chapters make it evident, as they also showcase African and Asian examples, where no regional responses are available. However, there are simultaneously promising developments in the regions. For example, as analyzed in one of the chapters, in May 2022, the African Commission on Human and Peoples' Rights adopted the Guidelines for the Protection of All Persons from Enforced Disappearances in Africa.[29]

### *1.2.2 The Universal System*

At the universal level, the right not to be subjected to enforced disappearances was first recognized in 1992 through the adoption of the Declaration on the Protection of all Persons from Enforced Disappearance (Declaration).[30] The already functioning Working Group on Enforced or Involuntary Disappearances (WGEID),[31] which operates under the UN Special Procedures, has been tasked with monitoring the Declaration's implementation. Established in 1980, the WGEID also helps relatives of disappeared persons to learn about their fate and serves as a channel of communication between sources reporting disappearances cases and relevant authorities. It also visits States worldwide and advises them on the implementation of the Declaration.

A major step to systematically work toward the eradication and prevention of enforced disappearances was made in 2006 with the adoption of the International Convention for the Protection of All Persons from Enforced Disappearance (ICPPED, Convention), which is the first binding universal treaty on enforced disappearances.[32] The ICPPED

[29] African Commission on Human and Peoples' Rights Sessions (achpr.org), see also Chapter 8.

[30] Declaration on the Protection of All Persons from Enforced Disappearance, A/RES/47/133, 18 December 1992.

[31] On the Working Group, see Baranowska, *Rights of Families of Disappeared Persons*, 186–95; G. Citroni, M. G. Bianchi, 'The Committee on Enforced Disappearances: Challenges ahead' (2012) 6 *Diritti umani e diritto internazionale* 127. For a perspective on the first years of the Working Group and its influence on the UN Special Procedures, see N. S. Rodley, 'United Nations actions procedures against "disappearances, summary or arbitrary executions and torture"' (1986) 8, 4 *Human Rights Quarterly* 700.

[32] For literature on the ICPPED, see M. L. Vermeulen, *Enforced Disappearance, Determining State Responsibility under the International Convention for the Protection of All Persons from Enforced Disappearance* (Intersentia, 2012); G. Citroni and

came into force in 2010 and created a monitoring body, the Committee on Enforced Disappearances, which oversees the implementation of the ICPPED. The CED uses the urgent actions procedure to request a State to take immediate measures to locate a disappeared person and reviews individual communications concerning an alleged violation of the ICPPED. Moreover, the CED examines interstate communications[33] and visits the States about which it receives reliable information that they 'seriously violate' the Convention.[34]

The Declaration and the ICPPED – as well as the WGEID and the CED – form the universal response to enforced disappearances aimed at preventing such events and supporting victims. However, there also are major differences between the two. The ICPPED is a binding international treaty, while the Declaration is a soft law instrument.[35] This also means that the CED can undertake actions regarding the States that have ratified the ICPPED, while the WGEID – just like all other UN special procedures – has a worldwide mandate. This is particularly relevant, as the ICPPED is still not widely ratified.

Both the CED and the WGEID received pleas from huge numbers of victims of enforced disappearances. During its over forty years of functioning, the WGEID has registered over 60,000 communications that allege enforced disappearances, out of which over 13,000 have been clarified.[36] In its first ten years of its functioning, the CED registered over 1,500 urgent actions that referred only to victims from the States that are parties to the ICPPED. While those numbers do not show the actual figures of enforced disappearances around the world, they indicate these two bodies' involvement with the victims. Moreover, the numbers

T. Scovazzi, *The Struggle against Enforced Disappearance and the 2007 United Nations Convention* (Martinus Nijhoff, 2007).

33 Claims submitted by a State party according to which another State party is not fulfilling its obligations under the Convention.

34 For a detailed analysis of CED's competences, see O. De Frouville, 'The Committee on Enforced Disappearances' in M. Alston (ed.), *The United Nations and Human Rights: A Critical Appraisal*, 2nd ed. (Oxford University Press, 2020); E. Decaux, 'Competences and functioning of the Committee on Enforced Disappearances' presented at the Conference on Enforced Disappearances, Berlin, 25 April 2012, Deutsches Institut für Menschenrechte, June 2012.

35 See the study by the WGEID arguing that the Declaration has been increasingly regarded as customary international law: WGEID 'Thirtieth anniversary of the Declaration on the Protection of All Persons from Enforced Disappearances', 31 August 2022, A/HRC/51/31/Add.3.

36 Working Group on Enforced or Involuntary Disappearances (WGEID), Annual Report for 2022, UN Doc. A/HRC/54/22, 30 July 2023.

reveal how the actions of those two UN bodies can touch on the lives of individuals. For example, thanks to the CED's urgent actions' mechanism, more than 100 persons have been located so far – more than 80 of them alive – which changed hundreds of lives of their family members, relatives and loved ones who suffered from enforced disappearances.

The relevance of the CED and WGEID is also recognized by domestic actors. In June 2021, the Mexican Supreme Court of Justice of the Nation declared the binding character of CED's urgent actions and obliged Mexican institutions to follow the measures ordered by the Committee.[37] In an innovative and much needed move, since 2019 the WGEID also reviews disappearances committed by non-State actors, called by the WGEID 'disappearances tantamount to enforced disappearances.' Finally, the CED even influenced some changes at the level of interstate cooperation in cases requiring the implementation of urgent actions.[38]

While the mandate to support families in inquiring about the fate and whereabouts of their disappeared loved ones is of crucial importance for the families that reach out to the CED and the WGEID, there are equally important areas of work of those two UN bodies. Thus, this book indicates their role as norm entrepreneurs.[39] They regularly adopt general comments, statements and thematic studies, which explain and develop existing standards about the most critical questions and challenges to combatting enforced disappearances. For example, disappearances in migration have recently become a worldwide phenomenon, posing huge challenges to both victims and States.[40] In 2017, the

[37] The Supreme Court of Justice of the Nation unanimously approved the lawsuit number 1077/2019 related to the Enforced Disappearance of Víctor Álvarez Damián who forcibly disappeared on 11 December 2013, in Veracruz's port. On 16 June 2021, the Supreme Court made the decision in which they stated that the CED urgent actions have a binding character for all authorities of the State party. The case was submitted by an NGO (IDHEAS) that has presented many urgent actions to the Committee. The NGO did this on behalf of a disappeared person and his mother after State authorities told the mother that they did not have any obligations to consider CED recommendations. See https://opiniojuris.org/2021/08/17/supreme-court-of-justice-of-mexico-the-urgent-actions-of-the-committee-on-enforced-disappearances-are-legally-binding/, DOA: 11 August 2022.

[38] E.g., this situation occurred in Honduras, in which authorities used the interstate cooperation mechanism to implement the CED urgent action. See, CED COB on Honduras CED/C/HND/CO/1, 31 May 2018, para. 29.

[39] See also, M. Lesch and N. Reiners, 'Informal human rights law-making: How treaty bodies use "General Comments" to develop international law' (2023) 2 *Global Constitutionalism* 378–401.

[40] See V. Azarova, A. D. Danson Brown and I. Mann 'The enforced disappearance of migrants' (2022) 40 *Boston University International Law Journal* 133; B. Duhaime and

WGEID produced a report on enforced disappearances in the context of migration, showing the direct link between migration and enforced disappearances. In 2023, the CED adopted a General Comment on enforced disappearances in the context of migration.

## 1.3 Aims of the Book

This book demonstrates the current challenges in the area of enforced disappearances and how they have been – or can be – addressed using international law and UN mechanisms. The challenges are not limited to a particular region, time or context. Throughout different parts of the globe, families of forcibly disappeared persons face similar problems, including ineffective search for the disappeared persons or utter lack of support. By bringing together different questions considered in the chapters highlighting universal or regional perspectives, the book contributes to the discussion on the protection from enforced disappearances from both an academic and practical viewpoint.

The frameworks developed in international human rights law at the universal level reside at the centre of this book's focus. At the same time, the book touches on other areas of international law that are relevant for enforced disappearances, in particular international humanitarian law[41] and international criminal law.[42] Some of the questions regarding the

A. Thibault, 'Protection of migrants from enforced disappearances: A human rights perspective' (2017) 99 *International Review of the Red Cross* 569; A. Gündoğdu, 'Border deaths as forced disappearances: Frantz Fanon and the outlines of a critical phenomenology' (2022) 5, 3 *Puncta. Journal of Critical Phenomoneology* 12; V. Laakkonen, 'Death, disappearances, borders: Migrant disappearability as a technology of deterrence' (2022) 99 *Political Geography* 102767; M. Tazzioli and N. de Genova, 'Kidnapping migrants as a tactic of border enforcements' 2020 *Society and Space* 867 (who frame enforced disappearances as 'kidnapping' and not enforced disappearance); E. Distretti, 'Enforced disappearances and border deaths along the migrant trail' in P. Cuttitta and T. Last (eds.), *Border Deaths: Causes, Dynamics And Consequences Of Migration-Related Mortality* (Amsterdam University Press, 2019) 117.

41 International humanitarian law and international human rights law have been influencing each other in the development of the rules, see G. Gaggioli, 'The prohibition of enforced disappearances: A meaningful example of a partial merger between human rights law and international humanitarian law' in R. Kolb and G. Gaggioli (eds.), *Research Handbook on Human Rights and Humanitarian Law* (Edward Elgar, 2013); on enforced disappearances and international human rights law, see also A. La Vaccara, *When the Conflict Ends, While Uncertainty Continues: Accounting For Missing Persons Between War and Peace in International Law* (Hart, 2019).

42 Which defines enforced disappearances differently from the international human rights law framework. See I. Giorgou, 'State involvement in the perpetration of enforced

overlap and influence between those areas of international law find elaboration in the chapters on enforced disappearances in war[43] and committed by non-State actors.[44]

As this book addresses universal challenges, it focuses on universal mechanisms and responses. However, the regional systems were central in developing universal standards, and so, the former continue to influence and dialogue with the latter. Consequently, the book also engages with regional frameworks, reflecting not only on the well-known European and Inter-American systems – recognized for addressing enforced disappearances – but also the African system.[45] Moreover, the book reflects on the standards set by another regional organization, the European Union, as it evaluates the painful experiences of the Western Balkans in the context of its attempts to join the European Union and achieve its rule of law standards.[46] Furthermore, the book explores the reasons for the insufficient influence of the universal mechanisms in the Asia and Pacific region.

Besides the role of universal and regional mechanisms, this book recognizes the variety of actors at the national level and their specific roles in the commission and eradication of enforced disappearances. Mindful of the above, the book deals with State and non-State actors, victims and human rights defenders.

Furthermore, our publication focuses on families,[47] which stems from several factors. First, enforced disappearances are chosen as means of violence precisely because they affect not only the disappeared person, but they also frighten their families and communities. Second, families endure unique forms of suffering in direct result of a disappearance (ambiguous loss).[48] Third, it is the families that have been at the forefront

disappearance and the Rome Statute' (2013) 11, 5 *Journal of International Criminal Justice* 1001.

43 Chapter 2.

44 Chapter 7.

45 Chapter 8.

46 Chapter 9.

47 The ICPPED recognized them as victims of enforced disappearances. In addition, international case law has predominantly recognized that rights of family members are violated, when enforced disappearances occur.

48 Boss, *Ambiguous Loss*; P. Boss, 'Ambiguous Loss: Working with families of the missing' (2002) 41 *Family Process* 14. For an overview of research on grief experienced by relatives of missing persons, see G. Klochok and C. Herrera-Espiñeira, 'The grief of relatives of missing migrants and supportive interventions: A narrative review' (2021) *Clinical Nursing Research* 1023.

of the fight against enforced disappearances.[49] Their involvement initially focuses on finding their family members, but it often transforms into broader human rights activism.[50] Therefore, this family-centred system strongly affects the approach of this book, emerging as a horizontal issue relevant to several of its chapters.

Finally, the book considers a gender-sensitive perspective. Most of the disappeared are men, while most of the left behind are women, whose economic situation deteriorates after the disappearances. Often, the disappearances stigmatize the women,[51] forcing them into low-paying, unstable jobs.[52] Thus, courts should also acknowledge the gender violence that accompanies enforced disappearance cases.[53]

Such complex scope of this book shows in its authors' diverse professional background and rich professional experience, which provides a comprehensive approach to addressing enforced disappearances. The authors are current and former members of the UN Committee on Enforced Disappearances, the UN Working Group on Enforced or Involuntary Disappearances and other UN treaty bodies. Besides their rich experience in UN mechanisms, their individual engagement in various professional fields ensures a rich expertise and different perspectives in the identification and addressing of relevant issues. Most are active members of the research community. Many participate in regional developments regarding enforced disappearances, NGO operations, along with domestic mechanisms and initiatives aimed at the eradication of enforced disappearances. Such a diverse group of contributors allows this book to become a strong and nuanced voice in the discussion on enforced disappearances.

[49] I. Kovras, *Grassroots Activism and the Evolution of Transitional Justice* (Cambridge University Press, 2017).

[50] I. Kovras and M. E. Burchianti, 'Building bridges of memory: The mothers of the Plaza de Mayo and the cultural politics of maternal memories' (2004) 15, 2 *History and Anthropology* 133; 'Interview with Estela Barnes de Carlotto, president of the Grandmothers of the Plaza de Mayo' (2017) 99, 2 *International Review of the Red Cross* 487.

[51] 'Families of Missing Migrants: Their Search for Answers, the Impacts of Loss and Recommendations for Improved Support', IOM Publications Platform.

[52] Working Group on Enforced or Involuntary Disappearances, Follow-up Report to the Recommendations, February 2014, available at https://trial.ba/wp-content/uploads/2016/02/Follow-upreportBiHFeb2014.pdf.

[53] R. Rubio-Marín and C. Sandoval, 'Engendering the reparations jurisprudence of the Inter-American Court of Human Rights: The promise of the Cotton Field Judgment' (2011) 33, 4 *Human Rights Quarterly* 1062.

## 1.4 Structure of the Book

The book is divided in two parts collecting analyzes of still insufficiently elaborated issues. The first part of the book, consisting of four chapters, considers horizontal issues: the application of enforced disappearances in armed conflicts, the impact of the Guiding Principles on the Search of Disappeared Persons, new technologies and enforced disappearances, as well as social rights. Three of these chapters closely zoom in on the two UN bodies dealing with enforced disappearances, the WGEID and the CED, showing their impact, contribution to the field, as well as pointing out areas for improvement. The second part of the book, consisting of five chapters, scrutinizes global challenges based on case studies, namely the role of NGOs, disappearances by non-State actors and of migrants, reparation and ratification of the ICPPED. Those chapters are all embedded in a regional case study, which allows for delving in more detail into examples, which showcase broader trends and challenges.

Chapter 2 analyzes enforced disappearances that occur during armed conflict, which is a worldwide phenomenon, raising many theoretical and practical questions. The author of the chapter, Ivan Jovanović, himself a practitioner, addresses the issue of enforced disappearances in armed conflicts through the lens of the ICPPED. The chapter explores the differences between enforced disappearances and the term 'missing persons' existing in international humanitarian law. It also demonstrates how the ICPPED fills gaps in IHL, highlighting the advantage of an international treaty in contrast to customary law – in particular for practitioners – as well as the potential of the continues nature of enforced disappearances for accountability efforts. Furthermore, limitations of the ICPPED in the context of armed conflict are shown, particularly by not including non-State actors among the potential perpetrators. While victims of enforced disappearances are a narrower group within the broader category of missing persons, the chapter argues for cautiousness not to exclude large numbers of families of missing persons from access to aid, services and reparation.

The CED's Guiding Principles on the Search for Disappeared persons adopted in 2019 are embedded in a similar approach, by stating principles that States are expected to apply in all instances, not just when it is clear that an enforced disappearance took place. Chapter 3, exploring the origins and assessing the impact of the Guiding Principles, was written by the two CED rapporteurs appointed to prepare the Guiding Principles, Maria Clara Galvis Patiño and Rainer Huhle. The authors highlight the autonomous obligation of searching for disappeared persons and explain how through its various instruments – urgent actions and State reporting – the CED became aware of the need to adopt guidelines on the search. The chapter's unique contribution is particularly the exploration of the impact the Guiding Principles have, during their first four years of existence (2019–2022), already made on public policies of States – both State parties and non-State parties to the ICPPED, case law, legislation, academic literature and civil society. The chapter shows the particularly significant impact in Latin American countries and the Inter-American system, while also being showcased in other regions, notably with the inclusion of the Guiding Principles in the Guidelines adopted by the African Union. The wide impact of the Guiding Principles can be explained by the highly participatory consultation process leading to its adoption, as well as efforts to widely distribute the Guiding Principles. It also is a tribute of the involvement and activities of families of disappeared persons, who were involved in the consultation process and are now demanding the Guiding Principles to be implemented domestically.

The search for disappeared persons and thus the efficient implementation of the Guiding Principles are strongly impacted by the development of new technologies. Gabriella Citroni, the author of the WGEID 2023 thematic study on the topic of new technologies and enforced disappearances wrote Chapter 4, showing both opportunities and challenges in the area. The chapter briefly analyzes the main finding from the work of UN Special Procedures on new technologies, including the WGEID, and then demonstrates the role new technologies have so far played in the activities of the WGEID, as well as areas for improvement. Citroni shows that there are still many questions as to which new technologies would be accepted – and how their credibility could be assessed – by the WGEID when reviewing cases under its humanitarian mandate. The chapter further explores how the WGEID could better engage with new technologies during its country visits. While highlighting the necessity of traditional approaches and techniques, the chapter shows also that new technologies can greatly enrich the functioning of the WGEID and argues that their opportunities outweigh the challenges. The questions posed and solutions proposed in this chapter can be equally relevant for the CED.

Chapter 5, written by Ariel Dulitzky, turns to social rights of disappeared persons. This often overlooked topic is crucial, as access to property, health care, education, religious facilities and other social and cultural rights can be restricted, discontinued or permanently blocked due to an enforced disappearance. Dulitzky demonstrates positive aspects in the CED's approach to social rights, as well as showcases gaps. He proposes to use approaches of the WGEID, Inter-American Court of Human Rights, UN treaty bodies and special procedures to seek alternative solutions. In particular, the WGEID 2015 thematic study on economic social and cultural has shown both how people who are unable to fully exercise those rights are more likely to become victims of enforced disappearances and that those who enforced disappearance have a particular negative effect on enjoyment of social rights by the disappeared persons and their families. The significant contribution of the Inter-American Court of Human Rights stems from its understanding of enforced disappearances as a multiple violation of multi-offensive nature and by being a pioneer in acknowledging families as victims of enforced disappearances. Dultizky argues that relying on those approaches would allow us to address the restrictive interpretations applied so far by the CED.

As mentioned above, the second part of the book analyzes the universal challenges from regional or domestic perspectives. It starts with Chapter 6, on the NGO contributions to eradicate enforced disappearances in Latin America. Born from the enormous suffering of mothers and grandmothers looking for their loved ones, the NGOs in Latin America have grown into one of the main forces to initiate, support and complement activities of the universal, regional and national institutional mechanisms that combat enforced disappearances. The chapter's author, Horacio Ravenna, was himself engaged with several of these crucial NGOs and provides a first-hand analysis of their background, current challenges and perspectives of their involvement in the eradication of enforced disappearances. The chapter is a tribute to the people and organizations that were substantial in pushing for an international treaty on enforced disappearances.

While the initial consolidation of NGOs was made because of widespread enforced disappearances of political opponents in Latin America, the reasons for more current disappearances are complex, covering particularly war on crime and migration. Chapter 7 by Lene Guercke demonstrates how contemporary disappearances in Mexico have become a conceptual challenge for the international framework on enforced disappearances. The country has experienced an unprecedented increase in disappearances since the adoption of the militarized approach to public security in 2006, commonly called the 'war on drugs'. One of the features of those disappearances is that they are often committed by criminal organizations, thus triggering questions on whether and how the enforced disappearances framework can be applied at all. The chapter's conceptual contribution is an analysis of whether a failure to identify dead bodies can be a form of enforced disappearances and under which circumstances impunity can be assessed as form of acquiescence. In the search for a response to the second question, the chapter engages in depth with the 2023 CED's statements on non-State actors.

Chapter 8 engages with another form of contemporary disappearances, that is, disappearances in migration, zooming in on Africa. As the contribution by Eva Nudd and Barbara Lochbihler makes clear, the continent is an important case study for this topic due to the widespread disappearances occurring to migrants and refugee seekers, as well as regional initiatives aiming at addressing precisely this topic. Among others, the African Commission adopted in 2021 a resolution addressing the problem of missing migrants in Africa and the impact on their families. The authors, both knowing and have worked on enforced disappearances on the continent, highlight also practical challenges, such as the lack of understanding of the very concept and distrust in authorities. They conclude that awareness raising and capacity building is a crucial step to overcome existing challenges.

Western Balkan countries have achieved incredible progress in establishing the fates and whereabouts of 30,000 (out of 40,000) missing persons after the wars in the 1990s and 2000s. Chapter 9 engages with an aspect that so far has received less scholarly attention than the search for the disappeared persons in this region: reparation. The authors of the chapter, Milica Kolaković-Bojović and Jasminka Džumhur, both researchers and practitioners from the Western Balkans, present an in-depth analysis of the complex legal situation on reparation in the region. They point out the impact of differentiation between family members of civilians and military members, as well as the challenges of families living currently in different States than where their loved ones disappeared. While the adopted laws differ between the three analyzed countries, namely Bosnia and Hercegovina, Serbia and Croatia, a common denominator is the absence of the crime of enforced disappearances, which appears particularly surprising in a region where the violation was so widespread.

Considering the undisputable importance of the universal applicability of the ICPPED, Chapter 10 is devoted to strategies of increasing ratification. Written by Koji Teraya, a human rights expert coming himself from the region with the least amount of ratification – the Asia-Pacific region – it takes such a regional focus. Teraya analyzes the impact of such a situation on the ratification coverage goals set by the CED and emphasizes that this imbalance suggests that focusing on bottleneck regions will be more effective for increasing ratification. The chapter concludes that the slow tempo of the ratification and the seriousness of enforced disappearances urge for the need to arrange symptomatic treatments, along with suggesting possible strategies to increase the number of ratifications in the Asia-Pacific region.

We expect that our assessment and contextualization of the most serious problems, recent achievements, current debates and rich experience of countries and regions with widespread problems of enforced disappearances in this book will influence the scientific and professional community – along with decision-makers at the national level – to recognize and address the challenges associated with this phenomenon in a most efficient manner. We sincerely hope this book will not remain exclusively on the shelves and in the hands of academic community members. After all, our overarching goal was to shed light on and explain the phenomenon of enforced disappearances and provide solutions for how to deal with them globally, regionally and locally through the joint efforts of the UN and regional mechanisms, national authorities, NGOs and the academic community.

# 2

## Enforced Disappearances in Armed Conflict through the Lenses of the International Convention for the Protection of All Persons from Enforced Disappearance

IVAN JOVANOVIĆ*

### 2.1 Introduction

Armed conflicts always result not only in mass deaths confirmed during or after the conflicts but also in large numbers of people who are considered missing or disappeared. They may be soldiers counted as 'missing in action', civilians whose bodies are not recovered who are killed in massacres, individual executions, or civilians not targeted as such but fallen during hostilities. Very often they may be civilians and combatants still alive but forcibly displaced or arrested and denied contact with families or their own party. Many armed conflicts where this is frequently happening become almost forgotten while they are still ongoing. Developments that are not only politically and morally shocking but are of global impact, like the full-scale invasion of Ukraine in February 2022 and the ensuing war, with many enforced disappearances among other international crimes documented or alleged there, remind us of the pertinence of the topic of enforced disappearances in the context of armed conflicts.

This contribution will address and discuss the applicability of the International Convention for the Protection of All Persons from Enforced Disappearance (hereinafter – ICPPED, or the Enforced Disappearance Convention, or the Convention) in armed conflicts, what the Convention brings to prevention of enforced disappearances in such situations and how different ICPPED is from international humanitarian law (IHL) norms designed specifically for armed conflicts.

* The views expressed herein are those of the author and do not necessarily reflect the views of their employer.

Besides laying out rules and aspects of the Convention and of IHL that are most relevant for the issue of enforced disappearances in armed conflicts, the chapter will highlight key differences between enforced disappearances and the broader notion of missing persons while trying to briefly capture their common societal impact. It will then proceed to discuss interoperability and mutual reinforcement between IHL and the Convention in armed conflicts, especially in relation to three issues, selected for their practical but sometimes neglected implications: limitations to application of customary IHL by national authorities, accountability for war-time enforced disappearances in domestic jurisdictions and addressing enforced disappearances by non-State actors.

The chapter will include and reflect experience and perspectives of the author as someone who is neither an academic nor an official directly applying the Enforced Disappearance Convention or IHL but a development practitioner involved in capacity building of national judicial and law enforcement institutions and civil society in affected countries and territories. In that vein, some of the examples referred to in the text will be coming from such experience and, in particular, because of their relevance, those related to two geographical and conflict contexts: the Western Balkans region – which has had by far the largest number of war crimes trials and investigations before national courts and a huge number of missing persons cases, including forced disappearances[1] – and Ukraine, where currently the caseload of IHL violations and missing persons and forced disappearances is immense and growing.[2]

## 2.2 Societal Impact of Conflict-Related Disappearances

The problem of missing persons, and victims of enforced disappearance as a part of that category (more on the differences between the two in Section 2.5), constitutes a very important element of political, legal and social transition processes during and following armed conflicts but also

[1] There were over 40,000 missing persons as the result of the Western Balkans armed conflicts of 1991–2001, with over 11,000 still unaccounted for, according to the Western Balkans regional data base of the International Commission on Missing Persons (ICMP), available at www.icmp.int/news/western-balkans-governments-launch-unique-public-database-of-missing-persons-cases/.

[2] According to an ICMP estimate, at least 30,000 people were considered missing in Ukraine at the end of 2022, with the number growing by the day, available at www.icmp.int/news/eu-supports-icmp-training-program-for-ukrainian-scientists-in-applying-dna-to-identify-thousands-of-missing-persons-from-the-war/.

after widespread political violence or following repressive regimes. This problem outlives wars and generates a strong impact on societies, communities and, most directly, victims. In this context, the notion of 'victim' includes not only the person who was subjected to enforced disappearance but 'any individual who has suffered harm as the direct result' of the crime of enforced disappearance.[3] This, first of all, includes families of the people that went missing.

The lack of knowledge of and prolonged uncertainty about the fate of the missing person and the sense of a mounting anxiety experienced as an effect of the disappearance have a long-lasting, damaging and often unique psychological impact on individuals and whole families, including trauma transfers within families and communities and across generations.[4] Families of the missing, and – especially when remaining the sole breadwinners – women, in particular, also very often have to cope with ensuing economic, legal and social problems.

Resolving the fate of missing persons, including victims of enforced disappearances, recovery and identification of their remains, and providing their families, but also the public, with credible information are of essential importance, first of all, for the families' own healing and closure. At the same time, this is also fundamental for human rights, the rule of law and democratic governance in a country, as well as for fact-based overcoming of the past and reconciliation and for social solidarity and cohesion as parts of post-conflict recovery and sustainable peace and human security.

State authorities need to enable the families of the missing to enjoy the rights and services they are entitled to, including, inter alia, access to psychosocial support and health services; economic support; fulfilment of

[3] International Convention for the Protection of All Persons from Enforced Disappearance (ICPPED), UN Doc. A/61/488, Annex, Arts. 12 and 24(1). UN Human Rights Council, Report of the Working Group on Enforced of Voluntary Disappearances (hereinafter – WGEID), General Comment on the right to the truth in relation to enforced disappearance, A/HRC/16/48, 26 January 2011, para. 4 at p. 16.

[4] Family members of missing persons develop, inter alia, more anxiety and suffer more often from PTSD than family members of those whose deaths have been conclusively established. M. Blaauw and V. Lähteenmäki, '"Denial and silence" or "acknowledgement and disclosure"' (2002) 84, 848 *International Review of the Red Cross* 767–83 at 771, citing the studies among the survivors in Cambodia, Bosnia and Herzegovina, Croatia and Honduras. Such are also personal accounts and experiences of aid workers, CSO activists, psychologists and other professionals working with missing persons' families in other post-conflict environments (including Cyprus, Serbia, Kosovo, Colombia, South Sudan, Syria, Timor Leste and Sri Lanka).

their right to know and other rights, including access to justice; and effective and inclusive reparations.[5] Justice, including criminal accountability of those responsible for enforced disappearances, is among the main needs and expressed desires of the families of the direct victims (usually not among their first and foremost priorities but becoming more prominent over time).[6]

Such impact of enforced disappearances at individual and societal level should also serve as a backdrop for analysis, including in this chapter, of the normative framework pertaining to enforced disappearances and for assessment of its effectiveness, especially with a view of accountability.

## 2.3 The Notion of Armed Conflict

Before turning to discussion about enforced disappearances and armed conflicts in legal terms, we should briefly define, for the purpose of this chapter, what armed conflict is.

The landmark *Tadic* decision by the International Criminal Tribunal for the former Yugoslavia (ICTY) defined that an armed conflict exists whenever 'there is a resort to armed force between states' (international armed conflict) or 'protracted armed violence between governmental authorities and organized armed groups or between such groups within a State' (non-international armed conflict).[7] For international armed conflict, occurrence of de facto hostilities is sufficient, no declaration or official acknowledgement of the conflict is needed. For non-international armed conflict,[8] in order to establish a threshold for 'protracted armed violence', two additional criteria, not needed for international armed

[5] According to the Updated Set of Principles for the Protection and Promotion of Human Rights through Action to combat impunity (Orentlicher-Joinet Principles), E/CN.4/2005/102/Add.1, 2005, available at https://documents-dds-ny.un.org/doc/UNDOC/GEN/G05/109/00/PDF/G0510900.pdf?OpenElement.

[6] Needs assessments by the International Committee of the Red Cross (ICRC) among families of missing persons conducted in Nepal, Timor Leste, Sri Lanka, and Colombia, as referred to in M. Crettol, L. Milner, A. La Rosa and J. Stockwell, 'Establishing mechanisms to clarify the fate and whereabouts of missing persons: A proposed humanitarian approach' (2017) 99, 2 *International Review of the Red Cross* 589–618 at 599.

[7] International Criminal Tribunal for the former Yugoslavia (ICTY), *Prosecutor* v. *Tadic*, Decision on the Defence Motion for Interlocutory Appeal on Jurisdiction, 1995, para. 70.

[8] Differences between thresholds for determination of those non-international armed conflicts in which Art. 3, common to all the Geneva Conventions, applies and those in which Additional Protocol II to the Geneva Conventions is applicable will be left aside for the purpose of this chapter.

conflicts, must be met: one is that the conflict should reach a certain *intensity*,[9] and the other is that the *organization of the parties* to the conflict must also reach a certain level.[10] The Tadic definition of armed conflict, such as the criteria of intensity and organization, has been regularly applied in the subsequent jurisprudence of the ICTY, International Criminal Tribunal for Rwanda (ICTR), International Criminal Court (ICC) and hybrid and many national courts and are widely regarded as reflecting customary international law.[11]

The situations remaining below the armed conflict thresholds are those of 'internal disturbances and tensions, such as riots, isolated and sporadic acts of violence and other acts of a similar nature'[12] or 'banditry, unorganized and short-lived insurrections, or terrorist activities'.[13] Such situations are not considered armed conflicts and are not subject to IHL.

The existence of an armed conflict, international or non-international, is always a factual determination, made by judicial or other bodies during or after a conflict, based on circumstances on the ground.

[9] The criterion is developed and explained in the ICTY jurisprudence: for example, *Tadic*, Trial Judgment (TJ), 1997, paras. 562–7; *Prosecutor* v. *Delalic et al.*, (*Celebici* case), Trial Judgment, 1998, paras. 188–90; *Prosecutor* v. *Limaj et al.*, Trial Judgment, 2005, paras. 135–70; *Prosecutor* v. *Haradinaj et al.*, Trial Judgment, 2008, paras. 49, 90–9. See also International Committee of the Red Cross (ICRC), Commentary on the First Geneva Convention, 2016, Art. 3, para. 439, available at https://ihl-databases.icrc.org/ihl/full/GCI-commentary.

[10] Also developed and explained in the ICTY jurisprudence: for example, *Haradinaj*, Trial Judgment, 2008, paras. 65–70, 83–9, *Limaj*, Trial Judgment, 2005, paras. 94–5, 101–24, 170; *Prosecutor* v. *Boskoski et al.*, Trial Judgment, 2008, paras. 185–92. Also Commentary on the First Geneva Convention, 2016, paras. 448–51.

[11] ICRC, Commentary on the First Geneva Convention, 2016, Art. 2, para. 218, Art. 3, paras. 421 and 435. See also, for example, International Law Association, Final Report on the Notion of Armed Conflict in International Law, 2008, p. 14; J. Grignon, 'The beginning of application of international humanitarian law: A discussion of a few challenges' (2014) 96, 893 *International Review of the Red Cross* 139–62 at 162.

[12] Protocol Additional to the Geneva Conventions of 12 August 1949 relating to the Protection of Victims of Non-International Armed Conflicts, Additional Protocol II, 8 June 1977, Art. 1 (all the Geneva Conventional and Additional Protocol available at ICRC Database, Treaties, States Parties and Commentaries, Geneva Conventions of 1949, Additional Protocols and their Commentaries, available at https://ihl-databases.icrc.org/en/ihl-treaties/geneva-conventions-1949additional-protocols-and-their-commentaries).

[13] For example, *Tadic*, Trial Judgment, 1997, para. 562; International Criminal Tribunal for Rwanda (ICTR), *Prosecutor* v. *Akayesu*, Trial Judgment, 1998, para. 625. ICRC, Treaties, States Parties and Commentaries, Protocol I and Protocol II Additional to the Geneva Conventions, Commentary of 1. January 1987, para. 6341, available at https://ihl-databases.icrc.org/en/ihl-treaties/api-1977/introduction/commentary/1987?activeTab=1949GCs-APs-and-commentaries.

## 2.4 Enforced Disappearance and the Convention

The Enforced Disappearance Convention, which entered into force on 23 December 2010, is the first universal treaty that prohibits enforced disappearances and provides for specific obligations for States Parties with regard to prevention, search and accountability.

The Convention defines enforced disappearance as 'arrest, detention, abduction or any other form of deprivation of liberty by agents of the State or by persons or groups of persons acting with the authorization, support or acquiescence of the State, followed by a refusal to acknowledge the deprivation of liberty or by concealment of the fate or whereabouts of the disappeared person, which place such a person outside the protection of the law' (Article 2 of the ICPPED).

The Convention obliges State parties to ensure that enforced disappearance constitutes an offence under their respective criminal legislations (Article 4), punishable by appropriate penalties (Article 7), and subject to *aut dedere, aut iudicare* principle (Article 9 and Article 11). The State parties have to ensure the individual right to report facts or allegations of enforced disappearances to the competent authorities and their obligation is to examine the allegations and investigate (Article 12). Some of these States' obligations will be also addressed in Section 2.6.

Enforced disappearance is understood as a complex and often composite and cumulative violation of different fundamental rights of the disappeared person: the right to life; the right not to be subjected to torture, cruel inhuman or degrading treatment or punishment; the right to liberty and security of a person; to recognition before the law; to humane conditions of detention; and to a fair trial.[14]

## 2.5 Differentiating between the Notions of 'Enforced Disappearance' and 'Missing Persons'

For a proper understanding of enforced disappearances in armed conflict, it is important to juxtapose it with the notion of missing persons, a

[14] For example, UN Human Rights Committee, *Bleier* v. *Uruguay*, UN Doc. CCPR/C/15/D/30/1978, 1982; *Sarma* v. *Sri Lanka*, UN CCPR/C/78/D/950/2000, 2003; Inter-American Court of Human Rights, *Velasquez Rodriguez* v. *Honduras*, IACHR Series C No. 4, 1988, *Juan Humberto Sanchez* v. *Honduras*, IACHR Series C No. 99, IHRL 1482, 2003; European Court of Human Rights (ECtHR), *Kaya* v. *Turkey*, 1998, Reports of Judgments and Decisions 1998-I, p. 324; *Gongadze* v. *Ukraine*, application 3456/02, judgment 8 November 2005.

phenomenon that is, as mentioned, a corollary of any war, causes significant societal and legal consequences and includes victims of enforced disappearances.

There is no mandatory or single definition of missing person under international law. The broadest and most widely applied one is the definition that the International Committee of the Red Cross (ICRC) uses and recommends for national legislations, by which a missing person is one 'whose whereabouts are unknown to his/her relatives and/or who, on the basis of reliable information, has been reported missing in accordance with national legislation in connection with an international or non-international armed conflict, or a situation of internal violence or disturbances, natural catastrophes, or any other situation that may require the intervention of a competent State authority'.[15] It covers situations of armed conflicts, which is of our interest, but also goes beyond that.

While the notions of missing persons and enforced disappearances overlap to an extent, they are often unnecessarily and sometimes wrongly conflated. Two legal and practical differences between these two categories will be outlined here.

The first main difference between missing persons and victims of enforced disappearances is that the ICPPED's definition of enforced disappearance includes an *unlawful act*: an arrest, detention, abduction, or other form of deprivation of liberty followed by a refusal to acknowledge the deprivation of liberty or by concealment of the fate or whereabouts of the person. All such acts – actions followed by intentional failure to provide information – are violations of human rights and, as required by the Convention, should constitute a criminal offence. In armed conflicts, however, people may often go missing not only as a result of unlawful acts but also as a consequence of military conduct that is lawful under IHL. For example, combatants, whether members of State armed forces or non-State armed groups, can go missing in action – after being shot dead or mortally wounded in a military action between combatants. This may also happen to civilians if they take a direct part in hostilities, who then, for such time, may be legitimately targeted.[16]

[15] ICRC, Guiding principles/model law on the missing; The Domestic Implementation of International Humanitarian Law: A Manual, Annex IV, available at www.icrc.org/en/doc/assets/files/publications/icrc-002-4028.pdf.

[16] Additional Protocol I, Art. 51(3); ICRC Database, Customary IHL, Civilians' Loss of Protection from Attack, r. 6, (all the Cusrommary IHL rules available at https://ihl-databases.icrc.org/en/customary-ihl/v1). See also N. Melzer, *Interpretative guidance on*

Civilians may also perish as a result of lawful combat operations – when incidental loss of lives of civilians occurs in a strike that is compliant with IHL requirements of distinction (an attack not directed at civilians or civilian objects as such or without distinguishing between military and civilian objectives), proportionality and precautions. In such situations, bodies of civilians and combatants may be left abandoned unintentionally, or buried in haste, or improperly disposed of or managed in an attempt of a burial, especially mass burials, which could then make their identification or discovery difficult or impossible, and such people could be reported as missing.

It may also happen that in the course of mass displacements of people during a conflict individuals become separated while fleeing, or lose communication with their families or are left behind; while many of them are usually traced and reunited, a number of such persons may remain missing.

This distinction, nonetheless, by no means renders the category of enforced disappearances dwarfed by the broader notion of missing persons or less relevant in armed conflicts. While it is a reality that during any war people can perish, go missing or be buried in mass graves as result of acts that are not per se unlawful, it is also true that people who are reported as missing and those found in mass graves are indeed often victims of forced abductions and summary executions. They are often intentionally thrown into unmarked man-made graves, or into such locations as pits, caves or dumping sites, which offer possibility of concealment of their remains. Persons that are counted as missing also often include those that have been captured or abducted and then held incommunicado in secret locations. Those whose remains are found in a mass grave are not always and necessarily victims of unlawful acts, but any mass grave found in connection with an armed conflict or mass violence should be carefully investigated with regard to the cause of the death.

The second main difference between the notions of missing persons and victims of enforced disappearances is that the ICPPED's definition of enforced disappearance also presupposes that a *State is behind the disappearance*: either representatives or agents of the State, or persons or groups of persons 'acting with the authorization, support or acquiescence

*the notion of direct participation in hostilities under international humanitarian law* (ICRC, 2009), available at www.icrc.org/en/doc/assets/files/other/icrc-002-0990.pdf.

of the State' (as the State's de facto agents).[17] Unlike victims of enforced disappearances under the terms of ICPPED, missing persons in the sense of the aforementioned broader notion under the ICRC's definition may also include those who went missing not due to acts by or attributable to a State or de facto State agent but by acts of non State actors. This is particularly relevant in contexts of non-international armed conflicts or violence and disturbances that are short of an armed conflict threshold, when perpetrators could be non-State armed groups. It is also relevant in situations when groups are State-controlled but their link to a State either cannot be easily legally proven, or proving such link would be intentionally avoided for political and other reasons or when one party in a conflict does not recognize the party responsible for disappearances as a State.[18]

Therefore, it is important not to use the term 'victims of enforced disappearance' as synonymous to 'missing persons'. While all victims of enforced disappearances or disappeared persons are also missing persons until their fate or whereabouts are established, not each and every missing person is a victim of enforced disappearance. Likewise, not every case of a person going missing in an armed conflict and not all the bodies found in a mass grave, even if such grave is improperly marked or not marked at all, should be considered or necessarily presumed as victims of war crimes, crimes against humanity or enforced disappearance as an autonomous crime. On the other hand, it is justified, fully legitimate and also mandatory under most of national laws that each body found should be not only examined for identification but also give rise to an investigation to establish the cause of the death and whether the person has fallen a victim of a war crime or any other unlawful act.

In the author's view, polices, legislation and development support actions, including reparation measures, to address needs, rights and status of families of missing persons should not be limited only to families of those considered victims of enforced disappearance in the sense of the ICPPED. Such support would then be unjustifiably limited only to cases where the fact of someone going missing could be proven as

[17] ICPPED, Art. 2. Working Group on Enforced Disappearance, Compilation of General Comments on the Declaration on the Protection of All Persons from Enforced Disappearance, A/HRC/7/2, para. 26 (para. 1 of the general comment on the definition of enforced disappearance).

[18] While international human rights law (ICPPED's) definition does not include non-State actors, definition of enforced disappearance under international criminal law does, but only with regard to crimes against humanity, as it will be explained in a section below.

resulting directly from unlawful acts behind which was a State, whereas families of all the missing persons, be them victims of enforced disappearance or not, as mentioned at the beginning of the chapter, share the same needs and expectations.

## 2.6 Enforced Disappearance, IHL and Armed Conflict

Before discussing the applicability and relevance of the ICPPED in armed conflict, we shall first briefly capture what IHL, as the primary normative source for situations of armed conflicts, offers to address enforced disappearances as well as missing persons as a broader notion.

The IHL conventions do not directly address enforced disappearance and do not even contain that term. Nonetheless, prohibition of enforced disappearance in armed conflict is a customary international law norm, according to the most reliable and authoritative source today on customary IHL – the Customary International Humanitarian Law Study by the ICRC (hereinafter: Customary IHL Study). In its Rule 98, the Customary IHL Study says that 'enforced disappearance is prohibited' and that 'state practice establishes this rule as a norm of customary international law applicable in both international and non-international armed conflicts'.[19] This prohibition encompasses, like in the ICPPED, a duty to investigate cases of alleged enforced disappearance.[20]

The prohibition of enforced disappearance in customary IHL has been regarded, as the Customary IHL Study explains, as a cumulative effect of the existence of a number of other IHL rules that the Study has also identified as having become a part of international customary law, most notably and most directly the prohibition of arbitrary deprivation of liberty (Rule 99), the prohibition of torture and other cruel or inhuman treatment (Rule 90) and the prohibition of murder (Rule 89). Some other customary rules also contributed to that formative cumulative effect, such as the rule, applicable only in international armed conflicts, concerning registration, visits and transmission of information with respect to persons deprived of their liberty (Chapter 37 of the Rules), and the rule, applicable only in non-international armed conflicts, requiring parties to a conflict to take steps to prevent disappearances, including through the registration of persons deprived of their liberty (Rule 123). As the Study also points out, the customary law prohibition of enforced

[19] ICRC, Customary IHL Study, Enforced Disappearance, r. 98.
[20] Ibid.

disappearance should also be viewed considering the rule requiring respect for family life (Rule 105) and the rule that each party to a conflict must take all feasible measures to account for persons reported missing as a result of the armed conflict and to provide their family members with information it has on their fate (Rule 117).

The Customary IHL Study, originally published in 2005 – hence before the adoption of the ICPPED in December 2006 – came to the customary law status of the prohibition of enforced disappearance in armed conflicts by examining a number of sources indicating State practice and *opinion iuris* in relation to the aforementioned rules. It deduced it, inter alia, from prohibition of enforced disappearance in the legislation and military manuals of a number of countries;[21] repeated condemnations by States and the UN bodies, including the UN Security Council, of enforced disappearances; the Inter-American Convention on the Forced Disappearance of Persons; international bodies' resolutions, as well as in the findings by human rights courts and bodies that enforced disappearance violates several other rights (Inter American Commission and Court of Human Rights, UN Human Rights Committee, European Court of Human Rights – ECtHR).[22] The universal customary prohibition was found to be based also on the inclusion of enforced disappearance as a crime against humanity in the ICC Statute and on the jurisprudence of the ICTY on enforced disappearance as a crime against humanity. Finally, the Study also found it confirmed by non-existence of official contrary practice: no State has ever claimed the freedom to enforce the disappearance of persons.[23]

There are several other rights embodied in the four Geneva Conventions and Additional Protocol I, also making a part of customary international law, that are directly related to missing persons in armed conflicts and that impose certain duties and standards of care to parties to armed conflicts that can prevent enforced disappearances or help in resolving the fate of those believed to be disappeared. In the event of death, all parties must use all means they can to identify the dead, including recording all available identifying information, before a burial

[21] Ibid. The ICRC's Customary IHL Study referred to the national legislation, in force at the time of the making of the Study, of Armenia, Australia, Azerbaijan, Belarus, Canada, Congo, El Salvador, France Germany, Mali, Netherlands, New Zealand, Niger, Paraguay, Peru and the United Kingdom, the draft legislation of Burundi, Nicaragua, and Trinidad and Tobago and military manuals of Colombia, El Salvador, Indonesia and Peru.

[22] Ibid.

[23] Ibid.

or disposal of the remains and marking the locations of graves.[24] The remains of the dead must be disposed of in a respectful manner and their graves properly maintained and respected.[25] In an international armed conflict, each party must endeavour to facilitate the return of the remains of the deceased.[26] All parties to an armed conflict, international or non-international, must take all feasible measures to account for persons reported missing as a result of the armed conflict and to provide family members with any information they have on the fate of their relatives.[27]

All the aforementioned treaty and customary norms of IHL, as the primary regulator in armed conflicts, create a substantially fair and adequate normative safety net for the prohibition of enforced disappearance and for the search for and identification of the disappeared and the missing in situations of armed conflicts. Nonetheless, as it will be explained below, there are potentially significant roles for the ICPPED to play besides and in conjunction with IHL in relation to armed conflicts.

### 2.6.1 *Applicability of ICPPED in Armed Conflicts*

The ICPPED, clearly, applies not only in peacetime but also in and to the situations of armed conflicts. The text of the Convention itself does not exclude any category of persons from its protection by guaranteeing, in Article 1(1), that 'no one shall be subjected to enforced disappearance'. Moreover, it explicitly says, in Article 1(1), that 'no exceptional circumstances', including '*a state of war or a threat of war*' (emphasis added), may be invoked as a justification for enforced disappearance, thus

24 Geneva Convention (I) on Wounded and Sick in Armed Forces in the Field, 1949, Arts. 16–7; Geneva Convention (II) on Wounded, Sick and Shipwrecked of Armed Forces at Sea, 1949, Arts. 19–20; Geneva Convention (III) on Prisoners of War, 1949, Arts. 120–2; Geneva Convention (IV) on Civilians, 1949, Arts. 129–31 and Arts. 136–9 (applicable to internees); For the customary law status of the rule: IHL Study, Accounting for the Dead, r. 116.

25 Art. 17 of Geneva Convention I; Art. 20 of Geneva Convention II; Art. 120 of Geneva Convention III; Art. 130 (applicable to internees) of Geneva Convention IV; Art. 34(2) of Additional Protocol I. Customary IHL Study, Disposal of the Dead, r. 115.

26 In particular, Arts. 34(2 and 3) of Additional Protocol I, and Customary IHL Study, Return of the Remains and Personal Effects of the Dead, r. 114, but also stemming from Art. 17(3) of Geneva Convention I, Art. 120(6) of Geneva Convention III, and Art. 130(2) of Geneva Convention IV.

27 Art. 122 of Geneva Convention III; Arts. 136 and 26 of Geneva Convention IV, Art. 33 of Additional Protocol I; Customary IHL Study, Accounting for Missing Persons, r. 117. Also Arts. 16–7 of Geneva Convention I, and Art. 19 of Geneva Convention II.

making prohibition of or protection from enforced disappearance one of the non-derogable international human rights.

Besides the text of the ICPPED itself, and even if there had been no such provisions in the Convention in the first place, another more general avenue for its applicability in armed conflicts is a general principle that international human rights law can be directly applied in situations of armed conflict together, in parallel or in interplay with IHL. In the words of the ICRC, 'in situations of armed conflict, human rights law complements and reinforces the protection afforded by international humanitarian law'.[28] This principle, gradually developing and growing in substance, and nuanced interplay between the two bodies of law, coming, inter alia, with the process of humanization of IHL through human rights law,[29] is generally widely accepted today. Espoused as a principle by the International Court of Justice in three of its cases[30] (though not without some inconsistencies), this has been a position also taken and maintained by a majority of States,[31] UN human rights treaty bodies and UN human rights special procedures,[32] by UN General Assembly and UN Security Council resolutions referring to both IHL and human rights law, by the ICRC and by overwhelming international academic opinion.[33]

While the answer to whether human rights law also applies in armed conflict is simple one – yes, it does – the interplay between human rights

28 ICRC, 'IHL and human rights law', 29 October 2010, available at www.icrc.org/en/document/ihl-human-rights-law.

29 On the humanization of law of armed conflict, see, in general, T. Meron, 'The humanization of humanitarian Law' (2000) 94 *American Journal of International Law* 239.

30 International Court of Justice (ICJ), *Legality of the Threat or Use of Nuclear Weapons*, Advisory Opinion, I.C.J. Reports 1996, p. 226, (*Nuclear Weapons*), para. 25; ICJ, *Legal Consequences of the Construction of a Wall in the Occupied Palestinian Territory*, Advisory Opinion, I.C.J. Reports 2004, p. 136 (*Wall*), para. 106; ICJ, *Armed activity on the territory of the Congo* (*Democratic Republic of the Congo v. Uganda*), Judgment, I.C.J. Reports 2005, p. 168, paras. 216–20.

31 With the US and Israel being the main explicit objectors in relation to a number of aspects of the IHL–IHRL relationship.

32 For example, UN Human Rights Committee, General Comment 29, States of Emergency, UN CCPR/C/21/Rev.1/Add.11, 24 July 2001, Art. 4, esp. para. 3; Concluding Observations of the Committee on Economic, Social and Cultural Rights, E/C.12/1/Add.69, 31 August 2001.

33 See, for example, M. Sassoli and L. Olson, 'The relationship between international humanitarian and human rights law where it matters: Admissible killing and internment of fighters in non-international armed conflicts' (2008) 90, 871 *International Review of the Red Cross* 599–627 at 600, 603–5; F. J. Hampson, 'The relationship between international humanitarian law and human rights law from the perspective of a human rights body' (2008) 90, 871 *International Review of the Red Cross* 549–72 at 550–1.

law and IHL in armed conflict, especially in concrete situations and with regard to concrete sets of norms, is not that simple. Even leaving aside the question of extraterritorial application of human rights treaties,[34] the issue of defining and determining relations between the two bodies of law, both in terms of applicable legal regimes and concrete applicable norms in a situation, has been much debated and not (conclusively) resolved. Undoubtedly, IHL is the first to look into when it comes to norms of conduct in an armed conflict. Using the *lex specialis* doctrine (a law governing a specific subject matter [*lex specialis*] overrides a law governing more general matters), with IHL being *lex specialis* as long as an armed conflict is ongoing, has been long held not as unimpeachable but at least a best answer to denote this interrelation.[35] Such position was held by governments and practitioners[36] and also maintained by the ICRC.[37] Many also persuasively argue against this,[38] suggesting other alternatives – not necessarily as approaches but more as tools for interpretation or notions capturing the substance of the IHL–human rights law relation and interplay, such as 'complementarity', 'cross fertilization', 'harmonization', 'parallel applicability', 'integration' or systemic interpretation.[39] The nature of the relation between the two bodies of law is not only a purely theoretical one but has practical implications on certain norm conflicts and on the legal interoperability of actors on the ground.[40] Still, this debated issue does not need to be dwelled on here for one

[34] See, for example, M. Milanović, *Extraterritorial Application of Human Rights Treaties: Law, Principles, Policy* (Oxford University Press, 2011).

[35] ICJ, *Nuclear Weapons*, para. 25; ICJ, *Wall*, para. 106; ICJ, *Congo* v. *Uganda*, paras. 2016–20; Sassoli and Olson, *The relationship between international humanitarian and human rights law where it matters*, pp. 600, 603–5.

[36] For an overview of such positions, K. Abbott, 'A brief overview of legal interoperability challenges for NATO arising from the interrelationship between IHL and IHRL in light of the ECHR' (2014) 96, 893 *International Review of the Red Cross* 107–37 at 110–16.

[37] ICRC, *International Humanitarian Law and the Challenges of Contemporary Armed Conflicts* (ICRC: 2011), p. 14.

[38] For example, W. Schabas, 'Lex specialis? Belt and suspenders? The parallel operation of human rights and the law of armed conflict, and the conundrum of jus ad bellum' (2007) 40, 2 *Israel Law Review* at 59; M. Milanović, 'A norm conflict perspective on the relationship between international humanitarian law and human rights law' (2009) 14 *Journal of Conflict and Security Law* 459.

[39] On the alternatives, see N. Lubell, 'Parallel application of international humanitarian law and international human rights law: An examination of the debate' (2007) 40, 2 *Israel Law Review* at 654–6. For an overview of the IHL–IHRL lex specialis debate, see C. Droege, 'The Interplay between international humanitarian law and international human rights law in situations of armed conflict' (2007) 40, 2 *Israel Law Review* 338.

[40] Abbott, 'A brief overview of legal interoperability challenges for NATO' 107–37.

substantial reason: unlike in relation to some other topics and rights that are regulated differently by IHL and international human rights law or regulated in such ways that are arguably mutually exclusive (such as rules on targeting, or preventive detention in armed conflicts or those regulating occupation), prohibition of enforced disappearance as a matter of human rights law does not encounter any conflicting IHL norm, principle or practice. They are mutually reinforcing. There are differences in terms of scope of what the Convention addresses as enforced disappearance and what IHL regulates in relation to missing persons – as discussed above – and some other differences that are not of great significance, which will be addressed in some details below.

### 2.6.2 *ICPPED vs. Ambiguous Advantage of Customary IHL*

An important advantage of the application of the Convention in situations of armed conflict is that it is an international convention. As previously explained, the IHL treaty does not contain a prohibition of or any reference to enforced disappearance, but IHL, by way of its customary law norms, does positively prohibit enforced disappearance and imposes a duty to investigate, as articulated in Rule 98 of the Customary IHL Study. Being a part of customary international law, the prohibition of enforced disappearance exceeds the reach of the ICPPED: it binds, in the situations of armed conflict, not only those seventy-one State parties to the Convention,[41] but, like most of customary law norms, all countries (as there have been no persistent objectors to the formation of this customary norm). This is especially important in light of the fact that many of the countries that did not ratify the ICPPED were or are engaged in armed conflicts in their own territory or abroad or deal with situations in which enforced disappearances are alleged to have or may occur.[42] The authority of the Customary IHL Study as a tool of telling us what customary IHL is has been widely recognized and is increasing and solidifying over time, due to, inter alia, the ICRC's expertise and special mandate vested to it by the States and the rigour and the extent of the

[41] As of early June 2023, the number of parties was 71 (with the latest ratification being by Finland, in March 2023). A high number of countries (41) signed but did not ratify the ICPPED. See the ratification status available at https://treaties.un.org/pages/ViewDetails.aspx?src=IND&mtdsg_no=IV-16&chapter=4&clang=_en.

[42] The non-State parties include, inter alia, the US, UK, Russian Federation, Belarus, Georgia, Azerbaijan, China, India, Myanmar, Pakistan, Afghanistan, Iran, Yemen, Saudi Arabia, Türkiye, Israel, Syria, Egypt, DR Congo, South Sudan, Ethiopia, Eritrea.

collection of practice and identification of the rules for the Study but also because of lack of repeated and consistent opposition by States.[43]

Still, I would submit, not only the Customary IHL Study as a source of knowledge of what customary law norms are, but even customary law itself as a source of law, have not been sufficiently recognized and understood by many, especially by practitioners, whose job is to apply IHL either during armed conflicts or in hindsight by resolving the cases of disappearances or enforcing criminal accountability. Namely, this author has twenty-year long experience with training and monitoring how officials from justice, law enforcement and institutions for searching for missing persons apply IHL and international criminal law in dealing with conflict-related atrocities and missing persons cases in national jurisdictions (mainly in the countries of the Western Balkans/former Yugoslavia, but also elsewhere, such as in South Sudan, Libya and recently in Ukraine). Based on numerous observations, first-hand reactions and feedback, the understanding of all these practitioners that customary international law is something they can and should apply was very rare.

The reasons are manifold why the vast majority of them, most of whom were lawyers by profession or training, lacked such understating and continued holding a firm professional belief or sense, even after attending international law trainings, that customary international law is either not really applicable or is a kind of exotic legal regime and, in their view, certainly secondary to treaties. Such reasons differ across various local professional and legal contexts, but some things can be observed as common. In legal education, customary international law is usually mentioned and taught about only rarely and only as part of (classes on) public international law and, partly, constitutional law, and only sketchily, without apparently being given proper explanations, especially in terms of customary law practical applicability. Another, practical reason is that practitioners, first of all judges, in national jurisdictions in most of the countries do not dispose of abilities and means (including technical) to research and identify customary law rules themselves as a product of State practice and *opinion iuris*. They are most often not

[43] See the recent empirical research that examines the authority of the Study within the international legal system, which concludes that it is held on par with treaty texts and judicial decisions: M. Milanovic and S. Sivakumaran, 'Assessing the authority of the ICRC Customary IHL Study, how does IHL develop?' (2022) 104, 920–1 *International Review of the Red Cross* 1856–97, and its Annex 1.

sufficiently aware of the usability or even the mere existence of the Customary IHL Study. Importantly, most of the practitioners are operating in the criminal law field, and criminal lawyers, especially theorists and academics in national jurisdictions, mainly traditionally hold that customary law cannot be a source in criminal law at all, or that it is, at best, inapt for such a role. Their position derives from traditional requirements that offences and punishments to be brought as a law must be written (*lex scripta* principle) and must be defined with sufficient clarity (*lex certa* principle), which, as they see it, customary law does not provide. They also use as a key argument that there are no prescribed concrete sanctions in customary law. Such position persists despite the fact that the International Covenant on Civil and Political Rights (ICCPR) and the European Convention on Human Rights (ECHR) allow for punishment for a criminal offence to be based not only on national but also international law.[44] In many national jurisdictions, domestic regulations of international crimes is done in such way, described by scholars as 'dynamic reference to international law by national criminal law provisions',[45] whereby national criminal law itself refers national courts to look into international law, which by default may include customary law, when defining elements of certain crimes. Typical examples of such national systems are or were criminal codes in the countries and jurisdictions of the Western Balkans, where, in relation to war crimes, the respective criminal codes make reference to 'international law', which should mean also customary law.[46] The respective courts, which have dealt with hundreds of such cases so far, have almost never invoked customary international law (with the Court of Bosnia and Herzegovina being the only one in that region inclined to look beyond the conventions and into customary law but mainly through the ICTY jurisprudence). In some countries, like Ukraine, where a dynamic reference to international law also exists in the national criminal code, the

[44] Art. 7 of the ECHR and Art. 15 of the ICCPR allowing for the trial and punishment for any act or omission that is considered criminal according, inter alia, to the general principles of law recognized by civilized nations.

[45] For example, H. Kreicker, 'National prosecution of genocide from a comparative perspective' (2005) 5 *International Criminal Law Review* 312.

[46] In the criminal codes of Bosnia and Herzegovina (in several country's internal jurisdictions), Croatia, Kosovo, Montenegro and Serbia, war crimes have been or are defined by a *chapeau* reading 'whoever, *in violation of international law* . . . orders . . . or commits . . .', thus requiring to look for determination of any of the underlying acts into prohibition of certain conduct by international law – treaty and customary law alike.

currently prevailing interpretation is that it is limited only to ratified treaties, thus excluding customary law.[47]

Therefore, while customary IHL legally enables the prohibition of enforced disappearance and all the related duties and rights and binds all States, not only the State parties to the ICPPED, when it comes to application and enforcement of the norm in domestic legal systems, customary law is not as recognized and appreciated as treaty law. In absence of enforced disappearance from IHL treaties, the ICPPED, hence, has an advantage over the customary law by being a legal ground, in all the ICPPED's State parties and where application of international treaties in domestic jurisdiction is constitutionally or otherwise possible, that is much better recognized by practitioners as a legal source for application within their own domestic legal systems.

### 2.6.3 *Enforced Disappearances in Armed Conflicts and Criminal Accountability*

Another important role for the ICPPED to fill a gap in IHL in relation to armed conflicts is to serve as a basis for criminal accountability for wartime enforced disappearances. Accountability in this context is not only an obligation under the Convention but also a mechanism that is arguably key in ensuring compliance with prevention of enforced disappearance and resolving the cases of disappearances (which will also be addressed in more detail below).[48]

#### 2.6.3.1 No War Crime of Enforced Disappearance

Enforced disappearance is not among the grave breaches (war crimes) of the Geneva Conventions and Additional Protocol I. They are not

[47] Criminal Code of Ukraine, Art. 438, defines war crimes by referring to several concrete underlying acts and to 'use of means of warfare prohibited by *international law*, or any other violations of laws and customs of warfare recognized by international instruments *consented to as binding by the Verkhovna Rada of Ukraine*'. Кримінальний кодекс України, Відомості Верховної Ради України (ВВР), 2001, nos. 25–6, ст. 131 (unofficial translation in English).

[48] On (disagreements on) the role of international criminal justice and accountability in fostering compliance with IHL and deterring crimes, see C. Jenks and G. Acquaviva, 'Debate: The role of international criminal justice in fostering compliance with international humanitarian law' (2014) 96, 895/896 *International Review of the Red Cross* 775–94.

included in war crimes under the Rome Statute (Article 8) either. International criminal tribunals and hybrid courts have not developed jurisprudence on prosecuting enforced disappearance as such as a war crime. While Rule 98 of the Customary IHL Study also entails a duty to investigate enforced disappearances, the Study does not include enforced disappearance among war crimes explicitly enumerated in its Rule 156 on definition of war crimes. What the Study does, though, is that it refers, at the end of its commentary to Rule 156, to enforced disappearance as an example of a *composite war crime* – as conduct that is criminal because it consists of a combination of several war crimes amounting in practice to depriving a person of a fair trial and often also to murder. This is indeed correct. Likewise, with the same arguments that enforced disappearance is a composite human rights violation, as previously explained, we can argue that accountability for enforced disappearances as a war crime may be reached also through the angle of the disappeared person's family members' prolonged suffering that can amount to torture, or inhuman or cruel treatment or outrages upon personal dignity (depending on the extent of the assessed suffering) of the relatives.

Nonetheless, we still cannot say that enforced disappearance as such is established as a war crime in international law – neither in treaty, nor, at the moment, in customary law. For this reason, and especially because the Rome Statute, which has served for the past two decades as a major single reference point for harmonization of national criminal legislation with international criminal and humanitarian law, does not count enforced disappearance as a war crime, States have not included enforced disappearance in their own domestic penalization of war crimes. (At least the author is not aware of any contrary example at the moment but allows that in some national jurisdiction such development might have already taken place.)

#### 2.6.3.2 Limitations of Enforced Disappearance as a Crime against Humanity

Enforced disappearance does exist as an international crime and in the Rome Statute as a crime against humanity. The Rome Statute, in Article 7 (2)(i), defines 'enforced disappearance of persons' as a crime against humanity in a manner that is largely similar to the ICCPED, with the key addition that, under the Rome Statute, 'a political organisation', not only a State, can be behind the crime. Enforced disappearance as a crime against humanity also appeared in the jurisprudence of the ICTY, as one of 'other inhumane acts' provided for in Article 5(1) of the ICTY Statute.[49]

The ICPPED also refers to enforced disappearance as a crime against humanity, but it did not introduce criminal responsibility in that respect; it only acknowledged what was already in international law.[50]

While crimes against humanity also often occur in armed conflicts, and there can be frequent substantive overlapping between war crimes and crimes against humanity, there is a significant difference too between these categories of crimes. Prosecuting enforced disappearance as a crime against humanity requires proving that there has been a *widespread or systematic attack*, carried out against any civilian population, with the perpetrator of the enforced disappearance acting with knowledge of such attack, as distinctive elements of crimes against humanity. Serious violations of IHL in armed conflict (war crimes), on the other hand, and enforced disappearances during an armed conflict can be and often are committed as single or isolated acts[51] or at least do not require proof of a widespread or systematic attack. In reality, a lot of enforced disappearances do occur in the context of or at the scale of widespread or systematic attacks, but this is not necessarily the case. In addition, during or after armed conflicts, authorities, including prosecution services and courts – especially in countries with a lack of independence thereof, may be reluctant, for political and other reasons, to go for proving or accepting evidence of widespread or systematic attacks or even to use such discourse or terminology. This may particularly be the case when the judicial, law enforcement or other institutions supposed to investigate enforced disappearance are from the country that has been behind the disappearances and the widespread or systematic attacks.

Besides the issue of distinctive elements of crimes against humanity, which may leave some instances of war-time enforced disappearances short of the crimes against humanity threshold, another obstacle may be the absence of domestic penalization, in many countries, of crimes

[49] ICTY, *Prosecutor* v. *Kupreskic et al.*, Trial Judgment, 2000, para. 2437.

[50] Travaux préparatoires confirm that States did not intend to give a 'definition' of enforced disappearances as a crime against humanity but mainly to recall that this qualification was accepted, WGEID Report, A/HRC/13/31, 2009, General Comment on enforced disappearance as a crime against humanity, para. 6. Also Art. 5 of ICPPED ('constitutes a crime against humanity as defined in applicable international law and shall attract the consequences provided for under such applicable international law').

[51] See also WGEID, Best practices on enforced disappearances in domestic criminal legislation, A/HRC/16/48/ Add.3, 28 December 2010, paras. 16–8.

against humanity as a separate crime or the non-retroactivity argument in the countries that at some point did introduce this offence in their criminal legislation. While there is a progressive process of inclusion of crimes against humanity as a crime under national law in many countries across the world, often through incorporation of the Rome Statute provisions as a perceived international law model, many still do not provide for domestic criminal responsibility for crimes against humanity. An example, currently very much under spotlights and with a large number of enforced disappearances, is Ukraine (despite, inter alia, its acceptance of the ICC jurisdiction since 2015). On the other hand, some countries envisaged crimes against humanity in their own criminal law, but notwithstanding this and despite facing themselves large number of potential cases of crimes against humanity, including enforced disappearances, from their own past, they do not investigate those cases as crimes against humanity because they had occurred before the amendments to the criminal code. The prime example of such position, given the load of potentially dozens if not hundreds of such cases, are the countries of the Western Balkans. They continue holding – with a notable exception of the Court of Bosnia and Herzegovina, which regularly enters convictions for crimes against humanity – that this would violate the principle of non-retroactive application of criminal law (*nullum crimen sine lege*). Such position in these jurisdictions prevails, based on a mixture of political considerations and legal conservativism, despite the fact that the ECtHR gave an unequivocal answer, and exactly in relation to accountability for crimes against humanity in the Western Balkans, that prosecuting for these crimes as a separate offence when committed before the criminal legislation amendments would be perfectly in line with international and domestic law and would not violate the principle of non-retroactivity.[52]

[52] ECtHR, *Boban Simsic v. Bosnia and Herzegovina*, Decision, App. No. 51552/10, 2012. The ECtHR held that the challenged conviction for crimes against humanity by the Court of BiH, entered for a conduct that took place (in the conflict in the 1990s) before crimes against humanity were introduced as a crime in the BiH Criminal Code (2003), was lawful and in accordance with ECHR's Art. 7 ('No punishment without law'), because the crime had already been a part of international law at the time of the commission. The Court of BiH remains the only in the Western Balkans that tries for crimes against humanity, while the courts from other jurisdictions from that region (other BiH courts, and courts in Croatia, Serbia, Montenegro, Kosovo) still do not.

#### 2.6.3.3 ICPPED's Enforced Disappearance as Autonomous Crime

In the absence of enforced disappearance codified as a war crime and with the aforementioned limitation of treating such conduct as a crime against humanity, the ICPPED does have a role in providing for accountability mechanisms for enforced disappearances in time of armed conflict. The Convention requires the State parties to take the necessary measures to ensure that enforced disappearance constitutes a separate offence under its criminal law (ICPPED's Article 4), covering various modes of liability (Article 6(1)a), including superior responsibility for failure to prevent or supress crimes of enforced disappearance by subordinates (Article 6(1)b, defined very much as in Article 28(b) of the Rome Statute). ICPPED does not establish direct grounds for individual criminal responsibility but obliges States to provide for enforced disappearance as a separate or autonomous crime that must be distinctive from similar offences commonly provided for in national legislation, such as deprivation of liberty, abduction, kidnaping, torture, incommunicado detention, etc.[53] Such codification of enforced disappearance in domestic criminal laws in the way the ICPPED requires, and not only as a crime against humanity (which, as explained, is insufficient and not commensurate to the nature of the offence),[54] would provide for a mechanism legally capable for investigation and holding accountable in domestic courts for a individuals involved in enforced disappearances both during and outside armed conflicts, independently of the context of the crime and a suspect. There are many States, parties to the ICPPED and States in general that are still to make such legislative changes at home.

Enforced disappearance is a continuous crime: as long as the perpetrator continues to conceal the fate and the whereabouts of the persons who have disappeared and these facts remain unknown, the violation is considered as ongoing.[55] The search for such person is a continuing

[53] Report of the WGEID, E/CN.4/1996/38, 1995; General Comment on Art. 4 of the Declaration, paras. 54–5; WGEID, Best practices on enforced disappearances in domestic criminal legislation, paras. 9–12.

[54] See also, WGEID, Best practices on enforced disappearances in domestic criminal legislation, para. 16.

[55] Art. 8(1)b) of ICCPED. UN Human Rights Council, Report of the WGEID, General comment on enforced disappearance as a continuous crime, UNA/HRC/16/48, 26 January 2011, pp. 10–12. Also IACHR, *La Cantuta* v. *Peru*, Judgment, 2006, para. 114.

obligation for the State.[56] For this reason, it is possible to convict someone without violating the non-retroactivity principle for enforced disappearance that had occurred (or, in other words, given the continuous nature of the crime, commenced) before a legal instrument introducing enforced disappearance as an autonomous crime was enacted domestically.[57] Therefore, codification of enforced disappearance as an autonomous crime would not only serve to hold future perpetrators accountable and thus, potentially, prevent or avert future disappearances but would also enable prosecution of the responsible for the past and ongoing disappearances.

Prosecution for enforced disappearance as a separate offence may often be the only option for criminal accountability but also for finding remains of disappeared or missing persons. A criminal investigation and trial for enforced disappearance may lead to establishing the fate of the missing and/or finding the person(s)' remains by, inter alia, generating evidence and information through the respective criminal proceeding. At the same time, even a mere possibility or likelihood that a criminal investigation is or may be open might lead to actual or potential suspects revealing information about the disappeared person's whereabouts or remains.

Namely, while people who have been taken away may well be believed to be killed, the absence of reliable evidence of the persons' death and the suspect(s)' involvement in their killing, torture or abduction would preclude prosecution for war crimes of murder or other such crimes. Information or evidence may often suggest the suspect's involvement in creation or, very often, concealment of a mass grave as provision of assistance (aiding and abetting) the main perpetrators, but in the absence of evidence that such assistance was promised or intended in advance, which is most often a standard requirement under national legislation or jurisprudence for that mode of liability, it can hardly if ever be proven. Participation in concealment of mass graves would be also considered, in most national jurisdictions, as a crime of removing the traces of criminal offence, or aiding evasion of justice, or the like; however, such crimes are subject, in most national jurisdictions, to statute of limitations, usually

[56] Committee on Enforced Disappearances, Guiding principles for the search for disappeared persons, CED/C/7, 8 May 2019, Principle 7.

[57] See also WGEID, General Comment on Enforced Disappearance as a Continuous Crime, para. 5.

relatively short, which would leave prosecution, when such acts occurred many years earlier, untenable.

On the other hand, because of its continuous nature, enforced disappearance, if provided in the law as an autonomous crime as required by the ICPPED, remains a viable option for the prosecution to break the silence about the destiny of the missing persons. This opens room for strategic use of enforced disappearance investigations and charges in order to resolve the fate of missing persons. Individuals involved in disposal and concealment of the bodies (e.g., often those who dug graves or disposed of the bodies in another way) and who were low in a chain of perpetrators or command, and who may be able to evade prosecution for commission or aiding and abetting war crimes for lack of evidence of their more direct and involvement, for the reasons just explained, may be subject to prosecution for enforced disappearance. For that, evidence pointing at their awareness of a mass grave, for example, would be sufficient to constitute 'concealment of the fate or whereabouts of the disappeared person' as a continuous act (provided, of course, that other elements of the crime are also fulfilled). In such case, a threat or a potential of their criminal prosecution, combined, if needed, with possible offer of immunity (if their responsibility is comparatively minor) or mitigation of punishment (as also allowed for under Article 7(2)a of ICPPED) may yield results. It may lead these individuals to reveal locations of mass or other graves, thus helping provide the families of the missing, and the society as a whole, with some answers and, possibly, the remains of the disappeared. They may also reveal and accept to testify against those who were higher up and/or more directly responsible for the disappearances.

### *2.6.4 An ICPPED's Limitation: Disappearances by Non-State Actors*

In one important aspect, the Convention provides a more narrow substantive protection from enforced disappearance than IHL, and this is with regard to disappearances in the hands of non-State actors. Such disappearances are common and frequent, especially in non-international armed conflicts, in particular if a non-State actor has significant power as party to the conflict or when a conflict is between two or more such groups. Such situations may also include instances when it is not possible to conclusively establish that a State had or has control over a non-State armed group.

The ICPPED requests the State parties to take appropriate measures to investigate and prosecute enforced disappearances when committed also by persons or groups of persons acting without the authorization of a State (Article 3). In this way, the Convention, as with the responsibility for enforced disappearance in general, imposes a certain duty on States and does not directly serve as the basis for the attribution of criminal responsibility to individuals that are not acting as de iure or de facto State agents. Moreover, the Convention nonetheless leaves the definition of enforced disappearance from Article 2 as it is – as a State agent perpetrated crime. This was in result a reflection of the ICPPED drafters' intention, inter alia, not to dilute the responsibility of the State as primary and of the traditional understanding that human rights violations can be committed only by States.[58]

The expansion to include non-State actors in a definition of enforced disappearance in international law came with the ICC's (Rome) Statute, which provides that the crime can be perpetrated by 'persons acting with the authorization, support or acquiescence of a State *or a political organization*' (Article 7(2)i) of the Rome Statute). However, this is only applicable when enforced disappearance can qualify as a crime against humanity and only in cases tried by the ICC (unless States have chosen to reflect such extension of the notion of enforced disappearance in their own national legislation).

The Committee on Enforced Disappearances adopted, in May 2023, a statement on non-State actors, emphasizing that the Convention is a living instrument and should be interpreted in the light of present-day conditions and the evolution of international law. It stated that acts fulfilling the international law definition of crimes against humanity are also enforced disappearance and, moreover, that enforced disappearance acts committed by non-State actors fall under article 3 of the Convention either when perpetrated in the context of a non-international armed conflict or when perpetrated by a non-State actor exercising effective control and/or government-like functions over a territory.[59]

[58] WGEID, Best practices on enforced disappearances in domestic criminal legislation, para. 26. See also A. Srovin Coralli, 'Working paper: Non-State actors and enforced disappearances: Defining a path forward, Geneva Academy of International Humanitarian Law and Human Rights' (2021) pp. 5–6, available at www.geneva-academy.ch/research/publications/detail/608-non-state-actors-and-enforced-disappearances-defining-a-path-forward.

[59] Committee on Enforced Disappearances, Statement on non-State actors in the context of the International Convention for the Protection of All Persons from Enforced

On the other side, without a need for any additional interpretation or progressive development of international law, it is clear that IHL norms bind not only States but also non-State armed groups. While there are different views on the exact legal basis or legal mechanism by which non-State entities are obliged to follow IHL rules,[60] it is not disputed that they are bound by them, including the rules of customary IHL such as the prohibition of enforced disappearance.

There are many arguments to push for expansion of definition of enforced disappearance in international law in general to include non-State actors, mainly based on better protection and rights of the victims.[61] International human rights law is moving in that direction, primarily through the practice of international human rights bodies and courts and most notably and recently through the aforementioned statement by the Committee on Enforced disappearances on non-State actors, while any hopes to address it at treaty level are unrealistically ambitious in a near future. Still, so far, until this becomes firmly established, and except for the context of crimes against humanity under the ICC jurisdiction, IHL provisions concerning missing and disappeared persons and its customary law prohibition of enforced disappearance remain the key normative protection against enforced disappearances by non-State groups in armed conflicts.

## 2.7 Concluding Observations

Enforced disappearances do not occur only in situations of armed conflicts, but they are most frequent and massive in such situations. Together with other causes of disappearances they leave, in most of the conflicts, huge numbers of missing persons. Resolving their destiny presents long, strong and enduring challenges and leaves a heavy psychological, health, economic and other impact on their families, as well as on the entire affected societies. Addressing the rights of the families of missing persons, including providing access to justice and enabling accountability, is a fundamental issue of upholding individual human rights but also the

Disappearances, CED/C/10, 2 May 2023. See also Chapter 7 discussing the statement and non-State actors in more length.

60 For an overview of various possible legal bases, see S. Sivakumaran, *The Law of Non-International Armed Conflict* (Oxford University Press, 2015), pp. 238–42, and in Commentary on GC I, 2016, paras. 507–8.

61 Coralli, 'Working Paper', pp. 10–15.

rule of law, social cohesion and post-conflict recovery in a society. Hence, a normative framework pertaining to enforced disappearances should be analyzed and its effectiveness assessed from the perspective of its potentially preventative effect as well as through the prism of addressing the aforementioned individual and societal impact of the disappearances, especially with a view toward accountability (which, in turn, can also have a preventive effect).

The ICPPED applies in times of peace and armed conflicts alike, as does its universal and treaty-based definition of enforced disappearances, which presupposes, first, unlawfulness of how the disappearance occurred and, second, direct or indirect involvement of the State. Due to the definition, not all persons going missing during an armed conflict are victims of enforced disappearances: some may be missing as a result of military or other actions that are lawful when judged by IHL rules, and/or they may be disappeared by non-State actors. Victims of enforced disappearance are a more narrow group within the broader category of missing persons. An implication of the difference may be politically or otherwise relevant, including, importantly, cautiousness not to exclude large number of families of missing persons, whose relatives may not be proven as victims of enforced disappearances, from access to aid, services and reparations.

Both treaty and customary IHL provides for a number of protections and duties on parties to armed conflicts that are preventive in relation to missing persons and enforced disappearances and enable active search and identification. Customary IHL prohibits enforced disappearance for State as well as non-State actors, unlike the ICPPED. Even with such a substantial IHL-based normative framework, the Convention nonetheless has its role and even some comparative advantages in armed conflict. While IHL prohibition of enforced disappearance as customary is, in theory, wider than the ICCPED's prohibition that binds only the seventy-plus State parties, applicability does not necessarily mean that something will be actually used in practice. When it comes to the application and enforcement of the respective customary IHL provisions, especially in criminal cases, national authorities often find customary law norms, *in concreto* or generally, elusive at best or do not recognize customary law at all, thus leaving ICPPED as a more direct and recognizable source.

When it comes to criminal accountability, there is an absence of enforced disappearance from the catalogue of war crimes. There are limitations of adjudicating enforced disappearance as a crime against humanity: they can be contextual (because of the 'widespread or systematic' requirement) and lack codification as crimes against humanity in national criminal legislations but also, as discussed, due to the prevailing (but erroneous) interpretations, in many national jurisdictions, relatively recent domestic codifications of crimes against humanity are not applicable to earlier crimes due to the non-retroactivity principle. This all makes the ICPPED's requirement for enforced disappearance as an autonomous and continuous domestic crime a possible way out, provided that the number of States adequately amending their criminal legislation grows more progressively. That would not only give a ground for accountability for enforced disappearance, potentially long-stretching timewise, but may also create inducement, through investigation, immunity and mitigation tactics, for those involved but not primarily responsible for the disappearances to break the silence and help resolve the cases.

The interplay and the mutual reinforcement between the ICPPED and IHL, together with the role and authority of the Customary IHL Study, may, hopefully, lead to more universal ratification and full implementation of the Convention. In addition, which this author finds desirable, it may lead to transformation of the human rights norm and definition of enforced disappearance to expand to cover equally State and non-State actors, in armed conflict and peace time alike, and to such norm obtaining customary law status.

# 3

## The Guiding Principles on the Search for Disappeared Persons

### Origins and Impact

MARIA CLARA GALVIS PATIÑO AND RAINER HUHLE

### 3.1 Introduction

In 2019, the Committee on Enforced Disappearances (hereinafter the Committee or the CED) adopted the Guiding Principles for the Search for Disappeared Persons (hereinafter the Guiding Principles or the Principles). The present chapter, written by the two rapporteurs appointed by the Committee for preparing the Guiding Principles, in its first part describes the considerations that led the Committee to discuss and redact these Guiding Principles, starting from the reaffirmation of the search of disappeared persons as an autonomous international human rights obligation under the Convention. An important element that took the CED to think about the need of some Guiding Principles for the search was the high number of 'Urgent Actions'[1] it had received under article 30 of the International Convention for the Protection of all Persons against Enforced Disappearances (hereinafter the Convention or the ICPPED). These urgent actions reflected, in the vast majority of cases, a dramatic failure of the authorities to comply with the obligation to search, reflected in deficient norms, inadequate institutions, lack of strategy to search and lack of cooperation with the victims. The dialogues held with States under article 29 of the ICPPED also gave the Committee valuable information on the deficiencies of the search in various countries. The Committee, following its obligation under articles 30.3 and 30.4 of the Convention to improve the search

[1] In accordance with the Convention, by means of an urgent action, the Committee requests a State party to immediately take measures to search for, locate and protect a disappeared person.

mechanisms, came to identify manifold obstacles to effective and appropriate search efforts. So, after just five years since it started functioning, the Committee decided, in March 2016, that the moment had arrived for it to give an answer to the urgent need of victims of forced disappearances to search for their loved ones and therefore to study more in depth the obligation to search in order to determine its content and scope with a view of adopting an instrument that would give an answer to the pressing need of victims of forced disappearances to search for their loved ones and at the same time be useful for overcoming obstacles that the Committee has already identified.

The Committee's own experience was enriched, once the decision to draft a document on the issue had been taken, through a highly participative process that preceded the adoption of the Principles. During more than three years, the Committee collected, through various conferences as well as a formal call for input, opinions and proposals on measures to strengthen the search processes. This input came from victims' organizations, National Human Rights Institutions (NHRI), NGOs, States, bodies of the UN and the Inter-American system, the International Committee of the Red Cross (ICRC) and academics. The final document (CED/C/7, 8 May 2019)[2] has been widely published and, so far, translated into the six official UN languages and three more.

The first part of this chapter reviews how the Committee reaffirmed the search of disappeared persons as an autonomous international human rights obligation under the Convention in the context of urgent actions and dialogues with States, as well as by holding discussions among Committee members and thematic debates with renowned experts. This part of the chapter also addresses the obstacles the Committee identified to an effective and appropriate search and describes the highly participative process that preceded the adoption by the Committee, in April 2019, of the Guiding Principles.

The second part of the chapter presents a first balance of the impact that the Principles have had, three years after their adoption as a UN document (2019–2022),[3] shaping public policies of States (member States of the ICPPED as well as non-State parties) and international bodies, of how they found their way into national and international jurisprudence

[2] Committee on Enforced Disappearances, Guiding principles for the search for disappeared persons, CED/C/7, 2019.

[3] Additionally, several instances that occurred in 2023 were added to the chapter.

and legislation, as well as in academic literature and, last but not least, in civil society.

## 3.2 The Reasons That Led the Committee on Enforced Disappearances to Adopt the Guiding Principles for the Search for Disappeared Persons

### *3.2.1 The Obligation to Search for and Locate Disappeared Persons in the Convention for the Protection of all Persons from Enforced Disappearances*

In the drafting of the Convention, there was agreement among States on the right of victims to know the fate and whereabouts of the disappeared person. To protect this right, the Convention enshrines the obligation of States to search for the disappeared person, addressing it not in a single article, as it did with the obligation to investigate (Art. 12), but in several articles (15, 19.1, 24.2 and 24.3, and 25.2 and 25.3). From this perspective, it might be misunderstood that the Convention would give less weight to the obligation to search and locate than to the obligation to investigate.

However, the international obligation to search for and locate disappeared persons is an autonomous one and is well developed throughout the Convention. The obligation to take all appropriate measures to search and locate disappeared persons, including that of cooperating among States and affording one another the maximum mutual assistance (article 15), is specified in more concrete obligations according to different situations, depending on whether the person is found alive, with another identity or dead. In the first case, the Convention establishes the obligation to release the person (articles 15 and 24.3). In the second case, related to the wrongful removal of children who are subjected to forced disappearance, or children whose father, mother or legal guardian is subjected to forced disappearance or children born during the captivity of a mother subjected to forced disappearance, States must identify them and return them their identity (articles 25.2 and 25.3). When the person is found dead, States have the obligation to exhume, identify, respect and return the body (articles 15 and 24.3).

The autonomous nature of the search is also reflected in the Convention when establishing that personal information collected or transmitted in the framework of the search shall not be used for purposes other than the search, without prejudice to the use of such information in criminal proceedings relating to the crime of forced disappearance (Art. 19). This provision can only be explained if the drafters of the Convention had in mind the autonomy of the search in relation to the criminal investigation.

The search as an autonomous international obligation is also manifest in the Convention by assigning to the Committee a specific mandate to urgently examine the petitions presented on behalf of a disappeared person in order for the State to search for and locate the person (article 30).

The autonomous nature of the search can also be seen in the provision of the Convention that establishes expressly the right of victims to know the fate of the disappeared person (article 24.2). To guarantee this right, conducting a criminal investigation is not enough. Only a specific obligation to conduct a search can guarantee that locating the disappeared person will be an integral part of the actions undertaken by the authorities. Accordingly, the Convention establishes that urgent action procedures will be kept open as far as the fate of the person being sought remains unresolved.

Under the International Convention, the obligation of States to search for and locate disappeared persons is clearly established as different from (yet related to) the obligation of States to conduct without delay a thorough and impartial investigation of the crime of forced disappearance, as stated in article 12.[4]

### *3.2.2 The Obligation to Search for and Locate Disappeared Persons in the Work of the Committee on Enforced Disappearances*

Receiving and considering urgent actions and monitoring States' compliance with the obligations established in the Convention are two mechanisms enshrined in the ICPPED that allow the Committee to receive information from victims, victims' organizations and NGOs as well as from States. Information received through these mechanisms enables the Committee to acquire knowledge regarding legal frameworks and institutional resources to conduct search processes as well as budgetary and personnel requirements of institutions charged with the search. This information has nourished the Guiding Principles.

4 R. Huhle, 'Fate and whereabouts: The two elements that make up the right to know about the victims of forced disappearance', in S. Mandolessi and K. Olalde Rico (eds.), *Disappearances in Mexico: From the 'Dirty War' to the 'War on Drugs'* (Routledge, 2022).

#### 3.2.2.1 Urgent Actions

By the time the Committee decided to create a working group charged with preparing a concept note on the obligation to search for the disappeared persons in accordance with the Convention and the jurisprudence of the CED,[5] and while the process of preparing the principles was underway, requests for urgent actions continued to increase. In 2017, the Committee received 86 requests for urgent actions, and 118 in 2018. As of April 2019, it had received 659 requests[6] for urgent actions from 15 countries[7] since the Committee was established.[8]

Through the urgent action mechanism, the Committee received valuable information illustrating obstacles in the searching processes related to institutional weaknesses and disrespect and ill treatment of victims.[9]

Institutional weakness often is expressed in deficiencies such as lack of authorities charged specifically with the search; fragmentation among investigations and lack of coordination among agencies, which cause excessive delays in the search processes; conducting the search without a strategy and carrying out isolated actions that are not part of a plan or a strategy previously defined; authorities that don't act unless relatives or representatives of the disappeared person take initiative; requests for information that remain unanswered and authorities charged with supervising those requests that don't take action; on-site investigations that are not carried out because the authorities do not have security measures; or even authorities charged with the search that are involved in the disappearances. In addition, the urgent action procedure brought to the Committee information about families and relatives of disappeared persons facing difficulties participating in the search.

[5] Committee on Enforced Disappearances, Report of the Committee on Enforced Disappearances, Doc. A/72/56, 2017.

[6] Committee on Enforced Disappearances, Report of the Committee on Enforced Disappearances, Doc. A/74/56, 2019.

[7] Argentina, Armenia, Brazil, Cambodia, Colombia, Cuba, Honduras, Iraq, Kazakhstan, Lithuania, Mauritania, Mexico, Morocco, Sri Lanka, Togo.

[8] As of 31 March 2023, the Committee had registered requests for urgent action concerning 1,578 disappeared persons since 2012. See Committee on Enforced Disappearances, Report of the Committee on Enforced Disappearances, Doc. A/78/56, 2023.

[9] Committee on Enforced Disappearances, Report of the Committee on Enforced Disappearances, Doc. A/73/56, 2018; chapter on urgent action procedure under Art. 30 of the Convention; and Report of the Committee on Enforced Disappearances on the 15th session, 16th session, chapter on urgent actions procedure under Art. 30 of the Convention.

Other problems seen by Committee members through urgent actions are those related to disrespect and ill-treatment of persons searching for their loved ones. On several occasions they have been prevented by authorities from formally denouncing the disappearance of a relative or have been contacted by the authorities in a manner that re-victimizes them. Authors of requests for urgent actions have faced threats, intimidation, pressure and reprisals.

The existence of these obstacles was confirmed during the process of drafting the Guiding Principles, in meetings and workshops with victims' families, human rights organizations, experts and even with State institutions.

#### 3.2.2.2 Dialogues with States and Concluding Observations

The obligation to search for and locate disappeared persons has been reaffirmed by the Committee in its concluding observations, issued after receiving States reports, information from victims and NGOs and having held constructive dialogues with States parties. Before the approval of the Guiding Principles, the Committee had interpreted the obligation to search and reaffirmed its autonomous nature in several concluding observations.

In line with the Convention, the Committee has recalled that determining the whereabouts of victims includes searching for and locating disappeared persons without delay.[10] It has also reaffirmed that the search must be launched even without a formal complaint.[11] For securing the effectiveness of the search, the Committee has recommended the adoption of measures such as the preservation and protection of mass

[10] See Committee on Enforced Disappearances, Concluding observations on the report submitted by Iraq under Art. 29 (1) of the Convention, CED/C/IRQ/CO/1, 13 October 2015; Concluding observations on the report submitted by Tunisia under Art. 29 (1) of the Convention, CED/C/TUN/CO/1, 11 March 2016; Concluding observations on the report submitted by Colombia under Art. 29 (1) of the Convention, CED/C/COL/CO/1, 27 October 2016; Concluding observations on the report submitted by Honduras under Art. 29 (1) of the Convention, CED/C/HND/CO/1, 21 June 2019; Concluding observations on the report submitted by Peru under Art. 29 (1) of the Convention, CED/C/PER/CO/1, 8 May 2019; and Concluding observations on the report submitted by the Plurinational State of Bolivia under Art. 29 (1) of the Convention, CED/C/BOL/CO/1, 24 October 2019.

[11] See Committee on Enforced Disappearances, Concluding observations on the report submitted by Spain under Art. 29(1) of the Convention, CED/C/ESP/CO/1, 12 December 2013.

graves and of all other sites where there is a suspicion that disappeared persons might be found.[12]

Furthermore, based on the situation seen by the Committee in dialogues with Spain, Iraq, Tunisia, Colombia, and Bosnia and Herzegovina, in the context of reporting processes, the Committee has recommended that States should allocate sufficient human, technical and financial resources for the search processes.[13]

Considering situations in Mexico, Colombia and Honduras, the Committee highlighted the importance of adopting search measures to increase the chances of finding persons alive. The Committee also emphasized the importance of continuing the search until the fate of the disappeared person has been established.[14]

## 3.3 A Highly Participative Process Led to the Approval of the Guiding Principles by the Committee on Enforced Disappearances

After the two rapporteurs appointed for preparing the Guiding Principles presented the first draft to the Committee, in November 2018, it set up a consultative process and invited all interested stakeholders to submit written contributions: families of disappeared persons and their associations; State parties; NHRI; special procedures of the United Nations, such as the WGEID, and regional human rights organizations, like the Inter-American Commission on Human Rights (IACHR); civil society organizations; experts and academics.

The Committee received a total of forty-six contributions, from four continents, that were presented in Spanish, English, French and Arabic. There were twenty-eight contributions from organizations of victims of

[12] See Committee on Enforced Disappearances, Concluding observations on the report submitted by Iraq and Committee on Enforced Disappearances, Concluding observations on the report submitted by Chile under Art. 29 (1) of the Convention, CED/C/CHL/CO/1, 8 May 2019.

[13] See Committee on Enforced Disappearances, Concluding observations on the reports submitted by Spain, Iraq, Tunisia, Colombia, above, and Committee on Enforced Disappearances, Concluding observations of the Committee on the report submitted by Bosnia & Herzegovina, under Art. 29(1) of the Convention, CED/C/BIH/CO/1, 7 October 2016.

[14] See Committee on Enforced Disappearances, Concluding observations on the reports submitted by Iraq, Tunisia, Colombia, Honduras, Peru and Chile, above.

forced disappearances and civil society organizations,[15] one from a NHRI,[16] one from United Nations offices,[17] two from specialized UN agencies,[18] nine from State parties to the Convention[19] and three from academia.[20]

From 2016 to 2019, several workshops were organized in Colombia, Mexico and Germany, where many persons and national, regional and international organizations presented a variety of proposals that nourished the Guiding Principles. All these contributions were organized and systematized by a team of experts led by Gabriella Citroni, renowned human rights lawyer and now member of the Working Group on Enforced and Involuntary Disappearances.

Throughout the process that preceded the adoption of the Guiding Principles, families of the disappeared persons, persons and organizations involved in the search processes as well as experts agreed that an instrument of a more practical nature such as a set of principles aimed at solving concrete problems was a better tool than an instrument only interpreting the obligations established in the ICPPED.

Based on all the information gathered in the consultation process, the two rapporteurs redacted and revised a draft of the Guiding Principles

[15] Grandmothers of Plaza de Mayo, Argentina; African Net against extrajudicial executions and forced disappearance (ANEKED); National Association for the Promotion and Protection of Human Rights (ANAPRODH), Cameroon; Association for the Recovery of Historical Memory of Catalunya (ARMH); Asia Justice and Rights (AJAR); Asian Federation against involuntary disappearances; Citizens in support of Human Rights (CADHAC) and Women's Human Rights Center (CED- HEM), Mexico; National Campaign against Forced Disappearance in Mexico (CNDF); Northern Pass Human Rights Center, Mexico; Center for Legal and Social Studies (CELS), Argentina; Committee of Families of Detained-Disappeared Persons in Honduras (COFADEH); Human Rights Commission (COMISEDH), Perú; Digna Ochoa Chiapas Grassroot Human Rights Committee, Mexico; Colombia-Europe-United Sates Coordination, (CCEEU); National Human Rights Coordination, Peru; ECCHR, Berlin; Argentine Team of Forensic Anthropology (EAAF); Equitas; Forensic Anthropology Foundation of Guatemala; Foundation for Justice and Democratic Rule of Law, Mexico; I(dh)eas, Mexico; Organization of Human Rights and Democracy Initiators (IOHRD), Iraq; Mothers of Plaza de Mayo, Argentina; National Movement of State Crimes (MOVICE), Colombia; Independent Romanian Society for Human Rights; Swiss Network of International Studies; Trudy Huskamp Peterson (archivist), United States; Truth Know, Chipre.

[16] National Commission for Human Rights from Mexico.

[17] OACNUDH Mexico.

[18] UNICEF, International Committee of the Red Cross.

[19] Argentina, Austria, Colombia, Ecuador, France, Morocco, Peru, Sri Lanka, Ukraine.

[20] University of Bournemouth (United Kingdom), Institute for Legal Studies of the Polish Academy of Sciences and Nestor Oswaldo Arias (Human Rights expert from Colombia).

for the Search for Disappeared Persons that was discussed and approved by the Committee in its session of April 2019. The Guiding Principles for the Search for the Disappeared Persons are available in the six official languages of the United Nations (Spanish, English, French, Russian, Arabic and Chinese) and so far also in German, Nepali and Serbian.

### 3.4 The Impact of the Guiding Principles for the Search for Disappeared Persons in State Norms and Actions, in Judicial Decisions, in Civil Society and in Academic Discussion

The Guiding Principles for the Search for Disappeared Persons, as shown above, have been developed in a highly participative process of many consultations with all kinds of stakeholders over more than three years. Since the demand for more effective search of disappeared persons and a clear formulation of States' obligations to search came to the Committee mainly from victims and organizations from Latin American State parties, especially Mexico, it is no surprise that in the beginning the Principles resonated in Mexico more than in any other country. It was in Mexico where they were first presented by the Committee to a broader public.[21] The OHCHR Office in Mexico, continuing its permanent support of the Committee in the preparation of the Principles, published together with the Office of the National Ombudsman for Human Rights (Comisión Nacional de Derechos Humanos – CNDH) an illustrated booklet of the Principles, which has been widely distributed.[22] With the support of the German agency for economic cooperation (GIZ) the 16 Principles were presented as videos through the voices of different personalities (including Michelle Bachelet,[23] who by then was the High Commissioner for Human Rights) on public screens in Mexico's subway and other places.[24]

[21] In the Auditorio del Museo Memoria y Tolerancia, Mexico City, on 29 August 2019, in presence of the head of the National Search Commission (CNB) and the vice-minister of the Interior. This presentation was followed by more events in Guadalajara, Monterrey, Chihuahua, Jalapa and other cities.

[22] Comité de la ONU contra la Desaparición Forzada, *Principios rectores para la búsqueda de personas desaparecidas* (ONU-DH, 2019).

[23] OACNUDH México, *Principios Rectores para la búsqueda de personas desaparecidas – Michelle Bachelet* (2021), available at https://youtu.be/ncuwienPVK8.

[24] The complete list of these videos (in Spanish) can be found at OACNUDH México, *Principios Rectores para la Búsqueda de Personas – Playlist* (2021), available at https://www.youtube.com/watch?v=VDalcPdekwU&list=PLeL4yp-msGcRKgVjXKuLLm-Ozcl7-zsB.

Responding to much input also from Colombian organizations, manifested in several workshops in Bogotá, the Principles received also public attention in Colombia and other Latin American countries. Although to a lesser extent, thanks to the efforts of the Asian Federation Against Involuntary Disappearances (AFAD) and the International Coalition Against Enforced Disappearances (ICAED), the Principles were echoed also in the Asian Region, for example, through an ICAED conference in Nepal in May 2019 or in February 2020 in Beirut, with the support of the Centre Libanais des Droits Humains (CLDH) and the Fédération euro-méditerranéenne contre les disparitions forcées (FEMED). Nevertheless, in accordance with the forces promoting the drafting of the Principles, the reception of these is still more visible in the Latin American region than in the rest of the world.

In the following sections, we will give an overview and outstanding examples of the impact of the Guiding Principles, considering their inclusion in legal and administrative texts as well as decisions by national and international bodies, their use by family and victims organizations and human rights defenders and organizations involved in the search of the disappeared and finally in an already rich academic discussion.

With regard to the impact of the Principles in national level decisions, we will present them starting with the countries where there have been more abundant references to the Guiding Principles in legal, administrative or judicial decisions. All the countries mentioned in the corresponding section are from Latin America, given that the demand for a more effective search of disappeared persons came to the Committee from organizations and victims from Latin American countries, as we mentioned before, and therefore, after the approval of the Principles, public debate involving legislative, administrative and judicial institutions was more intense than in other regions.

## 3.5 Impact of the Guiding Principles in Legal and Administrative Texts and in Judicial Decisions by National Bodies

While the Bournemouth Protocol has already gained much attention as a guideline that sets standards for the investigation of mass graves, it is still a civil society document. The Guiding Principles, as an official UN document, have already been referenced to in several legal documents and courts or treaty body decisions.

### *3.5.1 Mexico*

Already in August of 2019, the Federal Government of Mexico made a public pledge to apply the Guiding Principles as part of its public policies against forced disappearances.[25] The National Human Rights Commission (CNDH), the institution created in accordance with the Paris Principles, has edited, together with the UN Office of Human Rights in Mexico, a printed popular version of the Principles that has been very helpful in the outreach, even beyond Mexico in other Spanish language countries.[26]

The National Search Commission (CNB), the extraordinary search institution mandated in 2017 by the General Law on Forced Disappearance,[27] had already been vocal in the process of drafting the Guiding Principles and integrated them in many ways in their policies and norms. Soon after their adoption, the director of the CNB organized a formal outreach to all thirty-two Search Commissions in the federal States. When, after long debates in 2020, the basic Protocol that norms the activities of the CNB and the other institutions that have duties related to the search of disappeared had finally been adopted,[28] the basic norm established that the Guiding Principles 'must be transformed into concrete actions of specific authorities which can guarantee, in practice, the right of every person disappeared or not found to be searched'. A year later, an additional protocol was adopted, dealing in particular with disappearances of children and young adults, which again refers to the Principles as basic orientation.[29] Beyond these basic protocols, the Guiding Principles have become a permanent reference in many documents and internal guidelines of the CNB and some federal State search commissions.[30]

25 'Desaparición Forzada: tragedia y esperanza', La Jornada, 31 August 2019, available at www.jornada.com.mx/2019/08/31/edito/002a1edi.

26 Comité de la ONU contra la Desaparición Forzada, *Principios Rectores para la Búsqueda de Personas Desaparecidas* (Oficina del Alto Comisionado de las Naciones Unidas, 2019), available at https://www.ohchr.org/sites/default/files/Documents/HRBodies/CED/PrincipiosRectores_DigitalisedVersion_SP.pdf.

27 Ley General en Materia de Desaparición Forzada de Personas, *Desaparición Cometida por Particulares y del Sistema Nacional de Búsqueda de Personas* (México: 2017).

28 Protocolo Homologado para la Búsqueda de Personas Desaparecidas y No Localizadas, Acuerdo SNBP/002/2020, 6 November 2020, available at https://www.dof.gob.mx/nota_detalle.php?codigo=5601905&fecha=06/10/2020.

29 Protocolo Adicional para la Búsqueda de Niñas, Niños y Adolescentes, Acuerdo SNBP/002/2021, 15 July 2021, available at https://www.dof.gob.mx/nota_detalle.php?codigo=5623969&fecha=15/07/2021.

30 For example: Comisión Nacional de Búsqueda (CNB), Enfoque DH, USAID, *Manual de Capacitación para la Búsqueda de Personas, La Voz de la Academia* (CNB, 2020); CNB

In June 2021, the Supreme Court of Mexico rendered a landmark decision in which, among other important aspects, it defined the international obligations of the Mexican State in view of the human rights treaties to which it is a party.[31] Extending the jurisprudence referring to the Views of Treaty Bodies on individual complaints, the Court declared in this decision that also the recommendations of the CED responding to requests for 'urgent actions' on behalf of disappeared persons in Mexico are binding for the Mexican authorities, which implies that their fulfilment is also subject to judicial and constitutional control. Substantiating this victims-oriented approach, the Court found that in international human rights law and particularly in the Convention there existed a right to be searched for and that this right includes the duty for the State to comply with the urgent actions remitted by the CED, even when this procedure (Art. 30 of the Convention) is apparently of only a humanitarian nature.[32] In their unanimous Judgment, for the members of the Court 'it is clear that the search and its results constitute the essence of the right not to be forcibly disappeared and that they provide content and substance to the duties to prevent, investigate and repair the violations of human rights and their corresponding rights to the truth, justice and reparation' (para. 107).

In this path-breaking decision, the Supreme Court not only declared the Urgent Actions of the CED obligatory. It also found that the Principles have to be attended and observed[33] by the Mexican State, quoting the introduction to the Principles, particularly the statement that they 'seek to consolidate good practices in searching effectively for disappeared persons, arising from States' obligation to search' (para. 2

and USAID, *Guía de estudio. El ABC del Análisis de Contexto. Herramientas básicas de análisis de contexto orientado a la búsqueda de personas desaparecidas* (CNB, 2021); and *Estrategia para el Registro Nacional de Personas Desaparecidas o No Localizadas* (CNB, 2020).

31 Suprema Corte de Justicia de la Nación, Amparo en revisión 1077/2019, available (in Spanish) at www.idheas.org.mx/publicaciones-idheas/materiales-consulta-idheas/version-publica-amparo-en-revision-1077-2019/.

32 For a detailed discussion of the legal reasoning of the decision and its importance see G. Citroni, 'Supreme Court of Justice of Mexico: The urgent actions of the Committee on Enforced Disappearances are legally binding', *Opinio Juris*, 17 August 2021, available at https://opiniojuris.org/2021/08/17/supreme-court-of-justice-of-mexico-the-urgent-actions-of-the-committee-on-enforced-disappearances-are-legally-binding/.

33 'Resultan atendibles y observables'. Suprema Corte de Justicia de la Nación, Amparo en revisión 1077/2019, available (in Spanish) at www.idheas.org.mx/publicaciones-idheas/materiales-consulta-idheas/version-publica-amparo-en-revision-1077-2019/.

of the Introduction). In the following paragraph, the judges continue, referring now in detail to ten of the Principles they consider particularly relevant for their argument (para. 106).

Not in every case do the courts adopt fully the progressive pro persona language. In a case before the Higher Court of the federal State of Coahuila, a State with a particularly sombre record of disappearances, the majority of the Court rejected[34] the draft sentence redacted by the judge-rapporteur, which was oriented in many parts by the Guiding Principles.[35]

However, in 2022, Coahuila adopted an important constitutional reform, containing a whole section on the search of persons. The corresponding article 115Bis of the reformed constitution determines that the search must be carried out in accordance with international treaties, and particularly the Guiding Principles, which are written out in much detail in this paragraph.[36]

The Supreme Court's seminal sentence had a direct impact in a March 2022 initiative of the majority party in the National Parliament (Congreso de la República) aiming at adding three more paragraphs to Art. 17 of the Mexican Constitution in order to establish a 'Right to be searched' in cases of Forced Disappearance. The proposal copies language of the Principles and declares the right to be searched for as an autonomous right, distinct from the right to an investigation. In the

[34] See Poder Judicial de Coahuila, *Novena Sesión Ordinaria del Pleno del Tribunal Constitucional Local* (2021), available at www.pjecz.gob.mx/sesiones/tribunal-constitucional/2021/novena-sesion-ordinaria-del-pleno-del-tribunal constitucional-local-2021-10-27/. The original draft sentence is not public. The author holds a private copy as he had presented to the Court an Amicus Curiae. The Court, however, refused to accept any of the various Amicus offered to it.

[35] For a detailed critique of the decision see: I. Spigno, 'Quién debería buscar a las personas desaparecidas en Coahuila, México?', *Agenda Estado de Derecho*, 6 December 2021.

[36] 'La búsqueda de personas se regirá en todo momento por lo dispuesto en los tratados internacionales en la materia de los que el Estado mexicano es parte, las resoluciones de los organismos internacionales competentes en la materia, así como por los principios rectores para la búsqueda de personas desaparecidas emitidos por el Comité de la Organización de las Naciones Unidas contra la Desaparición Forzada, en el sentido de que la misma se realice bajo la presunción de vida; respete la dignidad humana; se oriente por una política pública; con un enfoque diferencial; respete el derecho a la participación; se inicie sin dilación; se conciba como una obligación permanente; se realice con una estrategia integral; en su caso, tome en cuenta la vulnerabilidad de las personas migrantes; se organice de manera eficiente; use la información de manera apropiada; sea realizada de manera coordinada; en condiciones seguras; sea independiente e imparcial y se lleve a cabo a través de protocolos públicos.'

argumentative part, it quotes large passages of the Supreme Court's decision, including one where the Court cites the Principles.[37]

The Principles have been adopted in norms and decisions in several more of the federal States that comprise the 'United States of Mexico'. In December 2019, the Congress of the Capital District adopted a Search Law for the City of Mexico, which established that all the measures and procedures foreseen in this Law shall be guided by a series of principles that have to be in line with the General Law on forced Disappearances and with the Guiding Principles of the CED.[38] The Human Rights Commission of Mexico City (CDHDF), too, relies for many of the definitions used in their decisions (recommendations) on those developed in the Guiding Principles.[39]

In October 2022, the Supreme Court of Justice of Mexico, together with the Federal School for Judicial Training, published a manual on the disappearance of persons. Various chapters mention the Guiding Principles, in particular one dedicated to forced disappearances in the United Nations Human Rights System.[40]

### *3.5.2 Colombia*

During the drafting process of the Principles, in Colombia, too, several consultations were held with different stakeholders about the text of the Guiding Principles. The Colombian government, in its latest report to the CED, committed itself to 'continue its efforts to implement the Guiding Principles for the search for disappeared persons'.[41] The most important avenue for this implementation are the institutions created following the

[37] Gaceta Parlamentaria, XXV, 5991-III, 29 March 2022, available at http://gaceta.diputados.gob.mx/Gaceta/65/2022/mar/20220329-III.html#Iniciativa28.

[38] Ley de Búsqueda de Personas de la Ciudad de México, Gaceta Oficial de la Ciudad de México, Art. 5. Similar laws with the same reference to the Principles have been adopted in other Mexican States, e.g., in Jalisco: Ley de Personas Desaparecidas del Estado de Jalisco, 5 March 2021.

[39] See, e.g., Comisión de Derechos Humanos de la Ciudad de México, Recomendación 2/2020 (Expedientes CDHDF/IV/122ffLAU13/D7502 y 8 otros).

[40] L. Eliud Tapia Olivares, *Manual sobre Desaparición de personas México* (Suprema Corte de Justicia de la Nación y Escuela Federal de Formación Judicial, 2022), available at https://www.supremacorte.gob.mx/sites/default/files/publicaciones_scjn/publicacion/2024-04/Manual%20sobre%20desaparicio%CC%81n%20de%20personas.pdf.

[41] Committee on Enforced Disappearances, Additional information submitted by Colombia under Art. 29(4) of the Convention, CED/C/COL/AI/1, 17 January 2020, para. 8.

mandate of the Peace Accord of 2016, in 2017, as parts of a comprehensive system for the implementation of the principal goals of the Peace Accord: The Integral System for Truth, Justice, Reparation and Non-Repetition (SIVJRNR for its Spanish denomination).[42] Within this System, there are two organs with specific responsibilities regarding the search of disappeared persons (with both mandates limited *ratione temporis* to the period of the armed conflict):

- The Special Jurisdiction for the Peace (JEP for its Spanish denomination).[43] The JEP is charged with the investigation of grave crimes committed during and in relation to the armed conflict and to try, under certain conditions, those responsible for these crimes. So, it is an extraordinary judicial organ, added to the existing (and continuing) regular organs of the justice system, the prosecutors, and the different kinds of Courts.
- The second institution is a non-judicial body, the Special Unit for the Search for Persons reported missing in the context of and due to the armed conflict (UBPD for its Spanish denomination).[44]

Both institutions have made efforts to integrate the Guiding Principles in their endeavours to find the disappeared persons and meet the need of the victims,[45] with a particular emphasis on Principle 13, which demands a constructive relationship between those institutions whose work should be mutually reinforcing. Indeed, both institutions have adopted the Principles in the design of their respective policies. The JEP, who had a representative participating in one of the Colombia workshops during the drafting process of the Principles, includes them in its list of 'national and international norms and jurisprudence' that orient its work.[46]

The UBPD whose mandate is exclusively directed towards the search is even more explicit. It made a pledge before the CED to observe the

[42] Sistema Integral de Verdad, Justicia, Reparación y No Repetición, Acto Legislativo No. 01/2017.

[43] Jurisdicción Especial para la Paz (JEP).

[44] Unidad de Búsqueda de Personas dadas por Desaparecidas en el contexto y en razón del conflicto armado (UBPD).

[45] V. Hinestroza, I. Jave and R. Huhle, *Comisiones de búsqueda en América Latina. Una apuesta extraordinaria por la integralidad en la investigación de las desapariciones* (GIZ, 2021) available at https://www.bivica.org/file/view/id/5968.

[46] See Jurisdicción Especial para la Paz (JEP), Sección de ausencia de reconocimiento de verdad y responsabilidad, Decisión AI-042 de 2021, 10 August 2021, para. 44, 54.

Guiding Principles in the implementation of its mandate and actions.[47] And it made many efforts to meet this pledge. Already in its first National Search Plan[48] of 2020, it refers to the Principles as one of the international standards to observe and makes systematic use of the Principles for the definition of the needs of the victims and the strategies developed by the UBPD. In its internal guidelines on specific aspects of its work, the UBPD also refers to the Guiding Principles as part of their normative framework, such as in the Guidelines on Victims Participation[49] or the Guidelines on a Differential Approach in the search for children and youth.[50] In May 2021, when news circulated about numerous forced disappearances in the context of social mobilizations, the UBPD published a statement on international standards on guarantees against this crime, again quoting the Principles along with the Convention.[51] Also in oral statements, the first director of the UBPD made frequent reference to the Principles. They form without doubt part of the institutional culture of the UBPD. In June 2022, the Colombia Office of the OHCHR supported this effort of the UBPD through a much-publicized public conversation between the director of the Office, Juliette De Rivero, and the then director of the UBPD, Luz Marina Monzón, on the orientation that the Principles provide for the search.[52]

47 Cancillería de Colombia, Anexo II al informe del Estado parte, Contribución de la UBPD a la elaboración del II Informe del Estado colombiano al Comité contra la Desaparición Forzada, INT_CED_AIS_COL_41954_S, 2019.

48 Unidad de Búsqueda de Personas dadas por Desaparecidas, *Plan Nacional de Búsqueda de la Unidad de Búsqueda de Personas dadas por Desaparecidas en el contexto y en razón del conflicto armado* (UBPD, 2020).

49 Unidad de Búsqueda de Personas dadas por Desaparecidas (s.f.), *Lineamientos para la participación de las personas que buscan y las personas dadas por desaparecidas encontradas con vida, durante el proceso de reencuentro, desde una perspectiva humanitaria y extrajudicial* (UBPD).

50 Unidad de Búsqueda de Personas dadas por Desaparecidas, *Lineamientos del Enfoque Diferencial de Niñez, Adolescencia y Juventud para el Proceso de Búsqueda de Personas Dadas por Desaparecidas en el Contexto y en Razón del Conflicto Armado* (UBPD, 2020).

51 Unidad de Búsqueda de Personas dadas por Desaparecidas, *Estándares internacionales sobre garantías para la prevención y protección de las personas frente a la desaparición* (UBPD, 2021), available at https://unidadbusqueda.gov.co/actualidad/estandares-internacionales-sobre-garantias-para-la-prevencion-y-proteccion-de-las-personas-frente-a-la-desaparicion/.

52 Oficina del Alto Comisionado de las Naciones Unidas en Colombia, 'La búsqueda de las personas desaparecidas a la luz de los principios rectores de la ONU', 16 June 2022, available at www.hchr.org.co/pronunciamientos/la-busqueda-de-las-personas-desaparecidas-a-la-luz-de-los-principios-rectores-de-la-onu/.

Another institution in charge of the protection of human rights in Colombia is the Ombudsperson (Defensor del Pueblo). On the occasion of the International Day of the victims of forced disappearance, the Ombudsperson declared on 30 August 2021 that the institution will push on the Principles through a national campaign.[53]

With the aim of building a route for finding all persons that have been subjected to forced disappearances, on 10 March 2023, the mayor of Buenaventura, a town in the Pacific coast of Colombia with high levels of serious human rights violations, adopted a decree creating an inter-institutional space for fighting against forced disappearances. The decree includes in its considerations several parts of Principle 3 of the Guiding Principles, which affirms that the search should be governed by a public policy.[54]

### 3.5.3 *Peru*

In Peru, the search for the persons disappeared during the years of internal war and political violence has been entrusted to a special department within the Ministry of Justice (DGBPD for its Spanish denomination).[55] It is in charge of designing a National Plan for the search of persons disappeared during the years 1980–2000. In 2021, the DGBPD revised its first Plan and adopted a larger Plan for the forthcoming years up to 2030.[56] This governmental document 'takes its direction from the guiding principles for the search for disappeared persons'[57] and integrates literally all of the 16 Guiding Principles, declaring them part of the Plan and refers in several details directly to them. In another important

[53] Defensoría del Pueblo, 'Defensoría del Pueblo impulsará los 16 principios para la búsqueda de personas desaparecidas de la ONU', 30 August 2021, available at https://www.defensoria.gov.co/-/defensor%C3%ADa-del-pueblo-impulsar%C3%A1-los-16-principios-para-la-b%C3%BAsqueda-de-personas-desaparecidas-de-la-onu.

[54] Distrito Especial, Industrial, Portuario, Biodiverso y Ecoturístico de Buenaventura, Decree 0047, 10 March 2023, available (in Spanish) at https://www.buenaventura.gov.co/images/multimedia/20230312_decreto_0047_del_10_de_marzo_de_2023.pdf

[55] Dirección General de Búsqueda de Personas Desaparecidas (DGBPD).

[56] Ministerio de Justicia y Derechos Humanos de Perú, *Plan nacional de búsqueda de personas desaparecidas al 2030* (Perú: 2021), available (in Spanish) at https://cdn.www.gob.pe/uploads/document/file/2145511/Plan%20Nacional%20de%20B%C3%BAsqueda%20de%20Personas%20Desaparecidas%20al%202030.pdf.pdf.

[57] See Committee on Enforced Disappearances, Information received from Peru on follow-up to the concluding observations on its report submitted under Art. 29 (1) of the Convention, CED/C/PER/FCO/1, 15 November 2021, para. 27.

document for its work, the guidelines for the psychosocial accompaniment of the families of disappeared persons,[58] the DGBPD had also declared that the Guiding Principles form part of its legal basis.

### *3.5.4 Chile*

With a view towards the fiftieth anniversary in 2023 of the coup d'état of Augusto Pinochet, the government of President Gabriel Boric decided to present a National Plan for the search of the persons disappeared during the dictatorship, to be executed by the Human Rights Program (Programa de Derechos Humanos – PDH) of the Ministry of Justice and Human Rights. In October 2022, the drafting process of the Plan was opened to a comprehensive dialogue with family and victims' organizations as well as experts from other countries. The first project presented by the PDH[59] was explicit in its reference to the Guiding Principles, particularly to the rights of the victims to participate in the search as stipulated in Principles 3.5 and 5.1. The PDH held consultations with experts about the implementation of the Principles. The National Plan for Search, Truth, and Justice, intended to search for those who were subjected to forced disappearances during the dictatorship, was signed and launched by President Boric on a symbolic day, 30 August 2023, the international day of the victims of enforced disappearances. The final version of the National Plan again has numerous and detailed references to the Guiding Principles in support of the dispositions of the Plan.[60] According to this document, the Guiding Principles are 'a basic reference

[58] Ministerio de Justicia y Derechos Humanos de Perú, 'Protocolo para el acompañamiento psicosocial a familiares en el proceso de búsqueda de personas desaparecidas con enfoque humanitario', 21 April 2021, available (in Spanish) at www.gob.pe/institucion/minjus/informes-publicaciones/1854676-protocolo-para-el-acompanamiento-psicosocial-a-familiares-en-el-proceso-de-busqueda-de-personas-desaparecidas-con-enfoque-humanitario.

[59] See Ministerio de Justicia y Derechos Humanos de Chile, 'Presentamos el diseño participativo del Plan Nacional de Búsqueda para víctimas de desaparición forzada en dictadura', 22 September 2022, available (in Spanish) at www.gob.cl/noticias/presentamos-el-diseno-participativo-del-plan-nacional-de-busqueda-para-victimas-de-desaparicion-forzada-en-dictadura/.

[60] Ministerio de Justicia y Derechos Humanos de Chile, Decreto 98, 2023, 'Aprueba plan nacional de búsqueda de verdad y justicia respecto de las personas víctimas de desaparición forzada ocurridas en Chile entre el 11 de septiembre de 1973 y el 10 de marzo de 1990, designa al programa de derechos humanos como órgano ejecutor y crea el comité de seguimiento y participación', available (in Spanish) at https://www.bcn.cl/leychile/navegar?idNorma=1197778&idVersion=2023-11-10.

for developing models for the search' and 'legitimize and guarantee the efforts of the families and their social position as agents of the search'.[61]

## 3.6 Impact of the Guiding Principles in International Organizations

### *3.6.1 United Nations*

The United Nations, as the tutelary organization on all the treaty bodies, including the CED, has made many efforts, in Geneva as well as through their regional and country offices, to support the drafting process and to promote their diffusion and application. In addition to using the Principles in the context of urgent actions as mentioned above, the CED has used them in its follow up concluding observations related to Colombia to encourage 'the State party to systematically incorporate the methods of the guiding principles for the search for disappeared persons in the design and implementation of comprehensive search strategies'. It also referred to the Principles in its report after the visit to Mexico in February 2022, the first visit under article 33 of the Convention, that allows the Committee to visit a country after receiving reliable information indicating that a State Party is seriously violating the Convention.

The Committee has also invoked the Guiding Principles for issuing recommendations in its concluding observations. After noting that an ordinance in Switzerland is not fully in line with the Convention, it recommended that the State, 'drawing the attention of the State party to guiding principles',[62] make the necessary amendments to the ordinance, that is, establishing a twenty-four-hour response time for any search, instead of the six days mentioned in the Ordinance or establishing safeguards to ensure that any person who may be involved or has links with a person involved in a forced disappearance 'does not participate in information gathering and is not in a position to influence the course of the investigation'. In this way, the Committee recalled principles 6 and 15. The Committee has also recommended the States of

[61] Ibid., p. 11. 'La relevancia de los Principios Rectores radica en ser un referente básico para desarrollar modelos de búsqueda, que incluyen no solo las ideas sustanciales para las buenas prácticas con enfoque de derecho, sino que también un modelo participativo que legitima y garantiza Ia labor de las familias y su lugar social de buscadores.'

[62] See Committee on Enforced Disappearances, Concluding observations on the report submitted by Switzerland under Art. 29(1) of the Convention, CED/C/CHE/CO/1, 21 May 2021.

Brazil, Niger and Mali ensure that its efforts to search for disappeared persons or that the search procedures implemented are aligned, in accordance or consistent with the Committee's guiding principles for the search for disappeared persons.[63]

In its first General Comment, on enforced disappearances in the context of migration, the Committee affirmed that for the purpose of ensuring the 'effectiveness of the search, States parties should implement the Committee's Guiding Principles'.[64]

Naturally, the 'sister body' of the CED, the WGEID, which had already given advice during the drafting process, also takes up the Guiding Principles regularly as orientation in their dealings with countries that are not State Parties to the ICPPED.[65]

In Mexico, the local branch of the OHCHR was extremely helpful not only supporting the drafting process of the Principles but also its dissemination. As mentioned, the Office printed an illustrated booklet with the 16 Principles, which was widely distributed even beyond the Mexican borders. And it cooperated in the production of a video on each one of the Principles that have been shown on screens in public spaces like the metro.

### 3.6.2 *Inter-American Human Rights System*

The Inter-American Commission on Human Rights (IACHR), which had already participated in the consultation on the draft of the Principles, included in their joint statement on behalf of the International Day of the victims of forced disappearance in 2021 an appeal to 'apply' the Guiding Principles.[66] For the same purpose of commemorating the International

[63] See Committee on Enforced Disappearances, Concluding observations on the report submitted by Brazil under Art. 29(1) of the Convention, CED/C/BRA/CO/1, 3 November 2021; Committee on Enforced Disappearances, Concluding observations on the report submitted by Niger under Art. 29(1) of the Convention, CED/C/NER/CO/1, 5 May 2022; Committee on Enforced Disappearances, Concluding observations on the report submitted by Mali under Art. 29(1) of the Convention, CED/C/MLI/CO/1, 4 October 2022.

[64] See Committee on Enforced Disappearances, General Comment No. 1 on enforced disappearance in the context of migration, CED/C/GC/1, 29 September 2023.

[65] In its report on communications and cases issued after the 126th session, A/HRC/WGEID/126/1, February 2022, the WGEID informs that it 'invited' several States to take into account their obligations to search for the disappeared, with reference to the Guiding Principles.

[66] Inter-American Commission on Human Rights, 'On the International Day of the Victims of Enforced Disappearances, the IACHR, the Committee on Enforced Disappearances and the Working Group on enforced or involuntary disappearances call on States to

Day of the victims of forced disappearances in 2022, the IACHR together with the CED and the WGEID called on States 'to adopt comprehensive policies on enforced disappearances that seek to make the rights to truth, justice, and reparation a reality' adding that those policies 'should also contemplate the economic and psychosocial impact that the disappearance and search has on victims' families, particularly women', and recalling that 'the CED's Guiding Principles note that it is States' duty to assess and provide the support needed by families during the search process. They should also require the search to follow a differential approach and be undertaken from a gender perspective and with adequately trained personnel'.[67]

The principles were also mentioned in at least one country report of the Inter-American Commission[68] where the Commission refers to Principle 3 (need of a public policy) to ask Brazil to structure its efforts in a coherent way (para. 407). The OAS to which the IACHR belongs had been asked by Peru to include in the long chapter of its regular Human Rights Resolution an express invitation for the member States to take the Guiding Principles as the source for their policies.[69] Although this direct mention did not make it into the final more concise text,[70] the Peruvian proposal showed the interest of governments in the Principles.

On its part, the Inter-American Court of Human Rights had mentioned the Guiding Principles in some of the latest cases related to forced disappearances. In *Garzón Guzman* v. *Ecuador*, the Court referred to principles 6 and 13 to reaffirm that the search must be initiated even

adopt and implement search and investigation strategies within the framework of a comprehensive policy on disappearances', 30 August 2021, available at www.oas.org/en/iachr/jsForm/?File=/en/iachr/media_center/preleases/2021/224.asp.

[67] Inter-American Commission on Human Rights, Inter-American Court of Human Rights, CED, and WGEID, 'States Must Prevent the Adverse Effects Faced by Relatives of Missing Persons and Respond to These from a Gender Perspective', 30 August 2022, available at www.oas.org/en/IACHR/jsForm/?File=/en/iachr/media_center/PReleases/2022/191.asp.

[68] Inter-American Commission on Human Rights and Organization of American States, *Situação dos direitos humanos no Brasil*, Ser.L/V/II, 12/2/2021, 12 February 2021.

[69] Organización de Estados Americanos. Consejo Permanente. Comisión de Asuntos Jurídicos y Políticos, *Párrafos propuestos para el tema 'Las personas desaparecidas y la atención a las necesidades de sus familiares' para su inclusión en el proyecto de resolución global 'promoción y protección de los derechos humanos' que se presentará a la Asamblea General en su quincuagésimo periodo ordinario de sesiones (Presentado por la delegación peruana)*, Doc. OEA/Ser.G, CP/CAJP/INF. 794/20, 30 June 2020.

[70] Organización de Estados Americanos, Promotion and Protection of Human Rights, AG/RES. 2961 (L-O/20), 21 October 2020.

without a formal complaint and that the search of the disappeared person and the criminal investigation should be mutually reinforcing and the comprehensive search process should be conducted with the same effectiveness as the criminal investigation.[71] In *Familia Julien Grisonas* v. *Argentina*, the Court resorted to the Guiding Principles to reaffirm the right of victims, representatives or any person authorized by them to participate in the search and to have access to information on the action taken and on the progress and results of the search.[72] In *Movilla Galarcio* v. *Colombia* and *Tabares Toro* v. *Colombia*, the Court deemed relevant that the Guiding Principles be considered in the implementation of the compliance with the reparation order given by the Court to establish the whereabouts of Mr Movilla and Mr Tabares, respectively, and expressly indicated the principles most relevant to each case.[73] In a case decided in October 2022, *Flores Bedregal* v. *Bolivia*, the Court, when reaffirming the different nature of the search and that of the criminal investigation recalled that the Guiding Principles established that the criminal investigation or the conviction or acquittal of those accused of having committed an enforced disappearance should not constitute an obstacle to the continuation of search activities or be invoked to justify their suspension.[74]

### *3.6.3 African Union*

In the course of its 73rd session (21 October–9 November 2022) in Banjul, Gambia, the African Commission on Human and Peoples' Rights adopted its Guidelines on the Protection of All Persons from Enforced Disappearances in Africa.[75] This is the first systematic elaboration on the issue of forced disappearances within the African System of Human Rights Protection. The ninety-page document draws extensively on the international normative advances on Forced Disappearance.

[71] Inter-American Court of Human Rights, *Garzón Guzmán* v. *Ecuador*, Judgment, Merits, Reparations and Costs, 1 September 2021, para. 75.

[72] Inter-American Court of Human Rights, *Familia Julien Grisonas* v. *Argentina*, Judgment, Preliminary Objections, Merits, Reparations and Costs, 23 September 2021, para. 219.

[73] Inter-American Court of Human Rights, *Movilla Galarcio* v. *Colombia*, Judgment, Merits, reparations and costs, 22 June 2022, para. 206–8; Inter-American Court of Human Rights, *Tabares Toro* v. *Colombia,* Judgment, Merits, Reparations and Costs, 22 May 2023, para. 139.

[74] Inter-American Court of Human Rights, *Flores Bedregal* v. *Bolivia*, Judgment, Preliminary Objections, Merits, Reparations and Costs, 17 October 2022, para. 78.

[75] African Commission on Human and Peoples' Rights, 'Guidelines on the Protection of All Persons from Enforced Disappearances in Africa' (2022).

Chapter 4.1.4 on the 'Obligation to search and investigate' is largely based on the Guiding Principles adopted by the CED, referring to several of them in detail.

## 3.7 Impact of the Guiding Principles in Civil Society

As mentioned before, the basic impulse for the CED to redact the Guiding Principles has come from the permanent complaint of victims' initiatives, human rights organizations and civil society in general that the search for the disappeared persons is mostly neglected by the responsible States. The Committee, while reaffirming that there is a clear States obligation already in the text of the Convention (see above) found it nevertheless necessary to issue a special document on the obligation of and good practices for the search of disappeared persons. This process resulted in the Guiding Principles, which was advanced in permanent exchange with civil society organizations. So, it is natural that these were the first to adopt the Principles as a new tool in their struggle to find the disappeared. The cases of Mexico and Colombia have already been highlighted. But first in Latin America and soon beyond that region, civil society began to use the Principles wherever there were disappeared persons to find. In the following paragraphs, we present just a few examples, highlighting the ones from countries that are not State parties to the Convention. We will present first the impact in civil society in Latin American countries, then in Asian and in European countries.

### 3.7.1 *Honduras*

In Honduras, one of the few Central American States that have ratified the Convention, civil society organizations have taken great interest in the Principles. One example is the Honduran Black Fraternal Organization (Organización Fraternal Negra Hondureña) (OFRANEH), that cares, among other issues, about the fate of disappeared members of the Garífuna communities in the Caribbean coast of the country. In its statement on behalf of the International Day of the Victims of Forced Disappearances in 2021, they sustained their claims on an extensive and detailed use of the Guiding Principles.[76]

[76] OFRANEH-SUNLA, '*OFRANEH* Communique: 'International Day of the Victims of Enforced Disappearances', 31 August 2018, available (in Spanish) at www.tortillaconsal.com/tortilla/node/12779.

### 7.2 *Peru*

An example of the wide dissemination of the Guiding Principles among civil society organizations is its mention in a text about memory and non-repetition, published in Quechua, by the National Association of Relatives of the Kidnapped, Detained and Disappeared in Peru (ANFASEP) together with the Catholic University of Peru (PUCP).[77]

### 3.7.3 *Cambodia*

In April 2022, fifty civil society organizations from Cambodia issued a joint statement denouncing forced disappearance in Cambodia, particularly the cross-border disappearance of Thai human rights activist Wanchalearm Satsaksit. Specifically, they declared that 'unconscionable delays in the search for a disappeared person are inconsistent with the Guiding Principles for the search for disappeared persons, including to presume the person is alive, respect human dignity, start the search without delay, use information in an appropriate manner, and respect that the search is a continuing obligation until the fate of the disappeared is known'.[78]

### 3.7.4 *Syria*

In March 2021, ethnic minority groups[79] from northern and eastern Syria founded a Coalition named 'Synergy' to represent all the victims of the wars in the region. A special focus of Synergy is directed towards the victims of forced disappearance. With a view towards existing and hopefully forthcoming international commissions for the search of these disappeared persons, Synergy developed a set of guidelines for the participation of victims in the international mechanism for the disappeared in Syria,[80] with the aim 'to consolidate the right to the participation of

[77] Instituto de Democracia y Derechos Humanos (IDEHPUCP), *YuyanaWasi 'Mana YapamantaKananpaq' Anfaseppa. riqsinapaq pusay,* 2020, available (in Quechua) at https://repositorio.pucp.edu.pe/index/handle/123456789/1.

[78] Sitanan Satsaksit and Family, 'Wanchalearm Satsaksit Remains Missing as UN Body Begins Review of Enforced Disappearances in Cambodia', Joint Statement, 4 April 2022, available at https://equitablecambodia.org/website/article/3-2471.html.

[79] Kurds, Arabs, Assyrians, Armenians, Syrians, Chechens, Circassians and Turkmens.

[80] Hevdesti et al., 'The guidelines for the participation of victims in the international mechanism for the disappeared in Syria', available at https://hevdesti.org/en/syrias-missing/.

victims and their families in the search for their disappeared and loved ones in Syria'. As the drafters manifest, the guidelines 'are based on articles 24 and 18 of the International Convention for the Protection of All Persons from Enforced Disappearance and the Guiding Principle no. 5 of Guiding Principles for the search for the disappeared persons developed by the Committee on Enforced Disappearance'. Indeed, this document can be considered an interesting, carefully drafted, adaptation of the principle of victims' participation in the search to the specific context and conditions of this region in Syria, a State that has not signed the ICPPED nor shows any concern about the protection from forced disappearance.

### 3.7.5 *Poland*

Although the Guiding Principles are based on the Convention, developing the duty to search contained in this treaty, they are an autonomous UN document at the service of any person, group or institution, including States that are not a party to the treaty. An interesting example on how the Principles thus can have an impact beyond the boundaries of the Treaty obligations is a document produced by the Polish Police Academy dealing with the 'Development of a database and tools for semantic search for information and knowledge management in the area of missing persons and search for persons'. The authors of the study emphasize that the proposed information system has been designed in line with the Guiding Principles, which they describe in detail adding that 'all these requirements, and others contained in the document, were taken into account when developing the system'.[81]

## 3.8 Academic Discussion of the Guiding Principles

Since some of the academics that for years have been involved in the topic of forced disappearances had also taken part in the drafting process, it is not surprising that they also published on the document once it had been adopted by the CED.[82]

[81] A. Swierczewska-Gasiorowska, M. Porwisz and P. Olber, 'Espozan electronic system supporting the polish police in the search for missing persons' (2020) 58, 3 *Journal of Criminology and Criminal Law (JCCL)* 69–80.

[82] See A. J. Ospina et al., *La búsqueda y la participación en los casos de desaparición forzada: marco legal en Colombia y El Salvador* (Dejusticia, 2021), available (in Spanish) at https://www.dejusticia.org/publication/la-busqueda-y-la-participacion-en-los-casos-de-desaparicion-forzada-marco-legal-en-colombia-y-el-salvador/, calling the Guiding Principles 'the

Several academic publications refer to the Guiding Principles in contexts that go beyond their immediate scope related to the search. For example, Bernard Duhaime, Juan E. Méndez and Pau Perez-Sales point to the Guiding Principle on the Respect for human dignity in the context of the relation between forced disappearance and torture.[83] Issa Cristina Hernández Herrera, when advocating for the need to interact in the search even with groups of organized crime in view of a 'humanitarian alternative' for the families victims of such groups, and decrying the 'false and unfair choice between justice and truth' that especially victims of these groups are confronted with, sees an avenue for victims in 'a complementarity logic' between investigation and search as demanded by Principle 13 of the Guiding Principles.[84] Britta Nicolmann points to the fact that the CED itself, once the Principles had been adopted, makes systematic use of them in its Urgent Action recommendations.[85] Lena Guercke finds in Principle 10, which deals with the efficient organization of the search an argument, 'that the CED considers "disappeared persons" as encompassing both victims of forced disappearances and victims of disappearances committed by non-State actors and considers the obligation to search to apply to all victims'.[86]

One aspect in which the Guiding Principles have found particular resonance is the disappearance of persons during flight or migration.

most promising document related to the search of the disappeared at the international level'; M. C. Galvis and N. O. Arias, 'Los Principios Rectores para la Búsqueda de Personas Desaparecidas: origen y contenido' (2019) 19 *Ideas Verdes. Análisis Políticos* 1–31, available at https://co.boell.org/sites/default/files/20190905_paper19_web.pdf.

83 B. Duhaime, J. E. Méndez and P. Perez-Sales, 'Current debates, development, and challenges regarding enforced disappearance as torture' (2021) 31, 2 *Torture. Journal on Rehabilitation of Torture Victims and Prevention of Torture* 8.

84 I. Hernández, 'Collaborating with organized crime in the search for disappeared persons? Formalizing a humanitarian alternative for Mexico' (2020) 102, 914 *International Review of the Red Cross* 607–28.

85 B. Nicolmann, *Preventing and Addressing Enforced Disappearances in the Context of International Migration. The Contribution of International Human Rights Mechanisms* (Geneva Academy, 2021), available at www.geneva-academy.ch/joomlatools-files/docman-files/working-papers/Preventing%20and%20Addressing%20Enforced%20Disappearances%20in%20the%20Context%20of%20International%20Migration.pdf.

86 L. C. Guercke, *Preventing and Addressing Enforced Disappearances in the Context of International Migration. The Contribution of International Human Rights Mechanisms* (Geneva Academy, 2021), available at www.geneva-academy.ch/joomlatools-files/docman-files/working-papers/Preventing%20and%20Addressing%20Enforced%20Disappearances%20in%20the%20Context%20of%20International%20Migration.pdf.

In her studies on disappearances in the context of migration,[87] Grażyna Baranowska draws systematically on the Principles for interpreting the norms of the Convention. Melanie Klinkner and Howard Davis, authors of a book on 'The Right to the Truth in International Law',[88] draw on article 9 of the Guiding Principles in a related essay published after the adoption of the Principles, in order to substantiate the duty to cooperate in effective investigations, understanding that Principle 9 'glosses the cooperation requirement in article 15' of the Convention.[89]

Special attention to the Principles comes from Chilean law professor Pietro Sferrazza who only weeks after the publication of the Principles discussed them in a first article dealing with problems of the search for the persons disappeared during the Pinochet dictatorship that are still not found.[90] Sferrazza stressed the importance of this 'soft law text' for the Chilean case, particularly with regard to the search as a continuing obligation (Principle 7) which he discusses in extenso. In another, larger essay published the same year, the Chilean expert sets out the existence of an autonomous fundamental right of disappeared persons to be searched for, along with a corresponding international obligation for all States.[91] He highlights the Guiding Principles as a 'landmark in the evolution of the interdisciplinary reflection about forced disappearance' and considers it an 'obligation for any State that seriously seeks to implement a public policy of search'. The CED, concludes Sferrazza, with the Principles has begun 'to promote a complementary model of search'. In this line, the author sustains throughout the text his argument quoting the different Principles. To these two important essays, Sferrazza added another in which he sets out directly to comment on the Principles article by article.[92]

87 G. Baranowska, *Disappeared Migrants and Refugees: The Relevance of the International Convention on Enforced Disappearance in their search and protection* (German Institute for Human Rights, 2020), available at https://www.institut-fuer-menschenrechte.de/fileadmin/Redaktion/Publikationen/Analyse_Studie/Analysis_Disappeared_Migrans_and_Refugees.pdf.

88 H. Davis and M. Klinkner, *The Right to the Truth in International Law. Victims' Rights in Human Rights and International Criminal Law* (Routledge, 2020).

89 H. Davis and M. Klinkner, 'Investigating across borders: The right to the truth in an European context' (2022) 26, 4 *The International Journal of Human Rights* 683–700.

90 P. Sferrazza, 'La búsqueda de personas desaparecidas en Chile: ¿Necesidad de un complemento humanitario?' (2021) *Revista Mexicana de Ciencias Políticas y Sociales* 243, 79–108.

91 P. Sferrazza, 'La búsqueda de personas desaparecidas: Derecho humano de las víctimas y obligación internacional del Estado' (2021) 19, 1 *Estudios Constitucionales* 265–308.

92 P. Sferrazza, 'Comentarios a los Principios Rectores para la Búsqueda de Personas Desaparecidas del Comité contra las Desapariciones Forzadas de Naciones Unidas' (2021) 21 *Anuario Mexicano de Derecho Internacional* 773–96.

He starts his analysis with a focus on one of the main concerns of the Principles, the difference and necessary complementarity of the two principal ways in which the search is normally conducted: through judicial and administrative (or 'humanitarian') procedures. In the main part of the essay, titled 'Critical analysis of the Guiding Principles for the Search for Disappeared Persons', the author comments on all the Principles, drawing often on related sources. He discusses first the principles that set the general frame, like the permanent character of the obligation to search, the presumption of life and the respect for dignity and the need for a comprehensive public policy. He notes that the Principles do not expressly call for an autonomous public institution for the search but leave it open to States whether they take this option or find a way that the competent judicial organs deal adequately also with the search, whereas in his opinion the need for a special administrative organ for the search is clear. In his discussion of the more technical recommendations contained in the Principles, Sferrazza comments that those related to forensic procedures are rather general and suggests some precisions like, for example, related to the preservation and documentation of unidentified remains. Without prejudice of these and some other features where Sferrazza sees a need for more extensive development of their content, the author summarizes his analysis stating that the Principles are a 'great advancement of the universal system of protection of human rights with regard to the humanitarian needs of the victims'.

In Colombia, already in 2020, a master's thesis sought to analyze the relevance of the Guiding Principles with regard to the work of the official institution charged with the search of the disappeared persons (Unidad de Búsqueda de Personas Dadaspor Desaparecidas – UBPD).[93] In her thesis, the author gives a detailed overview of the Principles and shows that they reflect largely the principles formulated in the legal norms that implement the Peace Accord of 2016. As a consequence, the author presents a series of specific proposals for direct application of the Principles in the work of the UBPD and their relations with other authorities created in the framework of the Peace Accord.

A comparative study between Colombia and El Salvador with respect to the rights of families to participate in the search considers the Guiding

[93] A. Rayo, *Principios Rectores para la Búsqueda de Personas Desaparecidas: una oportunidad para el fortalecimiento de la búsqueda humanitaria y extrajudicial desarrollada por la UBPD* (Universidad Santo Tomás, 2020), available (in Spanish) at https://repository.usta.edu.co/bitstream/handle/11634/30064/2020andrearayo.pdf?sequence=1&isAllowed=y.

Principles as 'the most promising instrument' in the international context and proceeds to a detailed scrutiny of their applicability in existing norms and the needs to enlarge and precise them.[94]

An even more expansive study on non-judicial search mechanisms in Latin America and Asia also discusses in much detail the Principles adopted by the CED.[95]

The number of academic texts referring more or less extensively to the Guiding Principles is growing fast and it is impossible to try to give an exhaustive list here. It should be of interest, though, that not only legal and social scholars pay attention to the Principles but also forensic scientists.[96] The latest specific protocol on forensic procedures, the 2020 Bournemouth Protocol on Mass Grave Protection and Investigation,[97] explicitly ranks the CED Guiding Principles among the 'International norms' in the field, referring repeatedly to them throughout the text. Another academic document proposing standards, in this case on the registry and documentation of forced disappearances, refers also to the Principles, particularly Principle 11.[98]

In Serbia, a State Party to the Convention, the Provincial Protector of Citizens – Ombudsman of the Autonomous Province of Vojvodina

94 A. J. Ospina et al., *La búsqueda y la participación en los casos de desaparición forzada: marco legal en Colombia y El Salvador* (Dejusticia, 2021), available (in Spanish) at https://www.dejusticia.org/publication/la-busqueda-y-la-participacion-en-los-casos-de-desaparicion-forzada-marco-legal-en-colombia-y-el-salvador/.

95 C. Collins, *An Innovative Response to Disappearances: Non-Judicial Search Mechanisms in Latin America and Asia* (Global Initiative for Justice Truth and Reconciliation, 2022), available at https://purc.ulster.ac.uk/ws/files/101225433/SearchComissions_Final_Research_Doc_PDF_13.5.22.pdf.

96 M. Salado Puerto et al., 'The search process: Integrating the investigation and identification of missing and unidentified persons' (2021) 3 *Forensic Science International*, available at www.sciencedirect.com/science/article/pii/S2589871X21000243; I. Biel-Portero and A. C. Mafla, Lipprint: A humanitarian forensification' (2021) 33, 1 *Revista Facultad de Odontología Universidad de Antioquia* 96–106, available at https://doi.org/10.17533/udea.rfo.v33n1a8.

97 M. Klinkner and E. Smith, 'From law to policy and practice – collaborative research amidst a pandemic: The creation of the Bournemouth Protocol on Mass Grave Protection and Investigation' (2021) 1, 1 *Journal of Legal Research Methodology* 26–49, available at https://doi.org/10.19164/jlrm.v1i1.1161. In another text, the authors call the Principles a 'standard-setting instrument': M. Klinkner and E. Smith, *The Bournemouth Protocol on Mass Grave Protection and Investigation* (Bournemouth University Press, 2020), available at www.bournemouth.ac.uk/research/projects/mass-grave-protection-truth-justice.

98 Universidad Alberto Hurtado et al., *Guidelines and Recommendations on the Registry and Documentation of Forced Disappearances* (Universidad Alberto Hurtado et. al., 2020), available at https://research.gold.ac.uk/id/eprint/30075/1/Guidelines%20and%20Recommendations%20on%20the%20Registry%20and%20Documentation%20of%20Forced%20Disappearances.pdf.

publishes a voluminous Yearbook. Its 2021 edition, dedicated to the Right to Life, offers an article by Milica Kolaković-Bojović on 'Disappeared Persons and the Right to be Considered Alive – The Current State of Play in the Western Balkans' in which the author, a member of CED, recurs to the Principles, among the International standards which proclaim the right to be searched for under the presumption of life, supporting this right. The author also informs that in 2021 the Serbian Government has established a working group to develop a draft Law on Missing Persons for which it used the Guiding Principles in detail.[99] The line between academic research, reports and similar documents by international human organizations is a fluid one. To give just a few examples, we mention the recent report of REDRESS on forced disappearance in Africa,[100] which makes extensive use of the Principles, and the interest of the International Commission of Jurists (ICJ) in understanding and disseminating the Principles.[101]

In Pakistan, which is not a Party to the Convention, the Guiding Principles were mentioned in an article published in 2021 entitled 'Dysfunctional Law against the Crime of Enforced Disappearances in Pakistan'. When referring to the continuous nature of the obligation to investigate a crime of forced disappearance, the authors recalled the continuous nature of this crime, enshrined in the Convention and in Principle 7 of the Guiding Principles.[102]

### 3.9 Conclusions

The Guiding Principles for the Search for Disappeared Persons have been the result of persistent claims from family organizations and civil society for a clear, detailed and legitimate interpretation of the right to be searched for and the right to search, according to international human

[99] M. Kolaković-Bojović, 'Disappeared persons and the right to be considered alive: The current state of play in the Western Balkans' in Z. Pavlović, *Yearbook Human Rights Protection. Right To Life* (Provincial Protector of Citizens – Ombudsman; Institute of Criminological and Sociological Research, 2021), p. 284; see also Chapter 9.

[100] Redress, The *forgotten victims: Enforced disappearance in Africa* (Redress, 2021) available at https://redress.org/publication/the-forgotten-victims-enforced-disappearance-in-africa/.

[101] Comisión Internacional de Juristas para América Latina, *Conversación sobre los Principios rectores para la búsqueda de personas desaparecidas* (2021), available at www.youtube.com/watch?v=RtMdP3Xjrs8.

[102] U. Hameed, K. Qaiser and Z. Qaiser, 'Dysfunctional Law against the Crime of Enforced Disappearances in Pakistan' (2021) 9, 2 *International Review of Social Sciences* 1–8.

rights law and stated in the ICPPED. The Principles were drafted with active and broad participation of many victims, in a process that let them feel that this instrument was theirs. It is no surprise then that those victims, their collective organizations and other human rights organizations from civil society make ample use of the Principles to sustain their continuing claims for a more efficient, respectful and participative search of the beloved family members or other persons close to them that continue disappeared.

The Principles were drafted, however, also with a view to giving better orientation and a more explicit interpretation of their obligations in the search process to those States that are willing to improve their practice that had and has been often criticized by the Committee in its recommendations on urgent actions and its concluding observations. It is encouraging to see that several States have quickly taken up this opportunity and integrated, in a constructive way, the Principles in the design of their public policies related to the search, in their legislation and, in one case, even made the Principles a constitutional norm for the search. Similarly, courts, including Supreme Courts, have adopted the Principles as a norm to measure the performance of the competent authorities in the search. The same is true for the most advanced jurisdiction for forced disappearance on the international level, The Inter-American Court of Human Rights, which has already integrated the Principles in its case law on forced disappearances. It is also notable to see that both the Committee on Enforced Disappearances and the Working Group on Enforced or Involuntary Disappearances continue to apply the Guiding Principles in their work.

The present chapter was concluded at the end of 2022, three years after the adoption and publication of the Guiding Principles. The balance of these first three years of the existence of the Principles is encouraging in many ways. While it is evident that the Principles have received most attention in the Latin American region, as it was there where the strongest impulse for their redaction came from, the Principles are making their way into other regions, too, and are clearly on the way to be universally recognized and integrated in the struggle for the search of disappeared persons. The examples presented here from civil society in Poland, Serbia, Cambodia, Syria and particularly the inclusion of the Principles in the recent Guidelines on the Protection of All Persons from Enforced Disappearances of the African Union show that the Principles can be adapted to situations everywhere where people are forcibly disappeared and where there is a will to do everything possible to clarify these disappearances and locate the missing persons.

# 4

# New Technologies and Enforced Disappearances

## The Working Group on Enforced or Involuntary Disappearances – Exploring a New World between Opportunities and Challenges

GABRIELLA CITRONI*

### 4.1 Introduction

Over the past decade, the subject of the human rights impact of new technologies[1] – both in terms of challenges posed by such technologies to the protection of fundamental rights and freedoms and of opportunities that they may offer to enhance the enjoyment of those rights – attracted increasing attention. Studies on the matter are growing in number and in the scope of the analysis of the multiple ramifications of the subject.[2] In the context of the Special Procedures of the United Nations Human

* The author is grateful to Elena Carpanelli, Ugo Cedrangolo and to the editors of the book for their invaluable comments on an earlier version of this chapter.

1 The expression 'new technologies' will be used in a broad sense across the chapter. For more details, see Section 4.3.

2 See, among others, J. Liddicoat, *Human Rights and the Internet* (Cambridge University Press, 2021); S. Dubberley, A. Koenig and D. Murray (eds.), *Digital Witness* (Oxford University Press, 2020); D. Lochak, 'Les fondements des droits de l'Homme au défi des nouvelles technologies: Conclusions générales', in O. de Frouville and J. Tavernier (eds.), *La Déclaration universelle des droits de l'Homme, 70 ans après: les fondements des droits de l'Homme au défi des nouvelles technologies* (Pedone, 2019), pp. 203–17; M. K. Land, J. D. Aronson (eds.), *New Technologies for Human Rights Law and Practice* (Cambridge University Press, 2018); L. Panella, *Nuove tecnologie e diritti umani: profili di diritto internazionale e di diritto interno* (Editoriale Scientifica, 2018); J. Coccoli, 'The challenges of new technologies in the implementation of human rights: An analysis of some critical issues in the digital era' (2017) 1, 2 *Peace Human Rights Governance* 223–50; A. E. Pérez Luño (ed.), *Nuevastecnologías y derechoshumanos* (Tirant Lo Blanch, 2014). See also the Special Issue (vol. 19, no. 1, 2021) of the *Journal of International Criminal Justice* on 'New Technologies and the Investigation of International Crimes', and the Issue (no. 913, 2021) of the *International Review of the Red Cross* on 'Digital Technologies and War'.

Rights Council, this has become a cross-cutting issue: mandate-holders have convened expert consultations, set guidance and provided recommendations to States and other stakeholders. More than 100 reports have been published by Special Procedures, addressing issues that span from the investigation of the use of digital technologies for surveillance – especially of human rights defenders – mass digital surveillance and internet shutdowns, to the use of digital technologies to contribute to the discovery and management of mass graves, to the emerging notion of 'cyber-torture'.

While some mandates, such as the Special Rapporteur on Extrajudicial, Summary or Arbitrary Executions, the Special Rapporteur on the Right to Privacy or the Special Rapporteur on the Promotion and Protection of the Right to Freedom of Opinion and Expression, have been at the forefront of the study of the subject concerned, as of 2023, the Working Group on Enforced or Involuntary Disappearances (WGEID) had never analyzed it in detail. In September 2021, the WGEID announced its intention to conduct a thematic study on new technologies and enforced disappearances, which, after two rounds of expert consultations (respectively held on 9 February 2022 and 11 May 2022) and the collection of inputs from interested stakeholders,[3] was eventually presented to the Human Rights Council in September 2023.[4]

After concisely illustrating the main results of the work of Special Procedures on human rights and technologies in general, this chapter will only briefly present the gestation and contents of the thematic study on new technologies and enforced disappearances of the WGEID. However, the principal aim of the chapter is to analyze a different aspect, namely the role played – if any – by new technologies, and in particular digital, information and communication technologies, in the regular activities of the WGEID. In this regard, the main functions of the WGEID (i.e., communications, prompt intervention letters, urgent appeals, general allegations and country visits) will be concisely illustrated and the opportunities that new technologies may offer to perform such activities will be explored. The impending consequences of the use of new technologies in the realm of country visits will also be considered, as well as the potential of awareness-raising and technical cooperation offered by the WGEID.

[3] The call for inputs circulated by the WGEID and the contributions received (excluding those for which confidentiality was requested) are available at www.ohchr.org/en/calls-for-input/2023/call-inputs-thematic-study-working-group-enforced-or-involuntary.

[4] WGEID, Study on New Technologies and Enforced Disappearances (WGEID Thematic Study), UN Doc. A/HRC/54/22/Add.5, 11 September 2023.

Furthermore, the challenges currently posed to the WGEID and its 'counterparts' by the use of new technologies in terms of security, verification and accessibility will be presented.

The chapter contains suggestions on how to seize the opportunities and to mitigate the challenges at stake with a view at identifying innovative methods to carry out the mandate of the WGEID that ultimately can enhance its effectiveness in the struggle against enforced disappearance and in assisting victims in the realization of their rights to truth, justice and reparations. The concluding remarks offer a reflection on how some of the findings and observations made with regard to the WGEID could be relevant also for the work of the Committee on Enforced Disappearances (CED) and should therefore be taken into account when imagining the future of this Treaty Body.

## 4.2 New Technologies and Human Rights as a Cross-cutting Issue for United Nations Special Procedures

New technologies and their impact – positive or potentially harmful – on the enjoyment of fundamental rights have been a subject of growing concern for the United Nations Human Rights Council,[5] which adopted several recommendations on the matter. Through resolution 41/11 of 11 July 2019, the Human Rights Council mandated its Advisory Committee to study the subject and this led, in 2021, to the publication of a report on the impacts, opportunities and challenges of new and emerging digital technologies with regard to the promotion and protection of human rights.[6] In the report, the Advisory Committee observed that 'new technologies are giving rise to profound new challenges and unforeseen human rights issues'[7] and concluded that 'the accelerating speed at which new technologies are developed and proliferate seems

[5] Albeit this chapter does not focus nor analyze in-depth this aspect, it is noteworthy that also the Office of the High Commissioner for Human Rights (OHCHR) and the United Nations High Commissioner for Human Rights have increasingly dealt with the subject of new technologies and human rights. Among others, see, respectively Report on Internet Shutdowns: Trends, Causes, Legal Implications and Impacts on a Range of Human Rights, UN Doc. A/HRC/50/55, 13 May 2022; and Report on the Impact of New Technologies on the Promotion and Protection of Human Rights in the Context of Assemblies, including Peaceful Protests, UN Doc. A/HRC/44/24, 25 June 2020.

[6] Advisory Committee of the Human Rights Council, Report on Possible Impacts, Opportunities and Challenges of New and Emerging Digital Technologies with regard to the Promotion and Protection of Human Rights, UN Doc. A/HRC/47/52, 19 May 2021.

[7] Ibid., para. 73.

inevitable, but the impact of new technologies on human rights can be effectively shaped through the joint efforts of multiple stakeholders'.[8]

The Human Rights Council's resolutions, as well as the mentioned initiatives and reports, coincide on the importance of a holistic, inclusive and comprehensive approach and the need for all stakeholders to collaborate in a more concerted way in addressing the subject. In particular, emphasis is placed on how the dialogue between technology and telecommunication companies, civil society organizations and United Nations human rights mechanisms (be they Special Procedures or Treaty Bodies) needs to be enhanced as a crucial component to ensure the development of adequate responses. However, at present, there seems to be a lack of regular communication and common background among these actors.[9]

Indeed, 'new technologies' have been identified as one of the cross-cutting thematic issues of concern for the Special Procedures of the Human Rights Council.[10] Over the past decade, Special Procedures mandate-holders have convened expert consultations and issued more than 100 thematic reports revolving around the subject, which provide recommendations to States and other stakeholders with a view at developing and implementing new technologies in a manner that complies with international human rights law. These reports span from the human rights impact of robotics and automation, artificial intelligence, drones and lethal autonomous weapon systems.[11]

The existence of a plethora of reports shows the complexity of the matter at hand, as well as a certain lack of coordination among mandate-holders, as, sometimes, the subjects examined in the reports seem to overlap and the reports themselves do not always cross-reference or build

[8] Ibid., para. 72.

[9] In this regard, it is noteworthy that that the United Nations High Commissioner for Human Rights has been reaching out and establishing partnerships with technology companies (e.g., www.business-humanrights.org/en/latest-news/technology-for-human-rights-new-partnership-between-un-high-commissioner-for-human-rights-microsoft/). However, as of today, a general framework and a coherent approach to the matter are missing. Since 2021, the International Service for Human Rights has launched an initiative to streamline the existing efforts and somehow 'bridge the gap' (see ishr.ch/latest-updates/business-human-rights-new-technologies-and-human-rights-mind-the-gap/).

[10] See www.ohchr.org/en/special-procedures-human-rights-council/cross-cutting-thematic-issues.

[11] For a non-exhaustive compilation of Special Procedures' reports relevant to new technologies, see www.ohchr.org/sites/default/files/Documents/HRBodies/SP/List_SP_Reports_NewTech.pdf.

upon each other. This aspect confirms that there is a need for a more holistic and coordinated approach, also to optimize the use of human, financial and technical resources.

A common trait of these reports is that they acknowledge the dual nature of the relationship between human rights and new technologies, whereby existing challenges are recognized, at the same time paying attention to how technologies can be instrumental in enhancing the promotion and protection of human rights.

Limiting here the scope of the examination to those reports that focus on gross human rights violations and international crimes and new technologies, a few seminal studies can be quoted, including three issued respectively in 2010, 2015 and 2020 by the Special Rapporteur on Extrajudicial, Summary or Arbitrary Executions on the relevance of new technologies in the context of human rights fact-finding, targeted killings and accountability and extrajudicial executions and robotic technologies;[12] the use of information and communication technologies to secure the right to life;[13] and on how digital technologies can contribute to the discovery and management of mass graves.[14] The approach followed in these three documents can be regarded as instrumental in paving the way for the WGEID to undertake similar research on the existing relationship between new technologies and enforced disappearances.

## 4.3 The Working Group on Enforced or Involuntary Disappearances Joins the Pack: The Thematic Study on New Technologies and Enforced Disappearances

In its first forty years of activity, the WGEID did not conduct any in-depth reflection on the subject of new technologies and enforced disappearances or on the impact that such technologies might have in carrying out its mandate. Hence, it is with some delay, compared to other Special Procedures that, at its 125th session, in September 2021, the WGEID

[12] Special Rapporteur on Extrajudicial, Summary or Arbitrary Executions, Report on the Relevance of New Technologies in the Context of Human Rights Fact-finding, Targeted Killings and Accountability, and Extrajudicial Executions and Robotic Technologies, UN Doc. A/65/321, 23 August 2010.

[13] Special Rapporteur on Extrajudicial, Summary or Arbitrary Executions, Report on the Use of Information and Communication Technologies to Secure the Right to Life, UN Doc. A/HRC/29/37, 24 April 2015.

[14] Special Rapporteur on Extrajudicial, Summary or Arbitrary Executions, Report on Mass Graves, UN Doc. A/75/384, 12 October 2020.

announced its intention to conduct a thematic study on new technologies and enforced disappearances.

The WGEID clarified that, for the purposes of the study, the expression 'new technologies' is used in a broad sense, to refer to technological innovations that occurred mostly over the past twenty years, including hardware and software information and communication technologies (ICT), encompassing satellite imagery, geographic information science and remote sensing, digital social networks and online datasets, the use of artificial intelligence and development of machine-learning, as well as digital forensic and biodata.[15] The same broad interpretation of the expression concerned will be applied for the purposes of this chapter.

As other Special Procedures have already done, the WGEID has also emphasized that new technologies have a dual relationship with human rights-related issues. On the one hand, repressive governments, as well as other actors, such as criminal networks, armed groups and non-State actors, can use new technologies against human rights defenders and activists to curb their fundamental rights, including through surveillance, monitoring, intrusion, disinformation campaigns and online harassment and cyber-attacks. In this realm, other stakeholders, such as technology corporations, also play a crucial – and so far somewhat under-analyzed – role through the development of hardware and software used to hamper the activity of human rights defenders. On the other hand, new technologies are today indispensable in documenting and investigating human rights violations, obtaining and preserving evidence and promoting accountability for human rights violations, including enforced disappearances.

Accordingly, the WGEID studied how new technologies (a) are being used against human rights defenders and civil society organizations, including relatives of disappeared persons and their representatives and which kind of protective strategies are – or can be put – in place; (b) can be effectively applied to facilitate the search for disappeared persons, ensuring that their fate and whereabouts are established promptly and in a reliable and secure manner; and (c) can be used to obtain evidence of the commission of enforced disappearance, especially bearing in mind that this crime under international law is by its own nature shrouded in secrecy and, as such, poses formidable evidentiary obstacles to identify and bring to justice perpetrators.

[15] WGEID Thematic Study, para. 3.

This chapter aims at exploring one of the matters not dealt with in the thematic study, that is the role played – if any – by new technologies, and in particular digital, information and communication technologies, in the regular activities of the WGEID.

### 4.4 New Technologies in the Regular Activities of the Working Group on Enforced or Involuntary Disappearances: Between Opportunities and Challenges

Indeed, does the fact that for several decades the WGEID did not expressly deal with new technologies mean that they do not play any role in its day-to-day activities and the way it discharges – or could discharge – its mandate? The following sections will analyze the current situation, as well as opportunities that could be explored for the future.[16] Furthermore, the cross-cutting main challenges – existing or potential – concerning the issues of security, verification and accessibility are illustrated.

While a detailed examination of the composition, mandate and functioning of the WGEID is beyond the scope of the present chapter, a general understanding is indispensable for present purposes. The WGEID is composed of five independent experts and meets in sessions three times per year. To discharge the mandate, the experts are supported by a Secretariat, composed of staff provided by the Office of the High Commissioner for Human Rights (OHCHR). While the experts serve in their personal capacity and are not staff of the United Nations, the members of the Secretariat are and they support the mandate-holders fulfilling their functions, through, among others, research and analysis, as well as legal, methodological and fact-finding expertise.

The WGEID was established by resolution 20 (XXXVI) of 29 February 1980 of the Commission on Human Rights with the mandate to examine questions relevant to enforced disappearance of persons.[17] The mandate

[16] For a broader reflection on the impact of new technologies, and especially ICTs, on the work of Special Procedures, see E. McPherson and T. Probert, 'Special procedures in the digital age', in A. Nolan, R. Freedman and T. Murphy (eds.), *The United Nations Special Procedures System* (Brill Nijhoff, 2017), pp. 261–70.

[17] The last relevant resolution to renew the mandate of the WGEID, Resolution 54/14, was adopted by the Human Rights Council on 11 October 2023. On the basis of its original mandate, the WGEID developed its methods of work: the version in use – and to which reference will be made in this chapter – is the one adopted on 10 February 2023 (UN Doc. A/HRC/WGEID/1, hereinafter, methods of work).

of the WGEID is articulated in various procedures that pursue two main aims: the 'humanitarian' one, that is, to assist families in determining the fate and whereabouts of their loved ones who are reportedly disappeared, and the 'monitoring' one, that is, to identify obstacles in the implementation of the 1992 Declaration on the Protection of all Persons from Enforced Disappearance, adopted by General Assembly resolution 47/133 of 18 December 1992 (the 1992 Declaration).

The WGEID performs its twofold mandate mainly through six procedures. In terms of communications transmitted, there are cases, urgent appeals, prompt intervention letters, general allegations and referrals. Communications on cases aim at assisting in the clarification of the fate and whereabouts of disappeared persons. Urgent appeals are transmitted when there are credible allegations that a person deprived of his or her liberty is at risk of being forcibly disappeared. Prompt intervention letters are used to deal with cases of intimidation, persecution or reprisal against relatives of disappeared persons, witnesses to disappearances or their families, members of organizations of relatives and other NGOs, human rights defenders or individuals concerned with disappearances. General allegations on obstacles encountered in the implementation of the 1992 Declaration are transmitted to States, with the request to comment thereon. Referrals are used when the WGEID receives claims of practices of enforced disappearance that may amount to crimes against humanity and it can refer them to the competent authorities, be they international, regional, sub-regional or domestic.

Furthermore, as with all the other Special Procedures, with prior agreement of the State concerned, the WGEID can carry out country visits, through which it aims at enhancing the dialogue with the authorities most directly concerned and the families of the disappeared or their representative and to assist in the clarification of the reported cases of enforced disappearance. Moreover, during the visits the WGEID examines the actions taken by States to prevent, investigate, punish and eradicate enforced disappearance, as well as the policies and measures adopted to implement the 1992 Declaration.

### *4.4.1 Receiving and Dealing with Communications, Prompt Intervention Letters, Urgent Appeals, General Allegations and Referrals*

In the context of its humanitarian mandate, the WGEID receives and examines communications (respectively handled under the 'urgent' or the 'standard' procedure, depending on when the alleged enforced disappearance commenced).[18] Pursuant to its methods of work, these communications must be submitted in writing, using a dedicated form, and, if the source of the communication is other than a family member, it must have the explicit consent of the family to submit the case on its behalf.[19]

Besides some general problems concerning security, verification and accessibility, which will be analyzed below,[20] the present section considers how new technologies, and in particular ICT, might have an impact on the format and modality of the submission of communications and on the expression of consent to submit a case, as well as the possibility that the WGEID applies new technologies, such as artificial intelligence or machine-learning, to analyze and deal with all the communications received and currently outstanding.

First, while today the submission of written forms can be processed either via email, regular post, the general online portal of Special Procedures[21] or fax, one may wonder whether other channels (e.g., social media or messaging applications) could or should be also allowed. For instance, would a communication submitted to the WGEID in the form of a comment left in its Twitter account (now X) be regarded as valid and processed accordingly? At present, the answer would most likely be in the negative,[22] but the rationale for such a response does not seem to be particularly solid or elaborated, besides the fact that 'this has never been done before.' Whilst it would be interesting to verify how many communications have been submitted by fax to the WGEID over the past five years, one may argue that setting up a dedicated channel via messaging applications (e.g., WhatsApp or Telegram) might facilitate the submission of communications and be met with favour by potential users and the general public.

[18] Methods of work, paras. 10–11.

[19] Ibid., para. 12. The form to be used to report a case is available at www.ohchr.org/en/special-procedures/wg-disappearances/reporting-disappearance-working-group.

[20] See Section 4.4.4.

[21] Available at spsubmission.ohchr.org.

[22] On 18 August 2022, the United Nations Special Rapporteur on Torture and other Cruel, Inhuman or Degrading Treatment or Punishment publicly affirmed that 'no action can be taken on basis of Twitter allegations alone'. Notably, this was announced through a Tweet (twitter.com/DrAliceJEdwards/status/1560189665151537152). Bearing in mind that Special Procedures are to be seen as a system that, to the extent possible, acts in a coherent and coordinated manner, it is likely that the WGEID would take the same stance.

The requested written format – confirmed, in more general terms, in the 2008 manual of operations applicable to all Special Procedures[23] – is somehow controversial. Would the WGEID consider a video clip an acceptable format for the submission of a communication? If so, under which conditions? Along the same lines, would a video be considered a legitimate manner to express consent (of the family or of the disappeared persons themselves) to the submission of the case?

Although the WGEID methods of work are silent in this regard and there does not seem to be any consolidated practice on these matters, the notorious case of princess Sheikha Latifa bint Mohammed Al Maktoum comes to mind.[24] In this instance, the princess had recorded a video,[25] whereby she explained why she was at risk of being subjected to an enforced disappearance: in the absence of the consent of her relatives (who, in this very peculiar case, were also the alleged responsible for her disappearance, and, at the same time, should be considered as State agents), could the said video be regarded as the consent of the victim herself to have her case considered by the WGEID? Interestingly, the family of the princess rebutted the allegations that an enforced disappearance was ongoing by submitting pictures that would show Sheikha Latifa in good health and free.

Without entering into the intricacies of the specific case, which, because of its features, is quite unique, the reported example begs at least four questions: If the WGEID considers videos and pictures as valid as formularies and consent forms, at a time where deep fake imagery is less than uncommon, would the WGEID have the technical means and skills to assess the veracity and reliability of these sources? Indeed, if the person who recorded the video then disappears and relatives cannot be considered as reliable sources, who could be considered the 'source' of the communication, with which the WGEID will maintain its correspondence? If the WGEID is to accept videos and pictures as sources of communication, will it do the same with the answers provided by States? Finally – and more in general – would the WGEID be competent and in a position to search, motu proprio, for videos, pictures or digital

[23] Manual of operations, para. 38, available at www.ohchr.org/sites/default/files/Documents/HRBodies/SP/Manual_Operations2008.pdf.

[24] E. Carpanelli, 'The mysterious abduction and confinement of two princesses: A tentative analysis under international law' (2021) 76, 2 *La comunità internazionale* 353–82.

[25] For a summary of the rather intricate case and the relevance played by pictures and videos, see edition.cnn.com/2018/12/24/middleeast/dubai-princess-sheika-latifa-photos-intl/index.html.

data, among other things, to corroborate or reject the allegations received? None of these questions finds an answer in the methods of work and existing practice of the WGEID and a reflection and the establishment of a clear policy in this regard could be useful.

A separate issue, that nevertheless somehow relates to the actual scope of initiatives that the WGEID can undertake motu proprio, concerns the use of new technologies, such as artificial intelligence or machine-learning, to deal with, and analyze, the remarkable number of cases under active consideration, which, as of 13 May 2023, stand at 47,774.[26] At present, the WGEID examines the communications received with a view at assessing whether they can be registered and transmitted. It equally reviews the responses received from States (or, where applicable, by other actors),[27] in order to evaluate whether they allow to clarify the cases by establishing the fate and whereabouts of the disappeared person concerned. However, the WGEID does not proactively seek additional information on a specific case (e.g., by cross-checking through satellite images or similar),[28] rather focussing on whether the allegations received are credible. Moreover, the WGEID has never examined the bulk of active cases as a whole or for each State to determine, for instance, the existence of specific patterns, relevant contextual elements or even information that may be instrumental in clarifying the fate and whereabouts of the disappeared and in promoting accountability for those responsible for the crimes.

It can be argued that these kind of proactive initiatives would most likely overstretch the boundaries of the mandate of the WGEID and, were they acceptable, they could have already been carried out by the Secretariat, without the need of any new technologies. The methods of work of the WGEID provide that the clarification of a case (i.e., establishing the fate and whereabouts of the disappeared person) can occur, among others, 'as a result of missions by the WGEID'.[29] While it is unclear whether such missions should be equated to the country visits[30]

[26] WGEID, Annual Report for 2022, UN Doc. A/HRC/54/22, 30 July 2023, para. 5.

[27] Since 2019, the WGEID documents also include violations tantamount to enforced disappearance perpetrated by non-State actors that exercise effective control or de facto government-like functions over a territory or population. Methods of work, paras. 32–8.

[28] Methods of work, paras. 24–6. In practice, the WGEID forwards the information received by the State (or other actors) to the source and expects the latter to confirm whether it agrees or not. Moreover, a case can be clarified by the source.

[29] Ibid., para. 27.

[30] See Section 4.4.2.

conducted by the WGEID (and it would not seem to be the case), the expression nevertheless suggests that the WGEID has some leeway to conduct investigations to clarify a case. It is however unlikely that the members of the WGEID and the Secretariat have the resources (human, technical and material) to perform these kind of investigations motu proprio on a systematic basis, especially bearing in mind the thousands of cases under active consideration.

Both for gathering information or conducting research that might clarify a case and for conducting a comprehensive and thorough contextual analysis of all the active cases before the WGEID, new technologies (in particular, the use of artificial intelligence, machine-learning tools and data mining techniques that can be set to process in a relatively short time-span a considerable volume of data and information) could be a game changer. If this is compatible with the mandate of the WGEID and feasible in terms of human and technical resources of the Secretariat remains to be determined and, in any case, seems worthy of consideration.

More in general, the questions formulated in the previous paragraphs and, in particular, the one concerning the admissibility and feasibility of research conducted motu proprio by the WGEID, may be referred also to its other procedures, namely urgent appeals, prompt intervention letters, general allegations, other communications and referrals.[31] These procedures range from communications sent to governments where a person is at risk of being forcibly disappeared (urgent appeals), to cases of intimidation, persecution or reprisal against relatives of disappeared persons, witnesses to disappearances or their families, members of organizations of relatives and other NGOs, human rights defenders or individuals concerned with disappearances (prompt intervention letters). They also encompass instances where there are alleged obstacles in the implementation of the 1992 Declaration (general allegations), or where detailed allegations are received that a State is practicing enforced disappearance or is about to adopt measures that could create obstacles to the implementation of the 1992 Declaration (other communications) or when the WGEID evaluates claims of practices of enforced disappearances that may amount to crimes against humanity and decides whether to refer them to international, regional or sub-regional authorities (referrals).

The procedures under consideration imply – to varying extents – the carrying out of information-gathering activities by the WGEID and the

[31] Methods of work, paras. 39–48 and 57–8.

corresponding evaluation of its reliability. Indeed, it is clear that the WGEID cannot be equated to mechanisms such as the commissions of inquiry or fact-finding missions mandated by the Human Rights Council. The mandate of these organs is inherently different, and they are expected to proactively search for, examine and evaluate information and data that can be regarded as evidence of the commission of international crimes and gross human rights violations, paving the way to holding perpetrators accountable. To fulfil their tasks, commissions of inquiry and fact-finding missions have taken advantage of new technology, added specialized expertise and refocused approaches to information collection and management. In particular, they appreciated that 'rapid changes in technology and ICTs have impacted investigations, opening up new channels of communication that in turn afford new kinds of access to sources'[32] and that 'telephone, internet based communication tools (e.g. Skype) or related technology may assist in reaching otherwise inaccessible areas.'[33] Accordingly, commissions of inquiry and fact-finding missions progressively incorporated in their staff (either counting on in-house knowledge or involving external experts) persons dedicated to conducting open source intelligence (OSINT), including on digital datasets or, where appropriate, satellite imagery.

For its part, the WGEID is not mandated, nor expected, to conduct investigations and collect evidence, be it to establish the fate and whereabouts of a disappeared person or to determine the identity of perpetrators or someone's involvement in the commission of an enforced disappearance.

Indeed, in carrying out its mandate, the WGEID regularly assesses the 'credibility' of the allegations received, as well as the 'reliability' of the sources, always guided by its humanitarian nature and the pro persona criterion. Neither the methods of work of the WGEID nor the code of conduct for Special Procedures[34] or the 2008 manual of

32 OHCHR, *Who's Responsible? Attributing Individual Responsibility for Violations of International Human Rights and Humanitarian Law in United Nations Commissions of Inquiry, Fact-finding Missions and Other Investigations* (OHCHR, 2018), p. 52, available at www.ohchr.org/sites/default/files/Documents/Publications/AttributingIndividualResponsibility.pdf.

33 Ibid., p. 54.

34 Human Rights Council, Resolution 5/2, 6 December 2007. Notably, Art. 6 (a) requires Special Procedures mandate-holders to 'always seek to establish the facts, based on objective, reliable information emanating from relevant credible sources, that they have duly cross-checked to the best extent possible'. Art. 8 (c) sets forth that, in carrying out 'information-gathering activities' the mandate-holders shall 'rely on objective and dependable facts based on evidentiary standards that are appropriate to the non-judicial character of the reports and conclusions they are called upon to draw up'.

operations[35] clarify in detail how mandate-holders are expected to conduct their due diligence in evaluating these crucial aspects. Leaving aside for the moment the underlying – yet pivotal – issue of verification, which will be considered below,[36] some considerations can be put forward on whether and how new technologies could be used in this crucial phase of the WGEID activities.

First, the WGEID performs research and information assessment, and, in this regard, as commissions of inquiry or fact-finding missions, it may benefit from, among others, OSINT. For such purpose, the WGEID should duly take into account the 2022 Berkeley Protocol on Digital Open Source Investigations, which contains a Practical Guide on the Effective Use of Digital Open Source Information in Investigating Violations of International Criminal, Human Rights and Humanitarian Law.[37] The Protocol – directed at a broad audience, which can encompass also the WGEID – is designed to assist open source investigators to conduct their work in accordance with a professional methodology that is broadly consistent with legal requirements and ethical norms.

Second, the fast-evolving nature of the technologies must be considered. If the WGEID includes the use of new technologies in its assessment of the credibility of the information received, there should be a broader reflection on whether the members of the WGEID and its Secretariat have the technical knowledge and skills and sufficient human resources to deliver. Alternatively, assistance on these matters could be outsourced,[38] although this might encounter – not necessarily insurmountable – problems in view of the confidential nature of most of the information dealt with by the WGEID.

Third, going beyond what the WGEID can – or should – do to ensure a broader use of new technologies in the performance of its mandate, in the context of most of the procedures here described, it regularly interacts with States and requests governments to carry out search activities and investigations and to inform it of the results. The WGEID will then assess the information provided by the State concerned, for instance, with a view to clarifying cases or evaluating the compliance with the 1992

[35] On 'sources of information' used by Special Procedures, see, in particular, paras. 23–7 of the manual of operations. The latter confirms that mandate-holders are expected to perform 'information-gathering' activities.

[36] See Section 4.4.4.

[37] Available at www.ohchr.org/sites/default/files/2022-04/OHCHR_BerkeleyProtocol.pdf.

[38] More on this point below in Section 4.4.3.

Declaration. As of today, it does not seem that the WGEID has systematically included in its exchanges with States questions and recommendations on the use of new technologies in search activities and investigations. This option could be explored, with a view to ensuring the addition of this issue in a comprehensive and systematic way in the dialogue with States, ideally promoting the enhancement of the applicable standards.

A final remark that can be made concerns the recipients of the WGEID's allegations or communications regarding obstacles in the implementation of the 1992 Declaration. In this sense, the traditional interlocutors of the WGEID are States.[39] Nevertheless, Special Procedures can – and many regularly do so – address their communications and allegations also to stakeholders other than States, including corporations and technology companies.[40] Hence, if the WGEID were to receive information according to which policies or practices of actors other than States – such as technology companies – are at odds with the 1992 Declaration or raise problems with regard to its implementation – for instance, through the use of digital tools of mass surveillance or spyware programmes[41] to target relatives of disappeared persons or their

39 For the 'exception' concerning non-State actors that exercise effective control or de facto government-like functions over a territory or population, see note 27.

40 Among others, see the joint allegation letter concerning Facebook, Instagram and WhatsApp sent in 2021 by the Special Rapporteur on the promotion and protection of the right to freedom of opinion and expression, the Working Group on the issue of transnational corporations and other business enterprises, the Special Rapporteur on the minority issues and the Special Rapporteur on the situation in the Palestinian territory occupied since 1967 (spcommreports.ohchr.org/TMResultsBase/DownLoadPublicCommunicationFile?gId=26567) or the one directed in 2021 to the 'NSO Technologies group' on measures of mass surveillance concerning the use of the Pegasus spyware sent by the Special Rapporteur on the promotion and protection of the right to freedom of opinion and expression, the Working Group on the issue of transnational corporations and other business enterprises, the Special Rapporteur on the rights to peaceful assembly and of association and the Special Rapporteur on human rights defenders (spcommreports.ohchr.org/TMResultsBase/DownLoadPublicCommunicationFile?gId=26564).

41 Spyware, also referred to as 'intrusion software' is a malware that allows an operator to gain access to a targeted device and extract, modify or share its contents. This is achieved by exploiting software vulnerabilities. Pegasus and Candiru are notorious examples of spyware programmes and their use to maliciously monitor the activities of, among others, human rights defenders, has been documented. In this sense, see, among others, High Commissioner for Human Rights, Statement on the Use of Spyware to Surveil Journalists and Human Rights Defenders, 19 July 2021, available at www.ohchr.org/en/2021/07/use-spyware-surveil-journalists-and-human-rights-defendersstatement-un-high-commissioner. Notably, spyware has been used to surveil relatives of disappeared persons, including, for instance, the wife and fiancée of Mr Jamal Khashoggi (www.theguardian.com/world/2021/jul/18/nso-spyware-used-to-target-family-of-jamal-khashoggi-leaked-data-shows-saudis-pegasus).

representatives[42] – it could address its allegations or communications to these other stakeholders concerned. At present, the methods of work of the WGEID neither contemplate nor rule out explicitly this possibility.

### *4.4.2 Country Visits*

Another core procedure of the mandate of the WGEID is that of country visits,[43] which it conducts upon invitation. Since 1980, the WGEID has carried out more than forty visits across the world.[44] The main purpose of these visits is to, inter alia, enhance the dialogue between the authorities most directly concerned, the families or their representatives and the Working Group and to assist in the clarification of the reported cases of enforced disappearance. The Working Group also undertakes visits to examine the actions taken by States to prevent, investigate, punish and eradicate enforced disappearances and to search for disappeared persons, as well as the programmes and measures adopted to implement the Declaration and to guarantee the rights of, among others, the victims.[45]

In practical terms, during a visit, the WGEID meets with national and local authorities (including members of the judiciary, the executive and parliamentarians), members of the National Human Rights Institution, NGOs, associations of relatives of disappeared persons, the United Nations and other inter-governmental agencies and the press. Moreover, the WGEID often uses the opportunity of being on site to visit detention facilities (former or functioning), sites where exhumations have been, or are in the process of being, carried out, as well as memorials.

As of today, country visits and the ensuing reports and follow-up procedure are one of the areas where new technologies have played a very limited – if any at all – role and where, arguably, more could and should be done.

First, it does not seem that the WGEID has regularly included in its visits meetings with authorities and institutions that have a pertinent

[42] These practices are actually well documented and among those analyzed in-depth in the WGEID Thematic Study, paras. 8–25.

[43] Methods of work, paras. 59–64. More in general, when conducting country visits, the WGEID must also adhere to the 2016 Revised Terms of Reference for country visits by Special Procedures mandate-holders of the United Nations Human Rights Council, based on Appendix V, E/CN.4/1998/45.

[44] For the list of country visits carried out and the corresponding reports and follow-up reports, see www.ohchr.org/en/special-procedures/wg-disappearances/country-visits.

[45] Methods of work, para. 59.

mandate (e.g., in charge of ICT, cyber-security, satellite imagery or development of artificial intelligence) or with experts in new technologies with knowledge of the country situation. The WGEID has not visited centres and sites that might hold valuable information and data related to these subjects. In view of future country visits, this is an aspect that holds some potential.

Second, more in general, pursuant to its methods of work, the WGEID's approach to the gathering of information prior, during and after a visit can be regarded as slightly 'passive' rather than 'proactive', in the sense that it is open to collecting data, reports, testimonies and information that is brought to it from different sources – including, often, in response to calls issued by the WGEID itself – but it does not seem to foresee any direct 'fact-finding' activity or autonomous search and investigation. It is however to be assessed whether initiatives by the WGEID to search for, and gather, data and information during country visits motu proprio is to be ruled out completely. In fact, the terms of reference for country visits common to all Special Procedures require that States visited must guarantee that mandate-holders have 'full access to all *documentary materials* relevant to the mandate'.[46] This phrase may be interpreted in the sense that mandate-holders can identify the material that they consider to be relevant to the mandate, request it to the authorities of the State concerned, and the latter would be under an obligation to provide full access to such material. While it is rather clear that the terms of reference were not drafted thinking of data and information that can be gathered or stored through new technologies, one could argue that the expression 'documentary materials' can encompass satellite imagery, datasets, digital data or biodata to which the WGEID might wish to have access during a country visit. Indeed, the WGEID would then most likely need the support of qualified experts to analyze and interpret the material collected, but this relates to a more general need – which will be examined more in-depth later – to count on persons knowledgeable on new technologies who can be consulted by the WGEID, where necessary and upon request.[47] Nevertheless, one can imagine that the kind of material mentioned, if duly analyzed, might shed light on crucial aspects of the search for disappeared persons, as well as provide useful information related to criminal investigations. This

[46] Revised Terms of Reference for country visits by Special Procedures, para. 5, emphasis added.

[47] See Section 4.4.3.

could be extremely useful in the assessment performed by the WGEID during a country visit and in the formulation of recommendations to be included in its report.

More in general, the WGEID could envisage systematically including a section in the reports on country visits whereby it examines the use (or lack thereof) of new technologies in the State concerned, duly reflecting its findings in the final recommendations. In this realm, the WGEID should consider the opportunity – prior, during and after a visit – to also gather information on the existing legislation (e.g., concerning data collection and management, regulation – including export and import – of digital surveillance programmes, or cybercrime), as well as on the contracts stipulated by the government concerned to acquire and apply, for instance, spyware programmes and data on the use and frequency of shutdowns or internet disruptions in the country. The information and data collected could be instrumental in the shaping of 'tailored' recommendations and eventually contribute to an overall better understanding of the relationship between new technologies and enforced disappearances.

Finally, it is worth mentioning that specific challenges related to new technologies might arise in the realm of country visits, especially with regard to security, but they will be analyzed below in the dedicated section.[48]

### 4.4.3 *Awareness-Raising and Technical Cooperation*

Like other Special Procedures, the WGEID is also mandated to engage in advocacy activities, raise public awareness and provide advice for technical cooperation. In particular, it can provide advisory services, when requested, and provide assistance to governments in the implementation of the 1992 Declaration. The thematic study on new technologies and enforced disappearances can certainly be regarded as a first concrete form of awareness-raising, but, bearing in mind the complexity and constantly evolving nature of the subject, it could be appropriate to design a more articulated strategy and set of activities over the next years.

The methods of work of the WGEID do not elaborate on the nature of the advisory services or the technical cooperation provided and the applicable requirements to activate them.[49] So far, this has taken various forms, including trainings on enforced disappearances for public officials

[48] See Section 4.4.4.

[49] Methods of work, paras. 4 and 6.

and law enforcement personnel, including judges; direct assistance to States in the process of drafting follow-up reports; or assistance on substantive matters such as draft legislation, the creation of mechanisms devoted to the search for disappeared persons or truth commissions.[50]

At the time of writing, the WGEID has not yet received requests to provide advisory services or technical cooperation on issues directly related to new technologies and enforced disappearances, be it on draft legislation or in the sense of how these can be used to hinder the work of civil society organizations and relatives of disappeared persons or to facilitate the search for disappeared persons and to obtain evidence of the commission of the crime and ensure accountability.

Arguably, it is rather likely that the WGEID will receive requests in this sense in the future, and it is therefore necessary to assess whether it counts on the resources and necessary expertise to deliver on a regular basis. The answer to this question will be somehow influenced by the composition of the WGEID and its Secretariat. Currently, members of the WGEID and of the Secretariat could undisputedly assist on human rights–related issues and may be apt to provide advice relating to the pertinent legal framework or the applicable criteria to assess evidence collected and secured through new technologies. However, they lack an actual background and deep technical expertise on technological matters. Similarly, even if one of the members or of the Secretariat were an expert on digital forensics and biodata, for instance, they may not be equally knowledgeable on artificial intelligence or machine-learning. This can indeed be seen as an area where capacity building and strengthening are in order, although it remains to be determined whether members of the WGEID or its Secretariat would be those better placed to provide advice or technical cooperation on technological matters, or they should rather rely, for such a purpose, upon experts with a different profile, either from within the OHCHR or, where appropriate, externally.

In one of the above-mentioned reports, the Special Rapporteur on Extrajudicial, Summary or Arbitrary Executions recommended to the OHCHR to appoint a digital content specialist[51] to provide advice with respect to information received from or produced by civilian witnesses

[50] WGEID, Report on the 30th Anniversary of the Declaration on the Protection of All Persons from Enforced Disappearances, UN Doc. A7HRC/51/31/Add.3, 31 August 2022, para. 25.

[51] At present, the OHCHR relies upon a consultant working on 'digital evidence preservation', as well as on a 'technology advisor'.

and to serve as an interface with external networks of expertise in that area.[52] However, the Special Rapporteur considered it as a 'stopgap solution to ensure quick movement', thus calling on the OHCHR, with the assistance of the appointed specialist, to establish a 'longer-term capacity'.[53]

As already mentioned above,[54] international commissions of inquiry and fact-finding missions today rely upon experts to analyze, for instance, the digital evidence received. However, this staff is appointed to serve these mechanisms and cannot be properly regarded as 'in-house expertise' that could support also other organs – including the WGEID – in performing their mandate.

Bearing in mind the fact that new and emerging technologies go beyond digital content and communication technologies, and that, as pointed out, it is virtually impossible to find one person who is proficient on all the relevant areas, the creation of a roster of experts in new and emerging technologies could be envisaged. Ideally, their support could be obtained on demand by the different United Nations' human rights mechanisms (Special Procedures and Treaty Bodies) in need. In the case of the WGEID, it could consider to team up with one or more experts for the purposes of, among others, providing assistance and technical cooperation to States or other stakeholders on issues related to new technologies and enforced disappearances.

### *4.4.4 Security, Verification and Accessibility*

As anticipated in the previous sections, in light of the current situation and the opportunities concerning the use of new technologies – admittedly, mostly ICT – in the performance of the mandate of the WGEID, the challenges – existing and potential – are cross-cutting and revolve around the three main areas of security, verification and accessibility.

With regard to security, the whole sphere of digital risks is to be considered, thus encompassing data security, as well as surveillance and digital threats both towards the members of the WGEID and the Secretariat and any person engaging with the WGEID.

52 Special Rapporteur on Extrajudicial, Summary or Arbitrary Executions, Report on the Use of Information and Communication Technologies to Secure the Right to Life, para. 114.

53 Ibid.

54 See Section 4.4.1.

The WGEID regularly receives, deals with and stores sensitive information that, if unduly disclosed, could seriously endanger the security of several people, including persons or groups of persons in situations of great vulnerability. One major challenge is therefore maintaining the confidentiality of such information and protecting it from any sort of threat, including cyber-attacks. The risk is – unfortunately – a very concrete one, as shown by the incident that occurred on 18 January 2022, where personal data and other confidential information concerning more than 515,000 people worldwide, stored in the systems of the Central Tracing Agency of the International Committee of the Red Cross were accessed.[55] On such occasion, among others, platforms containing data on missing and disappeared people, as well as their relatives (including the 'Family Links Answers' application and Website, and the platform 'Trace the Face') were compromised. The investigation on the attack showed that it was a very sophisticated one, conducted with the objective of data extraction.[56]

The WGEID holds very similar information, gathered for analogous purposes. This begs the question of preparedness: Has any measure been put in place, by the WGEID or the OHCHR more in general, to mitigate this risk? Was a cyber-attack on the WGEID database to happen, would there be a security scheme ready to kick in, while ensuring the continuation of critical functions? Fundamental measures of protection of the data received are certainly in place, but a reflection on whether they would be adequate and up-to-date in the face of rapidly emerging and ever-changing technological threats seems in order.

Moreover, it is pertinent to consider whether suitable measures are in force to protect both members of the WGEID and its Secretariat and all persons that engage with it – especially relatives of disappeared persons and their representatives – from forms of digital surveillance (such as spyware programmes) and disinformation or smearing campaigns, including on and through social media.

These kind of considerations shall be extended to those who engage with the WGEID in different contexts, including prior, during and after country visits, and, although the subject might have been dealt with on an ad hoc basis, a more systematic approach and a transparent policy seems

[55] On the incident see WGEID Thematic Study, para. 24.

[56] See the note circulated by the International Committee of the Red Cross in January 2022, available at www.icrc.org/en/document/sophisticated-cyber-attack-targets-red-cross-red-crescent-data-500000-people.

desirable and should be applied coherently in the implementation of all the procedures of the WGEID. Furthermore, especially with regard to interactions with human rights defenders, activists, civil society organizations and, in particular, relatives of disappeared persons, the WGEID might wish to adopt a more proactive stance and, when contact is established for the first time, share a general warning on the existence of digital threats, along with a reference to (external) resources that can help these stakeholders protect themselves and (more) securely engage in exchanges with the WGEID.

With regard to verification, it has already been pointed out on multiple occasions that, albeit lacking a full-fledged investigative mandate, the WGEID regularly evaluates the reliability of its sources and credibility of the information that it receives from sources, States and any other stakeholder. As with the other Special Procedures, the WGEID is requested to rely on 'objective and dependable facts based on evidentiary standards that are appropriate to its non-judicial character'.[57]

Hence, although the applicable standards are not those of a courtroom, the WGEID is expected to at least perform its due diligence in corroborating the information received.[58] In an era characterized by the use of fictitious accounts and deep fakes, or in situations of metadata paucity, this may prove especially challenging, in particular where there may be a lack of expertise of the members of the WGEID and its Secretariat on the matter, while, in parallel, relevant tactics and tools evolve at an extremely rapid pace.[59] So far, the WGEID has not encountered any specific obstacles in this realm, but for the future further reflection and consideration on how to mitigate potential risks, it could be desirable.

When it comes to accessibility, it must be pointed out that, while new technologies – in particular in the ICT sphere – may play a key role in facilitating access to the WGEID and the use of its procedures – this may not apply in the same terms worldwide. At a time where there still are several coverage gaps, internet shutdowns are increasingly used to curb dissent and to silence human rights defenders, and a significant uneven

[57] See note 34.

[58] See, among others, P. Alston, 'Hobbling the monitors: Should U.N. human rights monitors be accountable?' (2011) 52, 2 *Harvard International Law Journal* 561–649; and N. Rodley, 'On the responsibility of special rapporteurs' (2011) 15 *The International Journal of Human Rights* 319–37.

[59] See, among others, A. Toler, 'How to verify and authenticate user-generated content', in S. Dubberley, A. Koenig and D. Murray (eds.), *Digital Witness* (Oxford University Press, 2020), pp. 185–227.

adoption of ICT among population still exists, gearing all efforts of the WGEID to the use of digital technologies might result in being detrimental and discriminatory. In this sense, and more in general, bearing in mind the dual relationship between new technologies and human rights and the considerable – and certainly legitimate – expectations that the use of technologies may raise, the need for complementarity must be recalled. New technologies cannot – and should not – replace pre-existing strategies, procedures and approaches but must rather sum up them and enhance the likelihood to obtain significant results, in the case of enforced disappearance facilitating the clarification of cases, favouring accountability and enhancing the applicable legal standards.

Finally, another tenet of accessibility, equally regarding members of the WGEID, its Secretariat and all those stakeholders that engage with the WGEID, relates to the – arguably still limited – level of digital literacy and, more broadly, knowledge and understanding of new technologies – including others that go beyond ICT – and the corresponding implications. At the time of writing, this appears as a major loophole that would need to be adequately addressed before stepping up the use of, and reference to, new technologies, in the day-to-day activities of the WGEID.

## 4.5 Conclusions

> New technology is not good or evil in and of itself. It's all about how people choose to use it.
>
> —D. Wong

The previous sections show that, when dealing with enforced disappearance, as with other gross human rights violations, new and emerging technologies hold an equal amount of challenges and opportunities and, in broader terms, they cannot – and should not – replace pre-existing strategies, procedures and approaches, especially bearing in mind the risk of deepening the lingering digital divide and worsening instances of marginalization and exclusion or of exposing people to unprecedented threats.

These considerations are reflected in the thematic study of the WGEID:

> The Working Group emphasizes that there should not be over-reliance upon new technologies in this realm and expectations must be realistic: albeit they are going to facilitate the processes concerned, they are not going to solve all the existing problems. Traditional approaches and techniques to documenting, monitoring and reporting should not be

abandoned and cannot be entirely replaced by digital material and new technologies.

Complementarity between these strategies should be pursued and actively promoted and traditional human-centred processes must be fomented and strengthened accordingly. In parallel, access to new technologies shall be conceived in a way that does not reproduce or deepen existing digital divide and socio-economic differences and no developing country or relevant stakeholder can be left behind.[60]

While warning of the imperative to identify the existing risks and adequately address them, this chapter suggests that opportunities might actually outweigh challenges. In this sense, besides the adoption and dissemination of the thematic study on new technologies and enforced disappearances, it is here contended that the WGEID could benefit from a thorough reflection on how – and to what extent – new technologies could and should be used in its day-to-day activities. Similarly, it should consider how questions, remarks and recommendations concerning new technologies and enforced disappearances can be systematically included in its work and in all its tasks, including communications, urgent appeals, allegations, referrals, prompt intervention letters, country visits, awareness-raising and technical cooperation. The methods of work of the WGEID do not currently cover any of these matters and, when they will be revised in the future, they should reflect, to the extent possible, the outcome of this debate, also addressing the need for an increased technological literacy among the members of the WGEID and its Secretariat and the desirability to establish, and rely upon, a roster of experts on the multiple disciplines that can be related to new technologies.

At any rate, in its thematic study, the WGEID committed to 'regularly monitor the issue of new technologies and enforced disappearance and to systematically include remarks and recommendations concerning this subject in its activities, including in communications, urgent appeals, allegations, referrals, prompt intervention letters, country visits and awareness-raising. The Working Group also offers assistance to States on the subject through cooperation and advisory services'.[61]

Accordingly, the WGEID called on 'all concerned stakeholders to regularly engage and cooperate with it and report on the negative impact of new technologies in the enjoyment of human rights, especially of

60 WGEID Thematic Study, paras. 58–9.

61 Ibid., para. 63.

human rights defenders and relatives of disappeared persons, as well as on progresses made with regard to the use of new technologies in the search for disappeared persons and in the investigation and promotion of accountability'.[62]

More in general, recalling the importance of a holistic, inclusive and comprehensive approach and the need for all stakeholders to collaborate in a more concerted way in addressing the subject of new technologies and human rights, it is desirable that United Nations Treaty Bodies, including the Committee on Enforced Disappearances (CED), enhance their attention and work on the matter.[63]

Many of the considerations formulated here for the WGEID could apply, mutatis mutandis, to the CED and its functions, including the exam of State reports, urgent actions, inter-State and individual communications, country visits and the referral procedure.[64] Since the WGEID and the CED regularly exchange on matters of common interest and coordinate and cooperate,[65] the subject of new technologies and enforced disappearances, and, at the very least, of how the said technologies could be taken into account in the performance of the respective mandates, should be the subject of joint analysis and action.

In particular, both the WGEID and the CED should aim at systematically including the issue of new technologies in their considerations, observations and recommendations, and, when it comes to the workflow and concrete organization of the respective activities, they should consider the opportunity to adopt and offer up-to-date, secure and user-friendly tools to disappeared people, their relatives, representatives and civil society organizations, ultimately facilitating the work of all those concerned and helping in the eradication and prevention of this crime.

62 Ibid., para. 64.

63 In this sense, see also para. 69 of the conclusions of the WGEID Thematic Study.

64 See Arts. 29–34 of the International Convention for the Protection of All Persons from Enforced Disappearance, New York, 20 December 2006, 23 December 2010, UNTS 2716, UN Doc. A/61/448, C.N.737.2008 (ICPED).

65 See Art. 28 ICPED and para. 53 of the WGEID methods of work.

# 5

## The Fate and Whereabouts of Social Rights in the Practice of the Committee on Enforced Disappearances

ARIEL DULITZKY*

### 5.1 Introduction

The concept of enforced disappearance has undergone a multifaceted normative and jurisprudential evolution. This evolution occurred, among other areas, in the legal determination of which rights are violated in each case of enforced disappearances. In addition to the rights that were initially protected, other rights have arisen.[1] The victims, advocates, human rights bodies and the international community in general gained greater knowledge of elements that both define and enable enforced disappearance and of its effects.[2] Protection provided by international human rights bodies and by the international community is a process in constant evolution, achieved, among others, by the evolutive method or living instrument theory to human rights interpretation.[3]

The International Convention for the Protection of All Persons from Enforced Disappearance (the Convention) is the most modern instrument in this evolving process of responses to enforced disappearances. The Convention has created new rights including the right not to be forcibly disappeared, the right not to be secretly detained, the right of the

* Thanks to Ted Magee for helping, as always, with the editing of the text. Also, thanks to the editors of the book, for their insightful comments.

1 M. C. Galvis Patiño, 'Rights related to enforced disappearance: New rights in the International Convention for the Protection of All Persons from Enforced Disappearance' in A. Von Arnaud, K. Von der Decken and M. Susi (eds.), *The Cambridge Handbook of New Human Rights: Recognition, Novelty, Rhetoric* (Cambridge University Press, 2020), pp. 416–21.

2 Ibid., at 415.

3 See for instance, D. Keane, 'Mapping the International Convention on the Elimination of All Forms of Racial Discrimination as a living instrument' (2020) 2 *Human Rights Law Review* 236–68.

victims of (enforced) disappearance to be searched for, the right for appropriate measures to be adopted with regard to the legal situation of disappeared persons whose fate has not been established and the legal situation of their relatives and the right to establish and participate freely in organizations and associations whose objective is to contribute to clarifying the circumstances of enforced disappearances and the fate of disappeared persons.[4]

The Convention does not explicitly recognize the violation of economic, social and cultural rights (ESCR) in cases of disappearances. Nor has the Committee on Enforced Disappearances (CED or the Committee) made sufficient progress in recognizing the link between forced disappearances and ESCR. Article 28 of the Convention requires the Committee to 'cooperate' with all the relevant organs, offices and specialized agencies and funds of the United Nations, with the treaty bodies and the special procedures of the United Nations and with the relevant regional intergovernmental organizations, as well as with all relevant State institutions, agencies or offices and to 'consult' other treaty bodies and, in particular, the Human Rights Committee (HRC).[5] The CED Rules of procedure also refers to the cooperation with the Working Group on Enforced or Involuntary Disappearances (WGEID). Given this duty to cooperate and consult, it is useful to analyze the practice of the UN WGEID and the case law of the Inter-American Court of Human Rights (IACtHR or Inter-American Court) and other UN treaty bodies. Looking at the WGEID allows us to explore its more than forty years of experience dealing with enforced disappearances. The Inter-American Court is known for its leading role in developing jurisprudence in this area and particularly for its creative and forward-looking approach to enforced disappearances. Finally, the approaches of other treaty bodies to enforced disappearances present complementary methods from the perspective of those treaty bodies' specific mandates.

This chapter proceeds in the following way. The chapter starts (Sections 5.2–5.7) with a critical view of the CED current practice in approaching enforced disappearances from an ESCR viewpoint. Sections 5.8 and 5.9 present an analysis of the approaches taken by the WGEID and the IACtHR to the intersection of enforced disappearances and

[4] Galvis Patiño, 'Rights related to enforced disappearance', 422.

[5] O. Frouville, 'The Committee on Enforced Disappearances', in P. Alston and F. Megret (eds.), *The United Nations and Human Rights: A Critical Appraisal*, 2nd ed. (Oxford University Press, 2020), pp. 579–600.

ESCR. Section 5.10 explains the benefits of bringing an ESCR perspective when dealing with enforced disappearances looking, among other things, to the practices of other UN treaty bodies. The chapter offers some brief conclusions.

## 5.2 The Limitations of the Committee in Its Approach to ESCR and Some Possibilities

The Convention explicitly refers to the International Covenant on Economic, Social, and Cultural Rights in its Preamble.[6] However, in general, CED fails to specifically address ESCR. For instance, CED referred to 'health needs' rather than to health rights.[7] While there is no need to enter into the discussion on the relationship between needs and rights,[8] it is clear that a human rights–based approach requires a clarification of the scope of the rights implicated in any enforced disappearance and the corresponding State obligations.

In almost all of its Concluding Observations, the CED includes a paragraph emphasizing 'the particularly cruel effect of enforced disappearance on the rights of women and children'. Women relatives of a disappeared person are likely 'to suffer serious social and economic disadvantages and to be subjected to violence, persecution and reprisal as a result of their efforts to locate their loved ones'.[9] Children who are victims of enforced disappearance (whether they themselves were subjected to disappearance or due to the disappearance of a family member)

[6] The Preamble of the Convention cannot be considered legally inconsequential. According to Art. 31(2) of the 1969 Vienna Convention on the Law of Treaties, the context for the purpose of the interpretation of a treaty shall, inter alia, comprise the text of the treaty, which is defined to include its preamble. M. M. Mbengue, 'The notion of preamble,' in R. Wolfrum (ed.), *The Max Planck Encyclopedia of Public International Law* (Oxford University Press, 2008).

[7] Concluding observations on the report submitted by Tunisia under Art. 29(1) of the Convention, U.N. Doc. CED/C/TUN/CO/1, 2016, para. 22.

[8] See, e.g., O. O'Neill, 'Hunger, needs, and rights', in Steven Luper-Foy (ed.), *Problems of International Justice* (Routledge, 2019), pp. 67–83; L. T. Munro, 'Risks, needs and rights: Compatible or contradictory bases for social protection' in A. Barrientos and D. Hulme (eds.), *Social Protection for the Poor and Poorest* (Springer, 2008), pp. 27–46, or Hartley Dean, 'The translation of needs into rights: Reconceptualising social citizenship as a global phenomenon' (2013) 22 *International Journal of Social Welfare* S32–S49.

[9] See, e.g., Concluding observations on the report submitted by the Niger under Art. 29 (1) of the Convention, CED/C/NER/CO/1, 2020, para. 40, or Concluding observations on the report submitted by Mongolia under Art. 29(1) of the Convention, CED/C/MNG/CO/1, 2021, para. 45.

'are especially vulnerable to numerous human rights violations'.[10] The Committee therefore calls States to 'ensure that gender issues and the specific needs of women and children are systematically taken into account in implementing the recommendations … and the rights and obligations under the Convention'.[11] The paragraph identifies particular social and economic impacts of enforced disappearances and calls for a systematic approach to address the needs, consequences and cruel effect of enforced disappearances. This approach should lead the Committee to spell out the meaning more clearly of 'cruel effect' of a disappearance, the ways that the 'serious and economic disadvantages' are manifested, the specific manner in which children are 'vulnerable to numerous human rights violations', which 'numerous human rights' are being violated and in which manner those violations take place. Responding to those crushing impacts from a holistic emphasis on ESCR would provide a broader and more effective response to enforced disappearances. Of course, recognizing the intersectionality based on gender and age is crucial in this endeavour. In fact, in its only individual petition on enforced disappearances decided, CEDAW specifically recommended the adoption and implementation of a comprehensive 'national policy to prevent and eradicate disappearances of women which includes due diligence standards, a differentiated approach and a human rights-based approach as cross-cutting components'. The policy should address and combat the causes of enforced disappearances of women.[12]

## 5.3 Autonomous Right, Complex Act and Multiple Violation and Interdependency with Other Rights

The Convention recognizes a new autonomous right of any person not to be subjected to enforced disappearance. As a new right, this provision

[10] See, e.g., Concluding observations on the report submitted by the Niger under Art. 29 (1) of the Convention, CED/C/NER/CO/1, 2020, para. 40, or Concluding observations on the report submitted by Mongolia under Art. 29(1) of the Convention, CED/C/MNG/CO/1, 2021, para. 45.

[11] See, e.g., Concluding observations on the report submitted by the Niger under Art. 29 (1) of the Convention, CED/C/NER/CO/1, 2020, para. 40, or Concluding observations on the report submitted by Mongolia under Art. 29(1) of the Convention, CED/C/MNG/CO/1, 2021, para. 45.

[12] Committee on the Elimination of Discrimination against Women Views adopted by the Committee under Art. 7(3) of the Optional Protocol, concerning communication No. 153/2020, 22 November 2022, para. 9.b.iii.

should be interpreted in conjunction with the rest of the *corpus iuris* of international human rights law, including ESCR.

The CED had already recognized that enforced disappearance constitutes a complex offense.[13] However, it limited this analysis of complexity to the criminal aspects of enforced disappearances.[14] So far, the Committee has not spelled out the particular meaning that the phenomenon of disappearances constitutes a complex and multiple form of violation of numerous human rights. In some instances, referring to the crime of enforced disappearance, the Committee stated that the practice violates 'various rights' but described neither those rights nor how they are violated.[15] Most of CED considerations are around criminal investigations and the search for the disappeared rather than on the impact on other violations of human rights, including ESCR.

A more appropriate approach would be the one taken by the Committee on ESCR when it expressed its concerns 'about the daily challenges faced by the families and loved ones of disappeared persons in the effective enjoyment of their economic, social, and cultural rights'.[16] The ESCR Committee recommended that the State adopt measures that not only meet the needs of the victims but also 'ensure those persons effective enjoyment of their economic, social, and cultural rights, especially the rights to an adequate standard of living, health, and education'.[17]

## 5.4 Definition of Enforced Disappearance

The Convention defines enforced disappearances as 'the arrest, detention, abduction or any other form of deprivation of liberty by agents of the State or by persons or groups of persons acting with the authorization, support or acquiescence of the State, followed by a refusal to

[13] See, e.g., Concluding observation on the report submitted by Germany under Art. 29, para. 1, of the Convention, UN. Doc. CED/C/DEU/CO/1, 2014, para. 7; by Spain, UN. Doc. CED/C/ESP/CO/1, 2013, para. 9; by Belgium, UN. Doc. CED/C/BEL/CO/1, 2014, para. 11; by Burkina Faso, UN. Doc. CED/C/BFA/CO/1, 2016, para. 13; and by Gabon, UN. Doc. CED/C/GAB/CO/1, 2017, para. 12.

[14] See, e.g., Concluding observations on the report submitted by Kazakhstan under Art. 29 (1) of the Convention, UN. Doc. CED/C/KAZ/CO/1, 2016, para. 11; by Bosnia and Herzegovina, UN. Doc. CED/C/BIH/CO/1, 2016, para. 13; by Japan, UN. Doc. CED/C/JPN/CO/1, 2016, para. 13; and by Portugal, U.N. Doc. CED/C/PRT/CO/1, 2018, para. 14.

[15] Belgium, UN. Doc. CED/C/BEL/CO/1, 2014, para. 11.

[16] Concluding observations on the combined 5th and 6th periodic reports of Mexico, Committee on Economic, Social and Cultural Rights, E/C.12/MEX/CO/5-6, 2018, para. 43.

[17] Ibid., para. 44.

acknowledge the deprivation of liberty or by concealment of the fate or whereabouts of the disappeared person, which place such a person outside the protection of the law'.[18] This chapter might serve as the basis for the CED to construct a more robust practice in understanding that enforced disappearances affect social and economic rights.

Particularly relevant for our purpose is the reference to placing the disappeared person 'outside the protection of the law'. This reference should be considered or understood as a consequence of the commission of the crime of enforced disappearance, rather than as a necessary element of intent (animus) that would have to be present for the act to be considered criminal conduct.[19] A proper and expansive interpretation of the 'protection of the law' should include the protection of ESCR, such as the right to education or work or housing, as recognized both by domestic and international law. A good example comes from the Committee on the Rights of Persons with Disabilities (CRPD) in the case of the disappearance of two victims with psychological disabilities. The CRPD concluded that the State failed to discharge its positive obligation to ensure respect for the victims' rights to 'the enjoyment of the highest attainable standard of health'. The State did not provide information on any measures taken 'to ensure that they have access to adequate health care, taking into account their psychosocial disabilities and particularly vulnerable situation'.[20]

## 5.5 The Right to Truth Includes the Right to Know the Circumstances of an Enforced Disappearance

The Committee has been quite consistent in asserting that the right of the victims to know the truth includes the 'circumstances of an enforced disappearance'.[21] The CED has extended this right regardless of whether

[18] OHCHR, International Convention for the Protection of all Persons against Enforced Disappearances, UN. Doc. ST/HR/3/Rev.1, 20 December 2006, Art. 2.

[19] Concluding observations on the report submitted by Paraguay under Art. 29, para. 1, of the Convention, UN. Doc. CED/C/PRY/CO/1, 2014, para. 14; by Bolivia, UN. Doc. CED/C/BOL/CO/1, 2019, para. 13(a); and by France, UN. Doc. CED/C/FRA/CO/1, 2013, paras. 12–13.

[20] Committee on the Rights of Persons with Disabilities Views adopted by the Committee under Art. 5 of the Optional Protocol, concerning communications No. 67/2019 and No. 68/2019, 22 May 2023, para. 8.8.

[21] See e.g., UN. Doc. CED/C/ESP/CO/1, 2013, para. 32–3; Japan, UN. Doc. CED/C/JPN/CO/1, 2016, para. 25; Chile, UN. Doc. CED/C/CHL/CO/1, 2019, para. 17(b).

the crime occurred during a civil war, a dictatorship, an armed conflict, a communist regime, a 'dirty war', a 'post-election crisis' or a specific period.[22] The circumstances should be interpreted as including the causes and reasons of the disappearance and the impact of the disappearance on the ESCR of the disappeared and other persons.

The CED highlighted how the social and economic situation of the victims affects the right to know the truth. For instance, the Committee noted that the limited resources of a forensic institute has forced it 'to concentrate most of its campaigns for collecting genetic samples in urban areas'.[23] However, the recommendation to address the problem, 'conducting extensive campaigns to collect ante-mortem information and genetic samples from disappeared persons' relatives, with a special focus on rural areas',[24] does very little to spell out the particular situation of persons living in rural areas such as distance, language, daily work and childcare (to mention a few) that would have provided more clear guidance to the State. A slightly better approach to ESCR could be found in the same document where CED made a requirement for the State that 'all actions to identify and return remains duly take into account the traditions and customs of the peoples or communities to which the victims belong, in particular Indigenous peoples or Afro descendent communities'.[25]

## 5.6 The Duty to Investigate

The Committee has developed specific guidance on how to conduct investigations in cases of enforced disappearances. It referred to the duty to conduct a thorough, impartial, complete, diligent and effective investigation without delay, even if there has been no formal complaint.[26]

22 M. C. Galvis Patiño, *The Work of the Committee on Enforced Disappearances: Achievements and Jurisprudence Ten Years after the Entry into Force of the Convention* (The Geneva Academy of International Humanitarian Law and Human Rights, 2021), p. 12.

23 Concluding observations on the report submitted by Colombia under Art. 29(1) of the Convention UN. Doc. CED/C/COL/CO/1, 2016, para. 25.

24 Ibid., para. 26(b).

25 Ibid., para. 26(f).

26 Concluding observations on the report submitted by Mexico under Art. 29, para. 1, of the Convention, UN. Doc. CED/C/MEX/CO/1, 2015, para. 28; by Iraq, UN. Doc. CED/C/IRQ/CO/1, 2015, para. 20(a) and 23(a); by Colombia, UN. Doc. CED/C/COL/CO/1, 2016, para. 20(a); by Senegal, CED/C/SEN/CO/1, 2017, para. 28; by Gabon, UN. Doc. CED/C/GAB/CO/1, 2017, para. 25–6; by Honduras, UN. Doc. CED/C/HND/CO/1, 2018,

In this respect, it has requested that States Parties ensure that enforced disappearances are investigated as such and not as any other offence,[27] that investigations are not only initiated immediately after receiving information with reasonable grounds to believe that a person has been subjected to an enforced disappearance but also that investigations continue until the fate or whereabouts of the disappeared person have been clarified[28] and that the perpetrators are punished for the offence.[29]

The CED's approach appears to be limited to criminal investigation. When the Committee refers to the context, it appears to be circumscribing it to 'all lines of inquiry'[30] and to 'similar crime commission patterns and regional contexts'.[31] The investigation of 'all circumstances' of a disappearance appears to be limited to the criminal aspects rather than a holistic broad investigation (criminal or otherwise) of all the causes, modalities and consequences of the phenomenon.

The Committee has highlighted that in a particular State 'new cases of enforced disappearance in recent times [are] particularly targeting young persons in situations of extreme poverty and social marginalization'.[32] While CED is aware of the link between extreme poverty and social marginalization and the risk of becoming a victim of enforced disappearance, its recommendations delink the connection to extreme poverty and generically encourages the State 'to adopt all the necessary measures and to intensify its efforts to root out these contemporary forms of enforced disappearance'[33] and to 'promote institutional reform of the police forces so as to eradicate violence and ensure that police officers who commit

para. 25(a); by Japan, UN. Doc. CED/C/JPN/CO/1, 2016, para. 24 (b); by Argentina, UN. Doc. CED/C/ARG/CO/1, 2013, para. 17; by Spain, UN. Doc. CED/C/ESP/CO/1, 2013, para. 12; by Armenia, UN. Doc. CED/C/ARM/CO/1, 2015, para. 5; and by Bolivia, UN. Doc. CED/C/BOL/CO/1, 2019, para. 21(a).

27 Concluding observations on the report submitted by Uruguay under Art. 29, para. 1, of the Convention, UN. Doc. CED/C/URY/CO/1, 2013, para. 14.

28 Argentina, UN. Doc. CED/C/ARG/CO/1, 2013, para. 17); Spain, UN. Doc. CED/C/ESP/CO/1, 2013, para. 12; Iraq, UN. Doc. CED/C/IRQ/CO/1, 2015, para. 20; Tunisia, U.N. Doc. CED/C/TUN/CO/1, 2016, para. 23.

29 Uruguay, UN. Doc. CED/C/URY/CO/1, 2013, para. 14; Spain, UN. Doc. CED/C/ESP/CO/1, 2013, para. 12; Serbia, UN. Doc. CED/C/SRB/CO/1, 2015, para. 14; Iraq, UN. Doc. CED/C/IRQ/CO/1, 2015, para. 20(b); Montenegro, UN. Doc. CED/C/MNE/CO/1, 2015, para. 17; Bosnia and Herzegovina, UN. Doc. CED/C/BIH/CO/1, 2016, para. 22. Tunisia, U.N. Doc. CED/C/TUN/CO/1, 2016, para. 22.

30 Mexico, UN. Doc. CED/C/MEX/CO/1, 2015, para. 28(a).

31 Colombia, UN. Doc. CED/C/COL/CO/1, 2016, para. 20.

32 Argentina, UN. Doc. CED/C/ARG/CO/1, 2013, para. 14.

33 Ibid., para. 15.

such offences are duly investigated, prosecuted and punished'.[34] Again, the CED appears to take a limited criminal investigation response rather than addressing the root causes of the disappearances.

Recently, CED took a more sensitive approach. In its Concluding Observations on Brazil, CED recalled with alarm the information 'concerning enforced disappearance allegedly perpetrated in recent times, mostly against persons of African descent and persons living in slums or on the peripheries of large cities'.[35] The Committee did not limit the recommendation, as in the Argentine situation, to the criminal investigation but specifically required Brazil to 'redouble its efforts to tackle discrimination against certain targeted vulnerable groups as a means for preventing their disappearance and ensuring full access to their right to justice'.[36] However, the Committee then reverted to generic references to the fact that reparations need to be sensitive to the victims' specific needs[37] 'in view of, inter alia, their sex, sexual orientation, gender identity, age, ethnic origin, social status or disability'.[38] No references were made to the needs created by their economic situation, place of residency or structural racism.

## 5.7 The Right to Reparation and the Concept of Harm

States should take measures to guarantee that all persons who have suffered harm as a direct result of an enforced disappearance can effectively enjoy their right to obtain full and adequate reparation.[39] So far, the CED has not defined the scope or type of 'harm' that should be the reason for a reparation except stating the harm should be direct but not necessarily personal[40] and cover 'any natural person, without exception, who has suffered harm as the direct result of an enforced

34 Ibid.

35 Concluding observations on the report submitted by Brazil under Art. 29 (1) of the Convention, UN. Doc. CED/C/BRA/CO/1, 2021, para. 29.

36 Ibid., para. 23(c).

37 Ibid., para. 23(g).

38 Ibid., para. 29(b).

39 Germany, UN. Doc. CED/C/DEU/CO/1, 2014, para. 25; Paraguay, UN. Doc. CED/C/PRY/CO/1, 2014, para. 26(b); Serbia, UN. Doc. CED/C/SRB/CO/1, 2015, para. 26(b); Tunisia, U.N. Doc. CED/C/TUN/CO/1, 2016, para. 23(d); Colombia, UN. Doc. CED/C/COL/CO/1, 2016, para. 36(b); Chile, UN. Doc. CED/C/CHL/CO/1, 2019, para. 25(a); Albania, UN. Doc. CED/C/ALB/CO/1, 2018, para. 10(c).

40 France, UN. Doc. CED/C/FRA/CO/1, 2013, para. 35.

disappearance'.[41] The Committee has been consistent in embracing a broad concept of victim as defined by the Convention. Therefore, it has criticized restrictive domestic legislation.[42] However, sometimes it has limited the references to the relatives of the disappeared person.[43]

The right to reparation must include restitution, means and measures for rehabilitation,[44] satisfaction, guarantees of non-repetition[45] and a prompt, fair and adequate compensation. The broad categories, in particular the concepts of restitution, rehabilitation and satisfaction, represent recognition of the harm that enforced disappearances produce on the social, cultural, economic and family life of the victims. As such, it is necessary to understand that those impacts may constitute violations of ESCR and that the reparation is meant to amend such ESCR violations. Sadly, in *Yrusta*,[46] the first individual communication decided by CED, the Committee failed to properly spell out the content of specific measures of rehabilitation (for example, psychological support for the sisters of Mr Yrusta).[47] The Committee on the Rights of the Child, for instance, has been more specific in its recommendations requiring a State to provide 'psychological support to ... address trauma and other mental health issues ... to children who have been internally displaced and/or deprived of a family environment owing to violence and/or enforced disappearance'.[48]

[41] Concluding observations on the report submitted by Peru under Art. 29 (1) of the Convention, UN. Doc. CED/C/PER/CO/1, 2019, para. 29(a); Bolivia, UN. Doc. CED/C/BOL/CO/1, 2019, para. 33.

[42] France, UN. Doc. CED/C/FRA/CO/1, 2013, para. 34; Serbia, UN. Doc. CED/C/SRB/CO/1, 2015, para. 24; Montenegro, UN. Doc. CED/C/MNE/CO/1, 2015, para. 29; Lithuania, UN. Doc. CED/C/LTU/CO/1, 2017, para. 27; Honduras, UN. Doc. CED/C/HND/CO/1, 2018, para. 36; Japan, UN. Doc. CED/C/JPN/CO/1, 2016, para. 39; Peru, UN. Doc. CED/C/PER/CO/1, 2019, para. 28; and Bolivia, UN. Doc. CED/C/BOL/CO/1, 2019, para. 32.

[43] Mexico, UN. Doc. CED/C/MEX/CO/1, 2015, para. 28(a); Colombia, UN. Doc. CED/C/COL/CO/1, 2016, para. 20(c).

[44] Mexico, UN. Doc. CED/C/MEX/CO/1, 2015, para. 33(d); Albania, UN. Doc. CED/C/ALB/CO/1, para. 10(c).

[45] Serbia, UN. Doc. CED/C/SRB/CO/1, 2015, para. 26(b); Paraguay, UN. Doc. CED/C/PRY/CO/1, 2014, para. 26.

[46] CED, *Estela Deolinda Yrusta and Alejandra del Valle Yrusta* v. *Argentina*, Communication No. 1/2013, 11 March 2016.

[47] G. Citroni, 'The first years of the United Nations Committee on Enforced Disappearances: Achievements and future challenges' in M. Bidault, M. Boumghar, O. De Frouville and L. Trigeaud (eds.), *Réciprocité et universalité: sources et régimes du droit international des droits de l'homme: Mélanges en l'honneur du professeur Emmanuel Decaux* (Éditions Pedone, 2017), p. 402.

[48] Committee on the Rights of the Child Concluding observations on the combined fifth and sixth periodic reports of Sri Lanka, CRC/C/LKA/CO/5-6, para. 49(b).

Victims are particularly vulnerable rights holders and it is crucial to protect them from stigmatization, moral ill-treatment and security risks.[49] The respect for their human dignity also implies that the remains of a disappeared person should be handed over to the family under decent conditions, in accordance with the cultural norms and customs of the peoples or communities to which the victims belonged, keeping in mind that they are human remains and not objects.[50]

The Committee has specifically referred to social benefits and other measures of social support,[51] medical and psychological rehabilitation,[52] restitution and satisfaction, including restoration of dignity and reputation.[53] All those references appear to be related to ESCR, such as the right to health and social security, which deserve a proper recognition as rights violated by an enforced disappearance. However, CED has never mentioned explicitly the reparation of ESCR violations.

Article 24.6 of the Convention appears to make a distinction between rights and other areas when it refers to 'social welfare, financial matters, family law and property rights'. The Committee has been consistent in repeating this phrase in its Concluding Observations.[54] However, so far it has failed to explain in more detail if the reference to 'rights' is limited to property (an economic right but recognized in some civil and political treaties) or to the contrary if it includes all ESCR that were affected by an enforced disappearance. In fact, CED's practice appears to demonstrate a restrictive approach when it explicitly makes references to 'access to social welfare services and family and property rights'.[55] A more expansive interpretation could have added a reference to the enjoyment of ESCR.

The Committee on Enforced Disappearances has also insisted on considering that reparations be sensitive to the victims' individual characteristics, such as their sex, sexual orientation, gender identity, age,

[49] Guiding Principles for the Search for Disappeared Persons, UN. Doc. CED/C/7, Principles 2.2, 2.3.

[50] Ibid., Principle 2.4; Colombia, UN. Doc. CED/C/COL/CO/1, 2016, para. 26(f).

[51] Bosnia and Herzegovina, UN. Doc. CED/C/BIH/CO/1, 2016, para. 38.

[52] Paraguay, UN. Doc. CED/C/PRY/CO/1, 2014, para. 26(b); Montenegro, UN. Doc. CED/C/MNE/CO/1, 2015, para. 31.

[53] Montenegro, UN. Doc. CED/C/MNE/CO/1, 2015, para. 31.

[54] See for instance, Germany, UN. Doc. CED/C/DEU/CO/1, 2014, para. 27; Paraguay, UN. Doc. CED/C/PRY/CO/1, 2014, para. 30; Ecuador, UN. Doc. CED/C/ECU/CO/1, 2017, para. 22; Bolivia, UN. Doc. CED/C/BOL/CO/1, 2019, para. 37; Slovakia, UN. Doc. CED/C/SVK/CO/1, 2019, para. 27.

[55] Mongolia, CED/C/MNG/CO/1, 2021, para. 38.

ethnic origin, social status and disability.[56] These calls necessarily require States to consider the status of and level of enjoyment of certain ESCR in order to properly assess the needs and rights of the victims with a right to a reparation. Nevertheless, a more perceptive approach to ESCR could have led to references to the victim's situation such as employment status, education and literacy level, housing and food access, to mention a few relevant in many situations. The Committee on the Rights of Persons with Disabilities specifically recommended, on a case of enforced disappearance, the State to guarantee the victims' safety and access to medical care, including in relation to their disabilities.[57] The Special Rapporteur on housing, has made a reference to the direct connection between administrative problems that the families of disappeared persons must overcome to be able to take part in housing programs, obtain social security, enjoy the right to own and inherit property, and 'the direct impact of those problems on their right to housing'.[58]

The *Yrusta* case also reflects the limited approach to reparations. After determining Argentina's responsibility for the short-term disappearance of Mr Yrusta, the Committee included a series of redress measures for the violations suffered. For instance, CED urges the State to 'recognize the authors' status as victims, thereby allowing them to play an effective part in the investigations into the death and enforced disappearance of their brother'.[59] This recommendation and the CED's determinations[60] appear to be linking the status as victims to the participation in the criminal procedure, when the Convention takes a much broader concept of victim linked to the harm suffered. Similarly, the CED made a generic reference to measures of rehabilitation[61] without spelling out anything about the

[56] Colombia, UN. Doc. CED/C/COL/CO/1, 2016, para. 36(a); Cuba, UN. Doc. CED/C/CUB/CO/1, 2017, para. 32; Honduras, UN. Doc. CED/C/HND/CO/1, 2018, para. 37(b); Japan, UN. Doc. CED/C/JPN/CO/1, 2016, para. 40(b); Peru, UN. Doc. CED/C/PER/CO/1, 2019, para. 29(c); Bolivia, UN. Doc. CED/C/BOL/CO/1, 2019, para. 35(d); Slovakia, UN. Doc. CED/C/SVK/CO/1, 2019, para. 25.

[57] Committee on the Rights of Persons with Disabilities Views adopted by the Committee under Art. 5 of the Optional Protocol, concerning Communications No. 67/2019 and No. 68/2019, 22 May 2023, para. 9(b).

[58] Report of the Special Rapporteur on adequate housing as a component of the right to an adequate standard of living, and on the right to non-discrimination in this context, Raquel Rolnik, Addendum, Mission to Algeria, UN. Doc. A/HRC/19/53/Add.2, 26 December 2011, paras. 54 and 66.

[59] CED, *Estela Deolinda Yrusta and Alejandra del Valle Yrusta* v. *Argentina*, Communication No. 1/2013, 11 March 2016, para. 12(a).

[60] Ibid., para. 10.8 and 10.9.

[61] Ibid., para. 12(d).

specific harm suffered. The CED made no mention of the victims' right to health or whether it had been violated. These aspects need to be further developed in the future jurisprudence of the Committee.

## 5.8 The Innovative Approach of The UN Working Group on Enforced and Involuntary Disappearances

The WGEID, the only specialized body worldwide dealing with enforced disappearances for forty years, has played a crucial role in developing the understanding, scope, rights and obligations surrounding enforced disappearances.[62] Since its first annual report in 1980, the WGEID has considered that enforced disappearances may involve the denial or violation of many and very diverse human rights of the victims or their family, including both civil and political rights as well as economic, social and cultural rights. The WGEID added that when enforced disappearances occur, most economic, social and cultural rights are denied to a greater or lesser degree.[63]

In 2015, the Working Group published a Study on Enforced or Involuntary Disappearances and Economic, Social and Cultural Rights[64] (hereinafter the Study). The Study analyzes the relationship between enforced disappearances and economic, social and cultural rights in a comprehensive and systematic manner.[65] Given the inseparable, indivisible and interdependent nature of all human rights, the Working Group indicates that, by their very nature, enforced disappearances violate and have a particularly negative effect on the enjoyment of the ESCR of the disappeared person, their family and other persons. In addition, in many cases, people who are unable to fully exercise their ESCR are more likely to become victims of enforced disappearance.[66] States need to be able to effectively address enforced disappearances in a

[62] See, e.g., B. Duhaime, 'Multilateral human rights in a shifting world order: Perspectives from a UN special procedure mandate' (2018) 31, 2 *Revue québécoise de droit international* 213–18; and O. Frouville, 'Working out a working group: A view from a former working group member' (2017) *The United Nations Special Procedures System* 223–60.

[63] Report of the Working Group on Enforced or Involuntary Disappearances, UN. Doc. E/CN.4/1435, 1980, paras. 184 and 186.

[64] Report of the Working Group on Enforced or Involuntary Disappearances, Addendum, Study on Enforced or Involuntary Disappearances and Economic, Social and Cultural Rights (Hereinafter, Study), UN. Doc. A/HRC/30/38/Add.5.

[65] Study, paras. 3 and 5.

[66] Ibid., Summary, para. 2.

holistic manner, understanding the relationship between enforced disappearances and economic, social and cultural rights.[67]

The conditions of extreme poverty (considered to some extent as a lack of protection and enjoyment of ESCR) in which victims of enforced disappearances live are considered both a cause and a consequence of enforced disappearances. Hence, it is necessary to understand how the absence of an effective enjoyment of ESCR can be a factor that leads to or contributes to enforced disappearances, since individuals living in poverty are more vulnerable to becoming victims of enforced disappearance. Persons living in poverty often lack social integration, political and legal recognition and factual protection. This lack of security could mean insufficient protection with respect to several human rights violations, including enforced disappearances. In fact, in many conflict situations, a high percentage of enforced disappearances are concentrated in the poorest regions and most of the victims are poor.[68]

The Study adds that 'in many contexts, people who participate in the promotion or exercise of the enjoyment of ESCR are at a greater risk of becoming victims of enforced disappearance. In these circumstances, enforced disappearances are used as a tool to deter the population from promoting and exercising ESCR'.[69]

The WGEID then analyzes how enforced disappearances impact the ESCR of the disappeared person. Any person subjected to enforced disappearance is removed from the protection of the law, meaning that all kinds of protections, including those secured by and securing ESCR, cease to exist. In particular, the Group refers to violations of the right to work and the enjoyment of the highest attainable standard of physical and mental health.[70]

Enforced disappearances also have a negative impact on the ESCR of the victim's relatives and other dependents including their right to health, education, participation in a cultural life, the right to social security, property, family life and the right to housing. Such violations appear to be most evident when the person disappeared against their will is the

[67] Ibid., Section IV and para. 42.

[68] Ibid., paras. 2, 6, 8 and 9. See also, Report of the Working Group on Enforced or Involuntary Disappearances on its mission to Peru, U.N. Doc. A/HRC/33/51/Add.3, 2016, para. 69.

[69] Study, Summary, Section III and paras. 33 and 35.

[70] Ibid., paras. 17, 18, 19 and 21.

household 'breadwinner'.[71] For the Working Group, the effects on family members are not simply violations of their right to physical and mental integrity or suffering or damages. On the contrary, for the Working Group, in these circumstances, multiple ESCR such as the right to health, education, social security, property and a family life are infringed.[72]

A logical consequence of this approach is for States to consider the intrinsic relationship between enforced disappearances and ESCR. The effectiveness of prevention, eradication and reparation measures in the area of enforced disappearance requires a comprehensive approach that includes an adequate promotion or protection of ESCR. The Working Group considers that States should analyze 'the causes of enforced disappearances and ... the context in which they take place'.[73]

Measures to prevent, eradicate, investigate, punish and provide reparations for enforced disappearances must focus on the underlying context that produced vulnerability to enforced disappearance and that led to violations of ESCR after enforced disappearance. All measures to prevent, eradicate, investigate, punish, provide reparation and guarantee non-repetition must consider the factors that lead to an enforced disappearance, including the identification of those who could benefit from the act, as well as all the rights that the enforced disappearance violated.[74]

Measures to protect ESCR are necessary to prevent enforced disappearances or to address them should they occur.[75] Reparations must be holistic and must consider all rights violated. Reparation programs and measures must consider how enforced disappearances violate ESCR. Such measures should be designed as reparations for violations of ESCR suffered by victims of enforced disappearances and not simply as damage to physical or mental integrity or the aftermath of a disappearance.[76]

[71] See also, General comment on women affected by enforced disappearances, adopted by the Working Group on Enforced or Involuntary Disappearances at its 98th session, U.N. Doc. A/HRC/WGEID/98/2, 31 October–9 November 2012, para. 12 and General comment on children and enforced disappearances, adopted by the Working Group on Enforced or Involuntary Disappearances at its 98th session, 31 October–9 November 2012, para. 7.

[72] Study, paras. 23–4.

[73] Ibid.

[74] Ibid., para. 44.

[75] Ibid., Section III.A.

[76] Ibid., Section III.B.

## 5.9 The Case Law of the Inter-American Court of Human Rights

Since its first case on enforced disappearance, the Inter-American Court has established that the forced disappearance of a person constitutes a multiple and continuous violation of numerous rights recognized in the American Convention on Human Rights (the Convention).[77] Forced disappearance constitutes a multiple violation of several protected rights that entails 'other related violations'.[78]

The phenomenon of enforced disappearances requires a systemic and comprehensive analysis, due to the plurality of behaviours carried out for a single purpose (the disappearance).[79] Enforced disappearances should be treated as a complex form of human rights violation considering its multi-offensive nature.[80] An enforced disappearance should not be analyzed in an isolated, divided and fragmented manner but rather must cover the totality of all the facts.[81] The context in which the disappearances occurred needs to be analyzed to consider the prolonged effects over time and comprehensively focus on the consequences of an enforced disappearance.[82] The historical, social and political contexts are relevant to determine the State's international responsibility, better understanding the violations, as well as the scope of the reparations.[83]

The Inter-American Court has made references to economic, social, cultural, ethnic, gender or age circumstances that were contributing

[77] *Velásquez Rodríguez* v. *Honduras*, Merits, Judgment of 29 July 1988, Inter-Am. Ct. H.R. (ser. C) No. 4, para. 155.

[78] *Goiburú et al.* v. *Paraguay*, Merits, Reparations and Costs, Judgment of 22 September 2006, Inter-Am. Ct. H.R. (ser. C) No. 153, para. 84. Emphasis is ours.

[79] *Ibsen Cárdenas and Ibsen Peña* v. *Bolivia*, Merits, Reparation and Costs, Judgment of 1 September 2010, Inter-Am. Ct. H.R. (ser. C) No. 217, para. 57.

[80] *Heliodoro Portugal* v. *Panama*, Preliminary Objections, Merits, Reparations and Costs, Judgment of 12 August 2008, Inter-Am. Ct. H.R. (ser. C) No. 186, para. 106.

[81] *Gonzalez Medina and family* v. *Dominican Republic*, Preliminary Objections, Merits, Reparations and Costs, Judgment of 27 February 2012, Inter-Am. Ct. H.R. (ser. C) No. 240, para. 175.

[82] *Radilla Pacheco* v. *Mexico*, Preliminary Objections, Merits, Reparations and Costs, Judgment of 23 November 2009, Inter-Am. Ct. H.R. (ser. C) No. 209, para. 146 and IBAHRI and FLACSO, 'Violaciones, derechos humanos y contexto: herramientas propuestas para documentar e investigar, Manual de Análisis de Contexto para Casos de Violaciones a los Derechos Humanos' (2017), available at www.flacso.edu.mx/sites/default/files/violaciones-ddhh-y-contexto-herramientaspropuestas-para-documentar-investigar.pdf at 13–19.

[83] *Véliz Franco et al.* v. *Guatemala*, Preliminary Objections, Merits, Reparations and Costs, Judgment of 19 May 2014, Inter-Am. Ct. H.R. (ser. C) No. 277, para. 65.

factors to the damage caused by enforced disappearances or that condition the way violations occurred or how they should be remedied. Unfortunately, and similarly to the CED, the Court did not analyze those circumstances from the perspective of ESCR or find violations of Article 26 of the American Convention on Human Rights (The American Convention) related to economic, social and cultural rights or the Additional Protocol to the American Convention on Human Rights in the area of Economic, Social, and Cultural Rights (the Protocol of San Salvador).

For the Court, the disappearance of an indigenous leader affects not only their individual rights but also those of their community. The leader's disappearance removes that person from various areas of the social structure and prevents the leader from representing the community in its interactions with the State, which is a prerequisite for the realization of fundamental aspects such as inclusion, self determination and development of indigenous communities.[84] In a case of a massacre (with enforced disappearances), the Court referred to the deterioration of the cultural and spiritual life due to the impossibility of burying their dead according to their beliefs,[85] by the loss of spiritual guides and sacred places and by the deterioration in their social and family structure.[86] The disappearance of a leader and the displacement of the indigenous community causes a break with their cultural identity, affecting their bond with their relatives, their language, and their ancestral past requiring the State to adopt specific protection measures considering the particularities of indigenous peoples, as well as their customary law, values and customs to prevent and reverse the effects of such a situation.[87] However, the Court analyzed these effects from the perspective of personal integrity (article 5 of the Convention) and/or religious freedom (article 12 of the Convention) but not using article 26 on ESCR or the right to culture recognized in the Protocol of San Salvador.

The disappearance of a union leader intended to prevent the legitimate exercise of another right such as freedom of association, protected in

[84] *Chitay Nech et al.* v. *Guatemala*, Preliminary Objections, Merits, Reparations and Costs, Judgment of 25 May 2010, Inter-Am. Ct. H.R. (ser. C) No. 212, paras. 113–14.

[85] *Bámaca Velásquez* v. *Guatemala*, Merits, Judgment of 25 November 2000, Inter-Am. Ct. H.R. (ser. C) No. 70, paras. 136–7.

[86] *The Río Negro Massacres* v. *Guatemala*, Preliminary Objection, Merits, Reparations and Costs, Judgment of 4 September 2012, Inter-Am. Ct. H.R. (ser. C) No. 250, paras. 84, 153, 154 et seg.

[87] *Chitay Nech et al.* v. *Guatemala*, paras. 146–7.

article 16 of the Convention, is in turn an autonomous violation of this right.[88] Freedom of association recognizes the right and freedom to associate freely with other persons, without the authorities limiting or hindering such right. Freedom of association also derives positive obligations to prevent attacks against it, to protect those who exercise it and to investigate violations of that freedom.[89] The forced disappearance of a union leader most likely has a chilling and intimidating effect on other members of the union.[90] For this reason, the Court ordered the State to strengthen the protection mechanisms for trade unionists and trade union organizations.[91] So far, the Court has not found a violation of the union rights under article 26 or under the San Salvador Protocol. The textual differences between Article 16 of the American Convention and Article 8 of the Protocol indicate that the scope of the rights and the State obligations, although similar, are not identical.[92]

The Court, together with the Working Group, has been a pioneer in the analysis of family members as victims of enforced disappearance, considering that the suffering, anguish and uncertainty about the fate or

[88] *García and family members* v. *Guatemala*, Merits, Reparations and Costs, Judgment of 29 November 2012, Inter-Am. Ct. H.R. (ser. C) No. 258, paras. 116 and 121; and *Isaza Uribe et al.* v. *Colombia*, Merits, Reparations and Costs, Judgment of 20 November 2018, Inter-Am. Ct. H.R. (ser. C) No. 363, para. 145.

[89] *García and family members* v. *Guatemala*, paras. 116 and 121.

[90] Ibid.

[91] *Isaza Uribe et al.* v. *Colombia*, para. 197.

[92] Compare Protocol of San Salvador Art. 8 Trade union rights, '1. The States Parties shall ensure a. The right of workers to organize trade unions and to join the union of their choice for the purpose of protecting and promoting their interests. As an extension of that right, the States Parties shall permit . . . trade unions, federations and confederations to function freely, b. The right to strike . . .' with the plain text of the Convention Art. 16 Freedom of Association 'Everyone has the right to associate freely for . . . labor . . . purposes'. The Convention allows restrictions of this right for reasons of 'national security, public safety or public order, or to protect public health or morals or the rights and freedoms of others'. Meanwhile, the Protocol is more limited on the permissible grounds for restrictions including only 'public order or for protecting public health or morals or the rights and freedoms of others . . .' (excluding national security and public safety, two of the most often mentioned 'justifications' for ED). See particularly, I/A Court HR. Rights to freedom to organize, collective bargaining and strike, and their relation to other rights, with a gender perspective (interpretation and scope of Arts. 13, 15, 16, 24, 25 and 26 in relation to Art. 1(1) and 2 of the American Convention on Human Rights; Arts. 3, 6, 7 and 8 of the Protocol of San Salvador; Arts. 2, 3, 4, 5 and 6 of the Convention of Belém do Pará; Arts. 34, 44 and 45 of the Charter of the Organization of American States; and Arts. 2, 4, 14, 21 and 22 of the American Declaration on the Rights and Duties of Man. Advisory Opinion OC-27/21 of 5 May 2021. Series A No. 27, paras. 72, 73, 192.

whereabouts of the loved one generates a violation of the right to personal integrity of family members.[93] The Court presumes, without the need for proof, that immediate family members suffer harm and are entitled to reparation due to the disappearance of the person.[94] In several cases, given the specific circumstances of the disappearance, the Court has found an independent violation of the rights of the family as recognized by Article 17 of the Convention.[95] However, neither the effects related to family life,[96] nor the reparations ordered on this aspect were analyzed from the perspective of ESCR.[97] Specifically, the Protocol of San Salvador contains a different approach to family life than the American Convention. Article 15 of the Protocol, on the Right to the Formation and the Protection of Families, is not only much more detailed than the Convention but also broader in scope and in spelling out the State obligations.[98] Additionally, article 15 of the Protocol should be analyzed

[93] *Blake* v. *Guatemala*, Merits, Judgment of 24 January 1998, Inter-Am. Ct. H.R. (ser. C) No. 36.

[94] *Gudiel Álvarez et al. (Diario Militar)* v. *Guatemala*, Merits, Reparations and Costs, Judgment of 20 November 2012, Inter-Am. Ct. H.R. (ser. C) No. 253, para. 286.

[95] Art. 17 Rights of the Family. '1. The family is the natural and fundamental group unit of society and is entitled to protection by society and the state . . . 4. The States Parties shall take appropriate steps to ensure the equality of rights and the adequate balancing of responsibilities of the spouses as to marriage, during marriage, and in the event of its dissolution. In case of dissolution, provision shall be made for the necessary protection of any children solely on the basis of their own best interests . . ..'

[96] See, e.g., *R. Hernández et al.*, v. *El Salvador*, Merits, Reparations and Costs, Judgment of October 14, 2014, Inter-Am. Ct. H.R. (ser. C) No. 285, paras. 111–12; *The Members of the Village of Chichupac and neighboring communities of the Municipality of Rabinal* v. *Guatemala*, Preliminary Objections, Merits, Reparations and Costs, Judgment of 30 November 2016, Inter-Am. Ct. H.R. (ser. C) No. 328, para. 165; and *Contreras et al.*, v. *El Salvador*, Merits, Reparations and Costs, Judgment of 31 August 2011, Inter-Am. Ct. H.R. (ser. C) No. 232, paras. 116 and 121.

[97] I. de Paz Gonzalez, *The Social Rights Jurisprudence in the Inter-American Court of Human Rights: Shadow and Light in International Human Rights* (Elgar Studies in Human Rights, 2018), p. 115.

[98] Art. 15 Right to the Formation and the Protection of Families '1. The family is the natural and fundamental element of society and ought to be protected by the State, which should see to the improvement of its spiritual and material conditions. 2. Everyone has the right to form a family . . . 3. The States Parties hereby undertake to accord adequate protection to the family unit and in particular: a. To provide special care and assistance to mothers during a reasonable period before and after childbirth; b. To guarantee adequate nutrition for children at the nursing stage and during school attendance years; c. To adopt special measures for the protection of adolescents in order to ensure the full development of their physical, intellectual and moral capacities; d. To undertake special programs of family training so as to help create a stable and positive environment in which children will receive and develop the values of understanding, solidarity, respect, and responsibility.'

considering other norms of the same instrument such as social security, education, food or health.[99] For instance, an enforced disappearance clearly affects the State duty to see to the improvement of the spiritual and material conditions of the family, to adopt 'adequate' family protections or to create a 'stable and positive' family environment as specifically required by the Protocol but not by the Convention.

Enforced disappearance affects the right to health of both the disappeared person and their family members. The Court has understood that family members or other related persons should have access to prompt and effective judicial procedures or remedies as a means of determining not only the whereabouts of a disappeared person but also his or her state of health.[100] The violation of the mental and moral integrity of the next of kin is a direct consequence of such enforced disappearance.[101] For this reason, the Court usually orders as a measure of reparation the provision of appropriate, effective, immediate and free of charge care for the physical and psychological effects suffered by the victims.[102] However, the Court has never established a direct violation of the right to health of the disappeared persons or their relatives. The Court's failure is surprising given its compelling case law on the right to health in general.[103]

In several cases, alongside or in addition to an enforced disappearance, the home of the victim is affected. For instance, in a case the Court found that the military personnel, in the context of perpetrating a massacre including enforced disappearances, burned houses, destroyed and scorched crops and killed cattle. Therefore, the Court considered that the State violated the right to private property recognized in Articles 21.1 and 21.2 of the American Convention.[104] Again, the Court failed to

[99] See, for example, Inter-Am. Comm'n H.R., Rapporteurship on the Rights of the Child, The right of girls and boys to a family. Alternative care. Ending institutionalization in the Americas, OEA/Ser.L/V/II. Doc.54/13, 2013.

[100] *T. Millacura et al.* v. *Argentina*, Merits, Reparations and costs, Judgment of 26 August 2011, Inter-Am. Ct. H.R. (ser. C) No. 229, para. 114.

[101] *Gómez Palomino* v. *Peru*, Merits, Reparations and Costs, Judgment of 22 November 2005, Inter-Am. Ct. H.R. (ser. C) No. 136, para. 61.

[102] *Gomes Lund et al. ('Guerrilha do Araguaia')* v. *Brazil*, Preliminary Objections, Merits, Reparations and Costs, Judgment of 24 November 2010, Inter-Am. Ct. H.R. (ser. C) No. 219, para. 267.

[103] See M. Morales Antoniazzi and L. Clérico (eds.), *Interamericanización del derecho a la salud: Perspectivas a la luz del caso 'Poblete' de la Corte IDH* (Instituto de Estudios Constitucionales de Querétaro, 2019).

[104] *The Massacres of El Mozote and surrounding areas* v. *El Salvador*, Merits, Reparations and Costs, Judgment of 25 October 2012, Inter-Am. Ct. H.R. (ser. C) No. 252, para. 202.

consider the violation of housing rights as recognized, among others, in Articles IX, XI and XXIII of the American Declaration on the Rights and Duties of Man, Article 26 of the American Convention and 34.k of the OAS Charter. The Committee on Economic, Social and Cultural Rights understood housing as the right to live in a home in peace, security and dignity. This right, at a minimum, includes security of tenure, availability of services, affordability, habitability, accessibility, appropriate location and cultural adequacy. In the Committee's view, the right to housing should not be interpreted narrowly. It should not be equated with the shelter provided by merely having a roof, or considering shelter exclusively as a commodity.[105] This definition is even broader than the very broad and flexible understanding of the IACtHR of the right to property that includes material goods, intangible things, all movable and immovable property, corporal and incorporeal elements and any other intangible object of any value as well as any right that may form part of a person's assets and rights incorporated into a person's patrimony.[106]

The right to education can be affected in multiple ways. A disappeared person could be a student or teacher.[107] The Gómez Palomino case illustrates some aspects of the relationship between enforced disappearances and the right to education. In this case, due to the disappearance of the father, only one sister was able to complete secondary education. Some of the brothers had to abandon their studies to help their mother economically. Another sister, fourteen years old at the time, had to postpone her studies because her mother could not read or write, so she accompanied her in the search for the father, both to read documents and to help with the care of her younger sister. The Court found that, after the disappearance, all the brothers interrupted their studies, not only due to economic factors but also because of emotional factors such as depression, worry and sadness. The Tribunal ordered a series of

[105] Committee on Economic, Social and Cultural Rights, General comment No. 4: The right to adequate housing, Art. 11(1) of the Covenant, paras. 7 and 9.

[106] *Furland and Family* v. *Argentina*, Preliminary Objections, Merits, Reparations and Costs, Judgment, Inter-Am. Ct. H.R. (ser. C) No. 246, 31 August 2012, para. 220 57; *Ivcher-Bronstein* v. *Peru*, Merits, Reparations and Costs, Judgment, Inter-Am. Ct. H.R. (ser. C) No. 74, Feb. 6, 2001, para. 122.

[107] See for example, *La Cantuta* v. *Peru*, Merits, Reparations and Costs, Judgment of 29 November 2006, Inter-Am. Ct. H.R. (ser. C) No. 162 (University students and professors) or *Castillo Páez* v. *Peru*, Merits, Judgment of 3 November 1997, Inter-Am. Ct. H.R. (ser. C) No. 34 (student) or *Caballero Delgado and Santana* v. *Colombia*, Merits, Judgment of 8 December 1995, Inter-Am. Ct. H.R. (ser. C) No. 22 (teacher).

educational measures such as participation in special adult education programs, the possibility that such benefits could be transmitted to their sons and daughters, participation in a literacy program for the mother and a scholarship for the daughter of the disappeared.[108] While all these reparation measures are quite important, the Court once more failed to address the specific and autonomous violation of the right to education.

In several cases, the Tribunal recognized how the work of the families of disappeared persons is affected by such a situation. Relatives of a forcibly disappeared person had to leave the country and lost their jobs.[109] A mother who devoted herself exclusively to the search for her son had to abandon her work.[110] In these cases, unfortunately, the Court, despite recognizing the impact on the employment situation of the relatives of the victim of disappearance, did not make any special consideration of the right to work nor ordered reparations differentiated by the violation of such right. In another case, the relatives, partly due to the disappearance of their loved ones, had to move from their place of residence. As a result, they left their jobs and faced unemployment, in part due to the difficulties and stigmas of being displaced. The Court considered these situations proven. The Court, however, ignored a request to specifically guarantee the right to work without giving any explanation of the reasons why this request should not be accepted.[111]

## 5.10 Consequences and Challenges of the ESCR Approach to Enforced Disappearances

A new reading of enforced disappearances from an ESCR perspective is one of the possible strategies to respond to current demands. This approach could offer a fresh and deeper understanding of the causes and consequences of an enforced disappearance and a roadmap to properly revise the scope, duties and rights in terms of prevention, eradication, investigation, search, truth, reparation and memorialization.

[108] *Gómez Palomino* v. *Peru*, Merits, Reparations and Costs, Judgment of 22 November 2005, Inter-Am. Ct. H.R. (ser. C) No. 136, para. 144–8 .

[109] *Molina Theissen* v. *Guatemala*, Reparations and Costs, Judgment of 3 July 2004, Inter-Am. Ct. H.R. (ser. C) No. 108, para. 37.9 and 59.

[110] *Gómez Palomino* v. *Peru*, para. 127.

[111] *The Mapiripán Massacre* v. *Colombia*, Merits, Reparations and Costs, Judgment of 15 September 2005, Inter-Am. Ct. H.R. (ser. C) No. 134, para. 175 and seq. and 291. h. viii.

For instance, the Special Rapporteur on extreme poverty has explained that, in general but perfectly applicable to enforced disappearances,

> human rights experts and groups do not focus on any detail, either in their fact-finding or their assessments, specifically on the situation of persons living in poverty. As a result, neither the diagnosis of situations nor the resulting policy recommendations are tailored to address the distinctive ways in which people living in poverty are affected by police brutality ... left unprotected ... deprived of their liberty ... confined in their freedom of movement by the criminalization of homelessness ... to mention just a few of the major violations.[112]

In investigating and documenting violations of civil and political rights (including enforced disappearances), distinctions according to class or socio-economic status often are not made.[113] As a result, there is an inadequate capturing of either the diverse characteristics of those living in poverty or the very specific consequences of the varied forms of discrimination, oppression, stigmatization and violence many of them experience on a daily basis.[114]

If poverty and the lack of effective enjoyment of ESCR create situations of vulnerability to being victims of enforced disappearances, prevention measures must include combating poverty and guaranteeing ESCR. The Committee should consider, in conducting its analysis of the duty to prevent enforced disappearances, that, in many contexts, persons who do not fully enjoy economic, social and cultural rights may find themselves in a situation of greater vulnerability of being victims of enforced disappearances. In this regard, CEDAW has recommended the adoption of measures to prevent gender-based violence against women, including enforced disappearances of women, which requires 'addressing the root causes of such violence, such as ... poverty and the marginalization of women'.[115] Similarly, the Committee on the Rights of the Child has promoted the adoption of effective measures to prevent the killings and

[112] Report of the Special Rapporteur on extreme poverty and human rights, UN. Doc. A/72/502, 4 October 2017, para. 2.

[113] Ibid., para. 6.

[114] Ibid., para. 3. See also, Report of the Special Rapporteur on the promotion of truth, justice, reparation and guarantees of non-recurrence, Pablo de Greiff, UN. Doc. A/HRC/30/42, para. 34 (while the causes of violence or rights violations cannot be reduced to inequality or poverty, it is true that inequality and poverty are closely correlated with violence and violations of various rights, including ESCR).

[115] Committee on the Elimination of Discrimination against Women, Concluding observations on the ninth periodic report of Mexico, CEDAW/C/MEX/CO/9, para. 24(a).

disappearances of children and their recruitment by criminal groups and particularly addressing 'the root causes of violence and child recruitment such as poverty and discrimination'.[116]

In terms of truth and justice, ESCR's approach to enforced disappearances also poses innumerable challenges. The lack of protection or violation of ESCR (prior to or as a consequence of enforced disappearance) produces new and/or greater obstacles in the search for justice and truth.[117] In general, stigmatization and marginalization lead to poor people's complaints being taken less seriously and reduce those people's access to legal representation.[118] Therefore, it must be considered that combating poverty and promoting ESCR are necessary to ensure truth and justice. In parallel, ESCR obligations may involve considering that general and universal truth and justice policies may not be sufficient or effective for persons whose ESCR is not adequately guaranteed. This will require the adoption of special measures for such situations.

The incorporation of ESCR into the analysis of State obligations to investigate and guarantee the right to know the truth requires an inclusion of ESCR when investigating the 'circumstances' surrounding disappearances. It should be understood how the lack of protection of ESCR or the work in defence of ESCR was one of the causes of the disappearance. In addition, the circumstances of the disappearance require analysis of how ESCR were affected or their violations exacerbated as a consequence of the disappearance. In other words, what should be investigated and sanctioned must be rethought. At the same time, criminal investigation and sanction should be complemented by other types of judicial and administrative remedies to address ESCR violations in the context of enforced disappearances.

Taking into consideration ESCR violations in the context of disappearances draws attention to the question: Who were the perpetrators? Several UN human rights bodies have made references to the disappearances of persons due to their exercise[119] or

[116] Committee on the Rights of the Child, El Salvador, UN. Doc. CRC/C/SLV/CO/5-6, 2018, para. 23.

[117] Report of the Special Rapporteur on extreme poverty and human rights, UN. Doc. A/67/278, 9 August 2012.

[118] Report of the Special Rapporteur on extreme poverty and human rights, UN. Doc. A/72/502, 4 October 2017, para. 9.

[119] Report of the Special Rapporteur in the field of cultural rights, Visit to Maldives, UN. Doc. A/HRC/43/50/Add.2, 2021, para. 58. This is the case of a disappearance of a journalist and poet due to extremist ideology.

defence[120] of economic, social and cultural rights. Is it enough in those situations just to investigate the State agents who conducted the disappearance and those who may have ordered them or had control over the repressive apparatus? Or should the investigations extend to those who economically benefitted from such enforced disappearances?[121]

Similar or even greater challenges arise in terms of reparations. The perspective of ESCR, particularly in the analysis as a cause and effect of disappearances, should lead the Committee to require the adoption of transformative reparation measures. For example, the CEDAW has highlighted the difficulties of accessing proper reparations for enforced disappearances with reference to rural women. The CEDAW expressed its concern that many rural women are 'financially responsible for their families owing to the conflict-related killing or disappearance of their spouses [and] are unable to benefit from State support and protection, including access to basic services, such as potable water, housing, infrastructure, education, and health care, which are delivered in urban areas'.[122]

In the case of the right to health, there is a need to reevaluate the causal relationship between enforced disappearance and the impact on the physical and psychological health of family members in order to determine full and integral reparations. That is, what kind of health problems

[120] CERD, UN. Doc. CERD/C/THA/CO/4-8, 2022, para. 21 (expressing concern for the disappearance of those advocating for land rights, protection of the environment and the rights of ethnic and ethno-religious groups and indigenous peoples); Report of the Special Rapporteur on the Implications for Human Rights of the Environmentally Sound Management and Disposal of Hazardous Substances and Wastes, Visit to Canada, UN. Doc. A/HRC/45/12/ADD.1, 2020, para. 91) (allegations related to the disappearance of an indigenous woman who raised concerns of exposure to toxic pollution from oil sands operations); and CRC-OP-SC, UN. Doc. CRC/C/OPSC/LAO/CO/1, 2015, para. 19 (disappearance of a leading social activist who, inter alia, worked to tackle the root causes of child trafficking and exploitation by improving children's access to education).

[121] See, among others, J. Sarkin and G. Baranowska, 'Why enforced disappearances are perpetrated against groups as state policy: Overlaps and interconnections between disappearances and genocide' (2018) 2, 3 *Católica Law Review* 11–50, 33, available at https://doi.org/10.34632/catolicalawreview.2018.9098; Center for Legal and Social Studies, *Corporate responsibility in crimes against humanity: repression of workers during State terrorism (Responsabilidad empresarial en delitos de lesa humanidad. Represión a trabajadores durante el terrorismo de Estado)* (Ministry of Justice and Human Rights, 2015); H. Verbitsky and J. P. Bohoslavsky (eds.), *The Economic Accomplices to the Argentine Dictatorship: Outstanding Debts* (Cambridge University Press, 2016); L. Payne and G. Pereira, 'Corporate complicity in international human rights violations' (2016) 12, 20 *Annual Review of Law and Social Science*.

[122] CEDAW, U.N. Doc. CEDAW/C/SSD/CO/1, 2021, para. 44(a).

do enforced disappearances cause? What type of specialized care should be provided to secure the right to health for victims of enforced disappearances? If ESCR are violated, the reparations ordered must be consistent with the ESCR violated. The Rapporteur on the Right to Truth has called for a distinction between development interests in general, the duty to protect ESCR, the obligation to provide assistance under international humanitarian law and the need to provide reparations for human rights violations. It is extremely advantageous to increase the impact of these programs by linking them. However, it is important to be clear that the programs respond to diverse sources of obligation. In fact, the programs that achieve the best results are those that respond to the characteristics of the particular obligation on which they are based.[123]

Addressing the root causes and violations of ESCR in the area of enforced disappearance will produce important, albeit modest, contributions to promoting social change.[124] By recognizing that part of the cause of disappearances is due to the lack of enjoyment of ESCR, that the damage caused by disappearances is a violation of ESCR and that it is exacerbated in many cases by the lack of effective enjoyment of ESCR, there is clearly a need to remedy this situation. There are many reasons why this neglect matters. It renders invisible major groups of victims; it fails to expose the fact that many civil and political rights violations are rooted in poverty and that only by addressing this can sustainable solutions be found; it overlooks the fact that poor victims may suffer violations of a different nature requiring different reparations and responses.[125]

In short, the intrinsic link between enforced disappearances and ESCR demonstrates that the prevention of enforced disappearances is a fundamental element for the protection of ESCR and, in turn, the protection of those rights is at the same time an essential element for the prevention of enforced disappearances. Effective measures to prevent and eradicate enforced disappearances require a comprehensive approach that encompasses the appropriate promotion and protection of economic, social and cultural rights.[126]

[123] Report of the Special Rapporteur on the promotion of truth, justice, reparation and guarantees of non-recurrence, UN. Doc. A/69/518, para. 60.

[124] C. Sandoval, *Transitional Justice and Economic, Social and Cultural Rights* (United Nations Office of the High Commissioner for Human Rights, 2014), available at www.ohchr.org/Documents/Publications/HR-PUB-13-05.pdf.

[125] Report of the Special Rapporteur on extreme poverty and human rights, UN. Doc. A/72/502, 4 October 2017, para. 71.

[126] Study, para. 77.

## 5.11 Conclusion

This chapter, rather than being an exhaustive analysis of all possible links between enforced disappearances and ESCR, seeks to provide a first analytical framework on the positive aspects of the Committee's practice in this area as well as to make gaps visible and suggest possibilities for alternative analysis of ESCR considering developments provided by other human rights bodies. It also shows the possibilities already offered by the practice of the WGEID, the IACtHR and other UN organs that could serve as a model for the Committee's future developments.

The Committee's first decade or so has been enormously productive in deepening the development and understanding of enforced disappearance in the field of international law. Nevertheless, the Committee also has used a restrictive interpretation of some innovative Convention provisions. This restrictive approach is not consistent with the practice of other human rights bodies such as the WGEID or the Inter-American Court. The Committee will also have to address issues that remain unexplored given the limited number of individual complaints and concluding observations and the total lack of any general comment.

As the Convention is a victim-oriented treaty,[127] the Committee on Enforced Disappearances needs to interpret it in a more expansive way in order to properly recognize the interdependency and indivisibility of all human rights, including ESCR. To analyze enforced disappearances in a comprehensive manner means ultimately to consider that the interdependence and indivisibility of human rights denies any separation, categorization or hierarchy between rights for the purposes of their respect, protection and guarantee. Interpreting the Convention without considering economic, social and cultural rights detracts from the full effectiveness of these rights, distorting their essence. An analysis in the light of ESCR contributes to a greater clarification of State obligations, including those related to enforced disappearances. More importantly, it will provide analytical tools to respond more properly to the needs of the victims of enforced disappearances using a holistic view of human rights.

[127] E. Decaux, 'The International Convention for the Protection of All Persons from Enforced Disappearance, as a victim-oriented treaty' in Margaret M. de Guzman and D. M. Amann (eds.), *Arcs of Global Justice: Essays in Honour of William A. Schabas* (Oxford University Press, 2018), pp. 57–64.

# 6

# NGO Contributions to Eradicate Enforced Disappearances in Latin America

HORACIO RAVENNA*

## 6.1 Introduction

This chapter describes the long process of awareness that led to the creation of the International Convention for the Elimination of Enforced Disappearance, as well as the role and influence of non-governmental organizations (NGOs) on that process. For this purpose, research was carried out on the origins of some of the organizations of the civil society present in Latin America, which were created in the 1960s and 1970s in response to the Cold War, and which spread around the world after the end of the Second World War and the new division of the world agreed upon by the winning countries at the Yalta Conference of 1945 and the Paris Peace Treaties of 1947.

The analysis reviewed the national and international organizations that assisted developing countries and in turn allowed them to influence the model of society that was being developed under the threat of a third nuclear world war. During the Second World War, Nazi Germany issued a decree known as 'Night and Fog'[1] to fight against local resistance, whereby the system of enforced disappearance, torture and death was applied. It was also used in the colonies during liberation wars in the 1950s and 1960s.

When Latin America was almost completely under dictatorships, Chile, Argentina, Uruguay, Paraguay, Brazil, Peru and Bolivia in the Southern Cone, with tentacles extending outside Latin America to operate in the United States, Italy, France and Spain,[2] launched Operation Condor in order to persecute opposition activists and armed

* The cooperation of Maria del Pilar Gómez, Esq. in the research process of this work is appreciated.

[1] Issued on 7 December 1941 by Field Marshal Wilhelm Keitel.

[2] www.cipdg.gob.ar/pdf/Operacion-Condor.pdf.

organizations.[3] The Operation consisted in the coordination of governments and their intelligence agencies aimed at the detection in their territories of those who were escaping from their own countries. They were unlawfully arrested and, without any legal procedure, sent back to be tortured and then executed or thrown alive from planes into the sea.

> Operation Condor was a multilateral agreement between the national security dictatorships of the Southern Cone within the continental counterinsurgency system .... In November 1975, Argentina, Bolivia, Chile, Paraguay and Uruguay signed a pact that allowed their security forces to coordinate repression against Southern Cone political exiles outside their national borders and to target prominent leaders ... even in Europe and the United States ... Brazil joined soon after ... Ecuador and Peru subsequently joined.[4]

As a result, in 1980, the relatives of the victims began to seek a way to achieve first the identification of this offence as an autonomous offence and then the adoption of an international convention for its punishment. In this chapter, the testimonies about such actions were first analyzed first and then a description is provided about how, at the beginning of this century, a series of concomitant actions gained momentum, as a result of which, the United Nations (UN) convened a Drafting Group for what ended up being the long-awaited international convention. Finally, there is a brief analysis of the current state of those NGOs that fought hard for such Convention; the current solidarity organizations, their new perspective and interests; and the update of a utopian fight for the appearance of new challenges and the need for the recognition of new rights. Those people from the recent past who were essential creators of the present are herein remembered.

They base their accounts on memory. In this regard, Vera Carnovale[5] reminds us about the fact that: 'The past is remembered even if the memory is always contemporary; it is renewed every day, it is invented in order to develop its identity and erased to do without useless material.'

In *Historia, memoria y fuentesorales*, Carnovale et al. cite Mary Carruthers,[6] who reflects on the act of forgetting: 'To forget is another

[3] S. Calloni, *Operativo Cóndor, Pacto Criminal* (Ciencias Sociales UBA, 2001).

[4] Centro Internacional para la Promoción de los Derechos Humanos (CIPDH), Dirección Nacional del Sistema Argentino de Información Jurídica (2015), p. 18.

[5] V. Carnovale et al., *Historia, memoria y fuentes orales* (CeDinCi Editores, 2006).

[6] M. Carruthers, *The Craft of Thought, Meditation, Rhetoric, and the Making of Images* (Cambridge University Press, 1998), pp. 400–1200, cited by Carnovale.

aspect of the act of remembering because the act of forgetting on purpose allows for creativity. The disadvantage of memory is not the act of forgetting, but the disorder, the absence of guidelines, the dispersion or fate.'

This chapter consists of research about a historic stage of a generation that is giving way to new people with their new rights, their new fights and their new utopias.

## 6.2 International Solidarity in Latin America in the 1960s and 1970s

### *6.2.1 Solidarity Is the Tenderness of the People*

This section[7] briefly reviews the international solidarity organizations that helped the civil society in the different countries where there was resistance to authoritarianism.

#### 6.2.1.1 World Council of Churches (WCC)

The Human Rights Office for Latin America was created in 1975, at the 5th Assembly of the WCC held in Nairobi, whose theme was 'Jesus Christ Frees and Unites', in order to direct the collaboration of the evangelical churches with Latin American countries that were suffering brutal repression.[8]

Presbyterian Pastor Charles Harper, born in the United States, but who lived in Brazil since he was a child, was a leading figure responsible for the process of encouraging solidarity in Latin America. His mission was to support those churches and groups that were facing difficult situations in the repressive context of Latin America. Harper's commitment to human right defenders facing dictatorships in their countries considerably exceeded the responsibility for social care, and he was personally and physically involved in the actions performed.

On 4 October 1982, in Argentina, a *Marchapor la Vida* (March for Life) was organized by the existing human rights organizations: the Permanent Assembly for Human Rights (APDH, for its Spanish acronym), the Ecumenical Movement for Human Rights (MEDH, for its

[7] Based on Ministerio de Relaciones Exteriores, Comercio Internacional y Culto, Testimonios de la Solidaridad Internacional (2007), p. 120, cited by Belela Herrera.

[8] M. T. Piñero, *Iglesias Protestantes y Terrorismo de Estado* (Facultad de Ciencias Sociales, Universidad de Buenos Aires I), p. 10.

Spanish acronym), Madres de Plaza de Mayo (Mothers of the Plaza de Mayo), Abuelas de Plaza de Mayo (Grandmothers of the Plaza de Mayo), Familiares de Detenidos y Desaparecidos por Razones Políticas y Sociales (Relatives of Disappeared and Arrested People for Political and Social Reasons), Service, Peace and Justice (SERPAJ, for its Spanish acronym), the Liga Argentina por los Derechos del Hombre (Argentine League for Human Rights) and the Centre for Legal and Social Studies (CELS, for its Spanish acronym).

Since the march was prohibited, repression was expected. Harper travelled especially for this occasion and, on said day, he led the march together with the leaders of the different organizing NGOs and the representatives of the religious creeds. The march could not reach the seat of the executive power as planned, but it was not repressed, and it had a great national and international impact.

Based on the gathered information, the World Council of Churches filed complaints in different forums. The most important forum was the Commission on Human Rights of the United Nations, where the CMI has an advisory status. The Director of the Commission of the Churches on International Affairs (CIAI, for its Spanish acronym), Leopoldo Niilus, was in charge of the relationship with the United Nations. The CMI also had an office in New York, attended the United Nations General Assembly sessions and also filed complaints for human rights violations in Latin America.[9]

Furthermore, the presence of Latin American refugees in different countries led the local churches to participate in the actions against the military dictatorships. However, the member churches of the Council and the Council itself played a role of support and pastoral care with those who went into exile in such countries.[10]

In Chile, the WCC helped the Fundación de Ayuda Social de las Iglesias Cristianas (Christian Churches Social Aid Foundation, FASIC), an ecumenical organization; the Vicariate of Solidarity, together with the Catholic Church; and the Servicio Evangélicopara el Desarrollo (Evangelical Service for Development, SED), an institution of the Pentecostal Church. In Brazil, it took an active part in solidarity actions with the churches and the popular organizations.

The Human Rights Office of the Council helped the Coordinadora Ecuménica de Servicio (Service Ecumenical Coordinator, CES) and

[9] Ibid., p. 11.
[10] Ibid.

Clamor, an ecumenical organization created by Archbishop Paulo Evaristo Arns from São Paulo to assist the flood of refugees from Chile, Argentina and Uruguay who arrived in Brazil.

Protestants and Catholics worked together in the defence of human rights in the Comité de Iglesias para Ayudas de Emergencia (Churches Committee for Emergency Aid, CIPAE) from Paraguay, and in the Service, Peace and Justice from Uruguay. In Central America, an office of the World Council of Churches (WCC) carried out important work by filing complaints for the human rights violations in Nicaragua, Guatemala, Honduras and El Salvador, as well as by assisting the refugees who were escaping from political persecution and the killing of leaders and indigenous communities.

#### 6.2.1.1 Diakonia

Diakonia is a Swedish non-profit organization founded in 1966. In 1973, the Centro Evangélico de Acción Social (Evangelical Centre of Community Welfare, CEAS) was active. The Centre was formed by the Iglesia Evangélica del Río de la Plata (Evangelical Church of the River Plate, IERP), the Presbyterian Church and the Iglesia Evangélica Misionera Argentina (Argentine Evangelical Missionary Church, IEMA), which performed its actions among the people of shanty towns and the Comité Interluterano de Diakonía (Diakonia Inter-Lutheran Committee, CID), backed by the Lutheran Council of the River Plate composed of the IERP, Evangelical churches and the Lutheran and Scandinavian churches to respond to the floods in the northeast of Argentina. Just like the preceding commissions, the Comisión Argentina para los Refugiados (Argentine Commission for Refugees, CAREF) was also established to act in relation to the contingency, as a support for the activity in Chile and, at least at the beginning, the individuals involved planned the work for the short term.[11]

During the Latin American dictatorships, it was called Acción Ecuménica Sueca (Swedish Ecumenical Action, AES), and afterwards it was called Diakonia.[12] Paraguay, Peru, Bolivia, Guatemala, Honduras, Nicaragua, Colombia and Argentina were the Latin American countries in which Diakonia was present with local and Swedish workers.

[11] N. Casola, *Territorio de Refugio. Comisión Argentina para los Refugiados* (CAREF), p. 7, available at www.aacademica.org/000-040/15.

[12] A. Gauding, *Es mejor encender una luz que maldecir la oscuridad* (1991).

In line with such initiatives, in December 1974, Pastor Juan Cobrdo promoted the creation of the Diaconía Evangélica Argentina (Argentine Evangelic Diakonia, DEA). The goal was that the AED gradually be assigned all the tasks performed by the CEAS, CID and CAREF, to which new projects could be added. The aim of the initiative was to concentrate efforts and resources to make the task more efficient in view of the huge difficulties that existed for aid to be received.[13] Another common initiative was the creation of the Consejo Consultivo de Iglesias (Advisory Council of Churches, CCI) in 1978 as a response to the fact that it was not possible that all the members of the Federación Argentina de Iglesias Evangélicas (Argentine Federation of Evangelical Churches, FAIE) would pronounce against State terrorism.

A summary of Diakonia's role in the work for human rights, in relation to democracy and human dignity, states that:

> The human rights organisations and their representatives have saved many human lives . . .. For obvious reasons, there are no well-documented data on the number of people saved from being abducted, killed, tortured or exiled. However, it is not an exaggeration to note that the human rights organisations, in some cases, were especially relevant to the end of dictatorships and the return to democracy in several countries.[14]

Even during the dictatorships, Frikyrkanhjälper (Free Churches Aid) funded the aid that the victims of the dictatorships and their families received through informal channels, which were opened by Frikyrkanhjälper with the collaboration of different churches. Furthermore, Frikyrkanhjälper took part in the creation of different organizations that were useful for the coordination of actions against the repressive structure, which, through the Operation Condor, subjected the entire Latin American territory to unlawful repression. Frikyrkanhjälper called lawyers who were human rights activists in their countries and formed the Asociación de Abogados Latinoamericano spara la Defensa de los Derechos Humanos (Latin American Human Rights Lawyers' Association, AALA).

The Association was formed by Belisario Dos Santos Jr, from Clamor, São Paulo; Roberto Cuellar, a Salvadorian, who was a distinguished president of the Inter-American Institute of Human Rights (IIHR) after

[13] CAREF, Report, December 1974.

[14] Gauding, Es mejor encender una luz que maldecir la oscuridad, p. 18.

the return to democracy; and the author of this chapter, among other Latin American lawyers.

In some contexts, such as in Central America during the military dictatorships period in the 1980s, Diakonia created spaces of political action that must be analyzed within the social and political context.

As Anna Karen Gaudin said:

> A first reflection is that in Diakonia we enjoyed during the critical years of the military dictatorships, a very large autonomy on the part of our directors, to decide on projects that we considered a priority. In this way we also assumed very great responsibilities. The other side of this medal is that we were left alone to resolve eventual political, institutional and personal confrontations. Working in conflictive countries in matters ambiguously called 'internal affairs', requires taking precautions that, in difficult moments, became heavy .... Certainly, as the sharing of risks with others grew, so did the bonds of friendship. That is why, to a large extent, the human bonds created cannot be erased, neither by distance nor by time.[15]

#### 6.2.1.2 Ford Foundation

The Ford Foundation's solidarity was reflected in its support for human rights movements and its accompaniment during the transition to democracy.

The presidents and leaders of the Ford Foundation decided that human rights were an explicit and main priority in their agenda. Thereafter, the Ford Foundation worked explicitly on the creation of the so-called human rights lobby in Washington, DC, and supported organizations such as Amnesty International (created in 1961; winner of the Nobel Peace Prize in 1977); the Washington Office on Latin America (WOLA, founded in 1974 as a result of the coup d'état in Chile); and Human Rights Watch (previously known as Helsinki Watch in 1978), which were involved in the organization. Omar Torrijos (Panama), the Nicaraguan Sandinistas, Guillermo Ungo (El Salvador), Daniel Oduber (Costa Rica), Anselmo Sule (Chile) and Leonel Brizola (Brazil), among many others, were also actively involved.

The Ford Foundation funded the formation of the Asociación Latinoamericana de Derechos Humanos (Latin America Human Rights Association, ALDHU) composed of the subsequently elected president of

[15] Ibid., p. 19.

Colombia, Carlos Andrés Pérez;[16] César Verduga,[17] Secretary-General of ALDHU and then Minister of the government of Ecuador; the ever remembered leader of the APDH and co-founder of CELS, Emilio Mignone; and the author of this chapter, among many others.

According to Calandra,[18] who cites the Programa de la Fundación Ford para Latinoamérica y el Caribe (Ford Foundation's Latin American and Caribbean Programme), during 1959–83, the Ford Foundation gave 250 million dollars for programmes supporting the development of civil society organizations.[19] According to Richard Magat,[20] social sciences and interdisciplinary research – mostly intended for private and non-public entities, including independent NGOs – received support in those years.

At that time, the position was adopted by President Jimmy Carter and the policy, executed by the Secretary for Human Rights, Patricia Derian, was critically important for the fight against dictatorships. The refusal to sell weapons to the non-democratic governments of the region can be highlighted, as well as the talks held so that the Argentine dictatorship would accept the visit from the Inter-American Commission on Human Rights (IACHR) in 1979.

In 1985, Patricia Derian's in-person testimony at the Trial of the Juntas was particularly important, because she was President Carter's Secretary of Human Rights and in that capacity played a fundamental role in the relationship between the US government and the Latin American dictatorships. Her testimony in Case 13, for which the first three military juntas that governed Argentina between 1976 and 1983 were prosecuted and convicted, was particularly important.[21]

16 He had to resign after protests against his administration.

17 An economist and politician who was two times minister of the government of Ecuador.

18 Benedetta Calandra (PhD, Roma Tre University, 2005; MA, University of London, 2000). Researcher and Associate Professor in History of the Latin America, University of Bergamo, Italy, Department of Foreign Languages, Literatures and Cultures. Her lines of research are contemporary history of Latin America, memory and human rights, political exile, cultural relations between United States and Latin America.

19 The Ford Foundation's Latin American and Caribbean Programme, Discussion paper For the Board of Trustees Meeting as a Committee of the Whole, FFA No. 008856, 28 March 1984.

20 http://prabook.com/web/richard.magat/219083.

21 She recounted how they convinced the Argentine dictatorship to receive the IACHR in 1979. The IACHR report was lapidary for the dictatorship's aggressive foreign policy of denying the existence of the disappeared.

## 6.3 The Path of the International Convention

At the Coloquio de París (Paris Colloquium) of 1981,[22] exiles and jurists, including many from Latin America, presented their project for the Convention and set out the need for renewing the mandate of the Working Group on Enforced or Involuntary Disappearances (WGEID) created by the UN in 1980.[23] At that event, the first draft of the Convention was prepared and actions to promote its drafting were agreed upon. During the Colloquium, not only the legal discussions but also cultural activities were important. The Théâtredu Soleil from Arianne Mouchkine organized a march in the streets of Paris with the silhouette of the disappeared.[24]

Lawyers from Asamblea Permanente por los Derechos Humanos (APDH) and Madres de Plaza de Mayo also presented projects conceived by them for the creation of a Convention on Enforced Disappearance, among which was a project that had been conceived by the ever-remembered Alfredo Galletti, Esq. and Alberto Pedroncini, Esq., among others, can be highlighted. Emilio Mignone and Augusto Conte, members of APDH and then founders of Centro de Estudios Legales y Sociales (CELS), made a very well-founded presentation on the repressive strategy of the military dictatorship: 'La doctrina del paralelismo global.'[25]

Argentine writer Julio Cortázar was present at that event and, in an ever-remembered discourse expressed his opinion about the detained-disappeared: 'This meeting is about that ghostly population, so close and so far at the same time. Above and below the legal considerations, the analyzes and normative research in the field of domestic and international law, we are talking about that people of the shadows.'[26]

Rodolfo Mattarollo[27] describes that, from exile, work was done for the Colloquium, in two concomitant lines: (1) the filing of complaints and (2) political-legal reflection. Those in charge of such work were the

22 Held in the Senate and the National Assembly of Paris, 31 January and 1 February 1981.
23 Commission on Human Rights, Resolution 20 (XXXVI), 29 February 1980.
24 Cited by Rodolfo Mattarollo in *Estrategia represiva de la dictadura militar* (Colihue, 2006).
25 Mignone, Emilio, Conte, Augusto, Colihue, (2006).
26 J. Cortázar, *Negación del Olvido en Proyecto de Convención Internacional para la Protección de todas las personas contra las Desapariciones Forzadas, Serie Debates y Nuevos Desafíos* (Ministerio de Justicia y Derechos Humanos, 2006).
27 Ministerio de Relaciones Exteriores, Testimonios de la Solidaridad Internacional (2007), p. 235 et seq.

Comité Argentino de Información y Solidaridad or CAIS (Argentine Committee of Information and Solidarity); the Comisión Argentina de Derechos Humanos or CADHU (Argentine Commission on Human Rights) with representation in Spain, France, Mexico and the United States; and the Grupo de Abogados Argentinos Exiliados en Francia (Group of Argentine Lawyers Exiled in France, GAAEF).

The preparatory work for participation in the Paris Colloquium motivated the various human rights organizations that had been created in Latin America to connect and discover common interests.

In Latin America, the Federación Latinoamericana de Asociaciones de Familiares de Detenidos-Desaparecidos or FEDEFAM (Latin American Federation of Associations for Relatives of the Detained-Disappeared) was created in 1982, thus committing the victims' relatives to the vanguard of this fight.

There were many problems that had to be solved to achieve the drafting of the International Convention. Recognizing them, at a FEDEFAM's Congress held in 1985, the president of the Federation, Chilean Pamela Pereira, made a presentation in which she argued about the reluctance by the United Nations to draft a convention on enforced disappearance:

> Until now, the United Nations has devoted considerable effort. However, year after year, every time we go to Geneva, we are at odds with the two blocs of power .... The actual situation in the Commission on Human Rights is that no matter how many political criteria we present, we are at odds with the management of power by the big powers.[28]

The situation changed to another important person for the fight against enforced disappearances: Louis Joinet. The expert joined in 1988 the then Subcomisión de Promoción y Protección de los Derechos Humanos (Subcommission on the Promotion and Protection of Human Rights). His main responsibility was to assist the Commission on Human Rights at that time in performing studies on human rights affairs and make recommendations on prevention, discrimination and fundamental freedoms. As one of the 'experts of the Commission', he drafted a project for the Declaration on Enforced Disappearance,[29] which was one of the fundamental precedents for the drafting of the finally approved text.

[28] P. Pereira, *El desaparecimiento forzado como crimen contra la humanidad* (Lithobinder CA, 1987).

[29] Resolution 47/33.

In 1988, the Subcommission, through its Working Group on Detention, decided to take into account the project conceived by Joinet.

This was discussed in the context of a seminar organized in 1988 by the International Commission of Jurists (ICJ), with the participation of members of the Working Group on Detention, experts of the Subcommission and representatives of the relatives of the disappeared and civil society organizations from all over the world. The text that resulted from the seminar was approved by the Subcommission and then submitted to the Commission on Human Rights for its consideration. The Commission formed an Intersessional Open-ended Working Group to continue with the preparation of the document before it was submitted to the General Assembly for approval, which finally occurred on 18 December 1992, by Resolution 47/133, whereby the 21 Articles of the Declaration were enshrined.

This was not done until 2001, when the Commission on Human Rights issued a resolution whereby an expert was appointed to study the complete international law in force and to determine whether there were any gaps that would truly justify a specific Convention on the enforced disappearance offence. Manfred Novak, the appointed expert, stated categorically in his opinion that there were no appropriate defences against enforced disappearance in the international legal system. Therefore, the creation of a formal mechanism of meetings was approved by the Resolution of 2002 of the Commission on Human Rights, when Novak submitted his report.[30]

To approve the formation of an Intersessional Open-ended Working Group for the drafting of a legally binding instrument to punish the enforced disappearance offence, a resolution of the Commission on Human Rights was necessary. It was named like this to avoid mentioning the term 'convention' because there were many States that were against adopting another convention on the grounds that it would lead to greater reporting responsibilities for the States Parties.

The Open-ended Group met two or three times a year between 2003 and 2006. The drafting work was not easy, not only due to the strong opposition from some States but also because of the global mobilization of the victims that resulted from such opposition among NGOs around the world. The Asian Federation Against Involuntary Disappearances (AFAD) was chaired by Munir Said Thalib and its

[30] E/CN.47/2002/71, 8 January 2002.

Secretary-General was Aileen Bacalso. Both took a highly active part in the meetings for the drafting of the Convention. Munir was murdered on 7 September 2004, while on a trip from the Philippines to Geneva to take part in one of the meetings of the Drafting Group of the Convention. The Dutch authorities intervened and determined that he had been poisoned during the flight and reported it to the Philippines. Until now, this offence remains unpunished, and no investigations are being conducted.

The moment when the endearing French Ambassador Bernard Kessedjian announced the approval of the project for the International Convention for the Protection of All Persons from Enforced Disappearance was the end of four years of debates in which more than sixty States and dozens of NGOs from around the world took part.

Among the non-governmental organizations, the following are worth mentioning Federación Asiática contra las Desapariciones Involuntarias (Asian Federation Against Involuntary Disappearances AFAD), Madre de plaza de mayo (Mother of Plaza de Mayo), Asamblea Permanente por los Derechos Humanos (Permanent Assembly for Human Rights APDH), Comision internacional de jurisistas (International Commission of Jurists CIJ), Amnesty International, Human Right Watch and Fédération internationale des droits de l'homme (International Federation of Human Rights).

There were discussions about the definition of the enforced disappearance criminal offence, the commission of such offence by State agents and whether such offence can be committed by non-State agents as well. The agreements reached about such issues resulted in the current drafting of Articles 2 and 3 of the Convention.[31]

On 23 September 2005, the text of the International Convention for the Protection of All Persons from Enforced Disappearance was adopted by the Intersessional Working Group. Despite the initial opposition, the adoption of a Convention was approved during the years of debate.

[31] Art. 2 of the ICPPED: 'For the purposes of this Convention, "enforced disappearance" is considered to be the arrest, detention, abduction or any other form of deprivation of liberty by agents of the State or by persons or groups of persons acting with the authorization, support or acquiescence of the State, followed by a refusal to acknowledge the deprivation of liberty or by concealment of the fate or whereabouts of the disappeared person, which place such a person outside the protection of the law.' Art. 3 of the ICPPED: 'Each State Party shall take appropriate measures to investigate acts defined in Art. 2 committed by persons or groups of persons acting without the authorization, support or acquiescence of the State and to bring those responsible to justice.'

There was a strong opposition to keeping all the Committees of the Conventions in force and, in the same line of reasoning, it was proposed to disband them and unite them in a kind of Chamber with a few experts who would try to ensure that the States Parties complied with all the Conventions. The States were overloaded with work because they had to prepare more reports and, furthermore, the expenses of the Office of the High Commissioner for Human Rights or OHCHR were to be reduced.

In spite of the fact that these debates were concomitant with those held in the Drafting Group of the current Convention on Enforced Disappearance, the creation of a Committee composed of ten independent experts was finally agreed upon. As a result of the negotiation, an Article for the evaluation of the functioning of the Committee was approved, which provides that: 'A Conference of the States Parties will take place at the earliest four years and at the latest six years following the entry into force of this Convention to evaluate the functioning of the Committee and to decide ... whether it is appropriate to transfer to another body ... the monitoring of this Convention.'[32] The reasoning was not to create a new Committee, which would require the States Parties to prepare more reports.

The evaluating Conference took place in Geneva in December 2016 five years after the Committee was created and began to meet. At the Conference, the adoption of the following resolution was agreed upon: 'The Conference of the States Parties to the International Convention for the Protection of All Persons from Enforced Disappearance decides that the Committee on Enforced Disappearances continue to monitor the International Convention for the Protection of All Persons from Enforced Disappearance in accordance with the functions defined in Articles 28 to 36.'[33]

The Committee has jurisdiction over an urgent instrument called 'International Habeas Corpus' by jurist Rodolfo Mattarollo, which involves the power to receive communications from persons who are subject to the jurisdiction of one of the States Parties. If the Committee receives information about a serious breach of the Convention committed by a State Party, it may request the State Party to carry out a visit to the country concerned and present a report to the plenary of the

[32] Art. 27 of the ICPPED.

[33] Available at www.ohchr.org/es/events/2016/1st-conference-states-parties-international-convention-protection-all-enforced.

Committee on Enforced Disappearances (CED) with recommendations to the State Party.[34]

## 6.4 The Secret Procedure of Resolution 1503 and the Latin-American Dictatorships

The Chilean military coup of 1973 was characterized by the high international exposure of its repressive actions and the political actions taken by the exiled, which, with hard and coordinated work, got the United Nations to appoint a Special Rapporteur. The situation in Chile was discussed simultaneously by the Subcommission on Prevention of Discrimination and Protection of Minorities, the Commission on Human Rights and the General Assembly of the United Nations.[35] Upon the consideration of the case by the Subcommission,[36] the Commission was requested to analyze the situation in Chile at its annual session of February 1975. Due to the severity of the cases analyzed by the Commission on Human Rights in 1977 (known today as the Human Rights Council), Antonio Cassese from Italy was appointed as Special Rapporteur.

Furthermore, due to the huge number of complaints and the testimony of many Chileans who took up exile, investigations began to be carried out under the secret procedure established by Resolution 1503,[37] whereby the existence of 'a persistent context of clear and duly proven violations of human rights and fundamental freedoms' was analyzed. Within the context of the secret procedure, it was proposed and approved by a majority vote to take the case up in public consideration by the Commission on Human Rights. In February 1975, the then Commission created a special mechanism for Chile, a Working Group with the following five members: G. Allana (Pakistan), L. Benites (Ecuador), A. Dieye (Senegal), F. Ermacora (Austria) and J. Kamara (Sierra Leone). When the Working Group finished its work in 1979, the Commission appointed special rapporteurs.[38]

[34] Art. 33(1) of the ICPPED.

[35] S. Cerda, La situación de los derechos humanos en Chile (2022).

[36] Resolution 8 (XXVII), 21 August 1974.

[37] Procedure for examining communications relating to violations of human rights and fundamental freedoms Resolution 1503 (XLVIII) of the Economic and Social Council (ECOSOC), adopted in plenary session on 27 May 1970.

[38] A. Dieye (Senegal) 1979–83; R. Lallah (Mauritius) 1983–5; and F. Volio Jiménez (Costa Rica) 1985–90.

In addition, the General Assembly asked the Commission in 1974 to constantly monitor the situation in that country and took it up in public consideration in the Third Committee on an annual basis.[39] Thus, since 1974, the case has always been taken up in public consideration in the Subcommission and the Commission on Human Rights, both with headquarters in Geneva, and in the Third Committee of the General Assembly with headquarters in New York. In 1979–80, the Commission on Human Rights created a special mechanism along with an Independent Expert to examine the situation of disappeared persons or persons whose whereabouts were unknown.[40]

Furthermore, communications received under the secret procedure continued to be treated confidentially and only analyzed by the Situation Group. The role of the Protection Procedures of the United Nations is an example of the variety of alternatives that can be provided in situations of massive and systematic gross violations.

Among the activists and organizations defending human rights in Chile, the Vicaria de la Solidaridad (Vicar of Solidarity) stood out. It was a body of the Catholic Church created by Pope Paul VI at the request of Cardinal Raúl Silva Henríquez to replace the Pro Peace Committee. Its function was to provide assistance to the victims of the military dictatorship.[41]

In Argentina, a paradigmatic case was that of former legislators Mario Abel Amaya and Hipólito Solari Yrigoyen, who were disappeared and brutally tortured. Due to strong international pressure, the Argentine military dictatorship was forced to stop the disappearance of these political and social leaders. In order to do so, they simulated a procedure in which alleged irregular forces threw them out at a roadside. Thus, they pretended that they were rescued by the armed forces, but instead of being released, they were detained in official prisons without charge or trial. Mario Abel Amaya died in prison as a result of torture and Hipólito Solari Yrigoyen was expelled and took up exile in France. Upon his return, he was appointed Itinerant Ambassador by President Raúl Alfonsín, the first president after the return to democracy, who, upon taking office on 10 December 1983, set up, under decree, the National Commission on the Enforced Disappearance of Persons (CONADEP, for

[39] Resolution 3219, 6 November 1974.

[40] Austrian Expert F. Ermacora.

[41] http://archivodigital.londres38.cl/index.php/vicaria-de-la-solidaridad#.

its Spanish acronym) and ordered the prosecution of the Military Juntas. The political opposition was against both measures.

Argentina's case was considered under the same secret procedure as Chile's.[42] However, there was a big difference in the outcome because there was never a vote on whether to take up the case of the Argentine dictatorship. The reason for this was that the Soviet Union and the bloc of its allies always voted in favour of the dictatorship in order to prevent the case from being taken up in public consideration.[43] This support was based on the fact that the USSR was suffering a worldwide boycott of grain sales, which the Argentine military government did not comply with and thus negotiated trade in exchange for impunity.

## 6.5 Theo Van Boven and the Creation of the Working Group on Enforced or Involuntary Disappearances (WGEID)

Theo van Boven served as the UN Director of Human Rights (1977–82). His hierarchical position today would be comparable to that of High Commissioner for Human Rights. From his position, he promoted successful international action against Argentine State terrorism. According to the jurist's account to the author of this chapter, in 1980, after meeting a delegation from the Madres de Plaza de Mayo and after learning of the political reasons why the Argentine dictatorship could not be taken up in public consideration, he promoted the establishment of the Working Group on Enforced and Involuntary Disappearances to request all UN States Parties to provide specific information on the situation of disappeared persons in their territories. The WGEID still continues to work intensively against enforced disappearances around the world.

The eight organizations that are recognized as historical in Argentine are: La Liga Argentina por los Derechos del Hombre (The Argentine League for Human Rights)[44] created in 1937, Servicio de Paz y Justicia (Peace and Justice Service)[45] created in 1974, Asamblea Permanente por los Derechos Humanos (Permanent Assembly for Human Rights)[46] created in 1975, Movimiento Ecumenicopor los Derechos Humanos

42 M. T. Piñero, Exiliados, denuncias y organismos internacionales, p. 12.
43 K. McKeague, Extraña alianza: Relaciones cubano-argentinas en Ginebra, 1976–1983.
44 www.ligaporlosddhh.com.
45 https://serpaj.org.ar.
46 www.apdh-argentina.org.ar.

(Ecumenical Movement for Human Rights)[47] created in 1976, Madres de Plaza de Mayo (Mothers of Plaza de Mayo)[48] created in 1977, Abuelas de Plaza de Mayo (Grandmothers of Plaza de Mayo)[49] created in 1977, Familiares de Detenidos y Desaparecidos por Razones Politicas y Gremiales (Relatives of the Detained and Disappeared for Political and Trade Union Reasons) created in 1976 and Centro de Estudio Legales y Sociales (Center for Legal and Social Studies)[50] created in 1981. This measure would later cost him his job. He worked as a professor in his native Netherlands for many years, but he never gave up the fight for human rights. He also served as the chairman of the European Human Rights Foundation and the director of the Commission of the Churches on International Affairs of the World Council of Churches. In 2002, Theo van Boven joined the United Nations again but this time as Special Rapporteur against Torture.

The Commission on Human Rights was the main political body dealing with human rights issues at the United Nations. It was established in 1946 and was active until 24 March 2006, when the current Human Rights Council began its work.[51] As part of the reform process of the Commission towards the current Human Rights Council, the Subcommission on the Promotion and Protection of Human Rights was replaced by the Advisory Committee. The reform process of the Commission on Human Rights began in 2004. On 24 March 2006, the Commission met for the last time at its 62nd session and referred its pending work to the newly established Human Rights Council for consideration at its inaugural meeting in June 2006.[52] The General Assembly's decision to replace the sixty-year-old CHR with the Council stemmed from a proposal made in the Report of the High-Level Panel on Threats, Challenges and Change, which was presented in December 2004. This report was prepared by a commission appointed by Kofi Annan, UN Secretary-General at the time, which was tasked with

[47] www.derechos.net/medh/.

[48] https://madres.org.

[49] https://abuelas.org.ar.

[50] https://www.cels.org.ar/web/.

[51] See more in M. H. Halperin and D. F. Orentlicher, 'The New UN Human Rights Council' (2016) 13, 3 *Human Rights Brief*.

[52] Commission on Human Rights, Procedural resolution on the closure of the work of the Commission, UN Doc. E/CN.4/2006/L.2, 2, 4, 27 March 2006, available at www1.umn.edu/humanrts/closure.html.

assessing the best way in which the UN could face security threats.[53] In 2006, the General Assembly passed Resolution 60/251 by which the Council was created, and the Commission was terminated.[54]

The negotiation of this resolution was conducted in New York and almost no consultation with delegations in Geneva were conducted. There, the reduction from fifty-three to forty-seven Member States was agreed. As a result of these negotiations, the Latin American and Caribbean Group went from eleven members in the Commission to eight representatives in the current Council. Africa went from fifteen to thirteen Member States and the Western Group went from ten to seven Member States. When the Commission was active, the distribution of the fifty-three Member States was as follows: fifteen from Africa, twelve from Asia, five from Eastern Europe, eleven from GRULAC and ten from Western countries. As of 2006, the Council has forty-seven Member States: thirteen from Africa, thirteen from Asia, six from Eastern Europe, eight from GRULAC and seven from Western countries. This distribution has created a new balance that ensures a fairer distribution of power. Currently, both the GRULAC and the Group of Western countries must necessarily negotiate with Africa and Asia in order to move forward with proposals or projects.

A debate was held about whether the Council would be made up only of countries that respected human rights or whether it could be made up of all UN Member States. It was rightly decided that any State Party to the UN can be elected to the Human Rights Council for a four-year term, with only one consecutive re-election. In addition, the Universal Periodic Review (UPR) was established for all States Parties, in which all countries are reviewed by their peers on the human rights situation in their respective territories. On 7 April 2005, the Secretary-General expressed his support for the universal review by stating as follows: 'Its main task would be to evaluate the fulfilment by all States of all their human rights obligations. This would give concrete expression to the principle that human rights are universal and indivisible.'[55] It was made clear that the

[53] Report of the High-Level Panel [appointed by the UN Secretary General] on Threats, Challenges and Change (2004) A More Secure World: Our Shared Responsibility, available at www.un.org/secureworld/.

[54] Personal interview with Argentine diplomat Sergio Cerdá on 21 October 2022, who participated in all the negotiations in Geneva on the transformation of the Commission into a Council.

[55] Secretary-General's Address to the Commission on Human Rights, available at www.un.org/apps/sg/sgstats.asp?nid=1388#.

Council can also identify those who commit gross human rights violations and carry out a special review.[56]

During its many years of existence, the Commission met for forty-five days between February and March each year. It reported to the Economic and Social Council (ECOSOC) and was eventually elevated to a Council and so directly reports to the General Assembly. Its issues are considered by the Third Committee. In order to have more time and ability to address issues, the Council's agenda and the issues of concern were expanded. In addition, under a General Assembly Resolution,[57] it was established that: 'The Council shall meet regularly throughout the year and schedule no fewer than three sessions per year, including a main session, for a total duration of no less than ten weeks, and shall be able to hold special sessions, when needed, at the request of a member of the Council.'[58]

Currently, the Council meets three times a year, in March, June and September, to discuss a broad and varied agenda where the special procedures present their reports to the plenary of the Council and an interactive dialogue with States Parties and specialized NGOs is held. In this regard: 'The Human Rights Council has three main qualities different from the Commission: a) its quasi-permanent character, b) the fact that it is a subsidiary body of the General Assembly, and c) a greater vocation for universal monitoring of the protection of human rights.'[59]

The participation of non-governmental organizations has been maintained and they are still allowed to participate in the interactive dialogue, and the participation of National Human Rights Institutions (NHRIs) has been increased and strengthened.[60] The time allotted for speeches of one and a half minutes for all speakers is too short to allow for a more in-depth analysis of each topic. However, the variety of voices offers a variety that makes up for the limited time. Moreover, the Rapporteurs,

[56] The General Assembly 'decides also that the Council should address situations of violations of human rights, including gross and systematic violations, and make recommendations thereon'.

[57] AG Resolution 60/251.

[58] UN Doc. A/RES/60/251, 10, 3 April 2006.

[59] J. S. Cerda, *La Reforma de las Naciones Unidas en Nuevos Derechos del Hombre* (EUDEBA, 2011), p. 47.

[60] M. Abraham, *Building the New Human Right Council*, no. 33, August 2007, Friedrich Ebert.

the Committees of the Conventions and the Office of the High Commissioner have carried out outstanding work.

It should be noted that on 29 June 2006, in its first resolution, the Council adopted the International Convention for the Protection of All Persons from Enforced Disappearance,[61] which was subsequently approved by the General Assembly on 20 December 2006.[62]

## 6.6 The Elements of the Enforced Disappearance Criminal Offence in the International Convention, the Inter-American Convention and the Rome Statute

In 1994, the Organization of American States (OAS) adopted the Inter-American Convention on Forced Disappearance of Persons[63] (hereinafter referred to as Inter-American Convention), which precisely defines this criminal conduct as an autonomous offence.

In the preparation of the Convention, the OAS consulted the various NGOs registered as civil society organizations and those with consultative status at the United Nations on the elements of the crime of enforced disappearance. Many of them made written inputs that contributed to the definition adopted in Art. 2 of the Convention.

The American Convention establishes the following definition:

> Article II: For the purposes of this Convention, forced disappearance is considered to be the act of depriving a person or persons of his or their freedom, in whatever way, perpetrated by agents of the State or by persons or groups of persons acting with the authorisation, support, or acquiescence of the State, followed by an absence of information or a refusal to acknowledge that deprivation of freedom or to give information on the whereabouts of that person, thereby impeding his or her recourse to the applicable legal remedies and procedural guarantees.

Article 2 of the International Convention for the Protection of All Persons from Enforced Disappearance establishes:

> For the purposes of this Convention, 'enforced disappearance' is considered to be the arrest, detention, abduction or any other form of

61 Resolution 1/1 of the Human Rights Council, 29 June 2006.

62 GA Res. 61/177, UN Doc. A/RES/61/177, 20 December 2006. The General Assembly had deferred consideration of this Convention to its 61st session, where it was finally approved unanimously.

63 Adopted in Belém do Pará, Brazil, on 9 June 1994, at the twenty-fourth regular session of the General Assembly of the Organization of American States (OAS).

> deprivation of liberty by agents of the State or by persons or groups of persons acting with the authorisation, support or acquiescence of the State, followed by a refusal to acknowledge the deprivation of liberty or by concealment of the fate or whereabouts of the disappeared person, which place such a person outside the protection of the law.

Article 3 establishes the responsibility of the State in the event that a similar act is committed by non-State agents: 'Each State Party shall take appropriate measures to investigate acts defined in Article 2 committed by persons or groups of persons acting without the authorisation, support or acquiescence of the State and to bring those responsible to justice.'

According to the International Convention, the responsibility for enforced disappearance lies with the State and when it is committed by non-State agents, the State is obliged to investigate and punish the crime.

The Rome Statute was approved at the United Nations Diplomatic Conference of Plenipotentiaries on the Establishment of an International Criminal Court.[64] The Statute established the creation of the International Criminal Court. This made a qualitative leap in international criminal law. The International Criminal Court tries persons, inter alia, for the commission of crimes against humanity. The conventional and thematic international system for the protection of human rights protects persons from abuses committed by States through their agents.

Human rights analyze the responsibility of States and strive to ensure that they comply with international commitments to respect the universality of human rights. Article 7 of the Rome Statute establishes the crimes against humanity and determines that they shall mean 'any of the following acts when committed as part of a widespread or systematic attack directed against any civilian population, with knowledge of the attack'.

In turn, subsection (i) defines 'enforced disappearance of persons' as 'the arrest, detention or abduction of persons by, or with the authorisation, support or acquiescence of, a State or *a political organisation*, followed by a refusal to acknowledge that deprivation of freedom or to give information on the fate or whereabouts of those persons, with the intention of removing them from the protection of the law for a prolonged period of time' (emphasis added).

[64] It took place in Rome, 15 June–17 July 1988.

According to this author's opinion, the incorporation of 'a political organisation' among the possible perpetrators of enforced disappearance is a mistake. This definition sought to absolve States of their responsibility for acts of commission or omission in violation of human rights. This is a matter of international criminal law and not human rights, and it will be up to the Court to establish precedent that clarifies the true scope of the term.

Finally, international humanitarian law enshrined in the Geneva Conventions of 1949 governs the conventional law of war, and the Additional Protocols of 1977 deal with irregular armed forces, their responsibilities and rights. As regards the scope of the International Convention, for the first time in international human rights law, the right not to be subjected to enforced disappearance has been explicitly formulated with all the corresponding consequences and obligations for States. While the Convention was in force, this did not prevent the current chairperson of AFAD from being abducted and reported disappeared for more than a week, despite the vigorous international action requiring his safe return. This fortunately happened and he still serves as the chairperson of the Federation. His former Secretary-General currently serves as the president of the International Coalition against Enforced Disappearances (ICAED).

The Convention includes the right to truth as a collective value of society as a whole and the right of relatives to recover the mortal remains of their loved ones. It also establishes very important guarantees regarding the prohibition of secret detention, which is highly significant too as a fundamental principle of human rights.

The Convention incorporates a broad concept of victims by also including kith and kin and even lawyers. It confirms the right to obtain reparation and the right of children to recover their true identity, which is contained in Article 3 (1) of the Convention on the Rights of the Child that states that the best interests of the child shall always be a primary consideration.

The strong position of some States wishing to include non-State agents among those responsible for enforced disappearance provoked heated discussions. Finally, this was settled by establishing the concept of enforced disappearance in Article 2 of the Convention, which can be exclusively perpetrated by agents of the State or with the support or acquiescence of the State. It is clear that, at the time of its adoption, the criterion was that only agents of the State can violate human rights and it is the responsibility of States Parties to adopt legislation that provides for the punishment of conduct similar to enforced disappearance but committed by individuals.[65]

Another issue that prompted interpretation and an interpretative declaration by the CED was that the last paragraph of Art. 2, which states that the conduct punished places the person outside the protection of the law, led the same States Parties that opposed the Convention and wanted to incorporate non-State agents into the definition contained in Art. 2 to argue that placing the person outside the protection of the law is a fourth element required for the criminal conduct to be met and not a consequence of:

- deprivation of liberty
- by agents of the State
- followed by a refusal to acknowledge the deprivation of liberty.

Louis Joinet's report included the prohibition of amnesties and pardons for those responsible for enforced disappearances and their accomplices, as well as military[66]or special tribunals and the State's obligation not to restrict access to information.

## 6.7 Conclusion

This chapter has analyzed the significance of the NGO's involvement in fighting against enforced disappearances of Latin American dictatorships from the 1960s and 1970s to the present day. They have played an important role in the establishment of the WGEID, drafting the ICCPED, as well as demonstrated the strength of international solidarity. The NGOs in Latin America, while being at the forefront of developing legal solutions to address enforced disappearances, deeply benefitted from worldwide support. This solidarity is now brought forward by NGOs to other regions and contexts, in which people are experiencing widespread disappearances.

We live in a world with tremendous advances in sciences and arts that coexists with wars, massive displacements and great inequalities. Therefore, the new generations of social activists, politicians, scientists and academics committed to their time are called upon to keep alive the hope in this third decade of the twenty-first century. In this way, the old

[65] Art. 3 of the ICPPED.

[66] H. Ravenna, *Justicia militar: Juez natural o fuero especial, en educación y derechos humanos* (Centro Editor de América Latina, IIHR, 1989).

NGO structures are being replaced by new organizations with actions adapted to the new times.

However, when paths are closed or strength declines, the memory of those Madres de Plaza de Mayo, heartbroken and crying out for their children, continues to mark the path in the collective memory of the people.

# 7

# Contemporary Disappearances in Mexico

## A Conceptual Challenge for the International Framework on Enforced Disappearances

LENE GUERCKE*

### 7.1 Introduction

Since the adoption of a militarized approach to public security in Mexico in late 2006, commonly known as the 'war on drugs', violence has exploded and serious human rights violations, including enforced disappearances, have risen sharply. Mexico is currently the second country with most Urgent Actions before the Committee on Enforced Disappearances (CED/the Committee),[1] the treaty body created by the International Convention for the Protection of all Persons from Enforced Disappearance (ICPPED/the Convention),[2] and, in 2021, was the first country to be visited by the CED.[3] In its report on the visit, as well as in

* Part of this chapter is based on research that received funding from the European Research Council (ERC) under the European Union's Horizon 2020 research and innovation programme ('Digital Memories', grant agreement No. 677955).

[1] USAID, I(dh)eas, ONU-DH, El carácter vinculante de las Acciones Urgentes del Comité de la ONU contra la Desaparición Forzada en México (2023), p. 9, available at https://www.idheas.org.mx/publicaciones-idheas/el-caracter-vinculante-de-las-acciones-urgentes-del-comite-de-la-onu-contra-la-desaparicion-forzada-en-mexico/.

[2] International Convention for the Protection of All Persons from Enforced Disappearance, 1726 UNTS 3 (ICCPED), 23 December 2010. Urgent actions are a unique feature of the ICPPED. According to Art. 30 ICPPED, any person with a legitimate interest can present a request to urgently search for and find a person who has disappeared to the CED. The CED will then contact the State Party and request information about the person and their situation. See Office of the High Commissioner for Human Rights, Enforced Disappearances, Fact Sheet No. 6, Rev. 4, 2023, p. 56, available at *www.ohchr.org/en/publications/fact-sheets/fact-sheet-no-6-rev-4-enforced-disappearances*.

[3] Committee on Enforced Disappearances (CED), Report of the Committee on Enforced Disappearances on Its Visit to Mexico: Findings, UN Doc. CED/C/MEX/VR/1, 18 May 2022. According to Art. 33 ICPPED, the Committee can request to visit a State

prior and subsequent concluding observations, the Committee expressed 'deep' concern over the widespread nature of disappearances throughout the country and the prevalence of 'almost absolute impunity and revictimization'.[4] Disappearances in Mexico today are complex to understand and conceptualize from a legal perspective due to the involvement of both State and non-State actors as perpetrators, which implies that not all of these crimes can be categorized as *enforced* disappearances under international human rights law (IHRL). The legal questions that the phenomenon of disappearances in Mexico today raises can become equally relevant for other contexts where State and non-State actors are involved in the disappearance of persons, for example, in the context of migration.[5]

This chapter first provides a brief overview of the complexity of present-day disappearances in Mexico. It then zooms in on the issue of non-State actors as perpetrators of disappearances and explains how the Mexican domestic legal framework addressed the issue of different perpetrators by creating two distinct crimes. Further, it presents and discusses two questions that the Mexican context raises for IHRL: the State's failure to identify dead bodies as a form of enforced disappearance, on the one hand, and impunity as a form of acquiescence, on the other hand. The chapter's final section presents the CED's recently adopted 'Statement on non-State actors in the context of the International Convention for the Protection of All Persons from Enforced Disappearances' (Statement on Non-State Actors) and discusses how the definition of acquiescence provided by the CED could impact the categorization of disappearances in Mexico. It is argued that the CED's definition of acquiescence could and should be applied in such a way as to consider a large number of disappearances in Mexico today as enforced disappearances, due to the State's general awareness of risk of widespread disappearances and its failure to respond to clear patterns.

party after it has received 'reliable information indicating that a State Party is seriously violating the provisions of this Convention' and consulted the State party on the matter. Importantly, CED can only visit a State party if the latter agrees to the visit in accordance with Art. 33 ICPPED.

[4] Ibid., para. 24; CED, Concluding observations on the report submitted by Mexico, UN Doc. CED/C/MEX/CO/1, March 2015, para. 10, 5; CED, Observaciones finales sobre la información complementaria presentada por México con arreglo al artículo 29, párrafo 4 de la Convención, UN Doc. CED/C/MEX/OAI/2, 29 September 2023, paras. 5, 11(b).

[5] CED, General Comment No. 1 on Enforced Disappearances in the Context of Migration, UN Doc. CED/C/GC/1, 18 September 2023.

Based on the CED's Statement, the chapter proposes a presumption of acquiescence as the most appropriate approach in the Mexican context, as it places the burden of proof on the State in favour of the victims, thus potentially overcoming a seemingly arbitrary classification of victims into two categories. In that way, the State's contribution to the suffering of relatives could be more adequately reflected.

## 7.2 The Situation of Disappearances in Mexico

### *7.2.1 Contextualizing Disappearances in Mexico*

Mexico's history of enforced disappearances dates back to the so-called dirty war[6] period between the 1960s and mid-1980s. At the time, the then one-party State of the Institutional Revolutionary Party (PRI) pursued a strategy of repression against political opponents, including rural and urban guerrillas, that included enforced disappearances.[7] Alongside this legacy of enforced disappearances, whose victims are still demanding truth and justice,[8] since the onset of the 'war on drugs' in the country in late 2006 the number of disappeared persons has risen steeply. According to data provided by the National Search Commission (CNB for its Spanish initials) as of February 2024, over 114,000 persons had

[6] The term 'dirty war', while commonly used to describe the period of organized and widespread State repression against political opponents, is not without controversy. See M. De Vecchi Gerli, '¡Vivxs Lxs Queremos! The Battles for Memory around the Disappeared in Mexico', PhD Thesis, University College London (2018), p. 15, available at https://discovery.ucl.ac.uk/id/eprint/10064633/.

[7] For a historical analysis of State-sponsored violence and enforced disappearances in Mexico, see, for example, E. A. Montaño, C. V. Ovalle and J. S. Granada-Cardona, 'Recasting history to cast off shadows: State violence in Mexico, 1958–2018' in S. Mandolessi and K. Olalde Rico (eds.), *Disappearances in Mexico: From the 'Dirty War' to the 'War on Drugs'* (Routledge, 2022).

[8] Several official attempts to deal with the legacy of the 'dirty war' by creating specialized institutions, including a special prosecutor's office, have failed. Most recently, in October 2021, a truth commission was created by presidential decree to investigate and clarify political violence and human rights violations committed between 1965–90. However, the commissioners have already denounced the lack of full access to archives of one of the key security institutions involved in human rights violations. See P. Ferri, 'La Comisión de la Verdad para la Guerra Sucia denuncia la falta de colaboración del Centro Nacional de Inteligencia' (2023) *El País México*, available at https://elpais.com/mexico/2023-08-15/la-comision-de-la-verdad-para-la-guerra-sucia-denuncia-la-falta-de-colaboracion-del-centro-nacional-de-inteligencia.html.

disappeared or gone missing since 1962.[9] Among these, according to these data, 89,415 persons had been disappeared since 2006.[10]

The rise in disappearances, and violence more generally, cannot be attributed to a single cause. Nonetheless, experts agree that the militarization of public security as a means to fight drug-trafficking organizations played an important role in the sharp increase of human rights violations and violence more generally since late 2006. This relates, on the one hand, to the participation of the historically unaccountable Mexican armed forces in countering organized crime,[11] and, on the other hand, to the splintering of heretofore large criminal organizations into smaller warring groups following the initial strategy of removing the top leadership from large organizations.[12] To add complexity, the State and non-State actors involved do not always act independently but at times collaborate in the commission of crimes, including disappearances.[13]

[9] Available at https://versionpublicarnpdno.segob.gob.mx/Dashboard/ContextoGeneral. It is important to note that in December 2023, President López Obrador presented an alternative version of the statistics of disappeared persons, based on a recount ordered by him earlier in the year, alleging that there were fewer disappeared persons. The recount itself and the presentation of alternative figures led to an outcry among relatives' associations and non-governmental organizations, who have since presented several cases of disappeared persons who no longer appear on the register. Nonetheless, and in view of the methodological criticisms raised, this chapter uses the data provided on the original website of the National Register of Disappeared and Missing Persons (RNPDO). See, for example, Movimiento por Nuestros Desaparecidos en México, 'Nuestra lucha no se borra; exigimos transparencia y diálogo sobre el registro de personas desaparecidas y toda política que nos impacte', 19 December 2024, available at https://movndmx.org/nuestra-lucha-no-se-borra, E. Tzuc, 'Tiene Censo de AMLO Otros Datos … Equivocados Sobre Desaparecidos En México', *Animal Politico*, 22 January 2024, available at https://animalpolitico.com/sociedad/desaparecidos-censo-datos-equivocados; A. Daen and M. Nochebuena, 'Omisiones, Dudas y Opacidad: El Censo de Desaparecidos Del Gobierno de AMLO', *Animal Politico*, 15 December 2023, available at https://animalpolitico.com/verificacion-de-hechos/te-explico/omisiones-falsedades-nuevo-censo-desaparecidos.

[10] The total number of disappeared and missing persons for that period is 97,672. See https://versionpublicarnpdno.segob.gob.mx/Dashboard/Sociodemografico.

[11] See *Case of Alvarado Espinoza and Others v. Mexico*, Inter-American Court of Human Rights Series C No. 370, 2018, paras. 59ff.

[12] See M. Serrano, 'Mexico: A humanitarian crisis in the making' in W. G. Pansters, B. T. Smith and P. Watt (eds.), *Beyond the Drug War in Mexico: Human Rights, the Public Sphere and Justice* (Routledge, 2017).

[13] See, for example, CED, Report on Visit to Mexico: Findings, para. 13; Inter-American Commission on Human Rights (IACHR), Situation of Human Rights in Mexico, OEA/Ser.L/V/II.Doc. 44/15, 2015, paras. 34–52.

Indeed, given the pervasiveness of corruption, it is often difficult to draw clear lines between these actors, especially organized criminal groups and State actors.[14] Existing information about victims and perpetrators of disappearances compiled by civil society organizations, relatives, journalists and academia, while based on a rather limited number of cases in comparison to the overall number of disappearances, show that the modes of disappearances, the victims and the perpetrators differ depending on the time period and the geographic location. Consequently, it is not possible to provide a single, general account of disappearances across Mexico or of who the victims and perpetrators are.[15]

### *7.2.2 Victims*

Victims of disappearances in Mexico today are a heterogenous group and, contrary to assertions by authorities[16] and persisting criminalizing attitudes against victims and relatives by society at large, there is no evidence to suggest that most victims had ties to organized crime.[17] Social leaders or activists continue to be among the victims of disappearances today,[18] yet most current disappearances cannot be tied to any form of political or social activism. Moreover, and contrary to the traditional image of security forces as perpetrators, both police officers and members of the military have also been disappeared.[19] Although the

[14] See, for example, Fidh and I(dh)eas (2021) 'Mexico: Criminal Structure within the Public Prosecutor's Office of the State of Nayarit and Crimes Against Humanity', No. 769a, available at www.opensocietyfoundations.org/sites/default/files/corruption-that-kills-en-20180502.pdf.

[15] On this complexity, see also P. Calveiro, 'Disappearance and governmentality in Mexico' in S. Mandolessi and K. Olalde Rico (eds.), *Disappearances in Mexico: From the 'Dirty War' to the 'War on Drugs'* (Routledge, 2022), pp. 85–92. For a proposal of a typology of the different fates of victims of disappearances in Mexico today, see A. A. Pozos Barcelata, *El Cuerpo Ausente como Sujeto Político: El Proceso de Construcción de la Desaparición de Personas en México como un Problema de Acción Política (1969–2018)* (Université du Québec, 2018), p. 149ff.

[16] CED, Report on Visit to Mexico: Findings, para. 39.

[17] See, for example, Observatorio sobre Desaparición e Impunidad (ODIM), *Informe Sobre Desapariciones en el Estado de Nuevo León Con Información de Cadhac* (Facultad Latinoamericana de Ciencias Sociales, 2017), pp. 29–30.

[18] See C. Robledo Silvestre, 'Desaparecer por defender el territorio', A dónde van los desaparecidos, 18 March 2021, available at https://adondevanlosdesaparecidos.org/2021/03/18/desaparecer-por-defender-el-territorio/.

[19] In the north-eastern State of Nuevo León, for example, the first disappearance cases registered by the NGO CADHAC, were of police officers. See ODIM, *Informe sobre Desapariciones*, p. 25; '¿Les ha quedado grande el cargo? lanza madre de militar

majority of reported disappearance victims are male,[20] disappearances of women and girls have risen significantly in recent years, which can be the result of human trafficking, increased violence in general, as well as gender-based violence, such as femicides.[21] Finally, certain groups are especially vulnerable to becoming victims of disappearances, while at the same time being the least visible. This includes migrants, who risk falling victim to human trafficking or being kidnapped at the hands of organized crime, either acting alone or in collusion with immigration (or other) authorities,[22] as well as victims belonging to indigenous groups who experience high levels of exclusion, racism and marginalization and are often overlooked.[23] Communities living in territories of certain economic or extractive interests can suffer high levels of violence, including forced displacement and disappearances.[24]

desaparecido a Peña y Cienfuegos', Proceso, 8 May 2018, available at https://www.proceso.com.mx/nacional/2018/5/8/les-ha-quedado-grande-el-cargo-lanza-madre-de-militar-desaparecido-pena-cienfuegos-204640.html.

20 See https://versionpublicarnpdno.segob.gob.mx/Dashboard/ContextoGeneral.

21 Committee on the Elimination of Discrimination against Women, Concluding observations on the Ninth Periodic Report of Mexico, UN Doc. CEDAW/C/MEX/CO/9, 25 July 2018, paras. 23–4; see also K. Ansolabehere et al., *Nombrarlas para encontrarlas. Contexto, dinámicas y respuestas en torno a la desaparición de mujeres en el centro de México* (ODIM, FLACSO, 2021); A. Ayala Martínez, 'Buscando mujeres desaparecidas en vida: Entre trata de personas y violencia de género', A dónde van los desaparecidos, 5 March 2021, available at https://adondevanlosdesaparecidos.org/2021/03/04/buscando-mujeres-desaparecidas-en-vida-entre-trata-de-personas-y-violencia-de-genero/.

22 CED, Report on Visit to Mexico: Findings, paras. 18–20; *Informe presentado al Comité contra la Desaparición Forzada en vista del dialogo de seguimiento con respecto a México, en ocasión de la 15ªsesión* (Fundación para la Justicia y el Estado Democrático de Derecho and TRIAL International, 2018), available at https://trialinternational.org/wp-content/uploads/2018/11/Full-report-to-the-Committee-on-Enforced-Disappearances-Spanish.pdf.

23 See, for example, R. Aída Hernández Castillo, 'Las múltiples ausencias de los indígenas desaparecidos en México', A dónde van los desaparecidos, 25 April 2019, available at https://adondevanlosdesaparecidos.org/2019/04/25/las-multiples-ausencias-de-los-indigenas-desaparecidos-en-mexico/; X. Antillón Najlis, *Yo sólo quería que amaneciera impactos psicosociales del caso Ayotzinapa* (Fundar, Centro de Análisis e Investigación, 2018).

24 C. Jiménez-Damary, Visit to Mexico – Report of the Special Rapporteur on the human rights of internally displaced persons, UN Doc. A/HRC/53/35/Add.2, 27 June 2023; CED, Report on Visit to Mexico: Findings, para. 21; Silvestre, 'Desaparecer por defender el territorio'.

### 7.2.3 *Perpetrators*

Perpetrators are also heterogeneous and include State actors belonging to different security forces and a variety of non-State actors.[25] Among the latter, the most prominent are organized criminal groups. In some instances, disappearances are known to have been used in a strategic manner by such groups to ensure territorial control and intimidate local populations.[26] Conversely, some disappearances may also be perpetrated by individuals who are not part of either State security forces or organized criminal groups, for example, in the context of gender-based violence.[27] In yet other cases, victims of 'regular' kidnappings are not liberated after the family has paid the ransom, thus converting the kidnapping into a disappearance.[28] Disappearances committed by non-State actors in the Mexican context thus appear to be motivated by different factors, ranging from criminal purposes such as human trafficking and forced recruitment into criminal organizations,[29] to terrorizing the population as a means of securing territorial control, as well as to 'simply' getting of rid of dead bodies. This diversity of victims, perpetrators and motives, compounded by the general lack of effective investigations that could provide more clarity about the perpetrators and motives, complicates the understanding of disappearances in Mexico today.

### 7.2.4 *Forensic Negligence*

A final important aspect of the crisis of disappearances in present-day Mexico is the country's forensic crisis and the incapacity of forensic authorities to identify dead bodies and remains, as shown by the

[25] See CED, Report on Visit to Mexico: Findings, para. 13; IACHR, Situation of Human Rights in Mexico, paras. 34–52.

[26] This has particularly been documented in relation to the criminal group Los Zetas. See, for example, Human Rights Clinic, '*Control ... over the Entire State of Coahuila*' *An Analysis of Testimonies in Trials against Zeta Members in San Antonio, Austin, and Del Rio, Texas* (The University of Texas School of Law, 2017).

[27] See Ansolabehere and others, *Nombrarlas para encontrarlas.*

[28] J. A. Román, 'Familia veracruzana pagó rescate por un hijo y perdió a dos de sus miembros', La Jornada, 2 November 2015, available at https://www.jornada.com.mx/2015/11/02/politica/005n2pol.

[29] See, for example, A. Guillén and D. Petersen, 'El regreso del infierno: los desaparecidos que están vivos', A dónde van los desaparecidos, 4 February 2019, available at https://adondevanlosdesaparecidos.org/2019/02/04/los-desaparecidos-que-estan-vivos/.

existence of at least 52,000 unidentified bodies in the country.[30] Added to the failure to identify, there are numerous examples of mishandling of dead bodies by authorities, who, overwhelmed with the number of bodies they were receiving, buried them in official mass graves or disposed of them in other ways. In many instances, burials did not follow specific protocols and were conducted negligently without adequate documentation, resulting in the confusion of bodies and their exact location in cemeteries.[31] Such malpractice was discovered on a number of occasions during exhumation processes, for example, when exhumed bodies did not correspond to existing registers or when the number of bodies in exhumed graves was much higher than that officially documented.[32] Additionally, due to inadequate records and lacking databases, even identified bodies have been buried in official mass graves without notification of the families.[33] One particularly concerning example of mishandling is the cremation of 1,430 unidentified bodies without prior taking of DNA samples in the State of Jalisco between 2006 and 2015.[34] In several states, due to a lack of capacity in forensic institutions, the latter are sub-contracting private funeral homes to deal with bodies found in clandestine mass graves. These private companies are tasked with conducting the necropsies, which can lead to a loss of crucial data needed to identify the person.[35]

[30] Animal Político, 'El gobierno reconoce "crisis forense": Hay 52 mil cuerpos sin identificar', *Animal Político*, 17 March 2022, available at www.animalpolitico.com/sociedad/censo-base-encinas-cuerpos-identificar-mexico; E. Tzuc and M. Turati, 'Un País Rebasado Por Sus Muertos', Quinto Elemento Lab, 22 September 2020, available at www.quintoelab.org/crisis-forense/un-pais-rebasado-por-sus-muertos/.

[31] See, for example, F. Rodríguez, 'Desaparecer Dos Veces: La Burocracia Que Pierde Cuerpos', Quinto Elemento Lab, 28 September 2020, available at https://quintoelab.org/crisisforense/desaparecer-dos-veces-la-burocracia-que-pierde-cuerpos/.

[32] Tzuc and Turati, 'Un País Rebasado'.

[33] E. Tzuc, 'Cruce de datos: La clave para localizar a miles de personas desaparecidas', A dónde van los desaparecidos, 23 January 2023, available at https://adondevanlosdesaparecidos.org/2023/01/23/cruce-de-datos-la-clave-para-localizar-a-miles-de-personas-desaparecidas/.

[34] Centro de Justicia para la Paz y el Desarrollo (CEPAD), 'Incineraciones de Cuerpos No Identificados. Crímenes Sin Justicia', 30 Enero 2019, available at https://cepad.org.mx/2019/01/incineraciones-cuerpos-no-identificados-crimenes-sin-justicia/; D. F. Migues, 'Desaparecer Hasta Volverse Cenizas', Quinto Elemento Lab, 9 April 2019, available at https://quintoelab.org/project/volversecenizas.

[35] M. Vizcarra, 'Crisis Forense: Cuando Las Funerarias Suplieron al Semefo', Quinto Elemento Lab, 6 October 2020, available at https://quintoelab.org/crisisforense/crisis-forense-cuando-las-funerarias-suplieron-al-semefo/.

The forensic crisis led to the establishment in late 2019 of an Extraordinary Forensic Mechanism (EFM), in order to accelerate and support the identification of remains. However, due to a lack of funds, uncertainties about the members' contracts, insufficient political support and institutional collaboration, as well as internal disagreements, by early 2023 almost all members of the EFM had resigned and it is now to be replaced by another mechanism.[36] Notably, even with the establishment of extraordinary mechanisms, the identification of such a large amount of remains is likely to take decades, especially considering that violence and disappearances continue.[37] Moreover, in addition to the tens of thousands of known unidentified bodies, there are also thousands of clandestine mass graves spread across the Mexican territory, suggesting an even greater burden of identification of as yet unknown scale.[38] The mishandling of remains by authorities can be another effective cause for a person's disappearance in Mexico, which is very different from the 'original' terrorizing aim usually associated with the crime of enforced disappearance.[39] In these cases, even though non-State actors may have been responsible for killing the victim, their *disappearance* is the result of negligence by State actors, even though, as I discuss in Section 7.3, it is unlikely to be considered an enforced disappearance under international law.

The foregoing overview illustrates the complexity of disappearances in Mexico today. On the one hand, the heterogeneity of perpetrators, victims and manners in which persons are disappeared means that there are multiple explanations for the occurrence of disappearances. Furthermore, the lack of effective investigations into these cases implies that there is often very little information from which to draw on for the

[36] E. Cortez Morales, 'El Mecanismo Extraordinario de Identificación Forense: Un Proyecto Trunco', Instituto Mexicano de Derechos Humanos y Democracia (IMDHD), 9 March 2023, available at www.imdhd.org/comunicacion/blog/el-mecanismo-extraordinario-de-identificacion-forense-un-proyecto-trunco..

[37] Tzuc and Turati, 'Un País Rebasado'.

[38] Most recently, the estimated number of clandestine mass graves is above 5,600. See E. Tzuc, 'México Rebasa Las 5 Mil 600 Fosas Clandestinas', Quinto Elemento Lab, 9 October 2023, available at https://quintoelab.org/project/mexico-rebasa-cinco-mil-fosas-clandestinas.

[39] Javier Yankelevich makes a useful conceptual distinction between the state of *being disappeared* and being the victim of the crime of disappearance, which may or may not be the cause of this state. J. Yankelevich, 'El Concepto de Persona Desaparecida' in J. Yankelevich (ed.), *Manual de Capacitación para la Búsqueda de Personas. La Voz de la Academia.* (Comisión Nacional de Búsqueda, 2020), vol. I, p. 24. The effect, however, can be equally terrorizing. I thank María de Vecchi for raising this point.

purpose of analysis. Simultaneously, the forensic crisis further adds to the complexity of disappearances in Mexico today, because it shows that many persons who are disappeared may not be victims of a disappearance in a legal sense. In that sense, contemporary disappearances are difficult to comprehend and explain because they differ significantly from the traditional understanding of enforced disappearances as crimes committed by authoritarian – or otherwise repressive – States against political opponents.[40] Moreover, and perhaps relatedly, it also complicates their categorization from a legal perspective, which I discuss in Section 7.3.

## 7.3 Disappearances in Mexico from a Legal Perspective

The complexity of disappearances in Mexico today not only creates challenges for understanding and addressing the issue in practice. It also highlights questions from a legal perspective, which stem from the interrelated issues of involvement of non-State actors in the commission of disappearances, who may or may not have ties to State actors, and the issue of severe State omissions and malpractice. In this section, I briefly outline the legal consequences of non-State actor involvement in the commission of (enforced) disappearances from an IHRL perspective and discuss how the domestic Mexican legal framework addressed this matter. I then engage with two questions that the Mexican context raises from the IHRL perspective, concerning the mishandling of remains and the notion of acquiescence.

### *7.3.1 Non-State Actors as Perpetrators of Disappearances*

According to the definition in IHRL, enforced disappearances can only be committed by State agents or non-State actors who are in some manner connected to the State. This is illustrated by the definition of enforced disappearances contained in article 2 ICPPED:

> 'Enforced disappearance' is considered to be the arrest, detention, abduction or any other form of deprivation of liberty *by agents of the State or by persons or groups of persons acting with the authorization, support or acquiescence of the State*, followed by a refusal to acknowledge the deprivation of liberty or by concealment of the fate or whereabouts of the disappeared person, which place such a person outside the protection of the law. (emphasis added)

[40] M. R. Berman and R. S. Clark, 'State terrorism: Disappearances' (1982) 13 *Rutgers Law Journal* 531.

The UN Declaration on the Protection of All Persons from Enforced Disappearance (DPPED) and the Inter-American Convention on Forced Disappearance of Persons (IACFDP), instruments that predate the ICPPED, contain similar definitions.[41] Within International Criminal Law (ICL) the definition of enforced disappearance varies slightly: first, it requires an intention to remove the victim from the protection of the law for a 'prolonged period of time'. Second, it refers to the commission of an act 'by, or with the authorization, support or acquiescence of, a State *or a political organization*' (emphasis added),[42] which has led to the interpretation that, under ICL, certain types of non-State actors can commit enforced disappearances as crimes against humanity even without involvement of State actors.[43] While this is important to keep in mind, the main focus of this chapter lies on IHRL because the ICL definition only applies in the context of a systematic or widespread attack, as defined in the Rome Statute.[44] Although arguments have been made that violence in Mexico has reached this threshold in certain areas and during certain periods of time,[45] it is beyond the scope of this chapter to engage with this question.

41 The UN Declaration uses the phrase 'by officials of different branches or levels of Government, or by organized groups or private individuals acting on behalf of, or with the support, direct or indirect, consent or acquiescence of the Government', Preamble, Declaration on the Protection of All Persons from Enforced Disappearance, UN Doc. A/RES/47/133, 18 December 1992. The IACFDP wording is almost identical to the ICPPED and refers to acts 'perpetrated by agents of the State or by persons or groups of persons acting with the authorization, support, or acquiescence of the state', Art. II, Inter-American Convention on Forced Disappearance of Persons, 33 ILM 1529, 9 June 1994.

42 Art. 7(2)(i), Rome Statute of the International Criminal Court, 2187 UNTS 90, 17 July 1998.

43 CED, Statement on non-State actors in the context of the International Convention for the Protection of All Persons from Enforced Disappearances, UN Doc. CED/C/10, 2 May 2023, para. 17; O. de Frouville, 'Criminalizing or trivializing enforced disappearances? The issue of "non-State actors"' in O. de Frouville and P. Sturma (eds.), *La pénalisation des droits de l'homme* (Pedone, 2021), pp. 147–96; A. R. Wolffenbuttel, 'Enforced Disappearances: Applicable to Political Organizations?' (2021) 61 *Virginia Journal of International Law Online* 159.

44 Rome Statute, Art. 7(1).

45 'Criminal Structure within the Public Prosecutor's Office'; Fidh and Comisión Mexicana de Defensa y Promoción de los Derechos Humanos (CMDPDH), Art. 15 Communication under the Rome Statute to the International Criminal Court Regarding the Alleged Commission of Crimes against Humanity in Chihuahua, México between 2008 and 2010 (2018), available at www.fidh.org/IMG/pdf/mexique715anglais-1_final.pdf; Fidh, Centro Diocesano para los Derechos Humanos Fray Juan de Larios and Familias Unidas en Búsqueda y Localización de Personas Desaparecidas, Mexico Coahuila: Ongoing Crimes against Humanity (2017), available at https://www.fidh.org/

In addition to the attribution criteria of authorization, support or acquiescence listed in the definition of enforced disappearance, the ICPPED contains a separate article dealing explicitly with disappearances that do not reach this threshold. After much discussion during the drafting process, the inclusion of article 3 ICPPED was a compromise to address the reality that in certain contexts non-State actors were perpetrating disappearances, without diluting the responsibility of the State by calling such crimes 'enforced disappearances'.[46] Article 3 establishes obligations of States to 'take appropriate measures to investigate' and 'bring to justice' the perpetrators of disappearances committed by non-State actors acting 'without the authorisation, support, or acquiescence of the State'. Beyond this, disappearances falling within article 3 are not explicitly mentioned in the Convention. In this way, article 3 clearly indicates that there is a difference between enforced disappearances and disappearances committed by non-State actors falling within article 3 ICPPED. This understanding has been reiterated by the CED in its observations on reports by State Parties[47] and in its recently adopted Statement on Non-State Actors, which I discuss below.[48]

IMG/pdf/angmexico_coahuila_ongoing_crimes_against_humanity_fidh-final_a_revisar-1.pdf; OSJI, *Undeniable Atrocities: Confronting Crimes against Humanity in Mexico.* (Open Society Foundations, 2016); Fidh, CMDPDH and Citizens' Commission of Human Rights of the Northeast (CCDH), Mexico: Report on the Alleged Commission of Crimes against Humanity in Baja California between 2006 and 2012 (2014) 642a, available at www.fidh.org/IMG/pdf/mexique642ang2014web.pdf.

[46] Commission on Human Rights, Report of the Intersessional Open-Ended Working Group to Elaborate a Draft Legally Binding Normative Instrument for the Protection of All Persons from Enforced Disappearance, UN Doc. E/CN.4/2004/59, 23 February 2004, paras. 29–41; Commission on Human Rights, Report of the Intersessional Open-Ended Working Group to Elaborate a Draft Legally Binding Normative Instrument for the Protection of All Persons from Enforced Disappearance, UN Doc. E/CN.4/2005/66, 10 March 2005, paras. 29–35; Commission on Human Rights, Report of the Intersessional Open-Ended Working Group to Elaborate a Draft Legally Binding Normative Instrument for the Protection of All Persons from Enforced Disappearance, UN Doc. E/CN.4/2006/57, 2 February 2006, paras. 12–14. See also de Frouville, *Criminalizing or Trivializing Enforced Disappearances?*.

[47] See for example CED, Concluding Observations on the Report Submitted by Colombia under Art. 29 (1) of the Convention, UN Doc. CED/C/COL/CO/1, 27 October 2016, para. 15; CED, Concluding Observations on the Report Submitted by Iraq under Art. 29 (1) of the Convention, UN Doc. CED/C/IRQ/CO/1, 13 October 2015, para. 12.

[48] CED, Statement on non-State actors, para. 16.

## 7.4 Disappearances in Mexico from the Perspective of IHRL

Returning to the Mexican context, where both State and non-State actors commit disappearances, from an IHRL perspective not all of these disappearances can thus be considered as *enforced* disappearances. For example, an organized criminal group that abducts a group of construction workers, holds them at a secret location, executes them and buries their remains in a clandestine mass grave, thereby effectively disappearing them, is not committing an *enforced* disappearance because it is acting on its own account without any apparent connection to the State. If, however, the same group committed a massacre and buried the victims in a clandestine mass grave while a police convoy stood guard nearby – for example, because the officers had received a bribe – the State is acquiescing to the act,[49] and the case becomes one of *enforced* disappearance. In a third scenario, where the criminal group that commits the massacre is known to have close connections to the local police force and can therefore act undisturbed and without fear of being held to account, the indirect involvement of the State is less visible, and it is not clear whether acquiescence could be established. This example illustrates that the dividing line between different legal types of disappearances in the Mexican context is very thin.

The legal distinction is of relevance, however, because it implies that there exist two types of disappearances in Mexico today, and, consequently, two types of victims. To illustrate the difference, article 24 ICPPED, which provides a broad definition of victims and establishes their comprehensive rights to truth, reparation and participation, only applies to victims of *enforced* disappearances, excluding victims of disappearances falling within article 3 ICPPED.[50] The exclusion of victims of disappearances falling within article 3 ICPPED from the scope of article 24 implies that their relatives are also not considered victims under the Convention. Due to the detrimental impact of the agony of not knowing the fate or whereabouts of a loved one on the relatives of disappeared persons, regardless of the identity of the perpetrator, this exclusion has

49 See, for example, *Hajrizi Dzemajl et al.* v. *Yugoslavia*, Committee Against Torture, CAT/C/29/D/161/2000, 2002, para. 9(2).

50 This was confirmed by the CED in its recently adopted Statement on Non-State Actors. However, the CED does not explicitly exclude the applicability of Art. 24 ICPPED and emphasizes that: 'In order to comply fully with such obligations, States must ensure full respect for the rights of victims, including children'. See CED, Statement on non-State actors, para. 20.

been criticized.[51] Conversely, excluding victims of disappearances falling within article 3 may be justified from a legal perspective based on the lack of direct or indirect State participation in such disappearances. In a context like Mexico, however, where the State's actions and omissions are seen as perpetuating all types of disappearances and the State's failure to conduct effective investigations makes it impossible to clearly distinguish between them, a differentiation between types of victims seems somewhat arbitrary.

## 7.5 The Mexican Law on Enforced Disappearance

Domestically, in 2017, the Mexican government responded to pressure by relatives and civil society and adopted legislation to address the issue of disappearances in the country. The General Law on Enforced Disappearance, Disappearance Committed by Private Individuals, and the National Search System (General Law) deals with the problem of State and non-State perpetrators of disappearances by establishing two crimes, as indicated by its title: enforced disappearances and disappearances committed by private individuals. Notably, the definitions of the two crimes differ significantly in that the definition of enforced disappearance is almost equal to that contained in the ICPPED,[52] whereas the crime 'disappearance committed by private individuals' is defined as 'committed by anyone who deprives a person of their liberty with the aim of hiding the victim or the victim's fate or whereabouts.'[53] The

[51] See A. Srovin Coralli, *Non-State Actors and Enforced Disappearances: Defining a Path Forward*, (Geneva Academy, 2021), pp. 10–11, available at www.geneva-academy.ch/research/publications/detail/608-non-state-actors-and-enforced-disappearances-defining-a-path-forward; R. Huhle, 'Non-State actors of enforced disappearance and the UN Convention for the Protection of All Persons from Enforced Disappearance' (2013) 26 *Humanitäres Völkerrecht Informationsschriften* 21, 25. So far, no studies have been conducted that compare whether there are any differences in the suffering of victims depending on the perpetrator. See M. Bourguignon, A. Dermitzel and M. Katz, 'Grief among relatives of disappeared persons in the context of state violence: An impossible process?' (2021) 31 *Torture Journal* 14, 29.

[52] 'A public servant or private person acting with the authorisation, support or acquiescence of a public servant commits the crime of enforced disappearance of persons if they by any means deprive a person of their liberty, followed by the abstention or refusal to acknowledge this deprivation of liberty, or to provide information about the person or the person's fate, destiny, or whereabouts.' Author's translation. Art. 27 Ley General en Materia de Desaparición Forzada de Personas, Desaparición Cometida por Particulares y del Sistema Nacional de Búsqueda de Personas, 17 November 2017.

[53] Art. 34 LEDDCPI, author's translation.

difference between the two definitions has been criticized by the CED on the basis that article 3 ICPPED refers to 'acts defined in article 2', which, accordingly, would imply that both crimes should be defined in the same manner.[54] From a traditional criminal law perspective, however, this definition may be justified.[55]

Whereas the ICPPED only explicitly mentions State obligations to investigate and bring perpetrators to justice in relation to disappearances committed by non-State actors falling within article 3, the General Law clearly establishes obligations to search for *all* disappeared and missing persons[56] and conduct criminal investigations ex officio into all cases where a disappearance may be related to the commission of a crime, regardless of the perpetrator.[57] The General Law thus overcame the ICPPED's silence on additional State obligations regarding disappearances falling within article 3 by establishing equal general obligations in relation to enforced disappearances and disappearances committed by private individuals.[58] Importantly, the sections dealing with prevention (articles 158–73) establish preventive obligations without differentiating between the crimes of enforced disappearance and disappearance committed by private individuals, thereby going significantly beyond the ICPPED.

Regarding reparations, the General Law distinguishes between disappeared persons as direct victims and their relatives as indirect victims,[59] which differs from the definition of victims contained in article 24 ICPPED.[60] At the same time, relatives of both types of disappearances

[54] CED, Follow-up Observations on the Additional Information Submitted by Mexico under Art. 29, Paragraph 4, of the Convention, UN Doc. CED/C/MEX/CO/R.1/Add.1, 13 November 2018, paras. 10–11.

[55] See A. M. Mayo Flota, 'The Crime of Disappearance of Persons by Private Individuals in the New Mexican Legislation: An International Law Perspective', Master Thesis, Institute of International and Development Studies (2018), pp. 40–4.

[56] Art. 89, LEDDCPI.

[57] Art. 13, ibid.

[58] Art. 13–23, ibid. On how the General Law incorporates international standards on enforced disappearance in relation to investigation, see S. L. Morelos Zaragoza, 'The Mexican Law on the Forced Disappearance of Persons, Disappearances Committed by Individuals and the National Missing Persons System: How many steps forward?' (2019) *XII Mexican Law Review* 125, 141–3.

[59] Art. 137 LEDDCPI refers to the 'direct victims' of the crimes of enforced disappearance or disappearance committed by private individuals, whereas article 138 of the General Law refers to the 'relatives of victims' of the two crimes.

[60] According to article 24 (1) ICPPED, victims of enforced disappearance are 'the disappeared person and any individual who has suffered harm as the direct result of an

are considered as victims,[61] which is an important step beyond article 24 ICPPED, that, as discussed previously, only encompasses victims of *enforced* disappearance. Nonetheless, there remains a difference between victims when it comes to reparations also in the General Law: while all victims have the right to receive comprehensive reparation,[62] article 152 establishes that the Federation and federal entities have an obligation to ensure comprehensive reparation to victims of enforced disappearances. The obligation to compensate the harm caused to victims of disappearances committed by private individuals is only subsidiary in nature,[63] which reflects current international standards in relation to reparation obligations of States for acts committed by non-State actors.[64]

Mexican domestic law can thus be seen as going beyond the ICPPED in certain aspects. Nonetheless, some grey areas in the international framework are also reflected in the domestic realm given that the General Law adopted the definition of enforced disappearance from the ICPPED. Consequently, questions about the definition of terms such as support, authorization and acquiescence, which I discuss below, are of equal relevance, as there continues to be a small difference between victims of enforced disappearances and victims of disappearances committed by private individuals with regard to reparations also under the national framework. Moreover, clarifying the threshold for support, authorization and acquiescence at the international level could also provide useful guidance for domestic prosecutions.

## 7.6 Legal Questions Arising from the Mexican Context

Due to the general lack of effective investigation and search for the disappeared, regardless of the perpetrator, as well as prevailing impunity, *all* disappearance cases in Mexico, today and in the past, are connected by State omission. It is therefore unquestionable that, from the perspective of IHRL, the Mexican State bears some level of responsibility for all disappearances, at a minimum for its failure to investigate these acts, search for the victims and hold those responsible to account. The precise

enforced disappearance'. Consequently, there is no distinction between direct and indirect victims.

61 Art. 138, LEDDCPI.

62 Art. 150, ibid.

63 Art. 152, ibid.

64 Dinah Shelton, *Remedies in International Human Rights Law* (Oxford University Press, 2015), p. 75.

nature of this responsibility varies, however, because the State has different obligations depending on the type of disappearance and the international responsibility arising from a failure to investigate is less than that arising from direct or indirect State involvement. Nonetheless, given that impunity and corruption are key factors that perpetuate the commission of disappearances at the hands of both State and non-State actors in Mexico, and considering the active role of the State in the creation of the current crisis of disappearances through militarization, on the one hand, and forensic negligence, on the other, the question arises whether the Mexican State could be responsible in a more direct manner.

### *7.6.1 Forensic Negligence as Enforced Disappearance*

One question that arises concerns the implications of the State's negligence when it comes to the appropriate identification and handling of bodies, which, while technically part of the obligation to investigate and search,[65] is also a *direct* cause of the disappearance of tens of thousands of persons in Mexico, as outlined above. Could the State's utter negligence with regard to the handling of dead bodies constitute *enforced* disappearances because they are the direct result of actions and omissions by State agents? The answer to this question is most likely negative, given that the international definition of enforced disappearance contains three elements: deprivation of liberty, involvement of State agents and negation of information about the fate or whereabouts of the victim.[66] In cases of mishandling of dead bodies, the second and third elements are clearly present. However, if the reason that the body came into the hands of authorities was a homicide committed by a non-State actor, then the first element of an enforced disappearance, the deprivation of liberty at the hands of a State agent or a person acting with the authorization, support or acquiescence of the State, is lacking.[67] This is because a deprivation of liberty generally includes different forms of restrictions to a person's ability to move freely,[68] which implies that a person must be alive to exercise her right to liberty. Consequently, the mishandling, lack of

[65] See CED, Guiding Principles for the Search for Disappeared Persons, UN Doc. CED/C/7, 8 May 2019.

[66] T. Scovazzi and G. Citroni, *The Struggle against Enforced Disappearance and the 2007 United Nations Convention* (Nijhoff, 2007), pp. 271–2.

[67] I thank Grażyna Baranowska for bringing my attention to this issue.

[68] See Human Rights Committee, General Comment No. 35: Article 9 (Liberty and Security of Person), UN Doc. CCPR/C/GC/35, 16 December 2014, paras. 3–5.

identification and possible misplacement of a dead body would not constitute a deprivation of liberty and, as argued by Yankelevich, while the victims of such State negligence are in fact disappeared, they are not victims of the crime of disappearance.[69] In Mexican domestic law, the General Law criminalizes acts relating to hiding or destroying human remains as separate crimes.[70]

From a theoretical perspective, it is thus clear that the mishandling of human remains cannot constitute an enforced disappearance. Notwithstanding, the scale of the forensic crisis in Mexico today poses questions for the international framework on enforced disappearances. This is because thousands of persons would not be disappeared in Mexico today if it were not for the mishandling of their remains by the responsible authorities, yet, in the absence of a deprivation of liberty or evidence thereof, they cannot – strictly speaking – be considered victims of disappearances under IHRL. If this line of reasoning were to be followed, it would not even be possible to hold the Mexican State responsible for a failure to investigate under article 3 ICPPED because this article refers to 'acts defined in article 2' and therefore also requires a deprivation of liberty followed by a refusal to disclose the victim's fate or whereabouts.[71] If non-State actors kill a victim and hide the body, this act could fall within article 3. However, if the body is simply left in the street, the underlying crime is a murder and not a disappearance.[72]

While this approach makes sense in isolated cases, in situations where a State not only fails to identify victims but also actively obfuscates their fate or whereabouts by mishandling remains, it is counterintuitive to exclude them from the framework of enforced disappearances. This is because the very origin of the international legal framework dealing with both the missing and the disappeared is the detrimental impact on relatives of the uncertainty of not knowing what happened to their loved ones and where they are and, in the Mexican case, this uncertainty stems from the *State's* omissions.[73] Considering this, the international

[69] Yankelevich, *Manual de Capacitación para la Búsqueda*.

[70] Article 37, LEDDCPI.

[71] Note, however, that beyond the ICPPED framework, the State could still be held responsible for failing to investigate the death and identify the person, as well as for the damage caused to families as a result (often considered to amount to a violation of the relatives' right to physical integrity) under other IHRL instruments.

[72] Yankelevich, *Manual de Capacitación para la Búsqueda*, p. 22.

[73] For a discussion of how the origins of the international legal framework on enforced disappearances, see B. Finucane, 'Enforced disappearance as a crime under international

framework on enforced disappearances should be able to reflect the State's role in the effective disappearance of thousands of persons and leaving thousands of relatives in a limbo of uncertainty.[74] Further research is needed to explore the type of responsibility the State might incur under the framework on enforced disappearances in such cases, for example, whether the continuous obligation to search would apply even though the victim is, legally, not a victim of a disappearance.

### *7.6.2 Impunity as Acquiescence*

A second legal question regarding disappearances committed by non-State actors in the Mexican context concerns the meaning of acquiescence and the point at which a disappearance that ostensibly would fall under article 3 ICPPED could become an *enforced* disappearance in line with article 2 ICPPED on the basis of the State's omissions. This is because near-absolute impunity and systemic corruption are widely considered to be crucial perpetuating factors of the country's crisis of disappearances.[75] In view of this, arguments have been made that the State's persistent failure to investigate, and impunity more generally, would not 'only' imply a violation of the State's obligation to investigate but should also be viewed as a form of acquiescence when it reaches a certain threshold, such as systematicity.[76] The reasoning behind such arguments is that the systematic failure to search for the victims and to

law: A neglected origin in the laws of war' (2010) 35 *The Yale Journal of International Law* 171.

[74] For an example of such negligence, see the case of Cosme Humberto Alarcón Balderas in the north-eastern State of Coahuila. After years of searching for him, Cosme's mother was able to identify him on pictures from a homicide file, yet the State prosecutor's office had lost his body. To this day, and despite four exhumations, his remains have not been found. Given that the body was identified on pictures, the case is treated as a homicide and not a disappearance. See F. Rodríguez, '¿Cómo se despide una madre de un hijo cuyo cuerpo perdió el Estado?', A dónde van los desaparecidos, 23 October 2023, available at https://adondevanlosdesaparecidos.org/2023/10/23/como-se-despide-una-madre-de-un-hijo-cuyo-cuerpo-perdio-el-estado/.

[75] See, for example, International Federation for Human Rights (Fidh) and I(dh)eas, Litigio Estratégico en Derechos Humanos (2020) Situation of Impunity in Mexico, 750a, available at www.idheas.org.mx/wp-content/uploads/2020/05/Mexique750ang-1.pdf; OSJI, *Corruption That Kills*.

[76] See B. A. Frey, 'Conceptualising disappearances in international law' in K. Ansolabehere, L. A. Payne and B. A. Frey (eds.), *Disappearance in the Post-Transition Era in Latin America* (Oxford University Press, 2021).

identify and punish the perpetrators could be understood as endorsement and de facto authorization of such crimes.[77]

The main objection to these arguments is that a strict reading of the ICPPED would warrant maintaining a separation between articles 2 and 3 and that a failure to investigate disappearances committed by non-State actors (falling within article 3) would be a violation of article 3, rather than retroactively converting it into acquiescence.[78] Moreover, existing case law on acquiescence generally requires a certain level of awareness of risk to a specific victim and a possibility to *prevent* an act from occurring. Regarding disappearances, this means that the State would have to be aware of a risk in relation to the initial deprivation of liberty.[79] A less explored question is whether corrupt ties between criminal groups and State actors could be the basis for establishing acquiescence, or even support, to acts of such groups, even in cases where the State was not directly aware of a specific risk.[80] Having previously engaged with the issue of acquiescence in the Mexican context,[81] Section 7.7 focuses specifically on the CED's recently adopted Statement on Non State Actors and explores the extent to which it elucidates this question.

## 7.7 The CED Statement on Non-State Actors and the Mexican Context

### *7.7.1 The CED Statement on Non-State Actors*

In March 2023, the CED adopted the Statement on Non-State Actors with the aim of 'clarifying the scope of applicability of the Convention with regard to acts committed by non-State actors, the obligations of States parties in that regard, as well as implications for the functions entrusted to the Committee'.[82] The Statement is a key document because it outlines the Committee's position on several issues that were previously unclear, especially regarding disappearances falling within article 3 ICPPED. Regarding the latter, the Statement indicates that no Convention obligations

[77] Ibid.
[78] L. Guercke, 'State acquiescence to disappearances in the "context of Mexico's War on Drugs"' in S. Mandolessi and K. Olalde Rico (eds.), *Disappearances in Mexico: From the 'Dirty War' to the 'War on Drugs'* (Routledge, 2022), pp. 127–49.
[79] Ibid., pp. 136–40.
[80] Ibid., p. 141.
[81] Ibid.
[82] CED, Statement on non-State actors.

beyond those explicitly established in article 3 ICPPED, that is, to take appropriate measures to investigate and bring those responsible to justice, apply to article 3 disappearances.[83] At the same time, and in line with its Guiding Principles for the Search for Disappeared Persons,[84] the Committee made clear that States do have an obligation to search for all disappeared persons.[85] The Statement further clarifies that the Committee 'may register' cases falling within article 3 as Urgent Actions under article 30, receive communications relating to alleged violations of article 3 under articles 31 and 32 ICPPED and it may request a visit to a State party upon receiving reliable information of serious violations of obligations under article 3.[86] Finally, the Statement confirms that, following article 5 ICPPED, disappearances committed by non-State actors acting without the authorization, support or acquiescence of the State can be considered 'enforced disappearances' as crimes against humanity in situations where there is a nexus with a 'widespread or systematic attack against a civilian population'.[87]

One of the Statement's most ground-breaking contributions, also beyond the crime of enforced disappearance, is the definition of the terms 'support, authorisation and acquiescence' because it is the first time that a treaty body has provided such definitions. Whereas 'support' and 'authorisation' have received virtually no attention in cases concerning disappearances committed by non-State actors, existing jurisprudence encompassing an analysis of acquiescence is often confusing or even contradictory. In that sense, the adoption of a definition can be viewed as a welcome development. The extent to which the definition will be accepted and taken up in case law by bodies other than the CED remains to be seen, however, as the Statement is a soft law instrument whose legal authority is unclear.

### 7.7.2 *The CED's Definition of Acquiescence*

In light of the questions outlined above (Section 7.6.2), in particular the argument that impunity could constitute acquiescence, the CED's

[83] Ibid., para. 20(4).
[84] CED, Guiding Principles.
[85] CED, Statement on non-State actors, para. 20. Moreover, read together with the CED's recently adopted General Comment on Enforced Disappearances in the Context of Migration, the obligation to conduct ex officio investigations into a disappearance encompasses enforced disappearances and those falling within Art. 3. See CED, General Comment No. 1, para. 37.
[86] CED, Statement on non-State actors, paras. 24–6.
[87] Ibid., para. 17.

definition of acquiescence is of particular relevance for the Mexican context. The notion of 'acquiescence' is notoriously difficult to establish because it concerns silence from which consent can be inferred.[88] Perhaps due to this difficulty, jurisprudence on acquiescence by UN treaty bodies, as well as the Inter-American Court of Human Rights (IACtHR) and the European Court of Human Rights (ECtHR), is often vague, sometimes contradictory and generally does not include an in-depth analysis or explanation of the notion itself.[89]

In the Statement, the Committee defines 'acquiescence' as follows:

> 5. 'Acquiescence' means that the State knew, had reasons to know or ought to have known of the commission or of the real and imminent risk of commission of enforced disappearance by persons or groups of persons, but that one of the following applies:
>
> (a) The State has either accepted, tolerated or given consent to this situation, even implicitly;
> (b) The State has deliberately and in full knowledge, by action or omission, failed to take measures to prevent the crime and to investigate and punish the perpetrators;
> (c) The State has acted in connivance with the perpetrators or with total disregard for the situation of the potential victims, facilitating the actions of the non-State actors who commit the act;
> (d) The State has created the conditions that allowed their commission.
>
> 6. In particular, there is acquiescence within the meaning of article 2 when there is a known pattern of disappearance of persons and the State has failed to take the measures necessary to prevent further cases of disappearance and to investigate the perpetrators and bring them to justice.

This definition reflects existing jurisprudence in that it upholds the criteria of foreseeability, and imminence, which are commonly used in cases involving human rights violations committed by non-State actors and/or acquiescence. At the same time, it also goes beyond approaches in case law because it explicitly encompasses both the State's role in the creation of conditions that allowed the commission of such crimes and impunity for disappearances falling within article 3 ICPPED. Thus, a

[88] On the notion of acquiescence, see N. S. Marques Antunes, 'Acquiescence', *Max Planck Encyclopedias of International Law [MPIL]* (Oxford Public International Law, 2006).

[89] See, for example, M. Milanovic, 'State Acquiescence or Connivance in the Wrongful Conduct of Third Parties in the Jurisprudence of the European Court of Human Rights' (2019), available at http://dx.doi.org/10.2139/ssrn.3454007; Guercke, 'State Acquiescence to Disappearances', pp. 135–40.

State's failure to prevent a disappearance that was foreseeable and imminent can be considered as acquiescence if the State created the conditions for it to occur, or if it failed to investigate and bring the perpetrators to justice in contexts where there are clear patterns of disappearances falling within article 3 ICPPED. Furthermore, and distinct from case law on acquiescence by other human rights bodies, the definition is silent on the State's ability to prevent the disappearance. This is particularly relevant because there can be State acquiescence without physical presence or involvement of State actors. The question that remains for the CED, and other bodies applying this definition, is how, in a specific case, it will establish foreseeability and the existence of a real and imminent risk: Does the State's knowledge have to relate to the particular victim, or can it be more general contextual knowledge relating to a particular group of persons or a whole population?[90] At what point is the risk of a disappearance to occur 'real and imminent'?

### *7.7.3 The Statement on Non-State Actors and the Mexican Context*

Returning to the situation in Mexico, these questions are of crucial importance. All four elements listed in paragraph 5 as conditions for acquiescence could apply in relation to the Mexican State:

(a) if State forces let certain criminal groups operate freely, one could argue that they are giving implicit consent to their actions;
(b) the State continuously fails to investigate disappearances that are reported, and it also fails to take effective measures against the groups committing these disappearances, which could be seen as a failure to prevent[91];
(c) several high profiles cases, such as the disappearance of the 43 students from Ayotzinapa in 2014[92] or the 2011 massacre in Allende

[90] With regard to torture, some authors have argued that general knowledge of such acts being committed and failure to take measures against them would be sufficient to establish acquiescence. R. McCorquodale and R. La Forgia, 'Taking off the blindfolds: Torture by non-State Actors' (2001) 1 *Human Rights Law Review* 189, 206.

[91] I have developed this argument elsewhere. See L. Guercke, 'State responsibility for a failure to prevent violations of the right to life by organised criminal groups: Disappearances in Mexico' (2021) 21 *Human Rights Law Review* 329, 353–6.

[92] IACHR, Follow-up on the Ayotzinapa Case by the IACHR Special Follow-Up Mechanism (Organization of American States, 2018), Situation Report OEA/Ser.L/V/II. Doc, p. 82.

and Piedras Negras,[93] have shown connivance between State and criminal actors, and there are examples of criminal organizations in charge of security forces, for example, in the State of Nayarit;[94] moreover, the negligent behaviour of authorities in the forensic context could be described as the State acting 'with total disregard for the situation of the potential victims';

(d) finally, combining the persistence of impunity, as well as the role of State policies in causing the upward spiral of disappearances, it could be argued that the Mexican State 'has created the conditions that allowed their commission'.

Nonetheless, it still needs to be established that the State could have foreseen a disappearance and that the latter was imminent for there to be acquiescence.

Considering that the situation of disappearances in the country has been highlighted by Mexican civil society and regional and international human rights mechanisms for decades, and the Mexican State itself recognizes that there is a crisis of disappearances, there is clearly general knowledge of a real risk for persons to disappear. Notwithstanding, given the variations in the dynamics of disappearances across time and space, the level of risk for a disappearance to occur and its imminence also vary. Therefore, a blanket assumption of knowledge for all cases would be controversial. However, given that disappearances are 'widespread in much of [Mexico's] territory', as observed by CED itself since 2015,[95] it could be argued that there does exist a 'real and imminent risk of the commission' of a disappearance in those regions where disappearances are considered to be widespread. This interpretation would imply that in areas where disappearances are widespread, all disappearances could be considered as enforced disappearances based on acquiescence.

Furthermore, paragraph 6 of the Statement refers to State failure to respond to known patterns of disappearances falling within article 3 ICPPED. While this paragraph does not mention the criteria of foreseeability and imminence of risk, it must be presumed that the existence of a pattern implies the necessary foreseeability and imminence of risk, as it is unlikely that the CED intended to provide two different definitions of

[93] See, for example, S. Aguayo and J. Dayán, *El Yugo Zeta: Norte de Coahuila, 2010–2011* (Colegio de México, 2017).

[94] Fidh and I(dh)eas, 'Mexico: Criminal Structure within the Public Prosecutor's Office'.

[95] CED, Concluding Observations on Mexico, CED/C/MEX/CO/1, para. 10.

acquiescence. Paragraph 6 implies that the Committee agrees with the above-mentioned arguments (Section 7.6.2) in favour of considering State inaction, for example, as manifested in persistent impunity, as a form of acquiescence in certain circumstances. Returning to the example of an organized criminal group who abducts and executes a group of construction workers and buries the victims' remains in a clandestine mass grave, as per the definition of acquiescence provided by the CED, the crime could now also be categorized as an *enforced* disappearance in the following scenario: even if no State agents were present at the scene, State agents could be considered as acquiescing to the act if said organized criminal group was known to regularly abduct, execute and bury specific groups of persons, such as construction workers, constituting a pattern, and was able to engage in these activities undisturbed.

#### 7.7.3.1 A Presumption of Acquiescence?

A final important aspect of the Statement on Non-State Actors concerns what could be termed a 'presumption' of acquiescence. Consistent with recent case law concerning disappearances in Mexico by CED itself and the Human Rights Committee (HRC),[96] which concerned allegations of direct State participation, paragraph 7 of the Statement places the burden of proof on the State to show that there was no acquiescence:

> 7. In such cases, the State has the burden of proving that there was no acquiescence on its part, and it must demonstrate that it has taken concrete measures and action to prevent, investigate and punish the crime, and that such measures have been effective in practice.

While the definition of acquiescence provided in the Statement does not allow for a blanket categorization of all contemporary disappearances in Mexico as *enforced* disappearances on the basis of acquiescence, a *presumption* of acquiescence can be useful in a context of generalized State inaction. This is because if a case is brought alleging acquiescence, the State will have to show that it has taken measures to address disappearances in areas where there are patterns of disappearances, disappearances are widespread or where there are clear links between State officials and non-State actors. If the State fails to show that it has not acquiesced, victims will be considered as victims of enforced disappearance. In that

[96] See *Hidalgo Rea and Rivera Hidalgo* v. *Mexico*, Human Rights Committee, UN Doc. CCPR/C/131/D/3259/2018, 2021; *Berrospe Medina and Mendoza Berrospe* v. *Mexico*, Committee on Enforced Disappearances, UN Doc. CED/C/24/D/4/2021, 2023.

sense, a presumption of acquiescence may be the most appropriate approach to the Mexican context because it could avoid a differentiation between the victims of different types of disappearances in the international realm. This would reflect the Mexican State's overall responsibility based on its negligence towards all disappeared persons in the country and their relatives.

## 7.8 Conclusion

The issue of disappearances in Mexico highlights some of the legal questions surrounding disappearances committed by non-State actors and contexts of utter State failure to protect human rights and end impunity. Given that not all disappearances can be considered *enforced* disappearances in line with the ICPPED, the involvement of non-State actors can imply the coexistence of two types of disappearances and, subsequently, two types of victims. Yet, the Mexican context shows the potential issue with such a distinction due to the overall failure of the State to prevent disappearances, including those committed by non-State actors, as well as to investigate, search for the disappeared and ensure that perpetrators are brought to justice. Considering the detrimental impact on relatives of the uncertainty over the fate and whereabouts of their loved one, which gave rise to the international framework on the missing and disappeared in the first place, legal distinctions between categories of victims can seem arbitrary in such a context. Moreover, questions arise whether the State could not bear a higher level of responsibility for all disappearances due to its role in creating and perpetuating the country's disappearance crisis.

This chapter has shown that it is unlikely that the gross mishandling of dead bodies, one of the effective causes of disappearances in Mexico, could be considered as a type of enforced disappearance. Nonetheless, further research is needed to explore in what ways the State might be considered as more directly responsible for these crimes, given their impact on victims' relatives. Regarding the question of State inaction and impunity as a form of acquiescence, the CED's Statement on Non-State Actors for the first time provides a concrete definition of the term 'acquiescence', which is of great relevance to the Mexican context. The Committee's definition of acquiescence is broad and could apply to a very large number of disappearances in the country. This is because, according to the Statement, acquiescence can result from inaction in instances where there is a known pattern of disappearances, as well as when a State has created the conditions for the commission of disappearances and there exists a foreseeable risk that they will occur. Given that disappearances in Mexico have been considered as 'widespread' in many parts of the country for years, an argument could be made that there is always foreseeable and imminent risk in areas where disappearances are widespread. Additionally, where there are clear patterns of disappearances, the Statement can be read to presume the necessary foreseeability and imminence of risk, converting the State's inaction into acquiescence. Finally, the Statement provides for a presumption of acquiescence, which could be particularly important in the Mexican context to avoid seemingly arbitrary distinctions between victims.

These questions matter not just for Mexico but also for other situations in which State and non-State actors may be involved in the commission of disappearances and dead bodies are grossly mishandled, for example, in the context of migration. It will now be up to the CED to apply its own definition of the terms support, authorization and acquiescence and, regarding the latter, decide how it will determine the existence of knowledge or foreseeability and imminence of risk. If States are not to evade responsibility on the basis of legal nuance, a broad interpretation of these criteria based on knowledge of the risk itself and imminence based on an analysis of the context, rather than a specific victim, would be the most appropriate manner to approach this question.

8

# Disappearances of Migrants in Africa

EVA NUDD AND BARBARA LOCHBIHLER

## 8.1 Trends in Migration Movements in Africa and from Africa to Europe, Causes and Perpetrators

The history of migration on the continent of Africa dates back centuries, including the slave trade, trade of commodities and trading routes between East Africa and Middle East and bringing migrants to build infrastructure and work on sugar farms. In the last couple decades, many Africans have left their homeland due to poverty, lack of labour opportunities, war and famine, political insecurity and environmental degradation. At the same time, as the number of migrants on the continent has risen, migration has become much more dangerous, exposing many migrants to serious human rights violations, including enforced disappearances and torture. Migrants are particularly vulnerable, as they move often under precarious situations and rely on criminal networks to take them to the final destination. Further, enforced disappearances are often another reason for migrants leaving the country. Currently, international law does not have a definition of international migrant. In 2014, the United Nations Office of the High Commissioner for Human Rights introduced the term, noting that international migrants are all persons outside of the State of which they are a citizen or national, or in case of a Stateless person, their State of birth or habitual address, and who are not refugees. In this chapter, the term 'disappeared migrant' will also encompass people who are refugees as defined under the 1951 Refugee Convention as well migrants whose whereabouts remain unknown.

The phenomenon of enforced disappearances is often underreported in Africa and the statistics on migrants are even more difficult to obtain. The lack of proper data is due to several factors, including lack of understanding what enforced disappearances are, fear to report such crime to avoid retaliation and becoming victims of enforced disappearances themselves, as well as common distrust towards authorities to conduct search and effectively investigate the crime as they are often responsible for the commission of enforced disappearances. The United Nations Working Group on Enforced or Involuntary Disappearances (WGEID), whose mandate is to assist victims and families of enforced disappearances worldwide, has since its establishment in 1980 recorded only 4,873 active cases of forcibly disappeared individuals or slightly over 10% of all cases reported from the African countries.[1] While WGEID statistics focus on the reported cases of disappearance, the International Office of Migration (IOM) statistics are focused on migrants and note that since 2014, 11,376 migrants having gone missing on the African continent.[2] These data do not provide the full picture of the migrants suffering, as these statistics only compiled those who are recorded dead, leaving those who die without their deaths being recorded or gone missing. As a result, the available statistics unlikely represent the real number, as the African Union notes a close to 50% increase of migrants on the continent from 13.3 to 25.4 million people between a period of 2008 to 2017.[3]

In the last decade, the migration trends in Africa have changed significantly. Not only has the number of migrants almost doubled but also the routes and the profile of migrants have been changing. The African continent has the youngest populations in the world, with many countries having large segments of population below the age of thirty-five. However, the political strife, weak rule of law, war, poor socio-economic conditions and climate degradation force many young Africans to migrate as a matter of survival in some instances or seeking better opportunities in life.[4] Further, more women and girls are embarking on the migratory journey. The statistics show that nearly half of the migrants are women and girls, according to IOM reporting in 2019, 47.5% of migrants from Sub-Saharan Africa and 35.5% from Northern Africa and Western Asia were female.[5]

1 REDRESS, The Forgotten Victims: Enforced Disappearances in Africa, available at https://redress.org/wp-content/uploads/2024/08/20210824-Enforced-Disappearance-in-Africa-Report-6-for-digital-single-pages.pdf.

2 International Organization of Migration, IOM Missing Migrants Project, available at https://missingmigrants.iom.int/region/africa.

3 The African Union and International Organization of Migration, The Africa Migration Report: Challenging the Narrative, available at https://publications.iom.int/books/africa-migration-report-challenging-narrative.

4 Ibid.

5 UN Department of Economic and Social Affairs, International Migration 2019, available at https://www.un.org/en/development/desa/population/migration/publications/migrationreport/docs/InternationalMigration2019_Report.pdf.

## 8.2 Criminalization of Migration as a Risk Factor for Enforced Disappearances

The massive flow of the migrants on the continent, both moving to different African countries or leaving for Europe, has prompted many States to adopt harsh policies towards the migrants. Many African governments have used security and economic concerns to justify closing their borders and passing legislation that criminalizes migration, in particular illegal entry and working without a permit. Further, the Khartoum process, a political cooperation between Europe and States along the route of Horn of Africa with specific focus on addressing trafficking and smuggling of migrants, as well as prevention and fight against irregular migration, shifts the physical management of Europe's borders to African countries by funding projects that enhance border security, upgrade national legislation and disrupt or dismantle migrant smuggling and human trafficking networks in the Horn of Africa.[6] The negative perception of the migrants as a potential security threat precipitates the treatment and human rights violations migrants endure at the hands of the border patrol agents and other government entities. Further, corruption at the border and opportunities to extort money either at the border or in detention facilities lead to human rights violations, including enforced disappearances.[7]

Libya, one of the top transit countries to reach Europe, adopted harsh migration policies to control the migration. The law No. 19 of 2010 criminalizes 'illegal entry and exit from Libya' and provides for a basis of automatic detention noting that 'foreign illegal immigrants shall be penalized by detention with hard labour or by a fine not exceeding 1,000 LYD (approximately 200 USD).'[8]

Niger is another destination that migrants cross to reach Libya or Algeria. By 2017, close to 170,000 migrants passed through the town of Agadez, in the middle of the country. These numbers have fallen significantly because of external pressure mainly from the European Union that

6 Clingendal, 'The Khartoum Process: Shifting the Burden', 22 February 2016, available at www.clingendael.org/publication/khartoum-process-shifting-burden.

7 The African Union, African Union Migration Policy Framework for Africa and Plan of Action (2018–2030), available at https://au.int/sites/default/files/documents/35956-doc-au-mpfa-executive-summary-eng.pdf.

8 ECCHR, FIDH and LFJL, No Way Out: Migrants and Refugees Trapped in Libya Face Crimes Against Humanity (2021), available at https://www.ecchr.eu/en/publication/no-way-out-migrants-and-refugees-trapped-in-libya-face-crimes-against-humanity/.

caused the Niger government to criminalize irregular migration, forcing many migrants to cross at night or use smuggling networks, with many ending up disappearing.[9] The repressive approach of certain provisions of Law No. 2015-36 of 26 May 2015 on the smuggling of migrants encourages migrants to live in hiding in conditions that expose them to numerous abuses, which could include the risk of being a victim of enforced disappearance, as the UN Committee on Enforced Disappearances (CED) stated recently.[10]

Sudan, another transit country used by East Africans to reach Libya, has been reported to treat migrants with excessive brutality. The Sudanese government and the European Union have concluded a partnership agreement to distribute millions of euros to combat illegal migration and human trafficking with most of the money spent on technical equipment and training capacities of security and law enforcement agencies, including the Rapid Support Forces (RSF).[11] The RSF, led by General Hamedi, has been accused by the International Criminal Court of carrying out war crimes and crimes against humanity, including torture, enforced disappearances and other violations.

Burkina Faso, a transit country in West Africa that many migrants use to reach Libya through Niger, lacks legal and administrative guidance with regard to migration. A draft bill on migration (supposed to replace the 1984 Ordinance regulating the right of entry and leaving the country) was prepared in 2020 but still has not been introduced to the Council of Ministers. The UN Committee on Migrant Workers called on the government to step up its efforts to draft and enact the new migration bill that must be in line with the provisions of the Convention. A National Migration Strategy has been adopted, but the body that is supposed to monitor and evaluate the implementation of the national migration policy (Commissariat Général à la Migration) has still not been established.[12]

9 International Commission on Missing Persons, Global Report on Missing Persons 2020/21, available at www.icmp.int/wp-content/uploads/2021/08/ICMP_Global-Report_April_Digital .pdf.

10 The UN Committee on Enforced Disappearances, Concluding observations on the report submitted by the Niger under Art. 29(1) of the Convention, CED/C/NER/CO/1, 5 May 2022.

11 S. Baldo, Border Control from Hell: How the EU's migration partnership legitimatizes Sudan's Militia State (2017), available at https://enoughproject.org/reports/border-control-hell-how-eus-migration-partnership-legitimizes-sudans-militia-state.

12 The UN Committee on Enforced Disappearances, Observations finales concernant le deuxième rapport périodique du Burkina Faso, CMW/C/BFA/CO/2, 12 April 2022.

However, the recent coup that replaced the elected government with a military one may not take up the steps to address migration.

As a result of the adoption of laws that criminalize irregular migration and increased militarization of the borders, many migrants are now using irregular routes to avoid detection and detentions, relying on smugglers and human trafficking networks to reach the destination.[13] No region of the continent provides safe passage for the migrants.[14] The migrants from Sub-Saharan Africa must cross the Saharan desert to reach Morocco or Libya. In Western Africa, while the Economic Community of West African States (ECOWAS) allows free movement, the failed or weak governments and securitization of borders in Mali, Niger and Burkina Faso exposes migrants to serious human rights violations.[15] Migrants from East Africa trying to reach North Africa often undertake difficult journeys crossing to Sudan and especially on the borders between Libya and Sudan experiencing human rights violations at the hands of criminalized gangs.

The weak rule of law, insecurity and civil strife are not only the push factors for migration but also create an environment for non-State actors to occupy territories, exploit weak government structures and engage in human rights violations, including enforced disappearances and torture. In Libya, following the coup that brought down Muammar Khadafi in 2011, the country descended into a civil war with several factions fighting over political power. As a result, the UN-backed government, the Government of National Accord, controls mainly the western territories in Libya while most of eastern Libya is controlled or swayed by the Commander Khalifa Haftar and the Libyan National Army.[16] The law that criminalizes illegal migrations and sets up automatic detention of migrants, a political power vacuum and lack of a proper functional legal system have created an environment in Libya in which the government

[13] The African Union, African Union Migration Policy Framework for Africa and Plan of Action (2018–2030), available at https://au.int/sites/default/files/documents/35956-doc-au-mpfa-executive-summary-eng.pdf.

[14] The UN Refugee Agency (UNHRC), Protection, Saving Lives & Solutions for Refugees in Dangerous Journeys (UNHCR's 2022–2023) Updated Risk Mitigation Strategy and 2022 Appeal, available at https://reporting.unhcr.org/document/2247.

[15] The Missing Migrants Project, Migration in Africa, available at https://missingmigrants.iom.int/region/Africa.

[16] T. Perry, 'Libya's Eastern Commander Hafter announces election bid', Reuters, 16 November 2021, available at www.reuters.com/world/africa/libyas-eastern-commander-haftar-announces-election-bid-2021-11-16/.

as well as non-State actors exploit the migrants who often become victims of serious human rights violations. An Amnesty International Report concluded that refugees and migrants in Libya are often victims of enforced disappearances at the hands of State agents or militias affiliated with the State or by non-State actors, including armed groups. The refugees and migrants are deprived of their liberty in unofficial places of detention as well as other undisclosed locations.[17]

## 8.3 Enforced Disappearances and Related Human Rights Violations in the Context of Migration

The International Convention for the Protection of All Persons from Enforced Disappearance (ICPPED) defines enforced disappearances in Article 2 to be 'the arrest, detention, abduction or any other form of deprivation of liberty by agents of the State or by persons or groups of persons acting with the authorization, support or acquiescence of the State, followed by the refusal to acknowledge the deprivation of liberty or by concealment of the fate or whereabouts of the disappeared person, which place such person outside the protection of the law'.[18] Considering that, as illustrated above, non-State actors often are key actors with regard to the enforced disappearance of migrants, it is particularly relevant to note that the ICPPED in Article 3 also recognizes situations where acts tantamount to enforced disappearances can be committed by non-State actors and obliges State Parties 'to investigate acts defined in article 2 committed by persons or groups of persons acting without the authorization, support or acquiescence of the State and to bring those responsible to justice'.

Disappearances can occur in the context of detention or deportation or as a consequence of smuggling or trafficking. Further, every deprivation of liberty in the context of expulsions is an enforced disappearance when subsequently denied by authorities. This is relevant, irrespective of the duration and place of deprivation of liberty. A deprivation of liberty can

[17] Amnesty International, Between Life and Death: Refugees and Migrants Trapped in Libya's Cycle of Abuse (2020), available at www.amnesty.org/en/documents/mde19/3084/2020/en/.

[18] The International Convention for the Protection of All Persons from Enforced Disappearances, Art. 2, available at www.ohchr.org/en/instruments-mechanisms/instruments/international-convention-protection-all-persons-enforced.

also occur in places, like in vehicles, on boats or in other places not intended for detention.[19]

Many of the migrants recall horrific violations they experience in all stages of their journey. They speak of being tortured, subjected to electric shocks, engaged in forced labour and extortion. When speaking of the places of detention, they recall having almost no access to food, living in overcrowded cells with no proper sanitary facilities. As many of the migrants are being held in illegal detention or facilities run by non-State actors who are often supported by the States as is the case in Libya or act with the State's acquiescence, they do not have access to legal remedies and often only get released after their families pay the ransom. Libya is but one example of the significant role of non-State actors, where the standard attribution of acquiescence makes it particularly difficult to differentiate between enforced disappearances (Art. 2) and acts tantamount to enforced disappearances (Art. 3).

The OMCT report on torture interviewed several survivors who spoke of the subhuman treatment they were subjected to with one of the migrants:

> A week after my arrival in Libya, I was arrested in Sabha and jailed by the Medina Police. They beat me with their weapons every day. We barely had any food. I was only allowed a chunk of bread and a glass of water each evening. After three days, I was freed, having paid 200,000 CFA francs (approximately $330), which I had received from my family, On 16 November 2016, the shelter was attacked by the police and the Libyan army. All the migrants were transferred to the Misrata prison for three months, where we were beaten every day with whips.[20]

Female migrants, in particular, are at risk for sexual violence and rape. The migrants interviewed by Amnesty International recalled 'witnessing

[19] E. Decaux and J. Suela, 'The International Convention for the Protection of All Persons from Enforced Disappearance, a Human Rights Instrument of the 21st century: Reflections on its 10th Anniversary of the Entry into Force' (2021) 18 *Droits Fondamentaux*, available at www.crdh.fr/revue/n-19-2021/the-international-convention-for-the-protection-of-all-persons-from-enforced-disappearance-a-human-rights-instrument-of-the-21st-century-reflections-on-its-10th-anniversary-of-the-entry-into force/#:~:text=Introduction-,The%20International%20Convention%20for%20the%20Protection%20of%20all%20Persons%20from,instrument%20to%20fight%20enforced%20disappearances.

[20] OMCT, The Road of Torture: Cycle of Abuse against People on the Move in Africa (2021), available at www.omct.org/en/resources/reports/africa-new-report-exposes-torture-as-a-defining-feature-of-the-migration-journey.

the rape of women by traffickers and smugglers on multiple occasions during their journey and stay in Libya in 2017 and 2018. Two said they were forced to watch their wives being raped or otherwise sexually abused by traffickers while held in camp near Bani Walid'.[21] All this most often happens without anybody knowing the whereabouts of their relatives along their migration routes.

## 8.4 The Relevance of the ICPPED for the Protection of Migrants from Enforced Disappearances and the Contribution of the Committee on Enforced Disappearances

The United Nations has two bodies whose mandates explicitly include enforced disappearances. In 1980, the United Nations established the UN Working Group on Enforced or Involuntary Disappearances with a humanitarian mandate to assist families of the victims to obtain information on their whereabouts. In 2017, the WGEID issued a report on migration, discussing the phenomena as it relates to enforced disappearances. The report uses the term 'disappeared migrant' and notes that migrants in addition to leaving their countries for the fear of becoming victims of enforced disappearances also face enforced disappearances and other human rights violations along migratory routes within Africa and/or from Africa to Europe. The report further describes the migratory routes as often unsafe and less travelled, noting that many migrants end up in the hands of criminal elements patrolling the border areas or rogue States agents.[22]

The second UN body with a mandate encompassing enforced disappearances is the Committee on Enforced Disappearance, which is a treaty-based body created following the ICPPED coming into force. Since its creation in 2011, the CED has worked closely with the State Parties to ensure effective implementation of the obligations of the Treaty and accept individual complaints from the victims. The CED has, through review of the compliance with the Convention, provided

[21] Amnesty International, 'Between Life and Death: Refugees and Migrants Trapped in Libya's Cycle of Abuse', 24 September 2020, available at https://www.amnesty.org/en/documents/mde19/3084/2020/en/.

[22] UN Working Group on Enforced or Involuntary Disappearances, Report of the Working Group on Enforced or Involuntary Disappearances on enforced disappearances in the context of migration, 2017, available at https://www.ohchr.org/en/documents/thematic-reports/ahrc3639add2-report-working-group-enforced-or-involuntary-disappearances.

recommendations to African States on their obligations and standards to protect the migrants. The recommendations to Burkina Faso, Niger, Mali and Tunisia will be discussed in more detail further below.

The CED has paid increasing attention to enforced disappearances in the context of migration, as reflected in its regular work vis-à-vis State Parties and in Principle 9 of the 'Guiding Principles for the Search for Disappeared Persons'[23] adopted in 2019 and dedicated to search for the particularly vulnerable population of migrants. Most recently, on 18 September 2023, CED adopted its first General Comment on enforced disappearances in the context of migration. This was preceded by three years of research and broad consultation in writing and online meetings. During the regional consultation with national human rights institutions (NHRIs) and civil society from West and Sub-Saharan Africa as well as the Maghreb region, all participants described and confirmed the political, legal and institutional deficits that lead to the disappearance of migrants and prevent the clarification of their fates on the African continent. The work on the General Comment and its recent adoption was guided by CED's commitment to proactively respond to present-day realities, to assist State parties to fulfil their respective obligations under the ICPPED and to provide an authoritative and interpretative position on how to prevent and react to enforced disappearance in the context of migration. Key aspects of the General Comment will be elaborated below.

In addition to the above-mentioned bodies, there are several other special mandate holders and UN human rights bodies working on the issue of the rights of migrants. The Committee on the Protection of All Migrant Workers and Members of their Families (CMW) has been a vocal advocate for the rights of migrants by working with State parties to protect migrants' rights. Through its General Comment No. 5 on the migrants' rights to 'liberty, freedom from arbitrary detention,[24] the CMW addresses conditions that lead to enforced disappearances and specifically prohibit the use of secret detentions.

[23] The Committee on Enforced Disappearances, Guiding Principles for the Search for Disappeared Persons, CED/C/17, available at www.ohchr.org/en/documents/legal-standards-and-guidelines/guiding-principles-search-disappeared-persons.

[24] The Committee on the Protection of the Rights of All Migrant Workers and Members of Their Families, General comment No. 5 on migrants' rights to liberty and freedom from arbitrary detention, CMW/C/GC/5, available at www.ohchr.org/en/documents/general-comments-and-recommendations/general-comment-no-5-2021-migrants-rights-liberty.

## 8.5 States' Obligations to Prevent Enforced Disappearances in Migration

All States, under international law, have obligations to prevent human rights violations. However, parties to the ICPPED have additional obligations to search and take action to protect and prevent enforced disappearance. In 2019, with the world paying more attention to the plight of the migrants, the UN General Assembly adopted the biannual resolution on the protection of migrants and this time highlighted the States' obligations to protect the migrants and specifically referring to the ICPPED and States' obligations to search.[25]

The duty to prevent within the context of migration and enforced disappearances is fortified in Article 16 of the Convention that states 'No State Party shall expel, return ("refouler") surrender or extradite a person to another State where there are substantial grounds for believing that he or she would be in danger of being subjected to enforced disappearances.'[26] This prohibition of non-refoulement enshrined in all the major human rights treaties, is considered to be a customary international law[27] and it offers integral protection against torture and arbitrary deprivation of life.

In emphasizing that the prohibition of refoulement is a *jus cogens* norm under international law, CED has in concluding observations recommended to the States Parties to ensure, in law and in practice, the strict respect, without exception and not subject to any conditions, the prohibition of refoulement, which entails not to proceed with an expulsion, return, surrender or extradition whenever there are reasonable grounds to believe that a person would be in danger of being subjected to an enforced disappearance. CED has formulated specific recommendations for States Parties to ensure that there are clear and specific criteria and/or procedures for assessing and verifying the risk that a person may

[25] UNGA Resolution, Protection of Migrants, A/RES/74/148, available at https://documents-dds-ny.un.org/doc/UNDOC/GEN/N19/427/26/PDF/N1942726.pdf?OpenElement.

[26] The International Convention for the Protection of All Persons from Enforced Disappearances, Art. 2, available at www.ohchr.org/en/instruments-mechanisms/instruments/international-convention-protection-all-persons-enforced.

[27] Non-refoulement protection is enshrined in Art. 3 of the Convention against torture and other cruel, inhuman or degrading treatment or punishment and Art. 33 on the Convention relating to the Status of Refugee, available at www.ohchr.org/en/instruments-mechanisms/instruments/convention-against-torture-and-other-cruel-inhuman-or-degrading and www.unhcr.org/about-unhcr/who-we-are/1951-refugee-convention.

be subjected to enforced disappearance in the country of destination prior to expulsion, return or extradition, and that, if such a risk exists, the person is not expelled, extradited or returned. CED has requested strict compliance by the relevant authorities to extradition, expulsion, surrender and return procedures and that a thorough, comprehensive and individual assessment or examination of each case is carried out, impartially and independently, to determine whether there are substantial grounds to believe that the person would be at risk of enforced disappearance before extraditing, expelling, surrendering or returning him or her.[28] This position has been confirmed and further elaborated in the General Comment, that is, by asking States parties to explicitly incorporate this principle into national legislation.

Besides the specific obligations laid out in Article 16, the General Comment and the previously mentioned Principle 9 of the Guiding Principles for the Search of Disappeared Persons focus on the particular vulnerability and additional risks of enforced disappearances for migrants and persons trafficked. While all families of disappeared persons suffer not knowing whether their loved ones are alive or dead, there are additional obstacles for relatives of disappeared migrants related to the possible undocumented status of the disappeared person, language barriers, being in a country other than the one in which the disappearance presumably occurred and State authorities evading their responsibilities. In some cases, families of the disappeared migrant are reluctant to speak with authorities as the disappeared may not possess the necessary visa or documents to be in the country or because of general distrust of authorities, preventing many relatives from seeking answers. These particular difficulties are directly related – and thus to be considered by State Parties – to the obligations in the ICPPED to search, investigate and cooperate.

## 8.6 States' Obligations to Search and Cooperate Relating to Enforced Disappearances in Migration

The Guiding Principles seek to consolidate good practices in searching effectively for disappeared persons, arising from the States' obligation to

[28] M. Galvis Patino, The Work of the Committee on Enforced Disappearance. Achievements and jurisprudence ten years after the entry into force of the International Convention for the Protection of All Persons from Enforced Disappearances, available at https://www.geneva-academy.ch/joomlatools-files/docman-files/The%20Work%20of%20the%20CED.pdf.

search. In the context of migration, Principle 9 particularly highlights the necessity for cooperation between authorities in countries of origin, transit and destination and calls on States to 'adopt specific search mechanisms that take account of the difficulties associated with migration situations' and to 'develop cooperation agreements and establish competent authorities to allow for effective coordination in the search for disappeared persons at each stage of migration'.[29] The General Comment further underlines that as in migration contexts, cases of disappearance are often not reported, authorities should initiate search and investigation ex officio as soon as they have indications of a disappearance.[30]

Any public search policy adopted by a State party should be designed and implemented with the participation of victims and all persons and civil society organizations with experience and the willingness to cooperate in the design and/or implementation of the policy.[31] While enforced disappearances are prevalent on the continent of Africa, a considerable obstacle to effective search and investigation is the lack of technical capacities, making the search for disappeared migrants quite difficult. For example, the rapid and secure exchange of information and documentation that may help to locate disappeared persons in the country of transit or destination requires not only political will and preparedness – which is a challenge for destination countries in particular – but also administrative and technical provisions and sound knowledge about data protection. To develop and implement comprehensive search strategies, solid assistance from international and national civil society groups and other States in the context of collaboration can help bring the necessary skills to ensure a search is successful.

The ICPPED and the Guiding Principles outline obligations and recommendations for States to prevent, investigate, search and prosecute enforced disappearances and provide reparations to victims of enforced disappearances. However, both documents do not fully clarify situations of enforced disappearances in the specific migration context. A study on 'Disappeared Migrants and Refugees. The Relevance of the International Convention on Enforced Disappearances',[32] published by the German

[29] The Committee on Enforced Disappearances, Guiding Principles for the Search for Disappeared Persons, CED/C/17, available at www.ohchr.org/en/documents/legal-standards-and-guidelines/guiding-principles-search-disappeared-persons.

[30] Ibid., para. 37.

[31] Ibid., Principle 5.

[32] G. Baranowska, *Disappeared Migrants and Refugees: The Relevance of the International Convention on Enforced Disappearances in Their Search and Protection* (German Institute for Human Rights, 2020), available at www.ssoar.info/ssoar/handle/document/71589.

Institute for Human Rights in 2020 identified a number of uncertainties arising from the ICPPED on the protection and search of forcibly disappeared migrants that warranted the attention of the CED. These relate to legal issues that merit the Committee's interpretation, for example, on the obligation to undertake ex officio investigations or to ensure the right to report in transnational situations. This study as well as the growing trends of enforced disappearance in the context of migration initiated the CED's intensified work on these issues, which eventually brought about the adoption of its first General Comment.

In this authoritative document, CED elaborates in detail that, as disappeared migrants may cross many countries to reach their final destination, the cooperation and collaboration between States to prevent disappearances is essential. Article 15 of ICPPED outlines the principles of collaboration noting that, 'States Parties shall cooperate with each other and shall afford one another the greatest measure of mutual assistance with a view to assisting victims of enforced disappearance, and in searching for, locating and releasing disappeared persons and, in the event of death, in exhuming and identifying them and returning their remains.'[33] The General Comment translates this into migrations contexts by calling for 'effective interinstitutional cooperation and coordination … among institutions from countries of origin, transit, destination or return'.[34] The Guiding Principles transform these cooperation obligations into practical measures on the ground. Both the Principles and the General Comment emphasize the importance of mutual assistance and cooperation and the right of victims to report the disappearance irrespective of their migratory status.

In its ongoing work, CED has dealt with several individual cases related to migration and trafficking, in particular addressing the need for cooperation of States when searching and investigating cases of disappeared migrants in multiple circumstances. Among recent examples are confidential requests for urgent actions on behalf of domestic workers from country A who disappeared in country B and their relatives caught between authorities of both countries shifting the blame onto each other.

[33] The International Convention for the Protection of All Persons from Enforced Disappearances, Art. 2, available at www.ohchr.org/en/instruments-mechanisms/instruments/international-convention-protection-all-persons-enforced.

[34] UN Committee on Enforced Disappearances, General Comment No. 1 on Enforced Disappearances in the context of migration, CED/C/GC/1, available at https://www.ohchr.org/en/documents/general-comments-and-recommendations/cedcgc1-general-comment-no-1-2023-enforced.

There is also the huge dimension of disappeared migrants in Mexico that CED had to deal with on site during its visit to the country in November 2021. CED was confronted with multiple allegations of disappearances that occurred in prisons and migration centres and of migrants illegally detained at unknown locations, and it found this development facilitated by an almost absolute impunity.[35] The specific challenges related to trafficking of persons were taken up in preparation of the List of Issues for the review of Nigeria, a country with high levels of trafficking. To enable and facilitate the dialogue with the Nigerian government on this issue, CED asked for information on measures to improve the lack of official data of trafficking cases and identification of trafficking cases among the internally displaced population to ensure that all victims of trafficking are also protected from enforced disappearance.[36]

The common recommendation CED has issued to State Parties in the above-mentioned situations is very clear but far from implemented: to take measures in conjunction or in cooperation with countries of origin, transit and destination of migrants and of persons subjected to trafficking in persons, ensuring the participation of victims and civil society.

## 8.7 CED's Recommendations to African State Parties

One of CED's main tasks is to monitor State Parties' compliance with the ICPPED by reviewing the reports submitted by States Parties and adopt the Concluding Observations to provide guidance on meeting their obligations under the Convention. With regard to the migration context, the Concluding Observations on African State Parties that have been adopted so far mainly refer to the prohibition of non-refoulement pursuant to Article 16. Such specific recommendations were addressed to Tunisia and Burkina Faso in 2016, to Gabon and Senegal in 2017 and to Niger in 2022.

Vis-à-vis two of the reviewed African countries (Gabon and Senegal), CED regretted that it had received inadequate information on the

35 Committee on Enforced Disappearances, Mexico: Prevention must be central to national policy to stop enforced disappearance UN committee finds (2022), available at https://www.ohchr.org/en/press-releases/2022/04/mexico-prevention-must-be-central-national-policy-stop-enforced.

36 Committee on Enforced Disappearances, List of issues in relation to the report submitted by Nigeria under Art. 29(1) of the Convention, CED/C/NGA/Q/1, 2022; Human Rights Council, Visit to Nigeria, Report of Special Rapporteur on trafficking in persons, especially women and children, A//HRC/41/46/Add.1, 2019.

prohibition of refoulement, lacking details on the mechanisms in place and the criteria applied as part of expulsion, return, surrender or extradition procedures to assess and verify the risk that the person concerned runs of becoming a victim of enforced disappearance.[37] As CED carefully monitors developments in national legislations, it noted in regard to the Convention's implementation in Gabon, Tunisia and Burkina Faso that the States have no explicit prohibition of the expulsion, return, surrender or extradition of a person where there are substantial grounds to believe that he or she is at risk of becoming a victim of enforced disappearance as required pursuant to the Article 16 of the ICPPED.

On Burkina Faso, CED found that the principle of non-refoulement is not expressly provided for in legislation and, therefore, there is no guarantee of legal protection for persons who are at risk of enforced disappearance in the event of their return to another State. The Committee recommended taking the necessary steps to incorporate the principle of non-refoulement explicitly into its legislation, in order to ensure that individuals are not at risk of enforced disappearance in the event of their return to another State. Further, the Committee took note of the information concerning the various procedures for expulsion and extradition and the remedies available.[38]

To Gabon and Tunisia, CED recommended to consider introducing into domestic law an explicit ban on the expulsion, return, surrender or extradition of persons where there are substantial grounds to believe that they are at risk of becoming victims of enforced disappearance. It also recommended that the State Parties take the necessary steps to ensure that the principle of non-refoulement is respected in practice, including by carrying out an individualized assessment prior to expulsion, return, surrender or extradition in order to determine whether there are substantial grounds to believe that the person concerned is at risk of becoming a victim of enforced disappearance.[39] As Tunisia lacks a legal

[37] Committee on Enforced Disappearances, Concluding observations on the report submitted by Gabon under Art. 29, para. 1 of the Convention, CED/C/GAB/CO/1, 2017; Committee on Enforced Disappearances, Concluding observations on the report submitted by Senegal under Art. 29 (1) of the Convention, CED/ C/SEN/CO/1, 18 April 2017.

[38] Committee on Enforced Disappearances, Concluding observations on the report submitted by Burkina Faso under Art. 29, para. 1 of the Convention, CED/ C/BFA/CO/1, 2016.

[39] Committee on Enforced Disappearances, Concluding observations on the report submitted by Gabon under Art. 29, para. 1 of the Convention, CED/C/GAB/CO/1, 2017; Committee on Enforced Disappearances, Concluding observations on the report submitted by Tunisia under Art. 29(1) of the Convention, CED/C/TUN/CO/1, 2017.

framework on asylum, the Committee recommended to expedite the adoption of such on asylum and ensure that it provides for the guarantees necessary to prevent any risk of refoulement.[40]

In the recommendations to Senegal, CED again underlined that the principle of non-refoulement must be strictly observed in all circumstances. The Committee took note that it is possible to appeal with suspensive effect against an expulsion decision before the Administrative Division of the Supreme Court. It noted with interest the intention to include in the reformed Criminal Code an explicit prohibition against the expulsion, return, surrender or extradition of a person where there are substantial grounds for believing that he or she would be in danger of being subjected to enforced disappearance.[41] Unfortunately, until today this has not been implemented.

In addition to the issue of refoulement, in its Concluding Observations to Gabon, CED also raised concerns on reports of the scale of trafficking in persons, both foreign and Gabonese nationals, especially women and children who are particularly vulnerable to being placed outside the protection of the law and subjected to enforced disappearance, in particular when they are under the control of non-State actors. CED remained concerned at the current inadequacy of the legal framework to address this extremely serious situation and recommended the amendment of this legal framework in order to ensure that all forms of trafficking in persons are actually punished. Due to the high risk of migrants becoming victims of human trafficking, it is particularly noteworthy that CED raised this concern and recommended that Gabon, in cooperation with countries of origin and destination and victims of trafficking, redouble its efforts to prevent trafficking in persons and disappearances.

The most recent review took place in March 2022 when CED discussed the report of Niger with the State Parties' delegation. With regard to Article 16, Niger explained that extradition, return, expulsion or surrender may not be granted to the requesting State when the person is at risk of torture or other cruel, inhuman or degrading treatment or would be in danger of being subjected to enforced disappearance. The delegation further underlined that Act No. 97-016 of 20 June 1997 on the

40 Committee on Enforced Disappearances, Concluding observations on the report submitted by Tunisia under Art. 29(1) of the Convention, CED/C/TUN/CO/1, 2017.

41 Committee on Enforced Disappearances, Concluding observations on the report submitted by Senegal under Art. 29 (1) of the Convention, CED/ C/SEN/CO/1, 2017.

Status of Refugees governs the expulsion and return of refugees and asylum seekers and an accompanying decree lays down the procedures. All decisions are subject to appeal. The State Party delegation assured that all officials involved in making decisions on expulsion, return and extradition (public prosecutors, police officers, gendarmes, national guards and administrative officials) are trained on criminal procedure, law enforcement rules and compliance with international conventions on the promotion and protection of human rights.[42]

In its Concluding Observations, however, CED stressed its concern about allegations that individuals 'have been removed from Niger in the context of administrative or extradition procedures, despite proven risks that they would be exposed to torture or ill-treatment in the country of return'.[43] Due to the repressive approach of certain provisions of Law No. 2015-36 of 26 May 2015 on the smuggling of migrants, CED raised concerns that this may encourage migrants to live in hiding in conditions that expose them to numerous abuses, which could include the risk of becoming a victim of enforced disappearance and called on the State Party to revise this law in the light of relevant international standards. CED strongly referred to Article 16 of the ICPPED to strictly respect it under all circumstances and fully implement it into national legislation.[44]

As the ICPPED does not include an explicit provision on transnational disappearances, Article 16 is the most obvious relevant provision of the ICPPED with regard to migration. This can explain the almost exclusive focus of the CED's Concluding Observations on the implementation of Article 16 when reviewing enforced disappearances in the context of migration. However, this neglects the relevance of other ICPPED provisions for the prevention of enforced disappearances of migrants, which has now been elaborated in detail in the General Comment. For example, as shown above, secret or illegal detention centres entail great risks for migrants to become victims of enforced disappearances. The prohibition of secret detention, the guarantee of fundamental safeguards in all cases of deprivation of liberty and the proper maintenance of registers

42 The basis of the dialogue, as with all State Parties, is the Report submitted by the Niger under Art. 29(1) of the Convention, due in 2017, CED/C/NER/1, 28 January 2020, and the List of issues in relation to the report submitted by the Niger under Art. 29 (1) of the Convention, CED/C/NER/Q/1, 30 September 2020.

43 Comité des disparitions forcées, Observations finales concernant le rapport soumis par le Niger en application de l'article 29 (para. 1) de la Convention, CED/C/NER/CO/1, 2022.

44 Comité des disparitions forcées, Observations finales concernant le rapport soumis par le Niger en application de l'article 29 (para. 1) de la Convention, CED/C/NER/CO/1, 2022.

according to Article 17 is an issue in all Concluding Observations cited above but without reference to the particular risks for migrants. The obligations to ensure the right to report, to provide mutual assistances and to cooperate have also been identified as most relevant in migration contexts. Thus, when reviewing State Parties' reports, CED will hopefully integrate the findings of the General Comment in future reviews and Concluding Observations to raise awareness on the growing phenomenon of enforced disappearances in the context of migration. Following the most recent review of Greece, with a reportedly high number of migrants who have disappeared in Greek waters of the Mediterranean and the Evros river, CED adopted Concluding Observations that comprehensively reflect the various aspects of obligations[45] and thus could serve as good practice for other reviews ahead.

## 8.8 African Human Rights System and Enforced Disappearances

The African Human Rights system provides for the protection of migrants. The Banjul Charter, the basic human rights document for the continent, protects the right to life, prohibition of torture and cruel, inhuman and degrading treatment, right to personal liberty and protection from arbitrary arrest and freedom of movement.[46] While currently there is no single human rights instrument banning enforced disappearances, the scrouge of this horrific violation has not escaped the attention of the African Commission and the African Court. In 2018, the African Commission extended the mandate of the Working Group on Death Penalty, Extra-Judicial, Summary or Arbitrary Killings to include enforced disappearances.[47] In 2020, the Commission adopted another resolution paving the way for the Working Group to draft guidelines for

[45] Committee on Enforced Disappearances, Concluding observations on the report submitted by Greece under Art. 29, para. 1, of the Convention, CED/C/GRC/CO/1, 2022.

[46] The African Charter on Human and Peoples' Rights. Art. 5, available at https://au.int/sites/default/files/treaties/36390-treaty-0011_-_african_charter_on_human_and_peoples_rights_e.pdf.

[47] The African Commission on Human and Peoples Rights (ACHPR), Resolution on the expansion of the mandate and composition of the Working Group on Death Penalty and Extradjudicial, Summary or Arbitrary Killings in Africa. ACHPR/ Res. 408/ (LXIII), 2018, available at https://achpr.au.int/index.php/en/adopted-resolutions/408-resolution-expansion-mandate-and-composition-working-group.

the Protection of All Persons from Enforced Disappearances in Africa.[48] The Commission has adopted the guidelines in spring 2022 and a specific section is dedicated to the context of migration and disappearances on the continent. The Malabo Protocol and the African Union Convention for the Protection and Assistance of Internally Displaced Persons (the Kampala Convention) prohibit the use of enforced disappearances.

The African Commission also has a specifically dedicated office of the Special Rapporteur on Refugees, Asylum Seekers, Internally Displaced Persons and Migrants in Africa. In 2006, the Rapporteur's mandate was expanded to include migrants with a focus on monitoring of human rights violations, to undertake studies and fact-finding missions and assist member States in developing appropriate policies, regulations and law for the effective protection of migrants.[49]

In 2021, the Commission adopted a specific resolution highlighting the problem of missing migrants in Africa and the impact on their families. The Commission recalled that many refugees and migrants go missing during their journeys and are at risk of enforced disappearances, in detention in transit or destination countries or even in their country of origin when they are deported, including detention of a person in a secret/ unofficial place, which has consequences for the missing persons and their families, in particular women and children, and communities in the short and long term. Further, the resolution highlighted the obligations States have to prevent migrants from going missing in the first place, to facilitate search and identification as well as to support families so that they can know the fate of their missing relatives.[50] The Commission called on States to be more proactive in addressing migrants' situation and emphasized the obligations States have to protect human rights. In particular, the Commission called on the States to adopt measures to prevent migrants from going missing, respect the principle of non-refoulement regardless of

48 ACHPR, Resolution on the Drafting of the Guidelines on the Protection of All Persons from Enforced Disappearances in Africa, Res/448/LXVI, 2020, available at https://africanlii.org/akn/aa-au/statement/resolution/achpr/2020/448/eng@2020-09-17.

49 ACHPR, Mandate of the Special Rapporteur on Refugees, Asylum Seekers, Internally Displaced Persons and Migrants in Africa, available at https://achpr.au.int/en/mechanisms/special-rapporteur-refugees-asylum-seekers-internally-displaced-persons-and-migrant.

50 ACHPR, Resolution on Missing Migrants and Refugees in Africa and Impact on their families, ACHPR/ Res/486 (Ext.OS/XXXIII), available at https://achpr.au.int/en/adopted-resolutions/486-resolution-missing-migrants-and-refugees-africa-and-impact-their-fa.

the migrant status and to avoid enforced disappearances, the States should use detention as last resort.[51]

Finally, the African Union in 1969 adopted a Convention Governing Specific Aspects of Refugee Problems in Africa acknowledging the right to asylum and also codifying the principles of non-refoulment through article 2, which specifies that 'No person shall be subjected by a Member State to measures such as rejection at the frontier, return or expulsion, which would compel him to return to or remain in a territory where his life, physical integrity or liberty would be threatened for the reasons of race, religion, nationality, membership of a particular social group or political opinion.'[52]

While the African Human Rights system is independent from the United Nations, the African Commission has consistently applied the same standards to protect migrants and refugee seekers as the UN. Further, the collaboration between the bodies has been strengthened since the introduction of the Addis Ababa Road map in 2012 that creates synergies between the African Commission and the UN Special mandate holders to identify synergies, develop joint actions and ensure systematic information sharing on human rights on the continent.[53]

## 8.9 How to Fight the Enforced Disappearances in the Context of Migration in Africa

The international and the African human rights systems in principle provide good legal provisions and instruments to protect migrants from becoming victims of enforced disappearances and search and investigate the cases of this heinous human rights violation. The ICPPED clearly outlines the States' obligation on enforced disappearances. It is at the crossroads of international human rights law and international criminal law and can become a strong tool for the global prevention of enforced disappearance also in the context of migration. CED offers important guidance for State Parties and its work should also signal to the victims that their fate is being taken into account. The particularly vulnerable

[51] Ibid.

[52] The African Union Convention Governing Specific Aspects of Refugee Problems in Africa, Art. 2, available at https://au.int/sites/default/files/treaties/36400-treaty-0005_-_oau_convention_governing_the_specific_aspects_of_refugee_problems_in_africa_e.pdf.

[53] OHCHR, ACHPR and the UN Human Rights Special Procedures (2022), available at www.ohchr.org/sites/default/files/documents/hrbodies/special-procedures/2022-10-17/10-years_Addis-Ababa-Roadmap-brochure.pdf.

situation in which migrants and refugees find themselves, on the one hand, and the increasing defensive reflex of States when it comes to migration, on the other, do not make it an easy task for CED. However, dedicating its first ever General Comment to enforced disappearances in the context of migration clearly reflects its commitment to take on the challenge and to contribute to translating important questions of international law into political action.

This legal and institutional basis is undoubtedly an important but not the only part of an overall situation that needs more efforts from all States and the international community. The efforts should focus on the ratification and implementation of international and regional instruments, the necessary training of law enforcement personnel and relevant personnel in the countries and the need to increase awareness among civil society on the ground on enforced disappearance and migration.

As illustrated above, the implementation of the ICPPED by its State Parties is still far from perfect, which does not only apply for African States. Besides that, ratification in Africa lags behind other regions, with only nineteen out of fifty-four African States having ratified the ICPPED. Mali is the only one that has recognized the competence of the CED to receive communications from individuals or any other State Party in accordance with Articles 31 and 32 of the ICPPED. Despite the low numbers of States ratifying the ICPPED and having no regional treaty with specific focus on enforced disappearances, many African States are parties to other regional and international treaties that specifically address the rights violated by the crime of enforced disappearances. The ratification would provide the African States with a road map to protect their own citizens against enforced disappearance and to increase cross-border cooperation amongst them. The most recent ratification from Africa came from Sudan in 2021. This was a particularly welcome ratification, given the country's decades of dictatorship and its relevance as a transit country. But as with almost every State Party, ratification is only the first step. It will take a lot of work and political will until no more people – residents as well as migrants – forcibly disappear there. The ongoing violent conflict has significantly increased the challenges once more.

A recent illustrative example for the need for training of law enforcement personnel has been formulated by CED when it regretted in its Concluding Observations following the review of Niger that 'no court decisions relating to cases of enforced disappearance have been registered and that, according to the State party, the non-application of the

Convention is due in particular to the fact that judges and other judicial actors are unaware that the Convention exists'.[54] This is but one example of the recommendations to provide training of law enforcement personnel, civil or military, medical personnel, public officials and other persons who may be involved in the custody or treatment of any person deprived of liberty according to Article 23 that CED directs to State Parties in most Concluding Observations.[55] With regard to the specifics of enforced disappearances in the context of migration, training for all authorities and State officials dealing with migration is even more relevant and should include topics like the particular vulnerability of migrants and especially migrant children and the interconnection of migration, trafficking and disappearances.

The phenomenon of enforced disappearances is quite unknown despite the high occurrence of this crime on the continent. This is due to the lack of understanding of what an enforced disappearance is, reluctance of the families to report disappearance for fears of being harassed or becoming victims of human rights violations themselves, distrust in the authorities to carry out effective investigations and lack of laws and political will to eradicate this crime. While men are predominantly victims of enforced disappearances, they leave behind wives and children who often bear the brunt of the disappearance. The culture in Africa is no different, and women, who are often reliant on men to be breadwinners, find themselves without any financial support, unable to obtain jobs and support their families. Sometimes, the wives are blamed for the disappearance and ostracized, unable to move on, and continue to suffer for long periods.

Within the context of migration on the continent that has many porous borders and migrants have to cross several countries to reach their final destination, the awareness raising on the issues among the population and capacity building for the government entities interacting with migrants remains one of the challenges ahead.

[54] Committee on Enforced Disappearances, Concluding observations on the report submitted by the Niger under Art. 29(1) of the Convention, CED/ C/NER/CO/1, 2022.

[55] Patino, *The Work of the Committee on Enforced Disappearance*.

# 9

# Enforced Disappearances and the Right to Reparation in Western Balkans

MILICA KOLAKOVIĆ-BOJOVIĆ AND JASMINKA DŽUMHUR

## 9.1 Western Balkans and the Issue of Missing Persons

Two decades have passed since the last armed conflicts in the ex-Yugoslav region. It is estimated that about 40,000 people went missing in the armed conflicts in the former Yugoslavia.[1] In that period, various initiatives at the national and the regional level have been made to carry out search and identification processes, mostly with the support of the International Committee of the Red Cross (ICRC) and International Commission for Missing Persons (ICMP). Even if far from perfect, these initiatives have resulted in locating, exhumation, identification, hand over and a decent burial of the body remains of a significant number of the missing persons. Unlike the search process, the reparative mechanisms available to families of persons who disappeared in armed conflicts in ex-Yugoslavia have remained underdeveloped and largely differs within the region: 35,007 cases were reported to ICRC. According to the data of this organization from September 2023, 9,772 people were still missing as a result of the conflicts in the region. Of these, 6,233 cases are related to the conflict in Bosnia and Herzegovina, 1,924 to the conflict in Croatia and 1,615 to the conflict in AP Kosovo and Metohija.[2] Additional complexity of the situation is associated to the fact that, in some cases, persons who disappeared in the territory of one State may have family members, who are also victims, living in the territory of another State.

Even in the absence of precise estimation, we can say that a large number of those cases fulfil the conditions to be considered as enforced

[1] M. Kolaković-Bojović and E. Tilovska-Kechegi, 'Regional cooperation in the prosecution of war crimes as an EU accession benchmark' in G. Ilic (ed.), *Towards a Better Future: Democracy, EU Integration and Criminal Justice* (Faculty of Law – Kicevo, University 'St. Kliment Ohridski' – Center for Scientific Research at the Faculty of Law – Kicevo, 2019), p. 83.

[2] See more at www.kznl.gov.rs/latinica/dokumenta.php.

disappearances as defined in arts. 2 and 5 of the International Convention for the Protection of all Persons from Enforced Disappearances[3] (hereinafter, ICPPED). It is hard even to imagine the variety and seriousness of the consequences of the acts recognized as enforced disappearance – namely, when a person is arrested, detained, abducted or deprived of liberty by any other form of deprivation of liberty by agents of the State or by persons or groups of persons acting with the authorization, support or acquiescence of the State, followed by a refusal to acknowledge the deprivation of liberty or by concealment of the fate or whereabouts of the disappeared person, which placed such a person outside the protection of the law (Art. 2 of ICPPED) or as part of the widespread or systematic practice of enforced disappearance (Art. 5 of ICPPED). An extreme seriousness and gravity of enforced disappearances is not only associated with the possible consequences for the direct victim. It also strongly affects the family members of a disappeared person on multiple levels. Since they suffer a lot, victims of enforced disappearance need to be recognized, compensated, protected and supported in order to recover to the maximum possible extent. They need legal and institutional guarantees that perpetrators will be brought to justice, but also the guarantees of non-repetition. Even in cases when its duration is not so long, but especially when a fate of the disappeared person is unknown for months, or even for years, an enforced disappearance opens a dark circle of uncertainty.[4] To achieve this, the States shell establish comprehensive reparatory mechanisms based on the international treaties and the soft law.

## 9.2 The Right to Reparation

### *9.2.1 General Legal Framework on Reparations*

The victim's right to reparation has been well recognized and well developed within the UN Human Rights System. While there are some universal UN Human Rights treaties that include provisions that (in)

[3] International Convention for the Protection of all Persons from Enforced Disappearance, adopted on 20 December 2006 during the sixty-first session of the General Assembly in resolution A/RES/61/177.

[4] M. Kolaković-Bojović, 'Disappeared persons and the right to be considered alive – the current state of play in the Western Balkans', in Z. Pavlović and I. Stevanović (eds.), *Yearbook. No. 4, Human Rights Protection: Right to Life* (Provincial Protector of Citizens – Ombudsman and Institute of Criminological and Sociological Research, 2021), pp. 271–87.

directly concern this right,[5] it has been addressed in detail in most of the UN instruments of the new generation (developed since 2010).

The Rome Statute of the International Criminal Court (ICC) establishes an explicit right to reparation for victims of crimes prosecuted before it, as well as measures of protection for victims and witnesses (article 68) including restitution, compensation and rehabilitation (article 75).[6] In addition to the above-mentioned sources of international standards, an important role in recognition of the right to reparation is played by the soft law and jurisprudence of the UN treaty bodies and the special procedures, beyond those specialized in enforced disappearance.

According to the UN Special Rapporteur on the promotion of truth, justice, reparation and guarantees of non-recurrence in 2012, the right to reparation should be perceived as 'the full range of processes and mechanisms associated with a society's attempts to come to terms with a legacy of large-scale past abuses, in order to ensure accountability, serve justice and achieve reconciliation. These may include both judicial and non-judicial mechanisms, with differing levels of international involvement (or none at all) and individual prosecution, reparations, truth-seeking, institutional reform, vetting and dismissals, or a combination thereof'.[7]

Finally, the number and comprehensiveness of the regional legal instruments applicable in Europe, Africa and Asia deserve a special attention.

### 9.2.2 *Legal Framework on Enforced Disappearances and the Right to Reparation*

The very first initiative to establish a universal legal framework on enforced disappearance was adoption of the Declaration on the Protection of all Persons from Enforced Disappearance in 1992 (hereinafter, Declaration).

[5] This right is indirectly recognized in Art. 2(3(a)) of the International Covenant on Civil and Political Rights – ICCPR. At the same time, the Convention against Torture and Other Cruel, Inhuman or Degrading Treatment or Punishment (CAT) directly provides for the right to compensation for victims of torture Art. 14(1), just like the International Convention on the Elimination of All Forms of Racial Discrimination, which provides for this right in its article 6. The same applies for the Convention on the Rights of the Child (Art. 39) and the Hague Convention and Geneva Convention Protocol 1 also contain some references to reparations (Art. 91).

[6] See M. Kolaković-Bojović, 'Víctimas de desaparición forzada y derecho a la reparación' in *Desaparición forzada: Colección en temas de derechos humanos, Tomo I* (Centro Internacional para la Promoción de los Derechos Humanos bajo los auspicios de UNESCO [CIPDH], 2023), pp. 196–226.

[7] Ibid.

Article 19 of the Declaration provides for the right to reparation for the victims of acts of enforced disappearance and their families, who 'shall obtain redress and shall have the right to adequate compensation, including the means for as complete a rehabilitation as possible'. In the event of the death of the victim as a result of an act of enforced disappearance, their dependents shall also be entitled to compensation.

This article complements the rights under the Arts. 9, 10 and 13 of the Declaration, namely the right to a prompt and effective judicial remedy, the right to information and the right to investigation to be conducted and to take part in it. While the rights in these articles are designed to prevent, investigate, and terminate acts of enforced disappearance, the remedies in article 19 apply to victims of enforced disappearances and their families, after their fate and whereabouts have been established, be they alive or dead. In its General comment on article 19,[8] WGEID interpreted that States are 'under an obligation to adopt legislative and other measures in order to enable the victims to claim compensation before the courts or special administrative bodies empowered to grant compensation. In addition to the victims who survived the disappearance, their families are also entitled to compensation for the suffering during the time of disappearance and in the event of the death of the victim; his or her dependants are entitled to compensation' (E/CN.4/1998/43, paras 68–74). In addition to the right to compensation, the right to reparation includes the right to the various means of rehabilitation. The spectre of these means is wide, including medical care; psychological support; guarantees of non-repetition; restoration of liberty, family life, citizenship, employment or property; return to one's place of residence, etc. (WGEID, GC on Art. 19, par. 75)

The biggest step forward in establishing comprehensive legal protection in terms of the right to reparation of victims of enforced disappearances was adoption of ICCPED. Since it belongs to the new generation of UN human rights instruments, it recognizes well that protecting everyone from enforced disappearance, that is, the right not to be victims of enforced disappearance is detachable from the right to truth, justice and reparation for all victims of enforced disappearances.

The concept and scope of the right to reparation are defined in Article 24 of the Convention, which provides that for the purposes of the Convention, the term 'victim' means the disappeared person and any

[8] Working Group on Enforced and Involuntary Disappearances, General comment on Art. 19 of the Declaration on the Protection of all Persons from Enforced Disappearance, E/CN.4/1998/43.

individual who has suffered harm as the direct result of an enforced disappearance. Each victim has the right to know the truth regarding the circumstances of the enforced disappearance, the progress and results of the investigation and the fate of the disappeared person. In addition, the Convention guarantees that each State Party shall ensure in its legal system that the victims of enforced disappearance have the right to obtain reparation and prompt, fair and adequate compensation, covering material and moral damage and, if appropriate, other forms of compensation such as: (a) restitution; (b) rehabilitation; (c) satisfaction, including restoration of dignity and reputation; (d) guarantees of non-repetition.[9] The Convention also stipulates the obligation to continue the investigation until the fate of the missing person is clarified, as well as to take adequate steps regarding the legal situation of missing persons whose fate has not been clarified and the situation of their relatives, in areas such as social welfare, financial issues, family law and property rights.[10] The guarantee of establishment and free participation in organizations and associations that try to establish the circumstances of enforced disappearances and the fate of missing persons and to provide assistance to victims of enforced disappearances are also relevant in this regard, considering the important role that associations of victims play in memorialization actions.

The Convention does not provide for a comprehensive elaboration of the notion of 'reparation', since it introduces compensation as an autonomous term but not as an element of reparation. Therefore, a proper understanding of these notions is of the great importance. In that sense, so-called soft law could be a useful tool in proper understanding of the general terms.

In this sense, UN Basic Principles and guidelines of the right to a legal remedy and reparations for victims of grave violations of international human rights and serious violations of international humanitarian law (General Assembly resolution 60/147 15 December 2005) should be considered as the most useful tool to understanding the essential concept of reparation, where, according to principle of proportionality, this document provides for the State's responsibility for omissions attributable to it

[9] M. Kolaković-Bojović and Z. Grujić, 'Crime victims and the right to human dignity' in Z. Pavlović and I. Stevanović (eds.), *Yearbook Human Rights Protection: The Right to Human Dignity* (Provincial Protector of Citizens – Ombudsman and Institute of Criminological and Sociological Research in Belgrade, 2020), p. 240.

[10] M. Kolaković-Bojović, 'The synergy between criminal law and medicine under the International Convention for the Protection of All Persons from Enforced Disappearance' in I Stevanović (ed.), *Penal Law and Medicine* (Institute of Criminological and Sociological Research, 2019), pp. 387–98.

(para. 15), the State's obligation to establish national reparations programs and other assistance to victims in cases where the person liable for the damage is unable to meet his/her obligation or refusal to do so (para. 16), as well as to ensure the enforcement of domestic and foreign court decisions on reparations (para. 17). In addition, this document defines that reparation includes the following forms: restitution, compensation, rehabilitation, satisfaction and guarantees of non-repetition (para. 18). This provision obviously takes an approach that is different from article 24 of the Convention but is actually proper, considering the compensation as an element/modality of reparation, complementary with three other elements, all aimed at ensuring whenever possible, to return to a situation that preceded a grave violation of international human rights law or serious violations of international humanitarian law (para. 19).

It is important to underline that the Basic Principles could be considered as the most detailed, and therefore the most useful not only in terms of the 'proper reading' of the conventional law, especially of the Art. 24 of ICCPED, but also when developing domestic legislation and practices. The situation related to the exercise of the right to reparation requires States to take urgent measures, where the Basic Principles represent an extraordinary tool for developing those measures. Additionally, all relevant bodies and organizations within the United Nations have an obligation to help member countries in the implementation of their obligations (point 9), which opens up opportunities for States to ensure the necessary support.

### *9.2.3 UN Committee on Enforced Disappearances Practice and the Right to Reparation*

One of the primary UN Committee on Enforced Disappearances (hereinafter, CED) mechanisms aimed at overseeing the implementation of the convention in the State Parties is review of the State Parties' reports submitted in accordance with Art. 29(1) of ICPPED. The CED has established tangible progress in terms of overseeing the implementation of the right to reparation in practice.[11] When it comes to the most frequently raised concerns of CED, in addition to the way the definition of a victim has been recognized in the national legislation, one of the

11 See M. Kolaković-Bojović, 'Víctimas de desaparición forzada y derecho a la reparación' in *Desaparición forzada: Colección en temas de derechos humanos, Tomo I* (Centro Internacional para la Promoción de los Derechos Humanos bajo los auspicios de UNESCO [CIPDH], 2023), pp. 196–226.

most frequently repeated remarks of CED refers to the need to establish a system of reparation that is comprehensive.[12] This further means that it should include all forms of reparation in accordance with Art. 24 (5) of the Convention.[13] In addition to the comprehensiveness/variety of reparative measures, CED underlined that they should be based on a differential approach, which is adequate and fits the real needs of victims.[14]

The CED has also in its practice raised an issue of reparation through the lens of the State Party denial of crime, emphasizing the importance of complementing it with the right to truth and justice.[15]

The CED has been focused on the right to compensation, emphasizing several important elements of this right, like the length of relevant proceedings that need to be conducted to exercise this right in practice. The compensation received in such proceedings should be prompt, fair and adequate but also granted to all persons who have suffered harm as a direct result of enforced disappearance, regardless of their nationality. A decision on compensation should not be preconditioned by the rendering of a final decision in a criminal proceeding, even more, it should be applicable even if no criminal proceedings have been initiated. The compensation claim should not be subject to any statute of limitation or precluded by finishing the investigation stage of the criminal proceeding.[16]

The CED has also paid attention to the accessibility of compensation for victims of enforced disappearances in relation to the application of the territorial criteria, namely, CED recommended that the State party ensure that any person who has suffered direct harm as a result of an offence of enforced disappearance has the right to obtain reparation in accordance with article 24 (4) and (5) of the Convention, including when the person was abroad at the time of the event.[17]

[12] See, e.g., CED/C/GAB/CO/1, 12 September 2017, paras. 19–20; CED COB on Netherlands, CED/C/NLD/CO/1, 26 March 2014, paras. 32–3; CED COB on Honduras CED/C/HND/CO/1, 31 May 2018; CED COB on Niger, CED/C/NER/CO/1, 5 May 2022.

[13] See, e.g., CED COB on Italy, CED/C/ITA/CO/1, 17 April 2019, paras. 34–5; CED COB on Greece, CED/C/GRC/CO/1, April 12 2022, paras. 32–3; CED COB on Brazil, CED/C/BRA/CO/1, November 3 2022, paras. 28–9.

[14] See, e.g., CED COB on Greece, CED/C/GRC/CO/1, April 12 2022, paras. 32–3; CED COB on Brazil, CED/C/BRA/CO/1, 3 November 2022, paras. 28–9.

[15] See CED/C/JPN/CO/1, paras. 25, 26, 40.

[16] See CED/C/MNG/CO/1, paras. 36–7; CED/C/SVK/CO/R.1, paras. 24–5.

[17] See CED/C/CHE/CO/1, paras. 33–4.

It is important to mention that CED has also raised an issue of the accessibility of this right in practice from the perspective of the real effectiveness of the legal and institutional mechanisms.[18] At the same CoBs, the CED raised a very important issue, namely, the relation with the regional mechanisms.[19]

This issue is of special concern when it comes to the European Union Member States whose legislation is mostly based on the EU directives. However, the CED underlines the obligation of the State parties to comply with the provisions of the Convention, including in transposition of the definition of victim in their national legislation. This is well elaborated in the COBs for Italy, where CED clearly stated that the definition of victims in domestic law – including the legislation transposing Directive 2012/29/EU of the European Parliament and of the Council of 25 October 2012 establishing minimum standards on the rights, support and protection of victims of crime and replacing Council Framework Decision 2001/220/JHA[20] – is not in line with the definition of victims provided under article 24 of the Convention.[21]

The above-mentioned position of CED is of great importance considering the differences between the Western Balkans States (hereinafter, WBS) on their EU path. Namely, Croatia is already an EU Member State, while Serbia started the accession negotiations in 2016. Bosnia and Herzegovina has just attained the status of candidate country in 2022 and the start of the accession negotiation for it was approved in March 2024.

## 9.3 The Right to Reparation and the National Legislation of the Western Balkans Countries

Considering the previously elaborated background of WB countries in terms of the history of enforced disappearances, but also the need to establish an effective mechanism to address possible future cases, several questions appear to be relevant in terms of the legal regime applicable to the right to reparation for victim of enforced disappearances:

[18] See CED/C/BOL/CO/R.1, paras. 34–5.

[19] See CED/C/NLD/CO/1, CED/C/PAN/CO/1, para. 13.

[20] Directive 2012/29/EU of the European Parliament and of the Council of 25 October 2012 establishing minimum standards on the rights, support and protection of victims of crime, and replacing Council Framework Decision 2001/220/JHA.

[21] See CED/C/ITA/CO/1, paras. 32–3.

- Does the national legislation recognize enforced disappearance as an autonomous crime?
- How does the very nature of enforced disappearances as a continuous crime affect the right to reparation in view of *ex-tempore* applicability of criminal legislation, considering the earlier mentioned fact that the armed conflicts in Ex Yugoslavia occurred three decades ago?
- Is there is a statute of limitations applicable to this category of crimes?
- Does enforced disappearance constitute a crime against humanity (*ex-tempore* and regarding territorial criteria)?

### *9.3.1 Bosnia and Herzegovina*

According to the central register of missing persons of the Institute for Missing Persons of Bosnia and Herzegovina, of the 34,964 missing persons reported since the 1990s war in Bosnia and Herzegovina, 7,206 are still being sought. In Bosnia and Herzegovina, there is no law on torture on state level – which would define the status and rights of this category of citizens, including victims of the War, so the state lacks basic principles that should regulate this issue. The key issue for defining a right is the recognition of the holder of that right. It has resulted that Bosnia and Herzegovina has failed to establish a national legal framework and comprehensive administrative reparation programme to ensure comprehensive access to full reparation for all categories of civilian wartime victims. While several legislative attempts have been made to address this issue, they have been unsuccessful due to the lack of political agreement between authorities at different levels, who have conflicting agendas and narratives of the past. In the absence of a national reparations programme, victims rely on the existing social protection system and on individual proceedings before criminal and civil courts, both of which have shown considerable shortcomings.[22] Monthly support allowances can be shamefully low, and for some this can be a source of re-victimization. The situation of the group identified as 'women war victims of sexual violence' illustrates how multiple vulnerabilities are not adequately dealt with and thus how the state is failing to provide adequate reparation to victims.[23] Namely, many of those victims are at the same time family members of missing persons.

[22] Report of the Special Rapporteur on the Promotion of Truth, Justice, Reparation and Guarantees of Non-Recurrence, A/HRC/51/34/Add.2, para. 52.

[23] J. Džumhur, *Victimology in Theory and Practice in Post conflict Society: Perspective of Bosnia and Herzegovina* (University Press – Izdanja Magistrat, 2021).

#### 9.3.1.1 Most Important Laws and Institutions

Bosnia and Herzegovina has ratified almost all core United Nations human rights instruments and their facultative protocols as well as the Rome Statute. In relation to the issue of missing persons, it is important to note that Bosnia and Herzegovina ratified the ICPPED[24] in 2012 and recognizes the competence of CED in relation to receiving addresses from signatory States and individuals pursuant to articles 31 and 32 of the Convention.

Article II (2) of the Constitution of Bosnia and Herzegovina prescribes the obligation to 'ensure the highest level of internationally recognized human rights and fundamental freedoms'. It also stipulates that the European Convention for the Protection of Human Rights and Fundamental Freedoms together with its Protocols 'apply directly' and 'have priority over all other law'.

Bosnia and Herzegovina adopted the following laws and strategies that are relevant to missing persons:

- Criminal Code of Bosnia and Herzegovina;[25]
- Law on Missing Persons of Bosnia and Herzegovina, which came into effect in 2004 and applies to those persons who went missing between 30 April 1991 and 14 February 1996;[26]
- Law on the Witness Protection Programme in Bosnia and Herzegovina;[27]
- National War Crimes Strategy of Bosnia and Herzegovina, from 2008 and the Revised National War Crimes Processing Strategy from 2020
- The Criminal Code of Bosnia and Herzegovina adopted in May 2015, which introduced the offence of enforced disappearance as an autonomous crime in article 190 (a), but this new provision does not cover the responsibility of officials at the entity and district levels. The same articles in the Criminal Codes of the entity and district Brcko BiH levels contain elements related to enforced disappearance but they are not sufficient to adequately encompass all the constituent elements and

[24] See "Official Gazette of Bosnia and Herzegovina", International agreements, No. 3/12 dated 15 March 2012.

[25] Criminal Code of Bosnia and Herzegovina, Official Gazette of Bosnia and Herzegovina, No. 3/03, 32/03, 37/03, 54/04, 61/04, 30/05, 53/06, 55/06, 32/07, 8/10) 1

[26] Official Gazette of Bosnia and Herzegovina, No. 50/04, 17 November 2004.

[27] Official Gazette of Bosnia and Herzegovina, No. 36/14.

modalities of enforced disappearance, as defined in articles 2 and 6 of the Convention.

The experience of Bosnia and Herzegovina has particularly shown the importance of ensuring full support and cooperation of family members of missing persons in this process. This resulted in the adoption of the Law on Missing Persons in Bosnia and Herzegovina (hereinafter, LMP BiH), which is a single law to regulate the issue of missing persons. The Institute for Missing Persons was established in 2008 as the single national mechanism for the search, and other measures to improve process of searching missing persons have been taken.

**Law on Missing Persons** Bosnia and Herzegovina was among the first countries to regulate the issue of missing persons through a separate law. The content and arrangements of the LMP are certainly unique in every respect and completely new compared with the previous practice of searching for missing persons. This Law represents a combination of the standards set within humanitarian law and the standards for basic human rights and freedoms. Apart from guaranteeing and ensuring the right to know, the LMP also regulates the right to social protection and other rights of the members of the families of missing persons (Art. 11).[28] The LMP promotes a non-discriminatory and principled approach to all victims of the war – missing persons, defining a missing person in such a way that it includes not only civilians but also combatants and does not differentiate between these two categories. This is also important in terms of establishing the rights prescribed by the LMP, including the right to minimum financial support.[29] When it comes to the exercise of this right, it is proven that this right is defined too restrictively.[30] The WGEID

[28] Art. 11. 'In accordance with this Law, the family members of missing persons, as defined in Article 2, paragraph 2 of this Law, who were supported by the missing person and who are in need of support, shall be entitled to monthly financial support.'

[29] More precisely, this Law gives a general simplified definition of a 'missing person' whose disappearance relates to the period of their disappearance as set forth in the Dayton Agreement, which defines the period of the war and immediate war danger in Bosnia and Herzegovina as being from 30 April 1991 to 14 February 1996. When implemented, it has to be associated with the standards from the above-mentioned international sources.

[30] Art. 2.9 of the Law: 'The need for financial support is found to exist where a missing person's family member is not benefiting from any rights based on which s/he is supporting him/herself, such as: the rights of social protection, pension and disability insurance, veteran disability protection, work-related income, self-employed economic or other independent activity and other income that is considered as support under the applicable legislation.'

noted that there were some compensation programmes in Bosnia and Herzegovina for persons affected by the conflict but that these programmes relate mostly to individual monthly allowances for families of killed or missing persons and that it is necessary to introduce a comprehensive and detailed reparations programme. A particularly worrisome element is the fact that victims are not informed about these programmes and neither are the civil servants who are expected to implement the programmes. There is a need to change this particular provision in such a way that the family members who enjoy the right to pension under the pension and disability insurance provisions are not excluded from the right to financial support, particularly if the amount they receive is minimal, as it is an additional right given to members of the families of missing persons. This is also important, having in mind that a small number of citizens are familiar with the LMP, and the rights of their families are guaranteed by this Law. In the group of family members of missing persons that was part of this study, 61.3% were not even aware that the Fund for Support for Families of the Missing exists. The family members stressed the need to increase efforts to disseminate information on the Fund, since that will initiate lobbying for the creation of the Fund.[31]

**Institute for Missing Persons** The Institute for Missing Persons (hereinafter, IMP) was created for the purpose of locating missing persons and ensuring the rights of the victims of enforced disappearance in accordance with Article 8 of the Law on Missing Persons of Bosnia and Herzegovina. The co-founders of the IMP are the Council of Ministers of Bosnia and Herzegovina (hereinafter, CoM) and the ICMP. The IMP began its work on 1 January 2008, which was certainly too late in view of the basic intention and relevant provisions of the LMP.

**Fund for Support of Families of Missing Persons in Bosnia and Herzegovina** For the purpose of securing funds and realizing the rights of family members of missing persons, the Fund for Support of Families of Missing Persons in Bosnia and Herzegovina (hereinafter, Fund) is established as an independent administrative organization that has the status of a legal entity with its own seal and stamp (Art. 15 para. 1 of the LMP). The Fund was established by the Decision of the Council of

[31] International Commission on Missing Persons, *Persons Who Disappeared Due to Armed Conflicts during the 1990s: An Overview* (ICMP, 2014), pp. 120–1.

Ministers of Bosnia and Herzegovina,[32] with the basic purpose of ensuring and realizing the rights of family members of missing persons, which include the right to financial support, health care, assistance to associations of families of missing persons, marking of places of burial and exhumation of missing persons and other rights in accordance with the Law.

Paragraph 3 of Article 15, as well as Paragraph 2 of Article 1 of the Decision stipulate that the headquarters, method of financing, management and issues related to the work of the Fund shall be regulated by the Agreement that should be signed by the CoM, the Government of the Federation of BiH, Bosnia and Herzegovina, the Government of Republika Srpska and the Government of the Brčko District of BiH within thirty days from the date of entry into force of the Decision. As it was pointed out, the Decision entered into force on 12 December 2006, but unfortunately, the Agreement between the aforementioned entities has not yet been signed, and thus neither the Fund's headquarters nor its financing and asset management have not been determined. This has the consequence that the families of missing persons cannot exercise the rights established by the Law. The establishment of the Fund is particularly important due to the fact that most associations of families of missing persons depend in their work on the goodwill of entity governments and foreign donors, so the implementation of their programs is very difficult.

By establishing the Fund's financing system, that is, by enabling the basic needs of the families of missing persons to be financed from the Fund, primarily with monetary compensation and then other rights, it would enable the families themselves to directly influence the implementation of the LMP and the satisfaction of their basic needs. The Law also enables the Fund, in addition to the primary sources of financing from the budget, to be financed from secondary, additional sources (donations), which creates assumptions that certain goals from the law, especially the marking of places of burial and exhumation of the remains of missing persons and other social programs, which require larger financial resources, are solved in a faster and more efficient way.

Associations of families of missing persons throughout the country have voiced their deep concern over the situation and their loss of trust in

[32] Decision on the Establishment of the Fund for Support of Families of Missing Persons of Bosnia and Herzegovina, adopted by the CoM ('Official Gazette of Bosnia and Herzegovina'), No. 96/06, 4 December 2006.

domestic institutions. Many of their members die without being able to exercise any of their rights and without any support from the proposed Fund. Lastly, it is clear that the failure to establish the Fund also constitutes a failure to execute a significant number of rulings of the Constitutional Court of Bosnia and Herzegovina in relation to missing persons. In this context, the lack of payment of compensation to these families recognized as victims of serious human rights violations relates directly to the failure to establish the Fund, the establishment of which was ordered explicitly by the Constitutional Court of Bosnia and Herzegovina.[33]

There are two reasons for the delay in establishing the Fund. The first is the failure to agree on the location of the Fund and the second relates to the amount of money that each entity should pay to the Fund; the entities have differing opinions on this topic.

The WGEID and CED expressed their concern over the failure to establish the Fund and the fact that no state level law on access to social benefits has been adopted. Furthermore, there were also concerns regarding the lack of a centralized system and over the terms 'reparation' and 'social benefits for the families of missing persons' because these terms are deemed to be unnecessarily confusing. The lack of a centralized system continues to generate numerous cases of discrimination in the entities.[34] It recommended that the authorities in Bosnia and Herzegovina take steps to finally establish the proposed Fund for the Support of the Families of Missing Persons.[35]

Also, the Council of Europe Commissioner for Human Rights expressed grave concern over the failure of the government to meet the remaining obligations related to the LMP, such as establishing the Fund for the Support of the Families of the Missing, increasing the pace of the search for the missing and the provision of funds to support the operations of the associations of the families of missing persons.[36]

[33] Follow-up Report to the Recommendations made by the Working Group on Enforced or Involuntary Disappearances on its Mission to Bosnia and Herzegovina in February 2014, Submitted by TRIAL (Track Impunity Always), p. 7, available at https://trial.ba/wp-content/uploads/2016/02/Follow-upreportBiHFeb2014.pdf.

[34] Follow-up Report to the Recommendations made by the Working Group on Enforced or Involuntary Disappearances on its Mission to Bosnia and Herzegovina. A/HRC/27/49/Add.2, 8 September 2014, items 30 and 31 and Concluding Observations of the Committee on Enforced Disappearances, Item 37.b.

[35] Concluding Observations of the Committee on Enforced Disappearances, Item 38.b.

[36] For more information, see the report by Nils Muižnieks, the Council of Europe Commissioner for Human Rights, on his visit to Bosnia and Herzegovina on 12–16 June 2017, Item 41.

The LMP also constitutes the basis for the work of the associations of the families of missing persons Through the establishment of the Fund, all associations of missing persons would be able to request assistance from the Fund in compliance with criteria defined in the internal documents of the Fund (Art. 19 LMP). Delay in establishing of the Fund has serious impact on their functioning.

Related to implementation of international obligations, the WGEID recognized the substantial progress that Bosnia and Herzegovina has achieved in searching for and identifying missing persons, making reparation to victims and in the criminal prosecution of those responsible for such heinous crimes.[37] Also, CED in its Concluding Observations fully reflect the recommendations adopted by the WGEID.[38] At the same time, much remains to be done in order to realize the rights to truth, justice and reparation for the missing and their families, including establishment of the Fund for the Support of the Families of the Missing, as provided for under the Law on Missing Persons of Bosnia and Herzegovina.

The European Union constantly indicates that Bosnia and Herzegovina will have to thoroughly improve its legislative and institutional framework, in order to ensure the fulfilment of several priorities listed in the Opinion on BiH's request for membership in the European Union (hereinafter, Opinion on progress),[39] of which a significant number aimed at improving the overall state of the rule of law in the country. There are still unsolved cases of war crimes, and it is necessary to adopt a revised state strategy for working on war crime cases. Bosnia and Herzegovina needs to significantly improve the system of protection of civilian victims of war.[40] In this context, it was pointed out that Bosnia and Herzegovina lacks a nationwide strategy for transitional justice in order to ensure a political framework for dealing with the legacy of the past. It is necessary to significantly improve the compensation system for civilian victims of war, including the abolition of the statute of limitations

[37] See A/HRC/16/48/Add.1 and A/HRC/27/49/Add.2, Item 32.

[38] The Committee on Enforced Disappearances considered the report of Bosnia and Herzegovina submitted pursuant to Art. 29, para. 1 of the Convention (CED/C/BIH/1) during its 180th and 181st sessions (CED/C/SR.180 and 181), held on 4–5 October 2016. In its 191st session, held on 12 October 2016, the Committee adopted its Concluding Observations.

[39] European Commission, Opinion on BiH's request for membership in the European Union, COM(2019) 261, 29 May 2019.

[40] Opinion on progress, p. 9.

for claims for compensation in civil proceedings, the introduction of a mechanism for financing compensation from the budget where convicted perpetrators are insolvent and better protection of the identity of victims and witnesses in civil proceedings.

#### 9.3.1.2. Cross Cutting Issues Relevant for Missing Persons

**Compensation** Bosnia and Herzegovina has not adopted legislation to regulate right to compensation. The lack of implementation of the Law on Missing Persons prevents victims of disappearances to enjoy rights prescribed by this law. Some compensation programmes, mostly related to individual monthly allowances for families of killed or missing persons in Bosnia and Herzegovina have been established but not as a part of the comprehensive and detailed reparations programme. Any solution outside international standards creates opportunities for human rights violations. They can apply for rights defined by legislation on civilian war victims and can receive benefits in the form of monthly allowances pursuant to the existing entity-level or district-level social protection and disability schemes. However, the recognition of victim status – and therefore the requirements for accessing rights and the benefits guaranteed and the implementation of those rights – is regulated differently in each entity or district, pursuant to the legislation in force. These allowances are not intended as reparation for the damage suffered but rather as social protection measures without any link to the liability of the entity paying the benefit, or to the beneficiary's rights as wartime victim. In addition, access to this benefit is mainly linked to the place of residence.[41] Also, additional requirements prescribed by entity laws, such as a high threshold of disability,[42] documentation and short deadlines for submission,[43] have serious influence on realization of rights. Disability benefits received by civilian wartime victims remain significantly lower than those received by war veterans.

The cause of this problem is related to defining the concept of victim in BiH legislation. The CED considers that the term 'injured' does not cover every individual who has suffered harm as a direct result of an enforced disappearance. The CED is of the opinion that domestic laws do

[41] See A/HRC/51/34/Add.2, para. 53.

[42] Law on the Basics of Social Protection, Protection of Civilian Victims of War and Protection Families with Children, 'Official Gazette of the Federation of Bosnia and Herzegovina', No. 36/99.

[43] Law on the Protection of Victims of War Torture of Republika Srpska, 'Official Gazette of Republika Srspka', No 90/2018.

not include a definition of victim that is in accordance with the ICPPED, which is why it called on the state to make the necessary amendments to the law in order to ensure the harmonization of the term 'victim' with the term prescribed in the Convention.[44] Different laws adopted on entity's level have different definitions. This has significant impact on enjoyment of the right to reparation.[45] It is clear that not much has been done to avoid multiplication of concepts and approaches in solving this issue. Two of the causes are the absence of state-level legislation regulating the rights of victims and the lack of harmonization of those relevant laws that do exist.[46] This is exactly what creates space for further misuse of victims' sufferings and puts them in the position to be a tool for political campaigns, hate speech, etc. Furthermore, in recent years, the exacerbation of nationalistic discourses, marked by a rise in hate speech, the glorification of war criminals, rhetoric of national/ethnic division and the denial of the crime of genocide, crimes against humanity and war crimes – including calls for separation by some officials – have led to worrying levels of polarization and a virtual standstill in governance.[47] The status of mission persons and their family relatives has been partially solved by adoption of the Law on Missing Persons.

The victims are still habitually neglected, both nationally and globally. The lack of empathy for victims manifested also in the absence of adequate measures to ensure their protection and support remains very pronounced. In the context of BiH, this has been particularly evident in court proceedings in which victims' claims for compensation were rejected, invoking the statute of limitations, in circumstances where the damage was caused by war crimes that are not statute-barred. The obligation of the victims to pay the costs of the procedure of the defendant (entities) in the cases for compensation of damages is especially problematic, in the amount of the lawyer's costs, even though the defendant was represented by the attorney's office financed from the budget. Unfortunately, even when the Constitutional Court of Bosnia and Herzegovina and international mechanisms find violations of

[44] CED/C/BIH /CO/1, 2016, points 35 and 36.

[45] See: J. Džumhur, *Victimology in Theory and Practice in Post conflict Society: Perspective of Bosnia and Herzegovina* (University Press – Izdanja Magistrat, 2021).

[46] L. Pilegaar and J. Džumhur, 'Human rights shortcomings of the Dayton Peace Agreement', *Forced Migration Review*, 2015, www.fmreview.org/.

[47] Special Rapporteur on the Promotion of Truth, Justice, Reparation and Guarantees of Non-Recurrence, Preliminary Observations from the Official Visit to Bosnia and Herzegovina, 2–10 December 2021.

victims' rights in their decisions, their enforcement is often ineffective. In 2018, the State Court ruled that this practice constituted an excessive burden and a violation of the victim's right to property and access to remedy, prompting many payment exemptions before regular courts. Nevertheless, in a significant number of cases in the Republika Srpska, property seizures already underway have continued.[48]

The rejection of claims against the State and the entities in civil proceedings put victims in the position to ask for compensation in criminal proceedings against the perpetrators in which judges referred them to civil proceedings. This changed with a court judgment in 2015, after which sixteen judgments obliged the perpetrators to pay compensation, although payment was rarely enforced due to the perpetrators' reported lack of assets.[49]

The two Universal Periodic Review cycles,[50] in relation to missing persons and the prosecution of war crimes, recommended that Bosnia and Herzegovina, among others, continue its effort on fighting impunity for serious human rights violations committed during the armed conflict, adopt the Law on Reparation and Compensation to Victims of Torture during the War and amend the criminal legislation in order to harmonize it with obligations under international criminal law and obligations relating to criminal proceedings against the perpetrators of international crimes and war crimes in particular.[51]

**Memorialization** There is no comprehensive legal or policy framework regulating memorialization processes at the State level. Therefore, this matter is handled unevenly at local levels. A law on memorials adopted in the Republika Srpska in 2011 has been criticized for fostering discrimination.[52]

Article 20 of the LMP provides for the obligation to ensure that sites of suffering of missing persons in Bosnia and Herzegovina are marked,

[48] Report of the Special Rapporteur on the Promotion of Truth, Justice, Reparation and Guarantees of Non-Recurrence, A/HRC/51/34/Add.2, para. 56.

[49] TRIAL International, Bosnia and Herzegovina Study on Opportunities for Reparations for Survivors of Conflict-related Sexual Assault Violence, p. 63, available at https://trialinternational.org/wp-content/uploads/2022/03/GSFReportBiH_ENG_Web.pdf.

[50] The second UPR cycle on Bosnia and Herzegovina took place on 5 November 2014 and received a total of 167 recommendations.

[51] See more at www.ohchr.org/EN/HRBodies/UPR/Pages/BAIndex.aspx.

[52] Report of the Special Rapporteur on the Promotion of Truth, Justice, Reparation and Guarantees of Non-Recurrence, A/HRC/51/34/Add.2, para. 65.

which represents an important contribution to the process of facing the past. The legal provision regulating this issue is defined in very broad terms and the application of the prescribed right requires that the applicant meets the minimum requirements in order to be able to enjoy this specified right.

The families of missing persons or their associations may request that burial and excavation sites (individual or joint sites) be marked, regardless of the number of victims or missing persons.

In accordance with the Law, the appearance of markers or memorial plaques, financing and other issues are regulated by the Rulebook on Marking Places of Burial and Exhumation of Missing Persons (hereinafter, Rulebook), adopted by the CoM,[53] based on the proposal of the Ministry of Human Rights and Refugees of Bosnia and Herzegovina, in consultation with the competent ministries of the Federation of BiH, Republika Srpska, Brčko District of BiH and representatives of the association of families of missing persons.

The procedure for exercising the right to mark the place of burial and exhumation begins with the submission of a request to the IMP, as the competent authority for searching for missing persons, to issue a certificate that a body was exhumed at the specific location. This certificate, together with the request for marking the place of burial and exhumation, is submitted to the Fund, which, in cooperation with the competent state authorities, will obtain all the necessary documentation regarding the marking of the place (Art. 6 para. 1 of the Rulebook).

Article 20 para. 3 of the LMP and Article 6 para. 3 of the Rulebook prescribe that the competent authority of the municipality is the Department for Urban Planning and Spatial Planning and, in accordance with the laws in the field of urban and spatial plans, is obliged to issue appropriate permit for placing a memorial plaque or other appropriate sign.

The Law does not prohibit the marking of other places (e.g., the place where a missing person died, the place of a primary mass grave, etc.) with other means, provided that a permit has been obtained from the competent office for urban spatial planning.

Namely, the appearance of the marker/memorial plaque is regulated in a unified manner by Article 2 of the Rulebook, which establishes a unique text in the individual case and prescribes the method of marking the

53 Rulebook on Marking Places of Burial and Exhumation of Missing Persons, 'Official Gazette of Bosnia and Herzegovina', No. 83/06.

excavation site of multiple bodies. The Rulebook also defines the procedure for marking a site of joint or individual exhumation and the burial of unknown persons. The MPI is competent for submitting a request for marking a site of joint or individual exhumation or the burial of unknown persons (article 4 and 6 of LMP).

Great powers by the Rulebook are given to the Commission for the Selection of the Conceptual Design of the Memorial Plaque and Signs. The rights regulated by the Rulebook are financed by the resources of the Fund in accordance with the plan and priorities established by the Committee. The maintenance of the memorial is also financed from the resources of the Fund (Article 7 of the Rulebook). The failure to establish the Fund prevents creation of the Committee and implementation of the Rulebook. As a result, the families of missing persons do not enjoy the right to memorialization prescribed by the Law on missing Persons of BiH.

Also, there is concern that civil society efforts to memorialize victims belonging to national or ethnic minorities at the entity level, particularly in the Republika Srpska, have been hampered by local authorities (often belonging to the majority ethnic group) or by administrative requirements that delay or block the process for years. As a result, families of victims and survivors do not have the possibility to remember the harm suffered and to honour the victims.[54]

#### 9.3.1.3 Remaining Challenges

Therefore, in Bosnia and Herzegovina, there is not a state level reparations programme that includes compensation, allowances, restitution, rehabilitation, memorialization and the guarantee of non-repetition. Lack of implementation of the provisions of LMP that define establishment of the Fund prevents victims from accessing social benefits for the families of missing persons. Regulation of social benefits on the entity level for civilian war victims results in the overlapping of the terms 'reparation' and 'social benefits for war victims'. It also raises the issue concerning differences in access to and level of social benefits and other social protection measures resulting from the place of residence. Bosnia and Herzegovina should take measures with the aim to implement recommendations of WGEID, CED and other international bodies that victims

[54] Report of the Special Rapporteur on the Promotion of Truth, Justice, Reparation and Guarantees of Non-Recurrence, A/HRC/51/34/Add.2, para. 70.

of disappearances have access to the right to reparation in accordance to international standards.

### 9.3.2 *Serbia*

Making the search processes efficient and providing for reparation to the family members of the disappeared persons are highly dependent not only on national policies but also on regional cooperation, having in mind that most of the searched persons have gone missing in the territories of other States created by the disintegration of the former Yugoslavia and Kosovo.[55] In the territory of Serbia, a total of 1,402 remains were exhumed, of which 457 were exhumed in city cemeteries and 31 were exhumed in individual grave sites in connection with armed conflicts in the territory of the former Yugoslavia and 4 graves in connection with the conflict in Kosovo,[56] where 914 persons were exhumed and where the percentage of identification of the remains is greater than 97%. The Commission for Missing Persons of the Republic of Serbia (CMP) no longer has any information that would indicate the existence of a grave where the remains of the victims are buried in the territory of the Republic of Serbia.[57]

#### 9.3.2.1 The Most Important Laws and Institutions

Serbian legislation does not recognize the term 'reparation' itself, due to legal tradition, whereas the right to reparation is mostly seen in the context of compensation. However, specific elements of the right to reparation (restitution, rehabilitation and satisfaction, including restoration of dignity and reputation and guarantees of non-repetition) are guaranteed to victims through the set of rights provided to victims by Constitution,[58] ratified international agreements that consist of an integral part of the domestic legal order and by domestic legislation.

In accordance with Art. 194. of the Constitution, the Serbian legal and institutional system is governed by the Constitution, ratified

[55] This designation is without prejudice to positions on status and is in line with UN Security Council resolution 1244 and the International Court of Justice Opinion on the Kosovo declaration of independence.

[56] This designation is without prejudice to positions on status and is in line with UN Security Council resolution 1244 and the International Court of Justice Opinion on the Kosovo declaration of independence.

[57] See more at www.kznl.gov.rs/latinica/dokumenta.php.

[58] Constitution of the Republic of Serbia 'Official Gazette RS', No. 98/2006 and 115/2021.

international treaties and generally accepted principles of international law and Serbian laws. Generally accepted rules of international law and ratified international treaties shall be an integral part of the legal system in the Republic of Serbia, and they are directly applicable (Art. 16). Since Art. 167 provides that the Constitutional Court shall decide on the compliance of laws and other general acts with the Constitution, generally accepted rules of the international law and ratified international treaties, it's clear that national legislation is subordinated to the ratified international treaties and generally accepted principles of international law that are, as the integral part of the domestic legal order, directly applicable by Serbian authorities, together with the provisions of the domestic legislation.

Therefore, the obligation of Serbia to ensure an effective remedy to compensate damages to victims of enforced disappearances stems from the Constitution itself, from the generally accepted rules of the international law, directly applicable international treaties integrated in the domestic legal order by the ratification and the domestic legislation.

The Constitution of the Republic of Serbia guarantees that everyone 'shall have the right to compensation of material or non-material damage inflicted on them by the unlawful or irregular activity of a state body, entities exercising public powers, bodies of an autonomous province or local self-government' (Art. 35(2)), as well as the rights to receive assistance from the state in cases of 'social and existential difficulties' (Art. 69(1)).

Serbia ratified the ICPPED and other relevant international instruments (universal and regional) whose provisions supplements the ICPPED in terms of the right to reparation in 2011.[59] In addition to this, Serbia has ratified relevant regional legal instruments such as the European Convention for the Protection of Human Rights and Fundamental Freedoms[60] and the European Convention on the Non-Applicability of Statutory Limitation to Crimes against Humanity and War Crimes.[61] Therefore, the Serbian authorities are also guided by the European Court of Human Rights (ECtHR) jurisprudence.

59 Convention for Protection of all Persons from Enforced Disappearances 'Official Gazette RS– International Treaties', No. 1/11.

60 Arts. 13 and 41 of the European Convention for the Protection of Human Rights and Fundamental Freedoms, 'Official Gazette of the SaM – International Treaties', No. 9/03.

61 European Convention on the Non-Applicability of Statutory Limitation to Crimes against Humanity and War Crimes Strasbourg, 25 January 1974.

It is also governed by the following legislation: the Criminal Code of (S)FRY,[62] the Criminal Code (CC)[63] and the Criminal Procedural Code (CPC)[64]; the Law on Civil Procedure[65] (LCP); the Law on Contracts and Torts[66] (LCT) and the Law on Non-contentious proceedings,[67] with interpretation supported by the Guidelines for improving the case law with regard to procedures for compensation of damage to victims of serious crimes in criminal proceedings.[68]

In this regard, the issue of major concern is the legal status of enforced disappearances in Criminal Legislation, in accordance with Arts. 2 and 5 of ICPPED. Namely, Art. 371 of CC recognizes, as an autonomous crime, only enforced disappearances committed under the Art. 5 of the ICPPED, while those committed under the Art. 2 of the Convention are not recognized as autonomous crimes, but partially, under the other crimes such as abduction, illegal detention, abuse of power, etc. Therefore, the legal regime applicable to the right to reparation in criminal proceedings for enforced disappearances is one applicable to crimes against humanity.

In terms of the *ex-tempore* applicability of the penal legislation, it is important to reiterate that a crime of enforced disappearance is considered to be finished when the fate and whereabouts of the disappeared persons are known. Therefore, the provisions of the two criminal codes are relevant for cases of enforced disappearances: CC, SFRY and CC. The

[62] Criminal Code of SFRY 'Official Gazette SFRY', Nos. 44/76-1329, 36/77-1478, 34/84-895, 37/84-933, 74/87-1743, 57/89-1441, 3/90-63, 38/90-1217, 45/90-1340, 54/90-1773 and 'Official Gazette FRY', Nos. 35/92-651, 37/93-816, 24/94-273, 61/01 of 9 November). In 1992, the name of the law was changed from the Criminal Code of SFRY to the Criminal Code of FRY.

[63] Criminal Code, 'Official Gazette RS', Nos. 5/2005, 88/2005 – ispr., 107/2005 – ispr., 72/2009, 111/2009, 121/2012, 104/2013, 108/2014, 94/2016, 35/2019 and 27/2021 – CC decision i 62/2021 – CC decision.

[64] Criminal Procedure Code, 'Official Gazette RS', Nos. 72/11 of 28 September 2011; 101/11 of 30 December 2011; 121/12 of 24 December 2012; 32/13 of 8 April 2013; 45/13 of 22 May 2013; 55/14 of 23 May 2014; and 35/19 of 21 May 2019.

[65] Civil Procedure Law, 'Official Gazette RS', Nos. 72/11, 49/13, 74/13, 55/14 and 87/2018.

[66] Law on Contracts and Torts, 'Official Gazette SFRY' Nos. 29/78, 39/85, 45/89, 57/89, 'Official Gazette SRY', No. 31/93, 'Official Gazette SM', No. 1/2003.

[67] Law on Non-contentious proceedings, 'Official Gazette of the SRS', No. 25/82 and 48/88 and 'Official Gazette of the RS', No. 46/95 – other law, 18/05 – other law, 85/12, 45/13 – other law, 55/14, 6/15 and 106/15 – other law, 14/22.

[68] Guidelines for improving the case law with regard to procedure for compensation of damage to victims of serious crimes in criminal proceedings, available at www.podrskazrtvama.rs/en//posts/presentation-of-guidelines-for-damage-compensation-87.php.

first one was in force when the armed conflicts in the former Yugoslavia occurred and has not recognized enforced disappearances. The present one establishes the responsibility for enforced disappearances committed under Art. 5. of the Convention, but it could be applied only on enforced disappearances committed or still ongoing after entering the 2005 CC into the force.

#### 9.3.2.1 The Mechanisms to Get Compensation

**The Access to Compensation in Criminal Proceedings** In criminal proceedings, Serbia does not apply statutory limitations for war crimes and crimes against humanity. Article 2 (11) of the Serbian Criminal Procedure Code (CPC) defines a victim (injured party) 'as a natural or legal person who's personal or property right has been violated or jeopardized by a criminal offence'. This definition seems to be narrower than the definition provided in article 24 of the Convention, which provides that for the purposes of the Convention, the term 'victim' means the disappeared person and any individual who has suffered harm as the direct result of an enforced disappearance.

The rights of a victim (injured party) in criminal proceedings are listed in article 50 of the CPC. However, the CPC exclusively recognizes the notion of *injured person* whereas the Criminal Code refers to both concepts of *injured party* and *victim* without clear criteria for distinction, which creates some confusion.

Article 50 of the CPC includes a wide scope of the rights in line the EU *acquis* among which are the right to submit a motion and evidence for realizing a restitution claim and a motion for interim measures for securing it (Article 50 (1)). This mechanism allows a victim to claim compensation from an offender for material or non-pecuniary damage suffered, since a claim for restitution may relate to the compensation of damage, return of objects or annulment of a certain legal transaction (Art. 252 of CPC). In cases where the court assessed that rendering a decision on a compensation claim could result in the significant delay of the procedure, it can refer a victim to a civil proceeding (Art. 256 of CPC).

However, the implementation of the legal framework remains inconsistent. In order to harmonize the practice for deciding on compensation claims in criminal proceedings, the Supreme Court of Cassation (SCC) adopted Guidelines for improving the case law with regard to procedures for compensation of damage to victims of serious crimes in criminal proceedings in late 2019. Aside from this role of the courts, for the purpose of this analysis, it is important to mention an issue pertaining to the role of public prosecutors in obtaining compensation in criminal proceedings. Since the CPC from 2011 came into the force, public prosecutors have become those who lead the investigation. Considering this, the obligation of collecting evidence also lies with the public prosecutor at the investigation stage. Despite the great capacity of collecting evidence during the pretrial stage, whereby a court would have the capacity to decide not to prolong the procedure for collecting evidence during the main trial, it seems that prosecutors are either not aware of their role in this regard or they don't have sufficient administrative capacities and/knowledge to do so.

Therefore, despite these clear and adequate provisions of CPC, courts almost never use this mechanism of deciding on compensation claims in criminal proceedings. Instead, victims are regularly referred to submit a compensation claim in a separate civil proceeding. This is partially caused by the prosecutorial inactivity in terms of their role in collecting evidence relevant for a court to render decision not only on criminal conviction but also on the compensation claim.

As final outcome victims are pushed to initiate a new procedure before civil court, and

- engage additional costs in legal fees and in legal representation,
- face undue length of procedure for several years,
- potentially have to repeat their testimonies before the two different courts, hence causing re-traumatization and are
- not be able to benefit from any victim assistance, support or protective measures (including protection of the identity) when they are before civil courts as in civil proceedings, victims are a party equal to the offender from whom they are claiming a damage.

**The Mechanisms to Claim Compensation in Civil Proceedings** The LCT (Art.376) prescribes that the general limitation period to submit the lawsuit is three years from the moment that the victim has learned about non-material damage they have suffered as a consequence of a violent act, and/or the period of five years from the date on which the damage occurred.[69] When 'the claim for compensation against the person liable shall expire upon the expiration of the limitation period set forth in the statute of limitations of the criminal prosecution' (Art. 377 of the LCT).

[69] Judgment of the First Basic Court in Belgrade, 32 P br.70585/10, 15 June 2012.

The Supreme Court interpreted that the privileged statute of limitation is applicable on compensation claims based on the convictions in criminal proceedings – its length is connected with the statute of limitation applicable to the criminal proceeding for a certain crime. Therefore, since there is no statute of limitations applicable to international crimes, the same applies on compensation claims. In 2011, the Constitutional Court ruled an expansion of the application of the privileged statute of limitation (in cases of crimes against humanity, that means its non-applicability), not only to civil claims against the perpetrator but also against the State. In case a civil lawsuit is submitted prior to the criminal conviction, a general three years'[70] statute of limitation from the LCT is applicable. This solution is adequate from the legislative standpoint but could raise concerns when criminal proceedings are prolonged, preventing access to compensation in civil proceedings against the State, in absence of a criminal conviction against a perpetrator.

Therefore, in terms of the applicability, but also the length of the statute of limitation, the qualification of the crimes committed as international or ordinary crimes is paramount, which is directly dependent on the time and territorial borders of the armed conflict in which an enforced disappearance occurred.

The same issue relevant for the criteria that Serbian authorities take into account when deciding on reparation have been addressed in the ECtHR jurisprudence, mostly in *Fejzić and others* against Serbia[71] and *Kamenica and others* against Serbia.[72] Most importantly, the ECtHR addressed the issue of territorial criteria, more precisely, confirming that Serbian authorities consider crimes that occurred in the Serbian territory, during the conflict in Bosnia and Herzegovina, as an ordinary, not international crime.

In terms of the practical possibilities to enforce a decision on compensation from the perpetrator, it is important to mention that Serbia has established an efficient mechanism of enforcement through the bailiffs, but

[70] *Refik Hasani et al*, Judgment of the First Basic Court in Belgrade 84.P.46946/10, 6 June 2011, and Judgment of the Court of Appeal in Belgrade, Gž. 1771/12, 24 August 2012.

[71] *Fejzić and others* v. *Serbia*, Application No. 4078/15, 26 September 2017, inadmissibility of compensation cases for acts committed on the territory of Serbia out of 'state of war' – application of the statute of limitation.

[72] *Kamenica and others* v. *Serbia*, Application No. 4159/15, 4 October 2016, inadmissibility of compensation cases for acts committed out of 'state of war' on the territory of Serbia – application of the statute of limitation.

this cannot address the situations where, by referring the victim to civil proceedings, the court allows the offender enough time to sell all their property and therefore prevents the victim from getting compensation or where the offender is simply very poor. In that case, there are no alternative sources (e.g., State funds) from where compensation can be sought.

#### 9.3.2.3 Reparative Measures in Administrative Proceedings

By the adoption of the Law on the rights of veterans, military invalids, civilian invalids of war and members of their families (hereinafter, The Law on War Veterans, LoWV) in early 2020, a new legislative framework for acquiring the status of civilian victim of war for the family members of a missing person has been introduced to replace the procedure earlier ruled by the Law on the Rights of Civilian Invalids of War of 1996.[73] The law brings a wide scope of social benefits grounded in the fact that a person has suffered damage in the context of an armed conflict but without establishing the direct causal link between a crime against humanity committed and a damage suffered. The LoWV also recognized the rights of the family members of a missing person, providing them a status as family members of civilian victims or civilian invalids of war. Namely, according to Art. 27 of the same Law, a family member of a civilian war victim or invalid is considered a member of the family of a deceased civilian war invalid if they lived together in a joint household for at least one year before death and, therefore, this does not match the notion of victim as provided in Art. 24 of ICPPED.

Upon acquiring the status, victims become entitled to monthly cash benefits, subsidized public transport passes, health care, costs for care assistance and funeral costs (Art. 32 of the LoWV). The extent of the right and the amount of the monthly cash benefit for the family members of a victim are determined by the damage a victim suffered but also by various social characteristics of the family members associated with the status of vulnerability.

The competent authority for rendering a decision on the status of civilian victims of war is the local municipality/self-governments (the first instance) and the Ministry of Labour, Employment, Veterans, Social Affairs (hereinafter, the Ministry) as a second instance.

While listing the documents that need to be submitted by applicant a (family member of a missing person), LoWV requires, among others, to

[73] Law on the Rights of Civilian Invalids of War, 'Official Gazette of the RS', No. 52/96.

submit a declaration of death. This declaration/certificate could be issued to the family members as a result of a procedure for the declaration of missing person as dead or proof of death, according to the Law on Non-contentious proceedings. This law (Art. 57, par. 1(d)) provides that, among others, persons who disappeared during the war in connection with the events of the war, and about whose life there was no news for a year from the day of the cessation of hostilities, may be declared deceased. A proposal for declaring a missing person dead can be submitted by any person who has a direct legal interest in it, as well as by the public prosecutor (Art. 58).

Basically, this means that the family members of missing people are not considered as civilian victims of war until a declaration of death is issued (Art. 177), which is not in line with Art. 24(6) of the UN CPPED and prevents numerous potential family members of the victims of enforced disappearances to access the social protection measures. They are supposed to choose between upholding a presumption that their family member is alive and the right to access some social benefits.

#### 9.3.2.4 Rehabilitation and Symbolic Reparations

Rehabilitation plays an important role in reparation to victims, and it is preconditioned by establishing and operation of victim support services, specialized programs and adequate training of practitioners in contact with victims. The current legislative framework insufficiently deals with the rehabilitation of victims through victim support. According to the Law on the organization of courts[74], the Higher Court in Belgrade 'provides and provides assistance and support to witnesses and victims' (Art. 25(4)), while the Art. 52 of the same law provides that: 'In the judicial administration of higher courts, as well as other courts determined by the High Judicial Council [hereinafter, HJC], a service may be organized to provide support and assistance to witnesses and victims.' Organization and the operation of the victim support services are governed by the Court Rulebook (Arts. 38a–b)[75] and internal guidelines issued by the HJC[76] and Republic Public Prosecutor.[77]

[74] Law on the organization of courts, Official Gazette, No. 10/2023.

[75] Court Rulebook, Official Gazette, Nos. 110/2009-87, 70/2011-31, 19/2012-28, 89/2013-7, 96/2015-130, 104/2015-50, 113/2015-61 (corr.), 39/2016-44, 56/2016-56, 77/2016-57, 16/2018-34, 78/2018-161, 43/2019-16, 93/2019-275.

[76] www.podrskazrtvama.rs/lat/media/domaci/Uputstvo-o-nacinu-pristupa,sistemu-rada-i-nacinu-postupanja-sluzbe-za-pomoc-i-podrsku-svedocima-i-ostecenima-07.04.2015..pdf.

[77] www.podrskazrtvama.rs/lat/media/domaci/Opste-obavezujuce-uputstvo%20_Tuzilastvo.pdf.

There are also services at certain civil society organizations, legal clinics and social work centres, which offer support services to victims. There is a lack of exact data on the number and structure of service providers and programmes they offer, although it is known that their geographical coverage and the range of services they offer are highly inconsistent. What is also lacking are clearly defined criteria for professional qualifications of providers and the quality of services they provide. Needs assessment procedures, referral procedures along with procedural rules for provision of support have not yet been standardized. There are no formal mechanisms in place for maintaining liaison and cooperation between support providers nor has a system for coordination and funding of providers been established. This applies as well to a system for oversight of providers' activities. Training programmes in victims' rights have not been either standardized or established as part of initial and ongoing training for judicial office holders. Information regarding available types of support has not been systematized or made accessible via a single database.

Some preparatory steps have been made in order to amend relevant penal and judicial legislation in order to address requirements of the National Strategy for Enforcement of the Rights of the Crime Victims in Serbia (2020–5) in order to establish the nationwide network of support services, but legislation necessary to do that is to be amended yet.

Some activities of the Commission for Missing Persons, like an adoption and the implementation of the Framework Plan for Resolving the Issue of Missing Persons from the Conflict in the Former Yugoslavia (Framework Plan to Address the Issue of Persons Missing from Conflicts on the Territory of the Former Yugoslavia, 2018), also contribute to memorialization. All of these symbolic reparative measures have had a significant influence on the change of the general climate in terms of the public recognition of victims and the reconciliation. However, sporadically, there are still some public statements made by officials that jeopardize the principle of non-selective public recognition of victims, non-discrimination of victims and the spirit of non repetition.

#### 9.3.2.5 2021 Developments

In early 2021, the Serbian government established the working group to develop a draft Law on Missing Persons. A few months later, an initial draft was published, addressing the comprehensive scope of the rights of the persons missing in, or in relation to the conflict in the former Yugoslavia.[78]

As a basis for the draft, the working group used the CED's 2019 Guiding Principles for the search for disappeared persons[79] and reflected them, in detail, in the chapter of the law dedicated to the main principles and in the section that regulates the rights of the missing persons and the members of their families. In addition to the right to be searched, the Law provides for the wide spectrum of the rights of the family memebers, starting from the right to be informed about the progress and the results of a search, through monthly cash benefits and other social protective, assistance and support measures.

Assumption about the life of a missing person is ruled by the separate article (Article 3), which stipulates that a missing person shall be considered alive, until:

- he/she is found alive
- the remains are identified
- or until the missing person is declared dead in accordance with the regulation governing the declaration of a missing person as dead and proving death.

In order not to leave this presumption without legal effects, Art. 3, para. 2 provides that the rights of family members of a missing person or a person whose burial place is unknown shall not cease, in accordance with this Law, with the identification or declaration of the missing person as dead. Therefore, the draft law has introduced a kind of correctional mechanism in relation to the earlier mentioned requirements of the LoWV and the Law on Non-contentious proceedings, having in mind that it not only upholds the presumption that a missing person is alive but also upholds exercising the rights of the family members even if a missing person has been declared dead.[80]

[78] 'In terms of this law: 1) Missing person is a person about whom the family has no news, and whose disappearance occurred during or in connection with the armed conflicts in the territory of the former Socialist Federal Republic of Yugoslavia (hereinafter: SFRY) in the period from 1 January 1991 to 31 December 1995 and in the territory of the Autonomous Province of Kosovo and Metohija (hereinafter: AP KiM) in the period from January 1, 1998 to December 31, 2000 (hereinafter: armed conflicts) and which was reported on the basis of reliable disappearance data' (Art. 2).

[79] Committee on Enforced Disappearances, Guiding principles for the search for disappeared persons, CED/C/7, 8 May 2019.

[80] Kolaković-Bojović, 'Disappeared persons and the right to be considered alive', pp. 271–87.

Some efforts to rule activities in the field of memorialization have been made through the draft Law on Missing Persons (Arts. 60–5), which provides for the mechanisms of cooperation between the Commission and other relevant national, regional and international interlocutors to coordinate activities in connection with commemorating the International Day of the Disappeared and allocating funds to finance programs of associations of families of missing persons but also to promote the rights of missing persons. However, since the Draft was finalized in December 2021, no progress has been made in order to send it to the legislature, which strongly affects the family members who are patiently waiting to exercise their right to reparation in practice.

### 9.3.3 *Croatia*

In the territory of the Republic of Croatia, disappearances especially happened at the beginning and end of the conflict. Most Croatian victims disappeared in 1991, while most Serbian victims disappeared in 1995 during the operations 'Bljesak' and 'Oluja'. According to data provided by the Ministry of Veterans' Affairs of Croatia, 18,000 persons disappeared in 1991 and a further 1,226 persons disappeared in 1995.[81] The fate of more than 82% of registered cases of missing persons have been discovered. According to information submitted to the WGEID in 2018, the Republic of Croatia is searching for 1,945 missing persons, nationals of the Republic of Croatia or the mortal remains of persons killed from the beginning of the War.[82] They can be divided into two basic groups, based on the period of their disappearance: missing or killed persons from the period 1991–2 or 1,130 persons (95% of them are of Croatian ethnicity) and missing or killed persons from the period 1995 and later or 815 persons (98% of them are of Serbian ethnicity).

#### 9.3.3.1 The Most Important Laws and Institutions

The Republic of Croatia is a signatory to numerous agreements in the field of international humanitarian law and human rights. In 2022, the Republic of Croatia ratified the ICPPED.

[81] See A/HRC/30/38/Add.3 paras. 24 and 25.

[82] On 6 February and 14 August 2018, the government of the Republic of Croatia provided the Working Group on Enforced or Involuntary Disappearances with the information it requested concerning the implementation of the recommendations of the Working Group that were made following its visit to the Republic of Croatia. For more information, see Item 73 on p. 6 of the corresponding report.

The Constitution of the Republic of Croatia guarantees the highest level of international standards. The Law on Persons Missing in the Homeland War[83] (hereinafter, LPM) was adopted in 2019. The Homeland War Croatia is narrative in use based on a pervasive conception of self-defence against a larger Serbian aggressor. This opens a question of its relationship with the narrative of transitional justice that is focused on truth, justice and reparation. Especially, it opens questions of the position and treatment of civilian war victims. This Law constitutes the legal framework for defining a missing person, whereas respective rights are regulated under the Law on Civilian Victims from the Homeland War (hereinafter, LCVHW).[84] Article 8 of LCVHW, the Law on Civilian Victims from the Homeland War, defines civilian victims as civilian invalids and civilians killed, died or missing, that is, members of the immediate and extended family of a civilian killed, died or missing in the Homeland War. Also, Croatia has adopted the Act on the Rights of Croatian Homeland War Veterans and their Family Members and the Act on the Protection of Military and Civilian War-Disabled Persons. The acts establish a monthly stipend to the victims and families, although differences have been noted regarding the benefits received by families of veterans as opposed to families of civilians. A system of psychosocial assistance to families of missing persons has been set up.[85]

In accordance with Article 2, citizens of the Republic of Croatia are entitled to the rights prescribed by the Law. Exceptionally, foreign citizens may exercise rights under the Law, if they or the person on whose behalf they are submitting an application for exercising rights at the time of the injury had permanent or temporary residence in the territory of the Republic of Croatia; they do not obtain rights from the state of which they are citizens or from the state in whose territory they reside at the time of submitting a request for the exercise of rights under the Law. The citizens of the Republic of Croatia who also have foreign citizenship can apply for rights prescribed in the Law if they do not obtain them from another state of which they are citizens. Article 5 of the Law defines those who cannot enjoy the status and rights established by the Law. An element of the law that has raised concern is that it prevents the granting of benefits, including to 'members, helpers or associates of

[83] The Law on Persons Missing in the Homeland War, 'The Official Gazette', No. 70/19.
[84] 'The Official Gazette', No. 84/2021 (1555), 23 July 2021.
[85] The Report of the Special Rapporteur on the Promotion of Truth, Justice, Reparation and Guarantees of Non-Recurrence, A/HRC/51/34/Add.1.

enemy military and paramilitary units who took part in the armed aggression against Croatia, as well as members of their families'. Several interlocutors expressed concern that this broad notion could lead to inconsistent interpretations and unfair applications of the law.[86]

The LCVHW prescribed a set of rights for the following depending on victims′ categories: (a) rights of the disabled based on body damage; (b) rights based on the loss or disappearance of a family member and c) other rights.

The rights based on loss or disappearance of a family member are family disability allowance, increased family disability allowance, enlarged family disability allowance, family disability allowance after the death of a disabled civilian from the Homeland War I to IV groups and monetary compensation in the amount of family disability allowance and increased and enlarged family disability allowance. For victims of disappearances other rights prescribed by the Law are relevant. Those rights include monetary compensation for civilian victims from the Homeland War, the right to one time financial assistance, allowance for household appliances, the right to free textbooks, the right to a scholarship, preference for accommodation in student dormitories, the right to priority in hiring and filling a position, preference for placement in social welfare institutions, the right to use the services of veteran centres, the right to psychosocial assistance, the right to legal aid, special internships, exemption from payment of compensation for conversion of agricultural land, exemption from payment of court, administrative and notary fees and the right to the costs of transportation and burial of the remains of exhumed and identified civilians missing in the Homeland War on the territory of the Republic of Croatia.

#### 9.3.3.2 Compensation

In regard to the issue of damage compensation, the Republic of Croatia has adopted the Law on Liability of the Republic of Croatia for the Damage Caused by Members of the Croatian Army and Police Acting in their Official Capacity during the Homeland War (hereinafter, Liability Act).[87] This Law regulates the liability of Croatia in terms of

[86] Special Rapporteur on the Promotion of Truth, Justice, Reparation and Guarantees of Non-Recurrence, A/HRC/51/34/Add.1.

[87] Law on Liability of the Republic of Croatia for the Damage Caused by Members of the Croatian Army and Police Acting in their Official Capacity during the Homeland War, 'Official Gazette', No. 117/2003, 23 July 2003.

the damage caused over the period 17 August 1990 to 30 June 1996. It constitutes the legal basis for damage compensation for any damage caused to any person as the result of an act by a government official. However, the Law does not provide for the prior establishment of individual liability for the damage. The WGEID recognized that there were problems with the implementation of the Law. These problems have led to a situation where most compensation claims are rejected, except in the case of court disputes where criminal liability has already been established. The main reasons for the rejection of such claims are the Republic of Croatia's refusal to accept liability for damages caused during the war in the territory that was not under its control and its failure to prosecute the perpetrators. At the same time, there is an established practice, especially in cases of enforced disappearances, which shifts the burden of proof mostly to the plaintiff.[88] The WGEID recommended that a detailed analysis of the obstacles to the implementation of the Liability Act be conducted for the purpose of ensuring the effective application of this Law.[89] Despite this legislative framework, difficulties were still faced by victims trying to obtain compensation from the State. Moreover, attempts by many families of victims to receive compensation through lawsuits against the state have failed, and plaintiffs have been reportedly forced to pay substantial court fees, forcing some of them to sell their homes. This situation has reportedly disproportionally affected ethnic Serbs. Other measures to provide full reparation owed to victims beyond compensation, such as restitution, rehabilitation, satisfaction and guarantees of non-recurrence are not regulated under this legal framework.[90]

#### 9.3.3.3 Memorialization

According to observations of the Special Rapporteur on the Promotion of Truth, Justice, Reparation and Guarantees of Non-Recurrence, memorialization processes in Croatia have been mainly focused on the commemoration of the victory and the conduct of the war and in honouring Croatian veterans and victims. These efforts are welcomed; however, they show a prevalent focus on memorializing the victory in the conflict and Croatian victims, albeit the latter to a lesser extent. Memorialization efforts aimed at commemorating all victims, and in particular victims

[88] Report of the Working Group on Enforced or Involuntary Disappearances on its visit to Croatia on 15–18 June 2014, A/HRC/30/38/Add.3., 17 August 2015, para. 63.
[89] See A/HRC/30/38/Add.3. para. 96.
[90] See A/HRC/51/34/Add.1. paras. 46 and 47.

of Serb ethnic origin or other minorities, seem restricted to civil society efforts, with the notable exception of the commemoration of Day of Remembrance of Missing Persons in the Homeland War. The Special Rapporteur recognized the recent efforts from some high-ranking officials to commemorate all victims of the conflict and to recall violations suffered on all sides.[91]

#### 9.3.3.4 Remaining Challenges

The government of Croatia adopted certain measures in the areas of accountability, missing persons, reparations, and legal and institutional reform to address the legacy of the conflict. After the conflict, and particularly during Croatia's accession process to the European Union, some of these areas saw discernible progress, such as the prosecution of war criminals, the search for missing persons and the pace and quality of legislative and institutional reforms aimed at ensuring the rule of law, democracy and the promotion and protection of human rights. However, progress appears to have stalled in the last seven years since the accession to the EU and concerns have risen regarding the prospects of effective social reconciliation, particularly as a result of growing instances of hate speech, the glorification of war crimes and the relativization of the decisions of the ICTY and national tribunals.[92]

The WGEID, after visits to Croatia, recommended to authorities to continue its efforts in the search for missing persons and the identification of mortal remains in order to ensure the efficient prosecution of war crimes in compliance with international standards, adopt all necessary measures to fight impunity and establish a comprehensive programme of reparation.[93]

## 9.4 EU Integrations and the Issue of Disappeared People in the Western Balkans

Victims as witnesses should be provided with support in accordance with Resolution GS UN 60/147(2005) and the Directive 2012/29/EU. However, it is of the utmost importance to use EU integrations of the

[91] See: A/HRC/51/34/Add.1, paras. 56–61.

[92] See: A/HRC/51/34/Add.1.

[93] The Follow-up Report to the recommendations made by the Working Group on Enforced or Involuntary Disappearances on its missions to Croatia, Montenegro, Serbia and Kosovo. A/HRC/39/46/Add.2., 10 September 2018, p. 2.

WB countries as an effective mechanism not only to achieve the standards in terms of the protection of the victims' right to reparation but also to preserve the achieved level of the rights, once a state become the EU Member State, where the proactive role of the European Commission (hereinafter, EC) is crucial.

In that regard, the role of the EU accession processes in the Western Balkans should not be disregarded as a mechanism that can significantly contribute to the developments at the national level as through the regional cooperation. Namely, the mechanisms established by EC to measure the progress made by candidate countries based on the fulfilment of the interim and closing benchmarks in Cluster I (Fundamentals), more precisely, in negotiation of Chapter 23 (Judiciary and Fundamental Rights)[94] ensures that the progress towards the better protection of the rights of missing persons and their families influences the EC assessment of the Rule of Law state of play and therefore ensures fostering additional reforms.

In addition to the domestic reforms, progress and achievements in this field are also assessed by EC through the lens of regional cooperation under the ICMP and EU-WB mechanisms.

Namely, the regional dimension of searching for missing persons requires a regional approach.[95] In this context, the signatory member States should continue to fulfil their obligations assumed by signing the Declaration on the Role of the State in Addressing the Issue of Persons Missing as a Consequence of Armed Conflict and Human Rights Abuses in 2014, supported by ICMP (Mostar Declaration).[96] It is also necessary to ensure implementation of obligations from the final declarations of the EU-WB summits held in 2018 and 2019 in Sofia, London in 2018 and

[94] For more info on the new accession methodology, see M. Kolaković-Bojović and I. Simonovski, 'The accession negotiations of North Macedonia to the EU: Between new methodology and old challenges' in *International Scientific Conference 'Law between the Ideal and the Reality'* (Faculty of Law and Institute for Comparative Law, 2023), pp. 103–15.

[95] See more in M. Kolakovic-Bojovic and Elena Tilovska Kechegi, 'Regional cooperation in the prosecution of war crimes as an EU accession benchmark' in *International Scientific Conference 'Towards a Better Future: Democracy, EU Integration and Criminal Justice': Conference Proceedings* (Faculty of Law, Bitola: 2019), pp. 83–99; Kolaković-Bojović, 'Disappeared persons and the right to be considered alive, pp. 271–87.

[96] ICMP (2014). Declaration on the Mostar Declaration (Declaration on the Role of the State in Addressing the Issue of Persons Missing as a Consequence of Armed Conflict and Human Rights Abuses).

Poznan,[97] which address in detail the need for an individual commitment to improve the legislative and institutional framework and practice in accordance with relevant international standards but also their mutual cooperation in the field of war crimes prosecution, victims' rights and the search for missing persons and good neighbourly relations.

The above-described mechanisms have significantly contributed to raising the awareness of the general public on the issue of missing persons but also fosters the processes of the adoption of the national legislation dedicated to this issue. In this process, the WBs face various challenges, starting from a need to achieve a large number of international standards but also to avoid further regional conflicts through ensuring equal rights to all persons missing under the same circumstances associated to the armed conflicts. Finally, one of those challenges appears to be addressing the right to be considered alive until the fate of a missing person has been ascertained.

## 9.5 Conclusions

The issue of missing persons is regulated differently across the WBs, which also includes the legal regime of the crime of enforced disappearances and the different legal status of the victim. This has a huge impact, especially in the terms of whether the victim was a member of a military structure or a civilian. Regulation in this area is complicated further by the fact that persons who disappeared in the territory of one state may have family members, who are also victims, living in the territory of another state. This raises the question of who should ensure the rights of victims. The understanding of the concept of reparation is highly developed in the region, with the focus on compensation as an element of reparation. At the same time, the victims mostly seek recognition, namely, to be acknowledged under the law. The fact that in most of countries the relevant laws have still not been adopted points to an unwillingness to define the matter in accordance with international standards. In terms of compensation, this mostly relates to specific minimum social benefits, which complies with the prevailing challenges in the World in this regard.[98] There is a lack of memorialization, and it

[97] Sofia Declaration, 2018, retrieved April 15, 2020, available at www.consilium.europa.eu/media/34809/sofia-declaration_sr.pdf.

[98] G. Baranowska, 'The rights of the families of missing persons: Going beyond international humanitarian law' (2022) 55,1 *Israel Law Review* 25–49.

remains mostly unregulated, just as is the case of support to the associations of the families of missing persons. In addition to this, participation of victims in the various judicial and non-judicial processes, in parallel before the national, regional and international mechanisms, water down the concept of the efficiency of justice, keeping them trapped in the limbo of various standards and procedures.

The regulation of the right to reparation should be a part of a comprehensive, integrated process that includes the right to truth and justice. This process, from the perspective of disappearance, does not have solely a humanitarian purpose, but it is also a legal requirement and a factor that can improve inter-state relations and strengthen social cohesion in the societies in the region. The conclusion of the WGEID following its visits to the countries of the region was that despite the impressive results of the past, the level of progress in the search for missing persons has slowed down significantly in recent years A common gap at the regional level within the existing legal systems is the absence of the crime of enforced disappearance and the absence of an encompassing framework for compensation and reparation for the victims and their relatives.[99] It is important to adopt a national reparation policy aimed at implementing the existing legal framework in order to provide effective and timely reparations to all categories of victims, including compensation, rehabilitation, satisfaction, restitution and guarantees of non-recurrence. The reparations programme should be adopted in full consultation with victims and according to international standards and include a gender and disabilities perspective.

Also, it is necessary to ensure that national legal frameworks define a missing person and his or her rights in accordance with Article 24 of the ICPPED. The equitable distribution of existing resources for civilian war victims should be ensured in order to eradicate, among others, discrimination between civilian and military war victims. In terms of the specific challenges at the national level, in the context of Bosnia and Herzegovina, it is important to adopt comprehensive legislation on torture victims, including legislation on reparation. Government authorities should take action without delay to establish the Fund for the Support of the Families of Missing Persons. This requires a prior assessment of the potential number of beneficiaries, considering the limitations as set out in Article 2.9. of the LMP.

[99] See A/HRC/30/38/Add.1. and A/HRC/30/38/Add.3. paras. 8 and 13.

The analysis also revealed several shortcomings peculiar to each of the countries. For example, in Croatia it is crucial to eliminate the discriminatory policies in terms of the access to reparation in practice in order to comply with relevant international standards. In Serbia, the adoption of the Law on Missing Persons based on the 2021 Draft Law is the main prerequisite to comply with relevant standards and ensure that victims can access comprehensive reparative measures.

10

# The Strategies to Increase the ICPPED Ratification with Special Attention to the Asia-Pacific Region

## Being a Party as an Incessant Act of Treaty-Making

KOJI TERAYA[*]

## 10.1 Introduction

Agreeing with Emmanuel Decaux, the first chair of the Committee on Enforced Disappearances (CED), that the International Convention for the Protection of All Persons from Enforced Disappearance (the ICPPED, the Convention) is characterized as 'a very sophisticated and modern instrument',[1] one must also emphasize that it is true only if it has sufficient States parties. While the issue of increasing the number of States parties is not necessarily a point of contention in many other treaties, it is a very important issue. This is because the obligations of States can only be discussed once they have become parties to a treaty.

The ICPPED currently has seventy-one States Parties and ninety-eight signatories. This is second only to the International Convention on the Protection of the Rights of All Migrant Workers and Members of Their Families among the core UN human rights treaty bodies with ten monitoring bodies.[2] A campaign 'to double the number of States Parties' was

[*] Please note that this chapter is written in my personal capacity as an academic and is not the view of the organizations to which I belong(ed) in the past and present, in particular the Human Rights Committee and the Committee on Enforced Disappearances. Japanese-language references are translated into English by this author (Teraya) and not officially by the author of that document. This chapter has received technical assistance from Danni Zhang (PhD student, University of Tokyo). Any errors contained within are solely mine.

[1] Emanuel Decaux, 'The International Convention for the Protection of All Persons from Enforced Disappearance, as a victim-oriented treaty', in M. M. deGuzman and D. M. Amann (eds.), *Arcs of Global Justice* (Oxford University Press, 2018), pp. 57–63, at p. 58.

[2] For an up-to-date status on the number of States parties of the eighteen UN human rights treaties, see https://indicators.ohchr.org; for more details including information on the

launched in August 2017 during the period of Zeid Ra'ad Al Hussein, former High Commissioner for Human Rights, in response to the sluggish growth in the number of States Parties. At the start of the campaign, there were 57 countries, so the aim was to reach 114. There does not appear to have been sufficient strategy or foresight behind this simple quantitative target. There exists a significant disparity between the current reality and the aspirational goal, warranting critique for its overly optimistic indulgence.[3]

Apart from increasing the number of States participating in the ICPPED, there are other ways of exerting a norm against enforced disappearances on States. A typical one is to argue for the formation of customary international law and claim that it has become general law. The ICRC's attempt at customary international humanitarian law is a prime example. However, this is difficult in the absence of adequate State implementation, and customary law, by its nature, has no precise norms to begin with. No country would actively oppose it being a moral obligation, but the problem of the lack of State parties can only be solved by increasing the number of the States parties to the Convention.

This chapter examines the factors contributing to the small number of States Parties to the ICPPED. In doing so, it focuses both on the States that choose and on the conventions that are chosen. Next, it considers how the number of States Parties can be increased. Bearing in mind that ratification in practice has been gradual, this chapter also considers how the issue of enforced disappearances should be addressed even if the number of State parties remains relatively low.

In this chapter, particular attention will be paid to the Asia-Pacific region.[4] This is because the number of countries in the region that have ratified the ICPPED is extremely low. Of the 194 Member States of the UN, 55 are from Asia and the Pacific region, but only 10 States, or less than 20%, are parties to the ICPPED, while the African region has about 35% and the other three regions have around 50%. Even if the general objective of increasing the number of parties to the ICPPED is upheld,

status of each State party of the ICPPED, see https://treaties.un.org/pages/ViewDetails.aspx?src=TREATY&mtdsg_no=IV 16&chapter=4&clang=_en.

[3] Michelle Bachelet, the next High Commissioner for Human Rights, was realistic in setting a target, which was to increase the number of ratifications by 100 more overall human rights treaties, including the ICPPED, by 2018–21. However, it was unclear how many more States parties to the ICPPED should be targeted.

[4] In this chapter, 'Asia' refers to the fifty-five countries bracketed by the UN as Asia-Pacific (Asia-Pacific States), see www.un.org/dgacm/en/content/regional-groups.

the growth potential in other regions is not significant. In other words, geographically speaking, this issue is also a human rights issue for a specific region, the Asia-Pacific region. Conversely, the major problem of enforced disappearances in Asia, among the various issues, is first of all the problem of increasing the number of States Parties to the ICPPED, the flagship convention of this issue. This situation serves as a reminder of the 'Asian theory of human rights', which posits that Asia holds a unique perspective on human rights. This relativistic notion is not confined to Asia alone but is rather prevalent across various regions globally. Consequently, it prompts us to reevaluate the fundamental concept of the universality of human rights.

## 10.2 Analyzing the Status Quo

Factors leading to participation or non-participation in human rights treaties are complex. From an easy point of view, countries having not experienced enforced disappearances yet do not join because they are not interested, and countries facing enforced disappearances do not join because they do not want to be criticized. This seems to be particularly true in the case of the ICPPED. However, if this were entirely true, there would be no States ratifying human rights treaties in the first place. In reality, many States have ratified various human rights treaties. Also relevant is the question of the extent to which the articles of the ICPPED and the CED's management and interpretation of each issue are attractive to individual States.

Despite the complexity of the situation, cost-benefit calculation by countries is a necessary perspective when considering the increase in the number of ratifying countries. The term 'benefit'[5] is broad and ambiguous, but for a more precise understanding, it is better to divide them into two categories: 'practical benefit' and 'honour'. Here, 'practical benefit' refers to the protection and promotion of human rights made possible by human rights treaties, which can be further divided into external and internal benefits. Honour refers to the normatively high reputation of others for State behaviour, which does not include practical

[5] On the relationship between human rights and national interests, see generally Koji Teraya, 'Theory of human rights diplomacy: A consideration on the role of international law in diplomacy', in Shunji Yanai and Shinya Murase (eds.), *Putting International Law into Practice: In Memory of Ambassador Ichiro Komatsu* (Shinzansha, 2015), (in Japanese) pp. 626–31.

benefits. Honour has been pointed to as a national interest since the traditional era of State sovereignty. This type of benefit is transitive to the external real benefit through the concept of 'international contribution'.

More specifically, it is necessary to be able to have a subjective perception on the part of the State that the treaty will be 'beneficial' in a broad sense. It is not directly whether the treaty is intrinsically good, value-wise or morally, per se, but how the State decides on that and other aspects of it. It is also important who recognizes and judges this, which generally speaking means policymakers. However, this does not mean that the perceptions of different various legal actors within each State are not relevant, and indeed, in practice, especially in democracies, the perceptions of many legal actors are actually affected, especially through the electoral process.

### 10.2.1 *Perspectives from the State Side*

#### 10.2.1.1 The Status Quo

States can be broadly divided into three categories: (1) parties, (2) non-parties but signatories and (3) non-parties. There are ten State parties in the first category, in order of earliest ratification or accession: Kazakhstan (2009), Japan (2009), Iraq (2010), Samoa (2012), Cambodia (2013), Mongolia (2015), Sri Lanka (2016), Fiji (2019), Oman (2020) and Republic of Korea (2023). The States in the second category are, in order of earliest to latest, the following nine: Cyprus (2007), India (2007), Vanuatu (2007), Lebanon (2007), Maldives (2007), Lao People's Democratic Republic (2008), Indonesia (2010), Palau (2011) and Thailand (2012). All States having signed in 2007 were those that signed on 6 February, when signatures were opened in Paris. The third category includes thirty-six States other than those mentioned above, for example, Bangladesh, China, Myanmar, Pakistan, Philippines, Qatar, Saudi Arabia and Singapore.

The following discussion hypothetically takes up various factors, namely the States' political system, the real need to tackle enforced disappearances and the existence of alternative forums, which while not comprehensive, are highly relevant, as this section will discuss.

#### 10.2.1.2 Political System

It is difficult to draw certain conclusions from the above ratification situations, but first of all, the characteristics of the States, in particular its political system, may have an impact. Broadly speaking, the hypothesis is that States with mature democracies may tend to ratify the

ICCPED. Indeed, the Asia-Pacific region, with its weak treaty participation, is generally considered to have a low degree of democracy and generally overlaps. For convenience, a distinction is made here between liberal democratic and authoritarian regimes. Of the countries concerned, Japan and South Korea are the leading liberal democracies in the region. Among the signatories, only Cyprus, India, Indonesia and Thailand can be considered relatively democratic. However, States that are considered to have a relatively low degree of democracy, such as Cambodia, Iraq and Laos, are also parties. It seems fair to say that a rather clear feature is that the more authoritarian regimes such as China and DPRK are not in the ICPPED.

It is common to argue about such liberal-democratic/authoritarian dichotomies, for example, Eric Posner's much-discussed sceptical view of the usefulness of human rights treaties.[6] Arguments of this kind may seem too broad. 'Liberalism', 'democracy' and 'authoritarianism' are difficult to define strictly. It may look tautological, if one considers the conclusion of human rights treaties a consequence of liberal democracy. One would also find it of little usefulness to look at the fifty-five countries in Asia in terms of these two types. However, liberal democracy/authoritarianism is an excellent description of Sate behaviour and, as a first point of departure for qualitative classification, it is useful to organize the relationship between the complexity of reality. In this sense, this chapter uses these terms as ideal types in the sense of Max Weber, at the same time with reference to the quantitative analysis of democracy.[7] Additionally, it is not necessarily linked to treaty ratification. For a liberal democratic State, having ratified a human rights treaty is one important but not decisive indicator. The situation is not simple, as can be seen from the fact, for example, that the DPRK is a State party of the ICCPR.

[6] Eric Posner, *The Twilight of Human Rights Law* (Oxford University Press, 2014), esp. pp. 59–66. Other representative examples are John Rawls, who contributes to the present rise of international justice theories. When discussing the extension of the application of the 'law of peoples', he distinguishes between liberal peoples/States and decent peoples/States, as well as between ideal and non-ideal types. See John Rawls, *The Law of Peoples* (Harvard University Press, 1999), pp. 3–128.

[7] There are numerous studies using various indicators of democracy, see, e.g., EIU Report, available at https://www.eiu.com/n/campaigns/democracy-index-2023/. This chapter does not examine the validity of indicators or the appropriateness of inferences in various studies but rather explores the possibility of collaboration in relation to qualitative judgements.

Liberal democracies share liberal democratic values nationally and internationally, which are generally favourable conditions for treaty ratification. Referring to E. Posner's argument,[8] liberal democracies participate in human rights treaties primarily to exert pressure on authoritarian States or to help transitional States defend human rights. An explanation from democratic peace theory is introduced as to why they dare to get involved in the human rights of other States, which is that altruism and countries that do not protect human rights will start wars.[9] Although this does not immediately lead to the ratification of treaties of their own, additional reasons could be added, such as to increase the option of pressure through international organizations and to answer the criticism of double standards for not taking on international standards themselves.

Another type of 'benefit' to consider is honour. Even if a human rights treaty does not improve or make much difference to the human rights situation in their country, liberal democracies still value being a party to the treaty itself and seek to ratify it. Honour is more likely to work by ensuring freedom of speech. In some cases, as in Japan, it is incorporated into the Constitution (Preamble).[10]

Authoritarian States are not really intended to comply, either to avoid external pressure or for propaganda purposes. In terms of practical interests, the issue of enforced disappearances, as well as human rights in general, is not of paramount concern to authoritarian regimes. In the face of a wide variety of diverse and enormous political, security, economic and other challenges, the conclusion of human rights treaties that are not perceived to be of great practical interest is not a political priority. Even if a specific ruler felt a real benefit, it is difficult to say that it would be easily realized. As for the honour factor, it can be said that

[8] Posner also mentions 'transitional counties' as a third type, but this takes into account the temporal element, and from a generalization point of view it would be easier to distinguish between the two types.

[9] Posner, *The Twilight of Human Rights Law*, pp. 60–61.

[10] According to Preamble of the Constitution of Japan (1946), 'We desire to occupy an honored place in an international society striving for the preservation of peace, and the banishment of tyranny and slavery, oppression and intolerance for all time from the earth', available at https://japan.kantei.go.jp/constitution_and_government_of_japan/constitution_e.html. Though there is no explicit mention of 'hounor', a similar idea can be found in the Preamble of the Constitution of the Republic Korea, that is, 'To elevate the quality of life for all citizens and contribute to lasting world peace and the common prosperity of mankind', available at www.law.go.kr/LSW/eng/engLsSc.do?menuId=2&query=CONSTITUTION%20OF%20THE%20REPUBLIC%20OF%20KOREA#liBgcolor0.

authoritarian regimes do not care much about the honour factor in the first place. If this is the case, the incentive to enter into treaties will be scarce.

However, the argument is not simple. Costs also need to be taken into account. Paradoxically, even in liberal democracies, the costs are perceived to be greater when external interests are the main factor or when compliance with the treaty is taken more seriously, which can be a factor that discourages ratification. They cannot join a treaty when the breach of the treaty is too clear-cut, and the extent of the breach has to be moderate. On the other hand, for authoritarian regimes, no costs may arise, especially if there is no intention to comply with the treaty. This is particularly the case when treaty norms are ambiguous and difficult to comply with in the first place or when the supervisory body does not have sufficient enforcement powers.

#### 10.2.1.3 The Real Need to Tackle the Issue of Enforced Disappearances

Second, the question arises whether the problem of enforced disappearances exists in the State concerned. In the first place, if enforced disappearances appear to be unknown, there is little incentive to address them by law. Enforced disappearances are generally not found in liberal democratic regimes: the Western European Group of twenty-nine States has a high ratification rate of the ICPPED, but, interestingly, a closer look reveals no Anglo-American States in it. This includes Canada and Australia, which are parties to other human rights treaties. Australia and New Zealand, States not classified as Asian in this chapter but sometimes so classified, are not parties either. From the perspective of these practical countries, there seem little need to address a problem whose existence is not known in the country in the first place.[11] While the issue of enforced disappearances is a universal challenge, its existence is omnipresent. This is distinct from the reality that every country grapples with human rights challenges.

The 'existence' of the problem of enforced disappearances is not limited to typical circumstances. An interesting case is Japan. It is fair to say that in Japan there are no enforced disappearances by the government as is the case in other countries. However, Japan does have the issue

[11] The uneven distribution of enforced disappearances raises a fundamental question that should be considered prior to the promotion of treaty conclusion or even the adoption of a treaty: why do rulers resort to the practice of enforced disappearance? This also needs to be explored in order to assess 'real benefits'.

of abductions by DPRK, which remains a top priority, as evidenced by the then Prime Minister's first visit to North Korea in 2002, which coincided with the start of the drafting of the ICPPED. Liberal democracies generally emphasize foreign interests, and Japan has traditionally done so only moderately. However, this is not the case. Paradoxically, right-wing domestic forces, which normally have little interest in human rights, are enthusiastic. The same applies to South Korea, which is a major victim of abductions by DPRK. It is further complicated by the issue of reunification, however.

Authoritarian regimes also have different aspects. Not all authoritarian regimes resort to enforced disappearances. There are also implementation problems, such as in countries where enforced disappearances have become a problem at the local level, while the central government shows the will to improve. In any case, extreme problems may be a factor in a State's hesitation to ratify the ICPPED. The specific purpose of the Convention reinforces this tendency.

#### 10.2.1.4 The Existence of Alternative Forums for the Issue of Enforced Disappearances

Third, even if the need to legally address the issue of enforced disappearances is recognized, it is also relevant whether there are other alternatives. One alternative is the Working Group on Enforced or Involuntary Disappearances (WGEID), which developed from a thematic procedure established in 1980 during the time of the Human Rights Commission. While it does not have the usual procedure of human rights treaty bodies, such as the State reporting system, its most important strength is that, under the Human Rights Council, the WGEID reaches to States not party to the ICPPED. In this respect, for example, Japan has more benefit in approaching the WGEID for practical purposes, as the WGEID (and not the CED) can reach out to the DPRK.

Another alternative is the Human Rights Committee (CCPR), which is a UN treaty body, just as the CED. To begin with, the ICPPED could have been under the jurisdiction of other bodies, including the HRCt (Article 27).[12] Its functions are also common and, indeed, it has issued 'views' through the individual communication.[13] Of the ten countries that have ratified the ICPPED, all others have ratified the ICCPR, with

[12] Until the decision by State-parties to keep the CED in December 2017.

[13] See, generally, William A. Schabas, *Nowak's CCPR Commentary*, 3rd rev. ed. (N.P. Engel, 2019), pp. 454–8.

the exception of the Sultanate of Oman. Upon examination of non-State parties to the ICPPED, it becomes evident that Palau has signed the ICCPR, albeit it remains unratified. Among the thirty-six States that have neither ratified nor signed the ICPPED, twenty-three are parties to the ICCPR. Consequently, for twenty-four out of a total of fifty-five States, the ICCPR could serve as an alternative instrument.

The existence of alternative forums is an element that makes liberal democracies reconsider the need for ratification. If alternative measures appear to be working to a certain extent, there may be less incentive to ratify the ICPPED, a specific subject matter treaty created later. For example, it looks strange that the Philippines, having ratified up to the First Optional Protocol to the ICCPR, has not ratified the ICPPED, although the fact of enforced disappearance is known.[14]

When there is an alternative forum, the honour factor, which would normally function in liberal democracies, is less likely to do so. This is what might be termed 'the diminishing marginal utility' of honour, as liberal democracies are already parties to general conventions such as the ICCPR, and even if they do not ratify this later convention, their reputation will not be significantly damaged especially if the number of countries remains small at the time. From a practical point of view, the fact that the ICPPED deals with the specific issue of enforced disappearances could also be an obstacle to an increase in the number of States parties. For example, in a general human rights treaty, any liberal democracies would have more or less human rights problems, which would benefit from the protection and promotion of a more comprehensive framework such as the ICCPR. New human rights issues can also be addressed to a certain extent within existing interpretations of rights. Subject-specific treaties do not have these kinds of features and have the advantage of being subject-specific, but the significance of ratification may seem less significant if the issue does not exist in the first place.

On the other hand, of course, there is also the possibility of a positive attitude towards ratification, irrespective of the existence of alternatives. Specificity can also be a strength, involving the willingness to encourage other countries to ratify, with 'ratification' as one of the causes for momentum. Ratification has a symbolic function of displaying a

[14] E.g., Asian Federation against Involuntary Disappearances and Families of Victims of Involuntary Disappearance, 'Tears without Tombs: Enforced Disappearance in the Philippines, Joint Submission of AFAD and FIND to the Third Cycle of the UN Universal Periodic Review', 2017, available at www.afad-online.org/resources/reports/340-tears-without-tombs-enforced-disappearance-in-the-philippines.

commitment to value itself. The ICPPED may have a pragmatic function if it has an institutional appeal that differs from the existing system. Furthermore, if the size of the country is large, as in Japan and South Korea, the additional cost burden may not be perceived as relatively heavy.

Authoritarian States may decide that it is beneficial to pretend to respect international law even if more treaties are not observed. Regardless of the extent to which they do so intentionally, this is a position of disrespect for the treaties themselves. Such a suspicion may be raised in the case of ratifications by States that are parties to various other human rights treaties but do not submit reports or do not come to the review stage. However, for such States, the ICCPR alone is considered sufficient for a nominal commitment to a human rights treaty.

### *10.2.2 Perspectives from the ICPPED Side: The Correlation between the Number of State Parties and the Issues Interpreted by the CED*

The discussion so far has discussed the motivations from the perspective of the States Parties, but it is necessary to look more closely at the Convention on the part of the chosen party. The above discussion of the inherent appeal of the ICPPED concerns, in more detail, the provisions of the Convention and, furthermore, its interpretation.

A well-known technique to increase the number of States at the time was to recognize reservations, but for the ICPPED this should be as limited as possible. The HRCt is substantiated in asserting, as delineated in General Comment 24, that reservations to *jus cogens* and non-derogable rights are impermissible (paras. 8, 10).[15] It is imperative that positions align accordingly, particularly considering that the prohibition of enforced disappearances falls within these categories.

However, this view could be seen as depriving the ICPPED, and in practice, the interpretation of each of its provisions becomes more important. The drafting process is not always decisive in treaty

[15] CCPR General Comment No. 24: Issues Relating to Reservations Made upon Ratification or Accession to the Covenant or the Optional Protocols thereto, or in Relation to Declarations under Article 41 of the Covenant (UN Doc, CCPR/C/21/Rev.1/Add. of 4 November 1994).

interpretation, as not all issues are settled, and some are postponed due to 'constructive ambiguity'. It is particularly important how the committees of the supervisory bodies make their decisions. It is worth noting the fact that their decisions will be an important determinant for States considering accession/ratification at a later stage, while the treaty bodies should make decisions independently of whatever the number of States Parties may be.

#### 10.2.2.1 Definition of 'Enforced Disappearances' (Article 2)

The ICPPED provides a definition of enforced disappearance in Article 2, which States that (i) the actors are 'agents of the State' or 'persons or groups of persons acting with the authorization, support or acquiescence of the State'; (ii) the act is 'the arrest, detention, abduction' or 'any other form of deprivation of liberty' and; (iii) in terms of the manner of the act, it is followed by 'a refusal to acknowledge the deprivation of liberty' or 'concealment of the fate or whereabouts of the disappeared person'. Furthermore, (iv) it includes the provision to 'place such a person outside the protection of the law'.

Although there was a great deal of controversy at the time of drafting as to whether the fourth element was a requirement or a consequence of enforced disappearance, to the extent that 'constructive ambiguity' was mentioned in the drafting,[16] it is now established that the CED's position is to take the three-requirement theory. The scope of enforced disappearance is more widely considered than in the case when the fourth element is required. At the final stage of the drafting process, the position of considering the fourth requirement, or intention, as a requirement, was expressed by Asian countries such as China, Egypt and India, as well as by the UK, the US and Canada.[17] In other words, all these States prefer a narrower scope of enforced disappearance. It is noticeable that they all are not the State parties of the ICPPED.

[16] UN Doc.E/CN.4/2005/66 of 10 March 2005, para. 23. As for the drafting process, see also UN Doc.E/CN.4/2003/71 of 12 February 2003, para. 40; UN Doc.E/CN.4/2004/59 of 23 February 2004, paras. 24–6; UN Doc.E/CN.4/2005/66 of 10 March 2005, paras. 23–5; UN Doc.E/CN.4/2006/57 of 2 February 2006, paras. 91–7, Annex II, p. 49. See also Kimio Yakushiji, 'The reach of United Nations Human Rights Committee's precedents on cases of enforced disappearances and challenges for the Committee on Enforced Disappearances' in Kentaro Serita, Shigeki Sakamoto, Kimio Yakushiji, Masahiko Asada and Keikato Sakai (eds.), *Succession of International Law of Empirical: In Memory of Mr. Nisuke Ando* (Shinzansha, 2019), (in Japanese) pp. 43–89.

[17] UN Doc.E/CN.4/2006/57 of 2 February 2006, para. 92–5, Annex II, p. 49.

#### 10.2.2.2 Definition (Non-State Actors) (Article 2)

A possible further extension of the scope of 'enforced disappearance' is whether to allow it to be committed by non-State actors in relation to the first element. This was also a time of great controversy at the time of drafting.[18] Although, according to the ICPPED definition above, acts by non-State actors do not constitute enforced disappearances, on the other hand, the gravity of the act is not dependent on the actor, and the nature of the crime of enforced disappearance often makes it difficult to determine whether it is committed by a State or a non-State actor, so there is a strong awareness of the need to regulate this.

Interestingly, at the time of drafting, India, which took the position of establishing enforced disappearance only more narrowly, which requires all four elements, argued, on the other hand, that the exclusion of non-State actors was impractical.[19] The ICPPED provides for 'investigation' and 'appropriate measures to bring the case to trial' in Article 3, but how to go further is not well-established policy within the Committee and should be seen as an issue for the future.[20] Judging from a position such as India's, States are not necessarily averse to a broad mandate for the CED, and if the content is reasonable, a broader mandate may, on the contrary, facilitate ratification of the Convention.

#### 10.2.2.3 Criminalization as an Autonomous Crime (Article 4)

The State has an obligation to make enforced disappearance a crime under its domestic law (Article 4). The question is the manner in which this obligation is to be fulfilled, and specifically whether States are required to provide for it as an autonomous crime. Although there were disputes when drafting, the CED has established the position that it

[18] UN Doc.E/CN.4/2003/71 of 12 February 2003, para. 35; UN Doc.E/CN.4/2004/59 of 23 February 2004, paras. 31–41; UN Doc.E/CN.4/2005/66 of 10 March 2005, paras. 29–35; UN Doc.E/CN.4/2006/57 of 2 February 2006, paras. 12–15, 98. See also Kimio Yakushiji, 'Human rights violations by non-State actors and the responsibility of States parties under ICPPED' in Shigeki Sakamoto and Kimio Yakushiji (eds.), *The Challenge of Law for a Universal International Society: In Commemoration of Mr. Kentaro Serita's 70th birthday* (Shinzansha, 2013), (in Japanese) pp. 497–563.

[19] See UN Doc.E/CN.4/2006/57, Annex II. A comment made by States after the entry into force of the ICPPED is, for example, Mali's statement at the first meeting of States Parties in December 2016, see 'Conference of the States Parties, Summary record of the first meeting', UN Doc.CED/CSP/SR.1 of 28 December 2016, para. 53.

[20] As one of the authoritative introductions, see Mohammed Ayat, 'The controversial involvement of non-State actors in the Commission of Enforced Disappearances: An introduction' (2022) 60 *International Annals of Criminology* 309–316.

requires States to have an autonomous crime. Regulations that go as far as obligation of means reflect the recent trend in international law for stronger State involvement. For States, the cost for fulfilment goes up.

The question remains whether the pursuit for the obligation means a favourable control. Not many States actually discipline enforced disappearances as an autonomous crime in practice. This may be related to the fact that, at the time of drafting, there was an understanding that the 'duty of results' should be fulfilled, as well as the fact that the ICPPED is relatively new and there is not much time to develop national legislation. Above all, it can be said that countries where enforced disappearances are not known lack the incentive to legislate. China and Iran, as well as the United States, have shown opposition to making it an independent crime.[21] Generally speaking, it would be preferable to have an independent offence. One of the demands of the rule of law is clarity of rules, and a legal form that requires a combination of a large number of laws and regulations to be certain that obligations are being fulfilled is still inferior.

On the other hand, it is also worth considering the balance with other issues. Although the CED may ask about the direct applicability of the ICPPED in domestic court, the CED does not go so far as to say that the ICPPED should be so. On the other hand, the way in which the CED examines the conformity of national law with the ICPPED for each of the three requirements and asks whether the Convention has been applied before the Court, in search of an independent crime, seems to be tantamount to asking for the same effect as if the State concerned were, in practice, self-executing, whether by the general acceptance method or by a variant method. There is no balance to be struck.

States have little incentive to make it an autonomous crime in cases where there is no actual enforced disappearance, but the honour factor makes it a State party concern. Also, there are in fact cases where a number of domestic laws and regulations could be considered to cover all the obligations required by the ICPPED. Above all, it is not legitimate to end constructive dialogue by saying that the Convention is violated because the State does not make it an autonomous crime. Many States try to argue that they are fulfilling their obligations as a result of the combination and coverage of various domestic laws. Even if not as an independent crime, such an approach is at least the next best move. The

[21] UN Doc.E/CN.4/2006/57 of 2 February 2006, paras. 100–2.

CED would also examine whether the obligation of consequence is really fulfilled if it is not, even if it first seeks an independent crime.

It is important to acknowledge that this obligation operates on a spectrum. A clear distinction exists between the absence of an autonomous crime and the inability to address its consequences. If this particular aspect stands as the sole impediment to ratification, it casts doubt on the entire endeavour. Consequently, the formalistic dichotomy employed by the CED lacks the nuanced approach necessary to align with reality.

#### 10.2.2.4 Extraterritorial Application / Migration (Article 9)

There is little argument as to the extraterritorial application of the ICPPED. Jurisdiction is provided for in Article 9, but at the moment there is no situation in which it is actively discussed as 'extraterritorial application', as is prominent in the European Convention on Human Rights. In addition, the issue of interpretation of Article 2 of the ICCPR may be helpful, but it cannot be analogized or extended because it is about the relationship with the specific wording of the Covenant.[22]

However, the practical impact of making the ICPPED more effective in terms of widening its scope is not small. This is because it involves the violation of rights by other States. For example, the main reason why Japan recognizes a strong interest in the ICPPED is the issue of abductions by DPRK, which would bring such transnational acts of enforced disappearance within the scope of the Convention.

Interestingly, cross-border issues are now attracting significant attention in the context of enforced disappearances of migrants, although they do not fully overlap with issues of extraterritoriality. There has been ongoing interest[23] and the CED has adopted in 2023 its first General Comment on this subject.

#### 10.2.2.5 Military Courts (Article 11)

According to the Statement on the Jurisdiction of Military Courts adopted by the Commission at its eighth session, military jurisdiction

[22] See generally Yuval Shany, 'The extraterritorial application of international human rights law' (2020) 409 *Collected Courses of the Hague Academy of International Law* 21–152, esp. 52–101.

[23] Report of the Working Group on Enforced or Involuntary Disappearances on enforced disappearances in the context of migration, UN Doc.A/HRC/36/39/Add.2 of 28 July 2017. More recently, e.g., The Geneva Academy of International Humanitarian Law and Human Rights, 'Working Paper: Preventing and Addressing Enforced Disappearances in the Context of International Migration', May 2021, pp. 1–37.

should be excluded from enforced disappearances,[24] which is generally considered harsh for countries with existing legal systems and practices. This point could be an obstacle to participation in the ICPPED.

From a normative point of view, this interpretation appears to be supportable. Even if military commissions may make appropriate substantive judgments, procedural rights are themselves worth protecting. This can be balanced with the idea that the right not to be subjected to enforced disappearance is a non-derogable right (Article 1(2)) and that procedural rights are included in this.[25] Therefore, even if this is an obstacle to ratification, there is a strong demand that this interpretation should be maintained.

#### 10.2.2.6 Retroactive Effect (Article 35)

Enforced disappearances, by their inherent nature, constitute an ongoing offence, obligating a State Party to diligently search for and investigate all cases where the fate and whereabouts of individuals remain unknown. However, it's crucial to note that Article 35 regarding temporal jurisdiction stipulates that the competence of the CED pertains only to enforced disappearances that have occurred after its entry into force. This could be seen as an embodiment of the general content of Article 28 (non-retroactivity of treaties) of the VCLT, but it should be noted that the ICCPR and other instruments do not have such an explicit provision. Although the ICPPED could have been dealt with vaguely without provisions, the fact that it was adopted with an explicit prohibition of retroactive effect is significant. The application of this provision involves difficult practical problems in relation to the characteristics of the offence of enforced disappearance. Since enforced disappearances are carried out in secret, the starting point of the offence is not clear. The crime of enforced disappearance is also difficult to apply strictly due to its nature, which makes it difficult to determine the point of commencement and emphasizes its character as a continuing offence. In particular, it is undesirable to unduly bind the Committee's range, as is problematic in urgent action.

[24] Statement by the Committee on Enforced Disappearance and Military Jurisdiction: Report of the Committee on Enforced Disappearances fifth session, UN Doc.A/69/56 of 13 Feb 2016, Annex V, p.21, paras. 5, 10. See also Decaux, 'The International Convention for the Protection of All Persons from Enforced Disappearance, as a victim-oriented treaty', p. 62.

[25] See, Article 27 of the American Convention on Human Rights, San José, Costa Rica, 22 November 1969.

The CED issued a substantive statement on temporal jurisdiction at its fifth session. It confirms that the Commission is bound by Article 35, but that it should look to historical information when it is useful to fully understand current State reporting.[26] However, it must include delicate situations in relation to its actual application and this is another area where the Commission's practice is in flux. Wherever the balance is sought, it should not seem to extend to cases that have been expressly terminated or where the time of commencement or termination is historically clear. However, the practice of the CED seems adventurous in discussing it, as in the examination of Japan, as well as Spain.[27]

Broadening the scope of application in a manner that undermines the explicit wording of the article is not advisable. Even with changes in regime, the current administration may still face scrutiny regarding past events. Furthermore, regulations pertaining to enforced disappearances also apply to States that currently uphold the status of liberal democracies. More broadly, such actions could convey a perception that the CED treats the text of the article, and potentially other provisions, with a degree of levity, potentially discouraging ratification and membership. The burden of addressing historical legacies frequently serves as a deterrent to ratification, even among democratic States.

#### 10.2.2.7 Caveat

The CED's interpretation should essentially be a normative judgment that is decoupled from any increase or decrease in the number of ratifying States. It should not lower the human rights standards in order to increase the number of the State parties. It is also important to note that, contrary to the apologetic thinking, the setting of strict standards and the proactive work of the CED can also be a factor that makes States think positively about ratifying the ICPPED, rather than hesitating to do so. This is the case where practical benefits are found in the regulation of acts by private individuals or cross-border acts.

[26] Statement by the Committee on Enforced Disappearances on the *ratione temporis* element in the review of reports submitted by States Parties under the International Convention for the Protection of All Persons from Enforced Disappearance, see A/69/56, Annex V, paras. 1, 3.

[27] Concluding observations on the report submitted by Japan under article 29 (1) of the Convention, UN Doc.CED/C/JPN/CO/1 of 5 December 2018, paras. 25, 26; Concluding observations on the report submitted by Spain under article 29, paragraph 1, of the Convention, UN Doc.CED/C/ESP/CO/1 of 12 December 2013, paras. 31–3.

## 10.3 Strategies to Increase Ratification

### *10.3.1 Basic Strategies*

The right way to increase the number of States Parties is to emphasize the importance of the norm and to repeat the outreach in international fora such as the General Assembly, the Third Committee and the Human Rights Council. It is also important that there is greater recognition that the treaty system is in fact working effectively to combat crime. As the youngest UN human rights treaty with a monitoring body, the ICPPED should be publicized more widely, and the norms need to be known and understood as a precondition for States not just to implement their obligation under Article 23 but also to use honour as leverage to join the ICPPED.

Awareness raising seems a long way off but is the most reliable method. This is because, ultimately, adherence to any law hinges on the individual's own mindset. It can be assumed that if the activities of the CED are focused on through awareness-raising activities, the number of States parties to the ICPPED will increase, and as the number of States Parties increases, awareness-raising activities will also expand, creating a virtuous circle.

It is also important that the CED gains and promotes trust in the broadest sense. The conclusion of the ICPPED by State parties implies that they trust CED as the monitoring body and agree to submit to its supervision. There is probably no general distrust of the CED, but it could be just a reflection of the fact that only a small number of supporting States are parties.

In order to promote reliance, the CED has to provide sufficient information to States including non-State parties. The information provided should be clear and consistent, provide legal stability and predictability, as well as fairness and impartiality. It is also important to have the human and financial resources to do so. The same is true of the Commission's call for States to strengthen capacity building.

Efforts to lower the costs that the present and future State parties expect to incur in implementing the ICPPED will also be important. Administrative costs, such as submitting national reports after becoming a State party, are not small. This issue is notably problematic in under-resourced States, a concern that is particularly relevant in the Asia-Pacific region. Resources are an important issue regardless of the political regime. In particular, authoritarian States with fewer resources will not dare to join the Convention. This is a reform issue that is continually being discussed and should be debated by the UN and by the human rights treaty bodies as a whole.

### 10.3.2 More Specified Strategy

Having mentioned the basic strategies described above, this chapter points out some possible focus points to streamline the increase in the number of parties.

#### 10.3.2.1 Political Systems and Devising Methods of Persuasion

From the first possible factors of only a small number of ratifications examined in the previous section, the following more specific strategies may be derived. It is not immediately possible to turn a particular country into a democratic State. This is a long-term effect of treaty-making. However, it is important to vary the methods and strategies of persuasion for each target country's attitude.

In terms of regimes, appeals to honour and foreign interests remain useful in liberal democratic States. The crime of enforced disappearance can be a violation of several human rights, including the right to life and the prohibition of torture, which have *jus cogens* status. Large-scale violations also amount to 'crimes against humanity' (Article 5) and are in common with crimes covered by the ICC. It is easy to appeal to the honour factor to show that they are more important than other human rights in general. The method of enforced disappearances is connected to the politics of fear and to the international community's general drive against terrorism. In other words, it would be useful to emphasize commonality with other robustly supported objects.

Appeals to honour can be made in a variety of ways. The most straightforward is 'praise', for example, the reference to positive aspects at the beginning of the summary findings of the human rights treaty bodies. This reference cannot be achieved unless a State joins the treaty, but there can be a concerted effort among human rights treaty bodies to encourage States to ratify sister treaties. Non-participation can also be a disgrace. This is because participation in the ICPPED is the clearest proof of support for the values it stands for. Name and shame, a well-known method of compliance with human rights treaties, can be a way of appealing to honour in a negative way, provided that inadvertent repercussions are avoided.

Even in liberal democracies, which may often have no problems with enforced disappearances, it is worthwhile to appeal to internal interests.

In particular, the preventive effect can be emphasized, as retaliatory measures can be taken to extremes in the face of heightened domestic political conflict, and political conflict can switch sides between those in power and those not in power. The significance of political conflicts having a safety valve that does not lead to enforced disappearances can be more significant, depending on the maturity of the society concerned.

The approach to authoritarian States may be somewhat different: the main motivation for authoritarian States to join human rights treaties, as described by Posner, is in return for aid or in response to external pressure, which is also an external real benefit. External benefits also facilitate trade-offs with other external benefits, such as military and economic, and this is even more the case in authoritarian regimes. Even in authoritarian regimes, appeals to honour can have a certain effect. Indeed, not a few authoritarian regimes are simultaneously ratifiers of human rights treaties and assess other States on the basis of human rights, as seen in the Human Rights Council's Universal Periodic Review.

It might be said that authoritarian States, by their very nature, are not sincere in their inward interests, but this is a matter of degree. Indeed, authoritarian regimes can vary, and the benefits and costs vary according to the subject, as discussed above. There may be cases where other human rights are restricted on the grounds of stability of the political regime, but enforced disappearances are considered too extreme. The preventive effect in the above-mentioned liberal democracies can be emphasized here as well. The conclusion of ICPPED can be useful as part of capacity-building to prevent enforced disappearances. It is also important to demonstrate that the State reporting system of the ICPPED, in the first instance, is an 'examination' of the country's current system and status quo, but it is also a proposal for improvement in this way and, by extension, an external aid to forces wishing to reduce or eliminate enforced disappearances in the country.

#### 10.3.2.2 Defining Targets and Devising Methods of Persuasion: Targeting ICCPR Signatory Countries

The applicability of other relevant frameworks to non-State parties can significantly impact their decision-making process regarding the ratification of the ICPPED. Of the relevant other frameworks, WGEID covers all non-parties, so it is the relationship with the ICCPR that should be the focus here as the one that will show differences in persuasion.

One category is the case where non-parties to the ICCPED are parties to the ICCPR. In general, States Parties to the ICCPR are considered to have strong liberal democratic tendencies, which could be combined with the persuasion described in the section above. It should be noted then that the fact that a State is a non-party to the ICCPED not only raises the possibility that the State regards the ICCPED as an unnecessary alternative to superimposing it, but at the same time that it is a State that is good or willing to submit to international norms. This is the case for thirty-one out of fifty-five countries in the Asia-Pacific region. The Philippines, for example, is an exception in Asia, having also ratified the First Optional Protocol, which indicates the high probability of ratification despite, or because of, the known facts of enforced disappearances. Depending on how the States perceive their experience with other human rights bodies, it should be easier for the States to negotiate, not least in that it is not entirely new.

More specific targets within that group are the eight countries that have signed the ICPPED: India, Indonesia, Lao People's Democratic Republic, Lebanon, Maldives, Thailand and Vanuatu. Interest in the ICPPED has already been shown in these countries and they are also obliged as signatories (Article 18 VCLT). These countries have a relatively high degree of democracy, particularly India and Indonesia, which have large populations, and therefore have a high degree of influence in ratifying the ICPPED.

It should be noted, however, that all of these countries have been signatories for more than ten years and the momentum for ratification has been lost.

The other category is where a country is a non-signatory to the ICCPED and a non-signatory to the ICCPR: there are thirteen Asian countries, of which only one is a signatory to the ICCPR and the other is a signatory to the ICCPED. In addition to large States such as China, there are many Arab and Pacific States. The methods of persuasion for authoritarian States referred to in the section above are generally appropriate, but in addition, the specificity of the ICCPED may work in its favour. This means that fewer norms are targeted, which can be emphasized by the fact that the costs are less.

#### 10.3.2.3 'Rediscovering' Enforced Disappearances

The second hypothetical factor was the uneven distribution of the fact of enforced disappearances. What seems useful for countries that do not have enforced disappearances in their countries, or whose governments themselves do not see the need for such a method, is not only to highlight the seriousness of this violation but also the importance of this as a cross-border issue. Enforced disappearances associated with the movement of persons across borders are particularly important, and countries that do not have enforced disappearances within their own borders have no choice but to become involved. This is the case, for example, with enforced disappearances in migration. Even if the home government is not involved, there is an increased likelihood that its citizens will become victims of enforced disappearances by other countries, such as neighbouring States, or that problems will arise under its jurisdiction. An important issue that could be relevant here is the possible extraterritorial application of the ICPPED, which has not been discussed in earnest. In addition, there are a number of other transboundary issues, such as extradition (Article 13) and the operation of the non-refoulement principle (Article 16).

The subject of the General Comment 'enforced disappearances in the context of migration' is not only important in its own right but also very attractive in terms of encouraging non-parties to ratify it. It is particularly important for the South-East Asia region. This sub-region has a particularly low level of ratification but has a strong stake in the issue of trafficking in persons, because they 'export' more victims than other regions. Of the two protocols to the UN Convention against Transnational Organized Crime, all States in South-East Asia are party to the Protocol to Prevent, Suppress and Punish Trafficking in Persons, especially Women and Children, and many are party to the Protocol against the Smuggling of Migrants by Land, Sea and Air. As a regional flamework, the 2004 ASEAN Declaration Against Trafficking in Persons Particularly Women and Children is one of the key instruments for this issue, which advocates for the protection of victims common to the same spirit to the ICPPED. There is sufficient footing for joint action in this sub-region.

General Comment 1 can demonstrate the organic linkage between the ICPPED and these criminal instruments and others, which will lead to encouraging the States to ratify the ICPPED.

#### 10.3.2.4 Additional Strategies

Some specific actors can play a more effective role, even if all stakeholders should be involved in the call for ratification. The UN, in particular OHCHR, must be the focal point, but there could be several intermediaries. The active involvement of individual States Parties with influence on the actors is important, such as France, Morocco, Argentina and Japan. In the case of Japan and South Korea, which are already parties, the problem of cultural 'imposition' will be diminished. At the regional level, fields such as OHCHR's Bangkok will be important, but outreach through regional international organizations is also important and could facilitate ratification through such regional frameworks. The framework of Association of Southeast Asian Nations (ASEAN)[28] and the Organization of Islamic Cooperation (OIC)[29] will be particularly important in sub-regions with fewer parties. The expansion of 'judicial dialogues' in the region, even if they do not take the form of international organizations, should also be noted.[30]

The momentum is also important. Momentum itself is difficult to create from outside the target State, but it is possible not to miss such momentum. Momentum can manifest itself in various ways, but the most important trigger is regime change, where human rights treaties can be integrated into national regimes in the midst of new regime building.[31] In relation to the issue of enforced disappearances, international interest and norm-setting is centred on Latin American States, which adopted a regional convention on enforced disappearances, and the Inter-American Convention on Enforced Disappearances, in 1994, after a period of dictatorship in the 1960s and 1970s and a transition to democratic regimes in the late 1980s. If there is no crime in the first place, it is difficult to create incentives to deter it, and without regime change, normative engagement is difficult to achieve. East Timor ratified a number of human rights treaties when it gained independence as a new State in 2002, but this was at a time when the drafting of the ICPPED had just begun, and it is likely that it would have ratified the Convention had it been available. It is instructive that Benin ratified the Convention at the same time as the Genocide Convention in 2017, although this is an African example. The need for ratification would be felt to be higher if it were in conjunction with other important similar conventions, and the cost of the ratification process in the country concerned would be lower.

28 Available at https://asean.org/.

29 See www.oic-oci.org/home/?lan=en.

30 Yoichi Ito (ed.), *Judicial Dialogue: Cooperation and Competition among Courts and Tribunals* (Nihonhyoronsha, 2023) (in Japanese).

31 Examples of what Posner calls transitional States include Eastern European countries after the end of the Cold War, Latin American countries in the 1980s and South Korea, see Posner, *The Twilight of Human Rights Law*, p. 62.

#### 10.3.2.5 Caveat

The international environment for the promotion of human rights should be kept in mind. Even if ratification does not progress due to the international environment, it is not necessary to regard this as a problem for human rights as a whole. It is essential not to give up continuous efforts even if things do not go well. In particular, international peace in the region is a prerequisite, but this region faces many security issues such as the North Korean missile problem, China's maritime expansion, ongoing tensions between the nuclear-armed States of India and Pakistan and the Palestinian Issue. Russia, in the midst of its invasion of Ukraine, is part of Asia. If we recall that, in contrast to Asia, there is no conflict on this scale in Europe or Latin America, it is not surprising that the human rights framework in the region has taken a long time to mature.

### *10.3.3 Some Symptomatic Treatments*

#### 10.3.3.1 Cooperation with Other International Organizations

WGEID and the HRCt (CCPR) are alternative forums, as already mentioned. For countries such as DPRK and Turkmenistan, where human rights violations are widely suspected, it is important to address the issue of enforced disappearances through the ICCPR. It is also worth confirming that, whatever the human rights violations, remaining a State party to the human rights treaties is highly commendable. In cases where a State is not a party to the ICPPED, such as China, or where the scale of the damage is serious, the issue will be taken to a higher forum, such as the Human Rights Council or the General Assembly. Article 34 of ICCPED is based on the same idea in that it places certain more difficult or large-scale issues outside the treaty bodies. As institutions outside the UN framework, the ICRC and the ICC are particularly important as relevant bodies. While enforced disappearances are more likely to occur in areas of political instability, the ICRC has made particular achievements in the implementation of international humanitarian law. Article 7(1)(i) of the ILC lists enforced disappearances as a type of conduct that constitutes a crime against humanity.

The role of international organizations not specializing in human rights is also important. The ILC is in the process of codifying the recent 'Immunity of State officials from foreign criminal jurisdiction', which, although hotly contested, currently includes six target crimes that are not exempt from the prohibition of enforced disappearances.[32] Although it did not identify enforced disappearance as an established example of *jus cogens*, it is cited as *jus cogens* and presented as having widespread support. Although not directly related to the ILC, the Asian African Legal Consultative Organization (AALCO)[33] is notable for its Asian and African version. It is a framework of diplomats in the Asia-Africa region. The ICJ, the most authoritative court in International law, has made frequent references to human rights treaties in recent years, and developments in this area are expected.[34]

Norm-setting, an activity of the ILC and the ICJ, is also a central activity for the CED, which is characterized by works with deliberation. A major development in the CED's recent work was the Guiding Principles for the Search for Disappeared Persons (the Guiding Principles),[35] which provide more specific guidance on the various provisions around the duty to investigate (Article 12 of the ICPPED). Another important example is General Comment 1, which was adopted in September 2023. This is not only excellent in terms of choice of subject matter but is in itself a very good move to set about creating a GC. It should be said that the General Comment is an important means of ensuring consistency in the CED as an institution, whereas in the past the consistency of the Commission has relied on the experience of the Secretariat and the veteran members of the CED.

The two documents mentioned above can extend to non-parties in different ways. The Guiding Principles mentioned above are themselves technical in nature and are made available to any State, whether a State party or not, that wishes to make them available according to its needs and interests. The latter 'may give rise to, or refer to, a subsequent agreement or subsequent practice by parties under article 31, paragraph

[32] Draft article 7 (1): 'Immunity ratione materiae from the exercise of foreign criminal jurisdiction shall not apply in respect of the following crimes under international law: (a) crime of genocide; (b) crimes against humanity; (c) war crimes; (d) crime of apartheid; (e) torture; (f) enforced disappearance', in Report on the work of the sixty-ninth session, UN Doc.A/72/10, 2017, p. 176. As for the content of the argument: p. 164, para. 74.

[33] See https://aalco.int/. To call for the ratification, the author made a speech at the Fifty Seventh Annual Session of the Asian-African Legal Consultative Organization (AALCO), held in Tokyo, in October 2018.

[34] E.g, Conséquences juridiques de l'édification d'un mur dans le territorire palestinien occupé, avis consultative, C.I.J. Recueil 2004, paras. 110, 112, 136.

[35] Guiding principles for the search for disappeared persons, UN Doc.CED/C/7 of 8 May 2019.

3, or subsequent practice under article 32',[36] and could influence over identifying customary international law,[37] increasing the likelihood that customary international law will be binding on a State party as general international law.

#### 10.3.3.2 Mindset

It is important to note that when other international organizations are involved, the mindset is that while the CED has a specific mandate, it is part of the treaty bodies as a whole, the UN as a whole and the international community as a whole.[38] Hence, it can be seen that the previous arguments are part of the debate known as the 2020 Review on the strengthening of human rights treaty bodies in recent times.[39]

When it comes to norm creation in particular, first, care needs to be taken to clarify the legal status of the legal instruments to be created. In this regard, it is important to note that it was confirmed many times during the discussions that the Guiding Principles are not a general comment, and the Guiding Principles themselves state that they 'seek to consolidate good practices' (para. 2). This is an appropriate move that prioritizes practical usefulness, as it was particularly difficult for the CED,

[36] Draft Conclusion 13 of Draft conclusions on subsequent agreements and subsequent practice in relation to the interpretation of treaties, UN Doc.A/73/10 in *Yearbook of the International Law Commission* 2018, vol. II, Part Two, pp. 23–88 at pp. 82–88.

[37] Draft conclusions on identification of customary international law, UN Doc.A/73/10 in *Yearbook of the International Law Commission* 2018, vol. II, Part Two, pp. 89–113, does not mention clearly the role of pronouncements of the expert treaty body, but Conclusion 12 on resolutions of international organizations and intergovernmental conference may become relevant, see pp. 107–9.

[38] It should be recalled that the CED was confirmed as the body to carry out the mandate set out in the ICPPED at the first meeting of States Parties in December 2016, in accordance with Article 27. The institutional design of the ICPPED could well have been that the HRCt, which is specifically identified (Article 28(2)) as the consultative body to ensure the consistency of its views and recommendations, for example, would oversee the Convention. In the drafting process, there were many other ideas, including a proposal for the ICPPED itself to be an Optional Protocol to the Covenant on Civil Liberties, and a proposal to create a sub-committee of the HRCt. See UN Doc.E/CN.4/2004/59, paras. 143–8; UN Doc.E/CN.4/2005/66, paras. 147–68; UN Doc.E/CN.4/2006/57, paras. 69–84.

[39] The developments aimed at the 2020 Review, an important topic in recent times starting with the 2014 General Assembly resolution (UN Doc.A/RES/68/268 of 21 April 2014, para. 41) have many issues that have been discussed since then, but the scope is too comprehensive to be presented here. See, The Geneva Academy of International Humanitarian Law and Human Rights, 'Optimizing the UN Treaty Body System: Academic Platform Report on the 2020 Review', 2018, pp. 6–44, at pp. 17–26; Koji Teraya, 'Theory of human rights diplomacy', esp. at pp. 10–11.

which had little experience in implementing them, to argue the degree of establishment of individual legal norms. Second, care should be taken to avoid fragmentation of international law as multiple agencies become involved in the issue of enforced disappearances. The impression that they are doing things piecemeal is an element of disregard from States that are not part of the framework. The HRCt is specifically identified (Article 28(2)) as a consultative body to ensure consistency of the views and recommendations of the ICPPED, which could be positioned as a pioneering provision to address the issue of fragmentation. Attention should be paid not only to the HRCt but also to the wider community: it was very appropriate that the CED sent its views on consistency of jurisprudence to the ILC when the ILC's work on 'crimes against humanity' was underway.[40]

#### 10.3.3.3 Concluding Remarks

The preceding discussion has concentrated on potential factors and approaches for addressing the increase in the number of States Parties to the ICPPED, with a specific emphasis on Asia pacific countries. Two observations are warranted.

First, while the discourse has centred on the escalation of States parties, the considerations here are also important after the actual increase. This is because the motivation of States to ratify the ICPPED is closely linked to the extent to which they subsequently comply with it. The endeavour to augment the number of ratifying States is inherently intertwined with the imperative of ensuring effective implementation. Even upon resolution of the initial issue, the considerations elucidated herein retain significance in facilitating more streamlined implementation processes. In essence, the endeavour to boost the number of ratifying States serves as a gateway to the theory of observance, which grapples with delineating the fundamental issue, and the theory of implementation, which reframes the issue from a pragmatic standpoint. This, in turn, forms a component of the broader theory of international governance through treaties.

[40] CED, Statement on the draft articles on crimes against humanity, adopted by the International Law Commission, Adopted on 1 June 2018, during the 14th session of the Committee, available at www.ohchr.org/EN/HRBodies/CED/Pages/CEDIndex.aspx. Another important issue is in relation to the project of 'Immunity of State officials from foreign criminal jurisdiction'. The current status is available at https://legal.un.org/ilc/summaries/4_2.shtml.

The current situation regarding treaties in general is, on the one hand, that they are difficult to amend, and their interpretation has become increasingly important and contentious.[41] In parallel with these responses on the part of international organizations and (quasi-) tribunals, on the other hand, States are contesting how they behave while remaining parties and how current potential future signatories can engage from the outside, as withdrawal becomes a politically untenable option.[42] In turn, this dynamic feeds into normative theory. Just as marriage is a daily act of courtship and democracy is a daily act of voting, so compliance with treaties as a party to a treaty is an incessant act of treaty-making.

Second, regarding the perspective presented in this chapter, the framing of the 'Asian theory of human rights' is subject to scrutiny. As a matter of fact, there is no region or country that is not special. The illustrative examples of Asian nations provided in this chapter are broadly applicable across various regions. Therefore, singling out Asia as distinctive in this context is unwarranted. Such categorization should not serve as a basis for reluctance to ratify or adhere to international human rights standards, nor should it be utilized as rhetorical fodder by authoritative regimes. It is imperative to acknowledge that Asian countries are active participants in international bodies such as the UN, which espouses principles of human rights, and many have ratified treaties like the ICCPR. These actions demonstrate a level of commitment to upholding human rights standards. However, there remains a collective obligation for these countries to enhance their efforts significantly in this regard.

[41] One of the most recent outcomes is draft conclusions on subsequent agreements and subsequent practice in relation to the interpretation of treaties, see note 38.

[42] CCPR General Comment No. 26: Continuity of Obligations (UN Doc.CCPR/C/21/Rev.1/Add.8/Rev.1 of 8 December 1997) has not been challenged by States, as in the case of CCPR General Comment No. 24, see note 15. The impetus for the creation of this General Comment was the possibility of the DPRK leaving, but in the end the DPRK did not leave.

# BIBLIOGRAPHY

## Academic Sources

Abbott, K. 'A brief overview of legal interoperability challenges for NATO arising from the interrelationship between IHL and IHRL in light of the ECHR' (2014) 96, 893 *International Review of the Red Cross* 107–37.

Abboud, D., Baraybar, J. P., Salado, M., et al. 'The search process: Integrating the investigation and identification of missing and unidentified persons' (2021) 3 *Forensic Science International*, available at www.sciencedirect.com/science/article/pii/S2589871X21000243.

Abraham, M. 'Building the New Human Rights Council' (2007) 33 *Dialogue on Globalization*, available at https://repositorio.colmex.mx/concern/books/2f75r874m?locale=es.

Aguayo, S., and Dayán, J. *El Yugo Zeta: Norte de Coahuila, 2010–2011* (Colegio de México, 2017).

Allier Montaño, E., Vicente Ovallo, C., and Granada-Cardona, J. S. 'Recasting history to cast off shadows: State violence in Mexico, 1958–2018' in S. Mandolessi and K. Olalde Rico (eds.), *Disappearances in Mexico: From the 'Dirty War' to the 'War on Drugs'* (Routledge, 2022), pp. 50–72.

Alston, P. 'Hobbling the monitors: Should U.N. human rights monitors be accountable?' (2011) 52, 2 *Harvard International Law Journal* 561–649.

Antillón Najlis, X. *Yo sólo quería que amaneciera impactos psicosociales del caso Ayotzinapa* (Fundar, Centro de Análisis e Investigación, 2018).

Baranowska, G. 'The rights of the families of missing persons: Going beyond international humanitarian law' (2022) 55, 1 *Israel Law Review* 25–49.

*Disappeared Migrants and Refugees: The Relevance of the International Convention on Enforced Disappearance in their search and protection* (German Institute for Human Rights, 2020), available at www.institut-fuer-menschenrechte.de/publikationen/detail/disappeared-migrants-and-refugees.

Berman, M. R., and Clark, R. S. 'State terrorism: Disappearances' (1982) 13 *Rutgers Law Journal* 531.

Biel-Portero, I., and Mafla, A. C. Lipprint: A humanitarian forensic action' (2021) 33, 1 *Revista Facultad de Odontología Universidad de Antioquia* 96–106, available at https://doi.org/10.17533/udea.rfo.v33n1a8.

Blaauw, M., and Lähteenmäki, V. '"Denial and silence" or "acknowledgement and disclosure"' (2002) 84, 848 *International Review of the Red Cross* 767–83.

Bourguignon, M., Dermitzel, A., and Katz, M. 'Grief among relatives of disappeared persons in the context of state violence: An impossible process?' (2021) 31, 14 *Torture Journal* 29.

Calloni, S. *Operativo Cóndor, Pacto Criminal* (Ciencias Sociales UBA, 2001).

Calveiro, P. 'Disappearance and governmentality in Mexico' in S. Mandolessi and K. Olalde Rico (eds.), *Disappearances in Mexico: From the 'Dirty War' to the 'War on Drugs'* (Routledge, 2022), pp. 85–92.

Carpanelli, E. The mysterious abduction and confinement of two princesses: A tentative analysis under international law' (2021) 76, 2 *La comunità internazionale* 353–82.

Carruthers, M. *The Craft of Thought, Meditation, Rhetoric, and the Making of Images* (Cambridge University Press, 1998).

Cerda, J. S. *La Reforma de las Naciones Unidas en Nuevos Derechos del Hombre* (EUDEBA, 2011).

Coccoli, J. 'The challenges of new technologies in the implementation of human rights: An analysis of some critical issues in the digital era' (2017) 1, 2 *Peace Human Rights Governance* 223–50.

Crettol, M., Milner, L., La Rosa A., and Stockwell J. 'Establishing mechanisms to clarify the fate and whereabouts of missing persons: A proposed humanitarian approach' (2017) 99, 2 *International Review of the Red Cross* 589–618.

Davis, H., and Klinkner, M. 'Investigating across borders: The right to the truth in an European context' (2022) 26, 4 *The International Journal of Human Rights* 683–700.

*The Right to the Truth in International Law: Victims' Rights in Human Rights and International Criminal Law* (Routledge, 2020).

Decaux, E., and Suela, J. 'The International Convention for the Protection of All Persons from Enforced Disappearance, a human rights instrument of the 21st century: Reflections on its 10th anniversary of the entry into force' (2021) 18 *Droits Fondamentaux*, available at www.crdh.fr/revue/n-19-2021/the-international-convention-for-the-protection-of-all-persons-from-enforced-disappearance-a-human-rights-instrument-of-the-21st-century-reflections-on-its-10th-anniversary-of-the-entry-into-force/.

De Frouville, O. 'Criminalizing or trivializing enforced disappearances? The issue of "non-State actors"' in O. de Frouville and P. Sturma (eds.), *La pénalisation des droits de l'homme* (Pedone, 2021), available at www.ssrn.com/abstract=3798450.

De Vecchi Gerli, M. '¡Vivxs Lxs Queremos! The battles for memory around the disappeared in Mexico', PhD thesis, University College London (2018), available at https://discovery.ucl.ac.uk/id/eprint/10064633/.

Droege, C. 'The interplay between international humanitarian law and international human rights law in situations of armed conflict' (2007) 40, 2 *Israel Law Review* 338.

Dubberley, S., Koenig, A., and Murray, D. *Digital Witness* (Oxford University Press, 2020).

Duhaime, B., Méndez, J. E., and Perez-Sales, P. 'Current debates, development, and challenges regarding enforced disappearance as torture' (2021) 31, 2 *Torture Journal on Rehabilitation of Torture Victims and Prevention of Torture* 8.

Džumhur, J. *Victimology in Theory and Practice in Post conflict Society: Perspective of Bosnia and Herzegovina* (University Press – Izdanja Magistrat, 2021).

Finucane, B. 'Enforced disappearance as a crime under international law: A neglected origin in the laws of war' (2010) 35 *The Yale Journal of International Law* 171.

Frey, B. A. 'Conceptualising disappearances in international law' in K. Ansolabehere, L. A. Payne and B. A. Frey (eds.), *Disappearance in the Post-Transition Era in Latin America* (Oxford University Press, 2021).

Galvis Patino, M. 'The work of the Committee on Enforced Disappearance: Achievements and jurisprudence ten years after the entry into force of the International Convention for the Protection of All Persons from Enforced Disappearances' (2021), available at www.geneva-academy.ch/joomlatools-files/docman-files/The%20Work%20of%20the%20CED.pdf.

Galvis, M. C., and Arias, N. O. 'Los Principios Rectores para la Búsqueda de Personas Desaparecidas: Origen y contenido' (2019) 19 *Ideas Verdes. Análisis Políticos* 1–31, available at https://co.boell.org/sites/default/files/20190905_paper19_web.pdf.

Gauding, A. *Es mejor encender una luz que maldecir la oscuridad* (Diakonia, 1991).

Grignon, J. 'The beginning of application of international humanitarian law: A discussion of a few challenges' (2014) 96, 893 *International Review of the Red Cross* 139–62.

Guercke, L. C. *Preventing and Addressing Enforced Disappearances in the Context of International Migration. The Contribution of International Human Rights Mechanisms* (Geneva Academy, 2021), available at www.geneva-academy.ch/joomlatools-files/docman-files/working-papers/Preventing%20and%20Addressing%20Enforced%20Disappearances%20in%20the%20Context%20of%20International%20Migration.pdf.

'State responsibility for a failure to prevent violations of the right to life by organised criminal groups: Disappearances in Mexico' (2021) 21 *Human Rights Law Review* 353–6.

Hameed, U., Qaiser, K., and Qaiser, Z. 'Dysfunctional law against the crime of enforced disappearances in Pakistan' (2021) 9, 2 *International Review of Social Sciences* 1–8.

Hampson, F. J. 'The relationship between international humanitarian law and human rights law from the perspective of a human rights body' (2008) 90, 871 *International Review of the Red Cross* 549–72.

Hernández, I. 'Collaborating with organized crime in the search for disappeared persons? Formalizing a humanitarian alternative for Mexico' (2020) 102, 914 *International Review of the Red Cross* 607–28.

Howard, D., and Klinkner, M. 'Investigating across borders: The right to the truth in an European context' (2022) 26, 4 *The International Journal of Human Rights* 683–700.

*The Right to the Truth in International Law: Victims' Rights in Human Rights and International Criminal Law* (Routledge, 2020).

Huhle, R. 'Fate and whereabouts: The two elements that make up the right to know about the victims of forced disappearance' in S. Mandolessi and K. Olalde Rico (eds.), *Disappearances in Mexico: From the 'Dirty War' to the 'War on Drugs'* (Routledge, 2022), pp. 150–65.

'Non-State actors of enforced disappearance and the UN Convention for the Protection of All Persons from Enforced Disappearance' (2013) 26 *Humanitäres Völkerrecht Informationsschriften/Journal of International Law of Peace and Armed Conflict* 21.

Jenks, C., and Acquaviva, G. 'Debate: The role of international criminal justice in fostering compliance with international humanitarian law' (2014) 96, 895/896 *International Review of the Red Cross* 775–94.

Klinkner, M., and Smith, E. 'From law to policy and practice – collaborative research amidst a pandemic: The creation of the Bournemouth Protocol on mass grave protection and investigation' (2021) 1, 1 *Journal of Legal Research Methodology* 26–49, available at https://doi.org/10.19164/jlrm.v1i1.1161.

*The Bournemouth Protocol on Mass Grave Protection and Investigation* (Bournemouth University Press, 2020), available at www.bournemouth.ac.uk/research/projects/mass-grave-protection-truth-justice.

Kolaković-Bojović, M. 'Víctimas de desaparición forzada y derecho a la reparación' in *Desaparición forzada: Colección en temas de derechos humanos, Tomo I*, (Centro Internacional para la Promoción de los Derechos Humanos bajo los auspicios de UNESCO [CIPDH], 2023), pp. 196–226.

'Disappeared persons and the right to be considered alive: The current state of play in the Western Balkans' in Z. Pavlović (ed.), *Yearbook Human Rights Protection. Right To Life* (Provincial Protector of Citizens – Ombudsman; Institute of Criminological and Sociological Research, 2021), pp. 271–87.

'The synergy between criminal law and medicine under the International Convention for the Protection of All Persons from Enforced Disappearance', in I Stevanović (ed.), *Penal Law and Medicine* (Institute of Criminological and Sociological Research, 2019), pp. 387–98.

Kolaković-Bojović, M., and Grujić, Z. 'Crime victims and the right to human dignity' in Z. Pavlović and I. Stevanović (eds.), *Yearbook Human Rights Protection: The Right to Human Dignity* (Provincial Protector of Citizens – Ombudsman and Institute of Criminological and Sociological Research in Belgrade, 2020), pp. 239–70.

Kolaković-Bojović, M., and Simonovski, I. 'The accession negotiations of North Macedonia to the EU. Between new methodology and old challenges' in *Law between the Ideal and the Reality* (Faculty of Law and Institute for Comparative Law, 2023), pp. 103–15.

Kolaković-Bojović, M., and Tilovska Kechegi, E. 'Regional cooperation in the prosecution of war crimes as an EU accession benchmark' in G. Ilic (ed.), *Towards a Better Future: Democracy, EU Integration and Criminal Justice* (Faculty of Law – Kicevo, University "St. Kliment Ohridski" – Bitola, Center for Scientific Research at the Faculty of Law – Kicevo, 2019), pp. 83–99.

Land, M. K., and Aronson, J. D. *New Technologies for Human Rights Law and Practice* (Cambridge University Press, 2018).

Liddicoat, J. *Human Rights and the Internet* (Cambridge University Press, 2021).

Lochak, M. 'Les fondements des droits de l'Homme au défi des nouvelles technologies: Conclusions générales' in O. de Frouville and J. Tavernier (eds.), *La Déclaration universelle des droits de l'Homme, 70 ans après: les fondements des droits de l'Homme au défi des nouvelles technologies* (Pedone, 2019), pp. 203–17.

Lubell, N. 'Parallel application of international humanitarian law and international human rights law: An examination of the debate' (2007) 40, 2 *Israel Law Review* 654–6.

Marques Antunes, N. S. 'Acquiescence', *Max Planck Encyclopedias of International Law [MPIL]* (Public International Law, 2006), https://opil.ouplaw.com/display/10.1093/law:epil/9780199231690/law-9780199231690-e1373.

Mayo Flota, A. M. 'The Crime of Disappearance of Persons by Private Individuals in the New Mexican Legislation: An International Law Perspective', master's thesis, Institute of International and Development Studies (2018), pp. 40–4.

McCorquodale, R., and Forgia, R. L. 'Taking off the blindfolds: Torture by non-State actors' (2001) 1 *Human Rights Law Review* 189.

McPherson, E., and Probert, T. 'Special procedures in the digital age' in A. Nolan, R. Freedman and T. Murphy (eds.), *The United Nations Special Procedures System* (Brill Nijhoff, 2017), pp. 261–70.

Meron, T. 'The humanization of humanitarian law' (2000) 94 *American Journal of International Law* 239.

Milanovic, M. 'State Acquiescence or Connivance in the Wrongful Conduct of Third Parties in the Jurisprudence of the European Court of Human Rights' (2019), available at http://dx.doi.org/10.2139/ssrn.3454007.

*Extraterritorial Application of Human Rights Treaties: Law, Principles, Policy* (Oxford University Press, 2011).

'A norm conflict perspective on the relationship between international humanitarian law and human rights law' (2009) 14 *Journal of Conflict and Security Law* 459.

Milanovic, M., and Sivakumaran, S. 'Assessing the authority of the ICRC Customary IHL Study: How does IHL develop?' (2022) 104, 920–1 *International Review of the Red Cross* 1856–97, and its Annex 1.

Morelos Zaragoza, L. S. 'The Mexican Law on The Forced Disappearance of Persons, Disappearances Committed by Individuals and the National Missing Persons System: How many steps forward?' (2019) XII, 125 *Mexican Law Review* 141–3.

Nicolmann, B. *Preventing and Addressing Enforced Disappearances in the Context of International Migration. The Contribution of International Human Rights Mechanisms* (Geneva Academy, 2021), available at www.geneva-academy.ch/joomlatools-files/docman-files/working-papers/Preventing%20and%20Addressing%20Enforced%20Disappearances%20in%20the%20Context%20of%20International%20Migration.pdf.

Panella, L. *Nuove tecnologie e diritti umani: Profili di diritto internazionale e di diritto interno* (Editoriale Scientifica, 2018).

Pereira, P. *El desaparecimiento forzado como crimen contra la humanidad* (Lithobinder CA, 1987).

Pérez Luño, A. E. *Nuevastecnologías y derechoshumanos* (Tirant Lo Blanch, 2014).

Pilegaar, L., and Džumhur, J. 'Human rights shortcomings of the Dayton Peace Agreement' *Forced Migration Review*, 2015, www.fmreview.org/.

Pozos Barcelata, A. A. *El Cuerpo Ausente como Sujeto Político: El Proceso de Construcción de la Desaparición de Personas en México como un Problema de Acción Política (1969–2018)* (Université du Québec, 2018).

Ravenna, H. *Justicia militar: Juez natural o fuero especial, en educación y derechos humanos* (Centro Editor de América Latina, IIHR, 1989).

Rayo, A. *Principios Rectores para la Búsqueda de Personas Desaparecidas: Una oportunidad para el fortalecimiento de la búsqueda humanitaria y extrajudicial desarrollada por la UBPD* (Universidad Santo Tomás, 2020), available (in Spanish) at https://repository.usta.edu.co/bitstream/handle/11634/30064/2020andrearayo.pdf?sequence=1&isAllowed=y.

Rodley, N. 'On the Responsibility of Special Rapporteurs' (2011) 15 *The International Journal of Human Rights* 319–37.

Salado, Puerto, M. et al., 'The search process: Integrating the investigation and identification of missing and unidentified persons' (2021) 3 *Forensic Science International*, available at www.sciencedirect.com/science/article/pii/S2589871X21000243.

Sassoli, M., and Olson, L. 'The relationship between international humanitarian and human rights law where it matters: Admissible killing and internment of fighters in non-international armed conflicts' (2008) 90, 871 *International Review of the Red Cross* 599–627.

Schabas, W. 'Lex specialis? Belt and suspenders? The parallel operation of human rights and the law of armed conflict, and the conundrum of jus ad bellum' (2007) 40, 2 *Israel Law Review* 59.

Scovazzi, T., and Citroni, G. *The Struggle against Enforced Disappearance and the 2007 United Nations Convention* (Nijhoff, 2007).

Serrano, M. 'Mexico: A humanitarian crisis in the making' in W. G. Pansters, B. T. Smith and P. Watt (eds.), *Beyond the Drug War in Mexico: Human Rights, the Public Sphere and Justice* (Routledge, 2017), pp. 50–75.

Sferrazza, P. 'Comentarios a los Principios Rectores para la Búsqueda de Personas Desaparecidas del Comité contra las Desapariciones Forzadas de Naciones Unidas' (2021) 21 *Anuario Mexicano de Derecho Internacional* 773–96.

'La búsqueda de personas desaparecidas en Chile: ¿necesidad de un complemento humanitario?' (2021) *Revista Mexicana de Ciencias Políticas y Sociales* 243, 79–108.

'La búsqueda de personas desaparecidas: derecho humano de las víctimas y obligación internacional del Estado' (2021) 19, 1 *Estudios Constitucionales* 265–308.

Shelton, D. *Remedies in International Human Rights Law* (Oxford University Press, 2015).

Srovin Coralli, A. 'Working Paper: Non-State Actors and Enforced Disappearances: Defining a Path Forward, Geneva Academy of International Humanitarian Law and Human Rights' (2021) pp. 5–6, available at www.geneva-academy.ch/research/publications/detail/608-non-state-actors-and-enforced-disappearances-defining-a-path-forward.

Swierczewska-Gasiorowska, A., Porwisz, M., and Olber, P. 'Espozan electronic system supporting the polish police in the search for missing persons' (2020) 58, 3 *Journal of Criminology and Criminal Law (JCCL)* 69–80.

Toler, A. 'How to verify and authenticate user-generated content' in S. Dubberley, A. Koenig and D. Murray (eds.), *Digital Witness* (Oxford University Press, 2020), pp. 185–227.

Wolffenbuttel, A. R. 'Enforced disappearances: Applicable to political organizations?' (2021) 61 *Virginia Journal of International Law Online* 159.

## UN Treaties and Documents

Advisory Committee of the Human Rights Council, Report on Possible Impacts, Opportunities and Challenges of New and Emerging Digital Technologies with regard to the Promotion and Protection of Human Rights, UN Doc. A/HRC/47/52, 19 May 2021.

Commission on Human Rights, Procedural resolution on the closure of the work of the Commission, UN Doc. E/CN.4/2006/L.2, 2, 4, 27 March 2006, available at www1.umn.edu/humanrts/closure.html.

Report of the Intersessional Open-Ended Working Group to Elaborate a Draft Legally Binding Normative Instrument for the Protection of All Persons from Enforced Disappearance, UN Doc. E/CN.4/2006/57, 2 February 2006.

Report of the Intersessional Open-Ended Working Group to Elaborate a Draft Legally Binding Normative Instrument for the Protection of All Persons from Enforced Disappearance, UN Doc. E/CN.4/2005/66, 10 March 2005.

Report of the Intersessional Open-Ended Working Group to Elaborate a Draft Legally Binding Normative Instrument for the Protection of All Persons from Enforced Disappearance, UN Doc. E/CN.4/2004/59, 23 February 2004.

Declaration on the Protection of All Persons from Enforced Disappearance, 28 February 1992, E/CN.4/RES/1992/29.

Committee on Enforced Disappearances, *Berrospe Medina and Mendoza Berrospe* v. *Mexico*, UN Doc. CED/C/24/D/4/2021, 2023.

Report of the Committee on Enforced Disappearances, Doc. A/78/56, 2023.

General Comment No. 1 on Enforced Disappearance in the Context of Migration, CED/C/GC/1, 29 September 2023.

Observaciones finales sobre la información complementaria presentada por México con arreglo al artículo 29, párrafo 4 de la Convención, UN Doc. CED/C/MEX/OAI/2, 29 September 2023.

General Comment No. 1 on Enforced Disappearances in the Context of Migration, UN Doc. CED/C/GC/1, 18 September 2023.

Statement on non-State actors in the context of the International Convention for the Protection of All Persons from Enforced Disappearances, CED/C/10, 2 May 2023.

Concluding observations on the report submitted by the Niger under Art. 29(1) of the Convention, CED/ C/NER/CO/1, 2022.

Concluding observations on the report submitted by Mali under Art. 29(1) of the Convention, CED/C/MLI/CO/1, 4 October 2022.

Report of the Committee on Enforced Disappearances on Its Visit to Mexico: Findings, UN Doc. CED/C/MEX/VR/1, 18 May 2022.

Concluding observations on the report submitted by Niger under Art. 29(1) of the Convention, CED/C/NER/CO/1, 5 May 2022.

Concluding observations on Greece, CED/C/GRC/CO/1, 12 April 2022.

Observations finales concernant le deuxième rapport périodique du Burkina Faso, CMW/C/BFA/CO/2, 12 April 2022.

Concluding observations on the report submitted by Brazil under Art. 29(1) of the Convention, CED/C/BRA/CO/1, 2021.

Information received from Peru on follow-up to the concluding observations on its report submitted under Art. 29 (1) of the Convention. Doc. CED/C/PER/FCO/1, 15 November 2021.

Concluding observations on Brazil, CED/C/BRA/CO/1, 3 November 2021.

Concluding observations on Mongolia, CED/C/MNG/CO/1, 30 September 2021.

Concluding observations on Panama, CED/C/PAN/CO/1, 24 September 2021.

Concluding observations on the report submitted by Switzerland under Art. 29 (1) of the Convention, CED/C/CHE/CO/1, 21 May 2021.

Additional information submitted by Colombia under Art. 29(4) of the Convention, CED/C/COL/AI/1, 17 January 2020.

(2019). Guiding Principles for the Search for Disappeared Persons. CED/C/17, available at www.ohchr.org/en/documents/legal-standards-and-guidelines/guiding-principles-search-disappeared-persons.

List of issues in relation to the report submitted by Nigeria under Art. 29(1) of the Convention, CED/C/NGA/Q/1, 2022; Human Rights Council, Visit to Nigeria, Report of Special Rapporteur on trafficking in persons, especially women and children, A//HRC/41/46/Add.1, 2019.

Report of the Committee on Enforced Disappearances, Doc. A/74/56, 2019.

Concluding observations on the report submitted by the Plurinational State of Bolivia under Art. 29 (1) of the Convention, CED/C/BOL/CO/1, 24 October 2019.

Concluding observations on Bolivia, CED/C/BOL/CO/R.1, 9 October 2019.

Concluding observations on the report submitted by Chile under Art. 29(1) of the Convention, CED/C/CHL/CO/1, 8 May 2019.

Concluding observations on the report submitted by Peru under Art. 29(1) of the Convention, CED/C/PER/CO/1, 8 May 2019.

Guiding principles for the search for disappeared persons, CED/C/7, 8 May 2019.

Concluding observations on Italy, CED/C/ITA/CO/1, 17 April 2019.

Report of the Committee on Enforced Disappearances, Doc. A/73/56, 2018.

Concluding observations on Japan, CED/C/JPN/CO/1, 14 November 2018.

Follow-up Observations on the Additional Information Submitted by Mexico under Art. 29, Paragraph 4, of the Convention, UN Doc. CED/C/MEX/CO/R.1/Add.1, 13 November 2018.

Concluding observations on Slovakia, CED/C/SVK/CO/R.1, 7 October 2018.

Concluding observations on the report submitted by Honduras under Art. 29 (1) of the Convention, CED/C/HND/CO/1, 4 July 2018.

Concluding observations on Honduras, CED/C/HND/CO/1, 31 May 2018.

(2017). Concluding observations on the report submitted by Senegal under Art. 29 (1) of the Convention, CED/ C/SEN/CO/1.

Report of the Committee on Enforced Disappearances, Doc. A/72/56, 2017.

Concluding observations on Gabon, CED/C/GAB/CO/1, 12 September 2017.
Concluding observations on the report submitted by Burkina Faso under Art. 29, para. 1 of the Convention, CED/ C/BFA/CO/1, 2016.
Concluding observations on Bosnia and Herzegovina, CED/C/BIH/CO/1, 7 November 2016.
Concluding observations on the report submitted by Colombia under Art. 29(1) of the Convention, CED/C/COL/CO/1, 27 October 2016.
Concluding observations on the report submitted by Bosnia & Herzegovina under Art. 29(1) of the Convention, CED/C/BIH/CO/1, 7 October 2016
Concluding observations on the report submitted by Tunisia under Art. 29(1) of the Convention, CED/C/TUN/CO/1, 11 March 2016.
Concluding observations on the Report Submitted by Mexico (2015) UN Doc. CED/C/MEX/CO/1, March 2015.
Concluding observations on the report submitted by Iraq under Art. 29(1) of the Convention, CED/C/IRQ/CO/1, 13 October 2015.
Concluding Observations on Netherlands, CED/C/NLD/CO/1, 26 March 2014.
Concluding observations on the report submitted by Spain under Art. 29(1) of the Convention, CED/C/ESP/CO/1, 12 December 2013.

Committee on the Elimination of Discrimination against Women, Concluding Observations on the Ninth Periodic Report of Mexico (2018), UN Doc. CEDAW/C/MEX/CO/9, 25 July 2018.

Committee on the Protection of the Rights of All Migrant Workers and Members of Their Families, General comment No. 5 on migrants' rights to liberty and freedom from arbitrary detention, CMW/C/GC/5, available at www.ohchr.org/en/documents/general-comments-and-recommendations/general-comment-no-5-2021-migrants-rights-liberty.

Convention against Torture and Other Cruel, Inhuman or Degrading Treatment or Punishment, Adopted and opened for signature, ratification and accession by General Assembly resolution 39/46 of 10 December 1984 entry into force 26 June 1987, in accordance with article 27 (1).

Declaration on the Protection of All Persons from Enforced Disappearance, UN Doc. A/RES/47/133, 18 December 1992.

Department of Economic and Social Affairs, International Migration 2019, available at www.un.org/development/desa/pd/sites/www.un.org.development.desa.pd/files/files/documents/2020/Feb/un_2019_internationalmigration_wallchart.pdf.

Follow-up Report to the recommendations made by the Working Group on Enforced or Involuntary Disappearances on its missions to Croatia, Montenegro, Serbia and Kosovo. A/HRC/39/46.

General Assembly, Resolution 47/133, 18 December 1992.

Human Rights Committee, *Hidalgo Rea and Rivera Hidalgo* v. *Mexico*, UN Doc. CCPR/C/131/D/3259/2018, 2021.

Human Rights Committee, General Comment No. 35: Article 9 (Liberty and Security of Person), UN Doc. CCPR/C/GC/35, 16 December 2014.

Human Rights Council, Resolution 54/14, 11 October 2023.

Report of the Working Group on Enforced of Voluntary Disappearances, General Comment on the right to the truth in relation to enforced disappearance, A/HRC/16/48, 26 January 2011.

Resolution 5/2, 6 December 2007.

International Convention on the Protection of All Persons from Enforced Disappearance, UNTS 2716, UN Doc. A/61/448, C.N.737.2008, 20 December 2006.

Office of the High Commissioner for Human Rights, Report on Internet Shutdowns: Trends, Causes, Legal Implications and Impacts on a Range of Human Rights, UN Doc. A/HRC/50/55, 13 May 2022.

Report on the Impact of New Technologies on the Promotion and Protection of Human Rights in the Context of Assemblies, including Peaceful Protests, UN Doc. A/HRC/44/24, 25 June 2020.

Who's Responsible? Attributing Individual Responsibility for Violations of International Human Rights and Humanitarian Law in United Nations Commissions of Inquiry, Fact-finding Missions and Other Investigations (2018), available at www.ohchr.org/sites/default/files/Documents/Publications/AttributingIndividualResponsibility.pdf.

Report of the High-Level Panel [appointed by the UN Secretary-General] on Threats, Challenges and Change (2004) A More Secure World: Our Shared Responsibility, available at www.un.org/secureworld/.

Special Rapporteur on Extrajudicial, Summary or Arbitrary Executions, Report on Mass Graves, UN Doc. A/75/384 of 12 October 2020.

Report on the Use of Information and Communication Technologies to Secure the Right to Life, UN Doc. A/HRC/29/37, 24 April 2015.

Report on the Relevance of New Technologies in the Context of Human Rights Fact-finding, Targeted Killings and Accountability, and Extrajudicial Executions and Robotic Technologies, UN Doc. A/65/321, 23 August 2010.

Special Rapporteur on the human rights of internally displaced persons, UN Doc. A/HRC/53/35/Add.2, 27 June 2023.

Special Rapporteur on the promotion of truth, justice, reparation and guarantees of non-recurrence, Report A/ HRC/21/46, 9 August 2012.

UN Basic principles and guidelines of the right to a legal remedy and reparations for victims of grave violations of international human rights and serious violations of international humanitarian law, General Assembly Resolution 60/147, 15 December 2005.

UN Refugee Agency, Protection, Saving Lives & Solutions for Refugees in Dangerous Journeys (UNHCR's 2022–2023) Updated Risk Mitigation Strategy and 2022 Appeal, available at https://reporting.unhcr.org/document/2247.

UNGA Resolution, Protection of Migrants, A/RES/74/148, available at https://documents-dds-ny.un.org/doc/UNDOC/GEN/N19/427/26/PDF/N1942726.pdf?OpenElement.

Working Group on Enforced or Involuntary Disappearances, Study on New Technologies and Enforced Disappearances, UN Doc. A/HRC/54/22/Add.5, 11 September 2023.

Annual Report for 2022, UN Doc. A/HRC/54/22, 30 July 2023.

Methods of work, UN Doc. A/HRC/WGEID/1, 10 February 2023.

Report on the 30th Anniversary of the Declaration on the Protection of All Persons from Enforced Disappearances, UN Doc. A7HRC/51/31/Add.3, 31 August 2022.

Communications transmitted, cases examined, observations made and other activities conducted by the Working Group on Enforced or Involuntary Disappearances, A/HRC/WGEID/126/1, February 2022.

Report of the Working Group on Enforced or Involuntary Disappearances on enforced disappearances in the context of migration, 2017, available at www.ohchr.org/en/enforced-disappearances-context-migration-report.

Follow-up Report to the Recommendations, A/HRC/27/49/Add.2, 8 September 2014.

Follow-up Report to the Recommendations, February 2014, available at https://trial.ba/wp-content/uploads/2016/02/Follow-upreportBiHFeb2014.pdf.

Report of the Working Group on Enforced or Involuntary Disappearances on its visit to Bosnia and Herzegovina on 14–21 June 2010. A/HRC/16/48/Add.1, 28 December 2010.

Report of the Working Group on Enforced or Involuntary Disappearances 1997, E/CN.4/1998/43, available at https://documents-dds-ny.un.org/doc/UNDOC/GEN/G98/100/94/IMG/G9810094.pdf?OpenElement.

Working Group on Enforced Disappearance or Involuntary Disappearances, Compilation of General Comments on the Declaration on the Protection of All Persons from Enforced Disappearance, A/HRC/7/2.

## Regional Treaties, Documents and Jurisprudence of Regional Court

The African Commission on Human and Peoples Rights (ACHPR), Resolution on Missing Migrants and Refugees in Africa and Impact on their families, ACHPR/ Res/486 (Ext.OS/XXXIII), available at www.achpr.org/sessions/resolutions?id=517.

Resolution on the Drafting of the Guidelines on the Protection of All Persons from Enforced Disappearances in Africa, Res/448/LXVI, 2020, available at https://www.achpr.org/sessions/resolutions?id=479.

Resolution on the expansion of the mandate and composition of the Working Group on Death Penalty and Extradjudicial, Summary or Arbitrary Killings in Africa. ACHPR/ Res. 408/ (LXIII), 2018, available at https://achpr.au.int/index.php/en/adopted-resolutions/408-resolution-expansion-mandate-and-composition-working-group.

The African Union, African Union Migration Policy Framework for Africa and Plan of Action (2018–2030), available at www.ilo.org/africa/areas-of-work/labour-migration/policy-frameworks/WCMS_671952/lang–en/index.htm.

The African Union Convention Governing Specific Aspects of Refugee Problems in Africa, available at https://au.int/sites/default/files/treaties/36400-treaty-0005_-_oau_convention_governing_the_specific_aspects_of_refugee_problems_in_africa_e.pdf

Cancillería de Colombia, Anexo II al informe del Estado parte, Contribución de la UBPD a la elaboración del II Informe del Estado colombiano al Comité contra la Desaparición Forzada, INT_CED_AIS_COL_41954_S, 2019.

EU/2012/029, Directive 2012/29/EU of the European Parliament and of the Council of 25 October 2012 establishing minimum standards on the rights, support and protection of victims of crime, and replacing Council Framework Decision 2001/220/JHA.

European Convention on the Non-Applicability of Statutory Limitation to Crimes against Humanity and War Crimes Strasbourg, 25 January 1974.

Inter-American Commission on Human Rights and Organization of American States, Situação dos direitos humanos no Brasil, Ser.L/V/II, 12/2/2021, 12 February 2021.

Inter-American Commission on Human Rights, *Follow-up on the Ayotzinapa Case by the IACHR Special Follow-Up Mechanism* (Organization of American States, 2018), Situation Report OEA/Ser.L/V/II. Doc.

Inter-American Commission on Human Rights, Situation of Human Rights in Mexico, OEA/Ser.L/V/II.Doc. 44/15, 2015.

Inter-American Court of Human Rights, *Tabares Toro* v. *Colombia*, Judgment, Merits, Reparations and Costs, 22 May 2023.

*Flores Bedregal* v. *Bolivia*, Judgment, Preliminary Objections, Merits, Reparations and Costs, 17 October 2022.

*Movilla Galarcio* v. *Colombia*, Judgment, Merits, reparations and costs, 22 June 2022.

*Familia Julien Grisonas* v. *Argentina*, Judgment, Preliminary Objections, Merits, Reparations and Costs, 23 September 2021.

*Garzón Guzmán* v. *Ecuador*, Judgment, Merits, Reparations and Costs, 1 September 2021.

*Case of Alvarado Espinoza and Others* v. *Mexico*, Series C No. 370, 2018.

International Commission for Missing Persons, Framework Plan to Address the Issue of Persons Missing from Conflicts on the Territory of the Former Yugoslavia, 2018, www.icmp.int/wp-content/uploads/2018/11/FWP-eng.pdf.

Declaration on the Role of the State in Addressing the Issue of Persons Missing as a Consequence of Armed Conflict and Human Rights Abuses, 2014.

International Convention for the Protection of All Persons from Enforced Disappearance, 1726 UNTS 3, 2006.

adopted on 20 December 2006 during the sixty-first session of the General Assembly in resolution A/RES/61/177.

International Covenant on Civil and Political Rights – ICCPR, Adopted and opened for signature, ratification and accession by General Assembly resolution 2200A (XXI) of 16 December 1966, entry into force 23 March 1976, in accordance with Article 49.

Jurisdicción Especial para la Paz (JEP), Sección de ausencia de reconocimiento de verdad y responsabilidad, Decisión AI-042 de 2021, 10 August 2021.

Organización de Estados Americanos, Promotion and Protection of Human Rights, AG/RES. 2961 (L-O/20), 21 October 2020.

Organización de Estados Americanos. Consejo Permanente. Comisión de Asuntos Jurídicos y Políticos, Párrafos propuestos para el tema 'Las personas desaparecidas y la atención a las necesidades de sus familiares' para su inclusión en el proyecto de resolución global 'promoción y protección de los derechos humanos' que se presentará a la Asamblea General en su quincuagésimo periodo ordinario de sesiones (Presentado por la delegación peruana), Doc. OEA/Ser.G, CP/CAJP/INF. 794/20, 30 June 2020.

Protocol I Additional to the Geneva Conventions of 12 August 1949 on the protection of victims of international armed conflicts ('Official Journal of the SFRY – International Treaties', No. 16/78)

Rome Statute of the International Criminal Court, 2187 UNTS 90, 17 July 1998.

Sofia Declaration, 2018, retrieved April 15 2020, available at www.consilium.europa.eu/media/34809/sofia-declaration_sr.pdf.

## Domestic Legislative and Judgment

Agreement on Assuming the Role of Co-Founders of the Missing Persons Institute by the Council of Ministers of Bosnia and Herzegovina and the International Commission on Missing Persons. International Treaties, Official Gazette of Bosnia and Herzegovina, No. 13/05.

Civil Procedure Law, 'Official Gazette RS', Nos. 72/11, 49/13, 74/13, 55/14 and 87/2018.

Comisión de Derechos Humanos de la Ciudad de México, Recomendación 2/2020 (Expedientes CDHDF/IV/122ffLAU13/D7502 y 8 otros), available at https://directorio.cdhdf.org.mx/pdf/recos/Recomendacion_02–2020_1.pdf.

Constitution of Bosnia and Herzegovina, http://www.ccbh.ba/public/down/USTAV_BOSNE_I_HERCEGOVINE_bos.pdf.

Constitution of the Republic of Serbia Official Gazette RS, No. 98/2006 and 115/2021.

Court Rulebook, Official Gazette, Nos. 110/2009-87, 70/2011-31, 19/2012-28, 89/2013-7, 96/2015-130, 104/2015-50, 113/2015-61 (corr.), 39/2016-44, 56/2016-56, 77/2016-57, 16/2018-34, 78/2018-161, 43/2019-16, 93/2019-275.

Criminal Code, 'Official Gazette RS', Nos. 5/2005, 88/2005 – ispr., 107/2005 – ispr., 72/2009, 111/2009, 121/2012, 104/2013, 108/2014, 94/2016, 35/2019 and 27/2021 – CC decision i 62/2021 – CC decision.

Criminal Code of Bosnia and Herzegovina, Official Gazette of Bosnia and Herzegovina, No. 3/03, 32/03, 37/03, 54/04, 61/04, 30/05, 53/06, 55/06, 32/07, 8/10).

Criminal Code of SFRY 'Official Gazette SFRY', Nos. 44/76-1329, 36/77 1478, 34/84-895, 37/84-933, 74/87-1743, 57/89-1441, 3/90-63, 38/90–1217, 45/90-1340, 54/90-1773 and 'Official Gazette FRY', Nos. 35/92-651, 37/93-816, 24/94-273, 61/01 of 09 November).

Criminal Procedure Code, 'Official Gazette RS', Nos. 72/11 of 28 September 2011, 101/11 of 30 December 2011, 121/12 of 24 December 2012, 32/13 of 8 April 2013, 45/13 of 22 May 2013, 55/14 of 23 May 2014 and 35/19 of 21 May 2019.

Decision on the Establishment of the Fund for Support of Families of Missing Persons of Bosnia and Herzegovina, 'Official Gazette of Bosnia and Herzegovina', No. 96/06, 4 December 2006

Distrito Especial, Industrial, Portuario, Biodiverso y Ecoturístico de Buenaventura, Decree 0047, 10 March 2023, available (in Spanish) at www.buenaventura.gov.co/images/multimedia/20230312_decreto_0047_del_10_de_marzo_de_2023.pdf.

Gobierno de México, Protocolo Adicional para la Búsqueda de Niñas, Niños y Adolescentes, Acuerdo SNBP/002/2021, 15 July 2021, available at https://www.dof.gob.mx/nota_detalle.php?codigo=5623969&fecha=15/07/2021.

Gobierno de México, Protocolo Homologado para la Búsqueda de Personas Desaparecidas y No Localizadas, Acuerdo SNBP/002/2020, 6 November 2020, available at www.dof.gob.mx/nota_detalle.php?codigo=5601905&fecha=06/10/2020.

Law on Civilian Victims from the Homeland War, Official Gazette No. 84/2021, (1555), law, 23.7.2021.

Law on Contracts and Torts, 'Official Gazette SFRY' Nos. 29/78, 39/85, 45/89, 57/89, 'Official Gazette SRY No. 31/93, 'Official Gazette SM', No. 1/2003.

Law on Liability of the Republic of Croatia for the Damage Caused by Members of the Croatian Army and Police Acting in their Official Capacity during the Homeland War, 'Official Gazette' No. 117/2003, 23 July 2003.

Law on Missing Persons of Bosnia and Herzegovina, 'Official Gazette of Bosnia and Herzegovina', No. 50/04, 17 November 2004.

Law on Non-contentious proceedings, 'Official Gazette of the SRS', No. 25/82 and 48/88 and 'Official Gazette of the RS', No. 46/95 – other law, 18/05 – other law, 85/12, 45/13 – other law, 55/14, 6/15 and 106/15 – other law, 14/22.

Law on Persons Missing in the Homeland War, 'Official Gazette Croatia' No. 70/19.

Law on the organisation of courts, 'Official Gazette', No. 10/2023.

Law on the Rights of Civilian Invalids of War, 'Official Gazette of the RS', No. 52/96.

Law on the Witness Protection Programme in Bosnia and Herzegovina, 'Official Gazette of Bosnia and Herzegovina', No. 36/14.

Ley de Búsqueda de Personas de la Ciudad de México, Gaceta Oficial de la Ciudad de México.

Ley de Personas Desaparecidas del Estado de Jalisco, 5 March 2021.

Ley General en Materia de Desaparición Forzada de Personas, *Desaparición Cometida por Particulares y del Sistema Nacional de Búsqueda de Personas* (México: 2017).

Ministerio de Justicia y Derechos Humanos de Chile, Decreto 98, 2023, 'Aprueba plan nacional de búsqueda de verdad y justicia respecto de las personas víctimas de desaparición forzada ocurridas en Chile entre el 11 de septiembre de 1973 y el 10 de marzo de 1990, designa al programa de derechos humanos como órgano ejecutor y crea el comité de seguimiento y participación', available (in Spanish) at www.bcn.cl/leychile/navegar?idNorma=1197778.

Ministerio de Justicia y Derechos Humanos de Perú, 'Protocolo para el acompañamiento psicosocial a familiares en el proceso de búsqueda de personas desaparecidas con enfoque humanitario', 21 April 2021, available (in Spanish) at www.gob.pe/institucion/minjus/informes-publicaciones/1854676-protocolo-para-el-acompanamiento-psicosocial-a-familiares-en-el-proceso-de-busqueda-de-personas-desaparecidas-con-enfoque-humanitario.

*Plan nacional de búsqueda de personas desaparecidas al 2030* (Perú: 2021), available (in Spanish) at www.gob.pe/uploads/document/file/2145511/Plan%20Nacional%20de%20B%C3%BAsqueda%20de%20Personas%20Desaparecidas%20al%202030.pdf.pdf.

National War Crimes Strategy of Bosnia and Herzegovina, www.mpr.gov.ba/web_dokumenti/default.aspx?id=10809&langTag=en-US.

Oficina del Alto Comisionado de las Naciones Unidas en Colombia, 'La búsqueda de las personas desaparecidas a la luz de los principios rectores de la ONU', 16 June 2022, available at www.hchr.org.co/pronunciamientos/la-busqueda-de-las-personas-desaparecidas-a-la-luz-de-los-principios-rectores-de-la-onu/.

Revised National War Crimes Processing Strategy, www.mpr.gov.ba/web_dokumenti/default.aspx?id=10809&langTag=en-US.

Rulebook on Marking Places of Burial and Exhumation of Missing Persons, 'Official Gazette of Bosnia and Herzegovina', No. 83/06.

Suprema Corte de Justicia de la Nación, Amparo en revisión 1077/2019, available (in Spanish) at www.idheas.org.mx/publicaciones-idheas/materiales-consulta-idheas/version-publica-amparo-en-revision-1077-2019/.

## Other

The African Union and International Organization of Migration, The Africa Migration Report: Challenging the Narrative, available at https://reliefweb.int/sites/reliefweb.int/files/resources/africa-migration-report.pdf.

The African Commission on Human and Peoples Rights, Mandate of the Special Rapporteur on Refugees, Asylum Seekers, Internally Displaced Persons and Migrants in Africa, available at www.achpr.org/specialmechanisms/detail?id=5.

Amnesty International, Between Life and Death: Refugees and Migrants Trapped in Libya's Cycle of Abuse (2020), available at www.amnesty.org/en/documents/mde19/3084/2020/en/.

Animal Político, 'El gobierno reconoce "crisis forense": Hay 52 mil cuerpos sin identificar', *Animal Político*, 17 March 2022, available at www.animalpolitico.com/sociedad/censo-base-encinas-cuerpos-identificar-mexico.

Ansolabehere, K. et al., *Nombrarlas para encontrarlas Contexto, dinámicas y respuestas en torno a la desaparición de mujeres en el centro de México'* (ODIM, FLACSO, 2021).

Ayala Martínez, A. 'Buscando mujeres desaparecidas en vida: entre trata de personas y violencia de género', A dónde van los desaparecidos, 5 March 2021, available at https://adondevanlosdesaparecidos.org/2021/03/04/buscando-mujeres-desaparecidas-en-vida-entre-trata-de-personas-y-violencia-de-genero/.

Baldo, S. Border Control from Hell: How the EU's migration partnership legitimatizes Sudan's Militia State (2017), available at https://enoughproject.org/reports/border-control-hell-how-eus-migration-partnership-legitimizes-sudans-militia-state.

Centro de Justicia para la Paz y el Desarrollo (CEPAD), 'Incineraciones de Cuerpos No Identificados. Crímenes Sin Justicia', 30 Enero 2019, available at https://cepad.org.mx/2019/01/incineraciones-cuerpos-no-identificados-crimenes-sin-justicia/.

Citroni, G. 'Supreme Court of Justice of Mexico: The Urgent Actions of the Committee on Enforced Disappearances Are Legally Binding', Opinio Juris, 17 August 2021, available at https://opiniojuris.org/2021/08/17/supreme-court-of-justice-of-mexico-the-urgent-actions-of-the-committee-on-enforced-disappearances-are-legally-binding/.

Clingendal, 'The Khartoum Process: Shifting the Burden', 22 February 2016, available at www.clingendael.org/publication/khartoum-process-shifting-burden.

Collins, C. *An Innovative Response to Disappearances: Non-Judicial Search Mechanisms in Latin America and Asia* (Global Initiative for Justice Truth and Reconciliation, 2022), available at https://pure.ulster.ac.uk/ws/files/101225433/SearchComissions_Final_Research_Doc_PDF_13.5.22.pdf.

Comisión Internacional de Juristas para América Latina, Conversación sobre los Principios rectores para la búsqueda de personas desaparecidas (2021), available at www.youtube.com/watch?v=RtMdP3Xjrs8.

Comisión Nacional de Búsqueda, *Estrategia para el Registro Nacional de Personas Desaparecidas o No Localizadas* (CNB, 2020).

Comisión Nacional de Búsqueda and USAID, *Guía de estudio. El ABC del Análisis de Contexto. Herramientas básicas de análisis de contexto orientado a la búsqueda de personas desaparecidas* (CNB, 2021).

Comisión Nacional de Búsqueda, Enfoque DH, USAID, *Manual de Capacitación para la Búsqueda de Personas, La Voz de la Academia*, Tomo I (CNB, 2020)

Comité de la ONU contra la Desaparición Forzada, *Principios Rectores para la Búsqueda de Personas Desaparecidas* (Oficina del Alto Comisionado de las Naciones Unidas, 2019), available at www.ohchr.org/sites/default/files/Documents/HRBodies/CED/PrincipiosRectores_DigitalisedVersion_SP.pdf.

Committee on Enforced Disappearances, Mexico: Prevention must be central to national policy to stop enforced disappearance UN committee finds (2022), available at www.ohchr.org/en/press-releases/2022/04/mexico-prevention-must-be-central-national-policy-stop-enforced.

Cortázar, J. *Negación del Olvido en Proyecto de Convención Internacional para la Protección de todas las personas contra las Desapariciones Forzadas, Serie Debates y Nuevos Desafíos* (Ministerio de Justicia y Derechos Humanos, 2006).

Cortez Morales, E. 'El Mecanismo Extraordinario de Identificación Forense: Un Proyecto Trunco', Instituto Mexicano de Derechos Humanos y Democracia, 9 March 2023, available at www.imdhd.org/comunicacion/blog/el-mecanismo-extraordinario-de-identificacion-forense-un-proyecto-trunco/.

Council of Europe, Report of Nils Muižnieks, the Council of Europe Commissioner for Human Rights, on his visit to Bosnia and Herzegovina on 12–16 June 2017, 2018.

Daen, A., and Nochebuena, M. 'Omisiones, Dudas y Opacidad: El Censo de Desaparecidos Del Gobierno de AMLO', Animal Politico, 15 December 2023, available at https://animalpolitico.com/verificacion-de-hechos/te-explico/omisiones-falsedades-nuevo-censo-desaparecidos.

Defensoría del Pueblo, 'Defensoría del Pueblo impulsará los 16 principios para la búsqueda de personas desaparecidas de la ONU', 30 Augusto 2021, available at www.defensoria.gov.co/es/nube/comunicados/10375/Defensor%C3%ADa-del-Pueblo-impulsar%C3%A1-los-16principios-para-la-b%C3%BAsqueda-de-personas-desaparecidas-de-la-ONU-desaparici%C3%B3n-forzada Defensor%C3%ADa.htm.

Derechos Humanos Fray Juan de Larios and Familias Unidas en Búsqueda y Localización de Personas Desaparecidas, Mexico Coahuila: Ongoing

Crimes against Humanity (2017), available at www.fidh.org/IMG/pdf/angmexico_coahuila_ongoing_crimes_against_humanity_fidh-final_a_revisar-1.pdf.

'Desaparición Forzada: tragedia y esperanza', La Jornada, 31 August 2019, available at www.jornada.com.mx/2019/08/31/edito/002a1edi.

Eliud Tapia Olivares, L. *Manual sobre Desaparición de personas México*, (Suprema Corte de Justicia de la Nación y Escuela Federal de Formación Judicial, 2022), available at www.scjn.gob.mx/derechos-humanos/sites/default/files/Publicaciones/archivos/2022-10/Manual%20de%20desaparicion%20de%20personas.pdf.

European Center for Constitutional and Human Rights, International Federation for Human Rights and Lawyers for Justice in Lybia Home, No Way Out: Migrants and Refugees Trapped in Libya Face Crimes Against Humanity (2021), available at https://reliefweb.int/sites/reliefweb.int/files/resources/no_way_out_migrants_and_refugees_trapped_in_libya_face_crimes_against_humanity_en.pdf.

Ferri, P. 'La Comisión de la Verdad para la Guerra Sucia denuncia la falta de colaboración del Centro Nacional de Inteligencia' (2023) El País México, available at https://elpais.com/mexico/2023-08-15/la-comision-de-la-verdad-para-la-guerra-sucia-denuncia-la-falta-de-colaboracion-del-centro-nacional-de-inteligencia.html.

Franco, M. D. 'Desaparecer Hasta Volverse Cenizas' Quinto Elemento Lab, 9 April 2019, available at https://quintoelab.org/project/volversecenizas.

Guidelines for improving the case law with regard to procedure for compensation of damage to victims of serious crimes in criminal proceedings, available at www.podrskazrtvama.rs/en//posts/presentation-of-guidelines-for-damage-compensation-87.php.

Guillén, A., and Petersen, D. 'El regreso del infierno: Los desaparecidos que están vivos', A dónde van los desaparecidos, 4 February 2019, available at https://adondevanlosdesaparecidos.org/2019/02/04/los-desaparecidos-que-estan-vivos/.

Hernández Castillo Aída, R. 'Las múltiples ausencias de los indígenas desaparecidos en México', A dónde van los desaparecidos, 25 April 2019, available at https://adondevanlosdesaparecidos.org/2019/04/25/las-multiples-ausencias-de-los-indigenas-desaparecidos-en-mexico/.

Hevdesti et al., The guidelines for the participation of victims in the international mechanism for the disappeared in Syria, available at https://hevdesti.org/wp-content/uploads/2022/08/THE-GUIDELINES-FOR-THE-PARTICIPATION-OF-VICTIMS-IN-THE-INTERNATIONAL-MECHANISM-FOR-THE-DISAPPEARED-IN-SYRIA.pdf.

High Commissioner for Human Rights, Statement on the Use of Spyware to Surveil Journalists and Human Rights Defenders, 19 July 2021, available at www.ohchr.org/en/2021/07/use-spyware-surveil-journalists-and-human-rights-defendersstatement-un-high-commissioner.

Hinestroza, V., Jave, I., and Huhle, R. *Comisiones de búsqueda en América Latina. Una apuesta extraordinaria por la integralidad en la investigación de las desapariciones* (GIZ, 2021) available at www.identificacionhumana.mx/comisiones-de-busqueda-en-america-latina/.

Human Rights Clinic, *'Control . . . Over the Entire State of Coahuila' An Analysis of Testimonies in Trials against Zeta Members in San Antonio, Austin, and Del Rio, Texas* (The University of Texas School of Law, 2017).

*Informe presentado al Comité contra la Desaparición Forzada en vista del dialogo de seguimiento con respecto a México, en ocasión de la 15ª sesión* (Fundación para la Justicia y el Estado Democrático de Derecho and TRIAL International, 2018), available at https://trialinternational.org/wp-content/uploads/2018/11/Full-report-to-the-Committee-on-Enforced-Disappearances-Spanish.pdf.

Instituto de Democracia y Derechos Humanos (IDEHPUCP), YuyanaWasi 'Mana YapamantaKananpaq' Anfaseppa. riqsinapaq pusay, 2020, available (in Quechua) at https://repositorio.pucp.edu.pe/index/handle/123456789/1.

Inter-American Commission on Human Rights, 'On the International Day of the Victims of Enforced Disappearances, the IACHR, the Committee on Enforced Disappearances and the Working Group on enforced or involuntary disappearances call on States to adopt and implement search and investigation strategies within the framework of a comprehensive policy on disappearances', 30 August 2021, available at www.oas.org/en/iachr/jsForm/?File=/en/iachr/media_center/preleases/2021/224.asp.

Inter-American Commission on Human Rights, Inter-American Court of Human Rights, CED, and WGEID, 'States Must Prevent the Adverse Effects Faced by Relatives of Missing Persons and Respond to These from a Gender Perspective', 30 August 2022, available at www.oas.org/en/IACHR/jsForm/?File=/en/iachr/media_center/PReleases/2022/191.asp.

International Commission on Missing Persons, Global Report on Missing Persons 2020/21, available at www.icmp.int/wp-content/uploads/2021/08/ICMP_Global-Report_April_Digital.pdf.

Report on the Work of the Commission for Missing Persons for 2020 (2020).

*Persons Who Disappeared Due to Armed Conflicts during the 1990s: An Overview* (ICMP, 2014).

International Committee of Red Cross Database, Customary IHL, Civilians' Loss of Protection from Attack, available at https://ihl-databases.icrc.org/en/customary-ihl/v1.

International Committee of Red Cross Database, Guiding principles/model law on the missing; The Domestic Implementation of International Humanitarian Law: A Manual, Annex IV, available at www.icrc.org/en/doc/assets/files/publications/icrc-002-4028.pdf.

International Federation for Human Rights and Comisión Mexicana de Defensa y Promoción de los Derechos Humanos, Article 15 Communication under the Rome Statute to the International Criminal Court Regarding the Alleged Commission of Crimes against Humanity in Chihuahua, México between 2008 and 2010 (2018), available at www.fidh.org/IMG/pdf/mexique715anglais-1_final.pdf.

International Federation for Human Rights and I(dh)eas, 'Mexico: Criminal Structure Within the Public Prosecutor's Office of the State of Nayarit and Crimes Against Humanity', No. 769a, available at www.fidh.org/IMG/pdf/fidh-idheas_-_nayarit_report_english_.pdf.

International Federation for Human Rights and I(dh)eas, Litigio Estratégico en Derechos Humanos (2020), Situation of Impunity in Mexico, 750a, available at www.idheas.org.mx/wp-content/uploads/2020/05/Mexique750ang-1.pdf.

International Federation for Human Rights, Mexican Commission of Defense and Human Rights Promotion and Citizens' Commission of Human Rights of the Northeast, Mexico: Report on the Alleged Commission of Crimes against Humanity in Baja California between 2006 and 2012 (2014) 642a, available at www.fidh.org/IMG/pdf/mexique642ang2014web.pdf.

International Organization of Migration, IOM Missing Migrants Project, available at: https://missingmigrants.iom.int/region/africa.

Melzer, N. *Interpretative Guidance on the Notion of Direct Participation in Hostilities under International Humanitarian Law* (ICRC, 2009), available at www.icrc.org/en/doc/assets/files/other/icrc-002-0990.pdf.

Ministerio de Justicia y Derechos Humanos de Chile, 'Presentamos el diseño participativo del Plan Nacional de Búsqueda para víctimas de desaparición forzada en dictadura', 22 Septiembre 2022, available (in Spanish) at www.gob.cl/noticias/presentamos-el-diseno-participativo-del-plan-nacional-de-busqueda-para-victimas-de-desaparicion-forzada-en-dictadura/.

The Missing Migrants Project, Migration in Africa, available at https://missingmigrants.iom.int/region/Africa.

Movimiento por Nuestros Desaparecidos en México, 'Nuestra lucha no se borra; exigimos transparencia y diálogo sobre el registro de personas desaparecidas y toda política que nos impacte', 19 December 2024, available at https://movndmx.org/nuestra-lucha-no-se-borra.

Observatorio sobre Desaparición e Impunidad, *Informe Sobre Desapariciones en el Estado de Nuevo León Con Información de Cadhac* (Facultad Latinoamericana de Ciencias Sociales, 2017), pp. 29–30.

Oficina del Alto Comisionado de las Naciones Unidas en México, Principios Rectores para la Búsqueda de Personas – Playlist (2021), available at www.youtube.com/playlist?list=PLeL4yp-msGcRKgVjXKuLLm-Ozcl7-zsB.

OFRANEH-SUNLA, *OFRANEH* Communique: 'International Day of the Victims of Enforced Disappearances', 31 August 2018, available (in Spanish) at www.tortillaconsal.com/tortilla/node/12779.

Open Society Justice Initiative, *Corruption That Kills: Why Mexico Needs an International Mechanism to Combat Impunity* (Open Society Foundations, 2018), available at www.opensocietyfoundations.org/sites/default/files/corruption-that-kills-en-20180502.pdf.

Open Society Justice Initiative, *Undeniable Atrocities: Confronting Crimes against Humanity in Mexico.* (Open Society Foundations, 2016).

Ospina, A. J. et al., *La búsqueda y la participación en los casos de desaparición forzada: marco legal en Colombia y El Salvador* (Dejusticia, 2021), available (in Spanish) at www.dejusticia.org/publication/la-busqueda-y-la-participacion-en-los-casos-de-desaparicion-forzada-marco-legal-en-colombia-y-el-salvador/.

Perry, T. 'Libya's Eastern Commander Hafter Announces Election Bid', Reuteurs, 16 November 2021, available at www.reuters.com/world/africa/libyas-eastern-commander-haftar-announces-election-bid-2021-11-16/.

Poder Judicial de Coahuila, Novena Sesión Ordinaria del Pleno del Tribunal Constitucional Local (2021), available at www.pjecz.gob.mx/sesiones/tribunal-constitucional/2021/novena-sesion-ordinaria-del-pleno-del-tribunal-constitucional-local-2021-10-27/.

Proceso, '"¿Les ha quedado grande el cargo?", lanza madre de militar desaparecido a Peña y Cienfuegos', Proceso, 8 May 2018, available at www.proceso.com.mx/533346/les-ha-quedado-grande-el-cargo-lanza-madre-de-militar-desaparecido-a-pena-y-cienfuegos.

Redress, *The Forgotten Victims: Enforced Disappearance in Africa* (Redress, 2021) available at https://redress.org/publication/the-forgotten-victims-enforced-disappearance-in-africa/.

Robledo Silvestre, C. 'Desaparecer por defender el territorio', A dónde van los desaparecidos, 18 March 2021, available at https://adondevanlosdesaparecidos.org/2021/03/18/desaparecer-por-defender-el-territorio/.

Rodríguez, F. '¿Cómo se despide una madre de un hijo cuyo cuerpo perdió el Estado?', A dónde van los desaparecidos, 23 October 2023, available at https://adondevanlosdesaparecidos.org/2023/10/23/como-se-despide-una-madre-de-un-hijo-cuyo-cuerpo-perdio-el-estado/.

'Desaparecer Dos Veces: La Burocracia Que Pierde Cuerpos', Quinto Elemento Lab, 28 September 2020, available at https://quintoelab.org/crisisforense/desaparecer-dos-veces-la-burocracia-que-pierde-cuerpos.

Román, J. A. 'Familia veracruzana pagó rescate por un hijo y perdió a dos de sus miembros', La Jornada, 2 November 2015, available at www.jornada.com.mx/2015/11/02/politica/005n2pol.

Satsaksit, S. and Family, Wanchalearm Satsaksit Remains Missing as UN Body Begins Review of Enforced Disappearances in Cambodia, Joint Statement, 4 April 2022, available at https://equitablecambodia.org/website/data/LettersPress-Releases/2022/04/JS_Wanchalearm_Enforced_Disappearances_04042022_ENG.pdf.

Spigno, I. 'Quién debería buscar a las personas desaparecidas en Coahuila, México?', Agenda Estado de Derecho, 6 December 2021.

Trial International, Bosnia and Herzegovina Study on Opportunities for Reparations for Survivors of Conflict-related Sexual Violence, p. 63, available at https://trialinternational.org/wp-content/uploads/2022/03/GSFReportBiH_ENG_Web.pdf.

Tzuc, E. 'Tiene Censo de AMLO Otros Datos . . . Equivocados Sobre Desaparecidos En México', *Animal Politico*, 22 January 2024, available at https://animalpolitico.com/sociedad/desaparecidos-censo-datos-equivocados.

'México Rebasa Las 5 Mil 600 Fosas Clandestinas', Quinto Elemento Lab, 9 October 2023, available at https://quintoelab.org/project/mexico-rebasa-cinco-mil-fosas-clandestinas.

'Cruce de datos: La clave para localizar a miles de personas desaparecidas', A dónde van los desaparecidos, 23 January 2023, available at https://adondevanlosdesaparecidos.org/2023/01/23/cruce-de-datos-la-clave-para-localizar-a-miles-de-personas-desaparecidas/.

Tzuc, E., and Turati, M. 'Un País Rebasado Por Sus Muertos', Quinto Elemento Lab, 22 September 2020, available at www.quintoelab.org/crisis-forense/un-pais-rebasado-por-sus-muertos/.

Unidad de Búsqueda de Personas dadas por Desaparecidas (s.f.), *Lineamientos para la participación de las personas que buscan y las personas dadas por desaparecidas encontradas con vida, durante el proceso de reencuentro, desde una perspectiva humanitaria y extrajudicial* (UBPD, n.d.).

*Estándares internacionales sobre garantías para la prevención y protección de las personas frente a la desaparición* (UBPD, 2021), available at https://ubpdbusquedadesaparecidos.co/actualidad/estandares-internacionales-sobre-garantias-para-la-prevencion-y-proteccion-de-las-personas-frente-a-la-desaparicion/.

*Lineamientos del Enfoque Diferencial de Niñez, Adolescencia y Juventud para el Proceso de Búsqueda de Personas Dadas por Desaparecidas en el Contexto y en Razón del Conflicto Armado* (UBPD, 2020).

*Plan Nacional de Búsqueda de la Unidad de Búsqueda de Personas dadas por Desaparecidas en el contexto y en razón del conflicto armado* (UBPD, 2020).

Universidad Alberto Hurtado et al., *Guidelines and Recommendations on the Registry and Documentation of Forced Disappearances* (Universidad Alberto Hurtado, 2020), available at https://research.gold.ac.uk/id/eprint/30075/1/Guidelines%20and%20Recommendations%20on%20the%

20Registry%20and%20Documentation%20of%20Forced%20Disappearances.pdf.

USAID, I(dh)eas, ONU-DH, *El carácter vinculante de las Acciones Urgentes del Comité de la ONU contra la Desaparición Forzada en México* (USAID, 2023), available at www.idheas.org.mx/publicaciones-idheas/el-caracter-vinculante-de-las-acciones-urgentes-del-comite-de-la-onu-contra-la-desaparicion-forzada-en-mexico/.

Vizcarra, M. 'Crisis Forense: Cuando Las Funerarias Suplieron al Semefo', Quinto Elemento Lab, 6 October 2020, available at https://quintoelab.org/crisisforense/crisis-forense-cuando-las-funerarias-suplieron-al-semefo/.

World Organisation Against Torture, The Road of Torture: Cycle of Abuse against People on the Move in Africa (2021), available at www.omct.org/en/resources/reports/africa-new-report-exposes-torture-as-a-defining-feature-of-the-migration-journey.

# INDEX


African Union, 15, 68–9, 77, 182, 199
ambiguous loss, 3, 12
amnesties, 152
Amnesty International, 136, 186–7
Argentina, 6, 130, 132, 134–5, 137–8, 144–5, 262
armed conflict, 7, 14
  ICPPED, 24, 28–44
  notion of, 22–3
  societal impact, 20–2
association, of families, 6, 53, 70, 93, 104, 119–20, 139, 207, 214–17, 221, 233

Bosnia and Herzegovina, 17, 35, 39, 203, 211–18
Burkina Faso, 184–5, 195

child, 3–4, 6, 49, 57, 62, 105–6, 112, 125–6, 151
Committee on Migrant Workers, 184, 189, 242
country visit
  CED, 65, 154–5, 194
  WGEID, 93–5, 237
crime against humanity, 29, 37–9, 43–6, 85, 150, 174, 259
Croatia, 233–7

declaration of death, 229–30
Declaration on the Protection of all Persons from Enforced Disappearance, 8, 84–5, 164, 205–6

ECtHR, 29, 39, 175, 224, 228
exhumations, 93, 160–1, 203, 221–2

France, 130, 139, 144, 262

General Comment on enforced disappearances in migration, 66, 189, 191–4, 197–9, 255, 262, 265
Germany, 5, 54–5, 130
Guiding Principles on the Search for Disappeared, 47–77, 174, 191–3, 232, 265–7

Human Rights Committee, 104, 178, 249, 251, 264, 267
Human Rights Council, 78–9, 81, 90, 143, 146–7, 258
Human Rights Watch, 136

ICRC, 27–8, 31–3, 48, 203, 243, 264
identification, of remains, 21, 26–7, 30, 45, 162, 170–1, 203, 223–35, 237
Inter-American Commission on Human Rights, 53, 66–8, 137
Inter-American Convention on the Forced Disappearance of Persons, 7, 29
Inter-American Court of Human Rights, 104, 123, 175
International Commission for Missing Persons, 203
International Commission of Jurists, 140–1
International Commission on Missing Persons, 214, 238
International Committee of the Red Cross, 25
International Convention for the Protection of All Persons from Enforced Disappearance

International Convention for the Protection of All Persons from Enforced Disappearance (cont.)
  definition, 25–7, 42–4, 46, 152
  ratification, 14, 18, 46, 201, 242–68
  Travaux préparatoires, 38, 130–53
  victim, 7, 48, 104, 167, 169, 210, 219
international criminal law, 11, 34, 150, 200
international humanitarian law, x, 14, 28, 33–6
International Organization of Migration, x, 182

Kosovo, 1, 203, 223

Libya, 34, 183–6

Mexico, 4, 16, 53–5, 57–60, 66, 69, 139, 154–80, 194
missing migrants, 17, 66, 181–202
missing persons, 24–8
model law, 25
Morocco, 51, 54, 185, 262

Niger, 185, 189, 194, 197
non-governmental organization, x
non-governmental organization, 130–53
non-refoulement, 190, 194, 196, 199, 262
non-retroactivity, 39, 41, 46, 256

prevention of enforced disappearances, 8, 19, 128, 197
prosecuting perpetrators, 37–9

reparation, 4, 17, 22, 45, 58, 61, 80, 115, 203–41
right to truth, 6, 151, 206, 240
Rome Statute, 12, 37, 39–40, 43, 149–50, 164, 205, 212
Russia, 7, 264

Serbia, 55, 76–7, 223–33
Special Procedures of the Human Rights Council, 8–9, 15, 79, 85, 87, 93–7
Special Process on Missing Persons in the Territory of former Yugoslavia, 33–46, 203–41
Statement on non-state actors, 17, 43–4, 156, 173–9
statute of limitations, 41, 211, 217, 219, 227
Sudan, 21, 33, 184–5, 201

Ukraine, vii, 19–20, 24, 34–6, 39, 54, 264
urgent actions, 9–10, 15, 47–8, 50–1, 58, 65, 77, 102, 193

Working Group on Enforced or Involuntary Disappearances
  Thematic study on enforced disappearances and migration, 188
  Thematic study on enforced disappearances and new technologies, 82–102

Yrusta v. Argentina, 112, 115

Printed in the United Kingdom by TJ Clays Ltd.